Administering Human Resources

A BEHAVIORAL APPROACH TO EDUCATIONAL ADMINISTRATION

Compiled and edited by
Francis M. Trusty

Department of Educational Administration and Supervision
College of Education
University of Tennessee • Knoxville

McCutchan Publishing Corporation
2526 Grove Street
Berkeley, California 94704

ISBN 0-8211-1903-6
Library of Congress Catalog Card Number 71-146311

The Typography for this Book
is by the S. P. Miller Co., Oakland, CA

To Phyl

I wish to acknowledge with grateful appreciation the help of three friends and associates: John S. Reynolds, Frank W. Skinnell, and Mrs. Bette Leonard

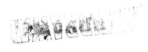

Preface

This book focuses attention on human issues in administration. Through selected material the reader is exposed to value concepts, administrative practices, and organizational developments that reflect the importance of human beings to the educational enterprise. The readings reflect a concern for the qualitative role of human beings as they authentically interact with other human beings in purposeful settings. Limiting the focus of administration in no way suggests that finance, facilities, planning, organizing, data gathering, and other technical demands of the administrative role are unimportant. It does indicate the high level of importance attached to the administrator's responsibility for improving the quality of human interaction and behavior in administrative and organizational settings.

Educational administration traditionally reflects a concern for "keeping school" more efficiently, maintaining order, and pacifying its various publics. These concerns still exist, but procedures such as PPBS, PERT, and hardware to facilitate computerized accounting and reporting have advanced administrative efficiency and effectiveness in technical areas considerably beyond the methods developed for improving human interaction and behavior.

The heightened visibility of unresolved and critical social, economic, political, and moral problems poses a new challenge to the public schools and sets the stage for this book of readings. These problems are reflected in the emergence of a humanitarian-oriented vocabulary that now includes the terms ecology, demography, pollution, racism, urbanization, poverty, relevance, dehumanization, and self-actualization. Emphasis on achieving uniform student behavior through standardized controls is declining. Procedures are being developed that recognize the importance of educating and accepting each human being as a unique and contributing member of an all-inclusive society. This task requires that leaders in service organizations and professions develop greater self-awareness, understanding of others, and skill and practice in working effectively with people of diverse beliefs and varying capacities for growth. Administrators particularly need to appreciate and accept people even as they provide for their human needs. The administrator must recognize his organization's objectives and how they can best be met by the available staff.

Administrators and those who study their concerns have begun to recognize that organizational problems are frequently related to socially inadequate responses by the organization's staff. However, these responses may not seem dysfunctional to the individual. This is the dilemma that administrators need training and experience to solve. It appears that understanding human behavior requires greater attention than the further development of technological skills. Our society's system of highly structured, interorganizational relationships reduces the opportunity for man to exist in any other context. Organizations are increasingly required to provide for more of man's hygienic and motivational needs. Attention to those needs is indeed a prerequisite to effective organization whether in a school, hospital, government agency, or factory. This book is intended to help those concerned with improving organizational productivity and the qualitative aspects of human existence within organizations. It is not intended to provide ammunition for those administrators and managers who view man as an object to be manipulated.

The selections in Part I reflect a concern for the values that govern our beliefs about the nature of man. They address themselves to the values implicit in basic policies related to education and administration. The authors explore issues of human resources development, human theories of administration, man and technology, the individual and society, the role of schools in society, the learning process, student-teacher relations, the role of the professional, economic and religious values, and the educational enterprise. Careful consideration has been given to including articles in which the author focuses on basic human needs and emerging environmental concerns.

Another area of concern is that of administrative practice and human behavior. Administrators are practitioners more than theoreticians, conceptualizers, creators of knowledge, and philosophers, although they are also all of these. They have a unique responsibility to know, to understand, and to do. In the past, administrators were given information about technological developments to help them be better doers, but their professional needs have now changed. Decisionmaking is now more a political process than an accounting procedure. Negotiation is replacing authoritative leadership. Coordination is more acceptable than supervision. Participation has affected the process of evaluation. Consistent with this changing focus of administrative practice is the need for administrators, and those who prepare administrators, to behave authentically and with consideration for human beings.

Part II presents articles on various administrative functions and concepts from the human behavior point of view. Some of the concepts to be dealt with include authority, leadership, power, decisionmaking, coordination, communication, evaluation, negotiation, conflict management, participation, planning, management, and the development of an effective organizational environment. Authority, for example, is a respected and longstanding concept in administration. Frequently, authority seems to be held by a person whose position was created by formal action of an organization that in turn legitimized by a common social value system. As such, authority is rarely viewed as a function of effective individual behavior. Writers have on occasion referred to authority based on competence or the informal power structure, but this recognition has rarely been sufficient to legitimize human behavior that is inconsistent with organizational values.

Organizational development is a concept that is rapidly gaining stature. This reflects a growing concern for the quality of organizational life available to most professional, semiprofessional, supervisory, and administrative personnel. Early organizational studies were concerned with worker productivity. This concern legitimized ensuing efforts to analyze organizational pathologies. Present efforts, while continuing to receive philosophical support based on the need to increase worker productivity, have in fact shifted toward an analysis of the relationship between the individual and the organization. The goal is to increase the employee's satisfactions, extend his opportunity to be creative in personal growth and self-expression, and make use of dormant democratic values. Evidence of this trend is seen in the low regard people have for "bureaucratic" behavior. Consistent with this analysis is the creation by policymakers of organizational development divisions for the purpose of self-renewal and maximizing the contributions of employees: Terminology such as crisis management, task forces, management by objectives, flattening the hierarchy, target-setting, job enlargement, organizational environment, and systems analysis attests to the changes taking place in organizations and the new demands being placed on administrative personnel. Basic to these changes are the impact of new technologies with emphasis on efficiency and the potential dehumanizing effects of technology when it is applied.

The articles in Part III reflect an increasing concern with dehumanization. They deal directly with some of the specific human problems created in organizations by overemphasis on organizational needs or underattention to human needs.

The selections discuss organizational climate, status systems, role-differentiation, innovative behavior, organizational renewal, personnel motivation, target-setting, task forces, and reward systems. It is hoped that this section will help the reader acquire greater insight and understanding and perhaps some conceptual tools for dealing more effectively with human potential in organizations.

Contents

1

Administration
and
Human Values

Human values strongly affect the attitudes and behavior of administrators. Therefore, in attempting to educate students better, administrators should seriously consider student's values, attitudes, and beliefs to provide motivation for learning. This recognition is behind the selection of articles for this part.

Karier's article provides an historical and analytical approach to the question of the nature of man and the role of education in our society. Hartley attempts to formulate an alternative to the present scientific, empirical approach to administrative conduct. He explores the concept of existential humanism and suggests its appropriateness for contemporary urban school administration.

A general survey of the educational scene in American society is provided by Schrag's article, "End of the Impossible Dream." The future function of schools is suggested by Kelley and Combs in "The Fully Functioning Self" and "Fostering Self-Direction."

School administrators are no less influenced by their values in administrative decisionmaking than are administrators in the fields of business and government. Jourard suggests a starting point: self-disclosure. Here perhaps is a more open approach to valuing. The ethical dilemma of all administrators is brought into focus with Kelman's article about manipulating human behavior.

The last two articles by Maslow and Rogers suggest a way of looking at the behavior of human beings through a "person" orientation rather than through a "thing" orientation.

HUMANIST CONCEPTIONS OF MAN AND SOCIETY

Clarence J. Karier

There are two laws discrete,
Not reconciled—
Law for man, and law for thing;
The last builds town and fleet,
But it runs wild,
And doth the man unking.[1]
Ralph Waldo Emerson

At the center of much of the social and educational conflict in twentieth-century America lie some basically conflicting positions with respect to the nature of man and the good society. From the standpoint of those who believe in a pluralistic society, this condition is as it should be. A society that is truly pluralistic should reflect differences at a fundamental as well as a superficial level. There are, however, inherent dangers in such a social system. If, for instance, basic differences are allowed to immobilize a society and prevent action, then such a society is committed to its own self-destruction. A pluralistic social ideal assumes free, open debate on fundamental issues, but is also assumes that man will strive for consensus in terms of action even though they may never reach consensus on basic questions.

In this respect, it was the pragmatist, James B. Conant, in the midst of the stormy educational debate at mid-century, who sought consensus for educational action, not by analyzing the virtues and defects of fundamentally conflicting positions with respect to educational thought, but rather by purposely focusing attention on those educational practices on which he could obtain the greater consensus. Conant, as the great compromiser of mid-twentieth century, was a pragmatist who believed in a pluralistic society. While Conant sought consensus in practice, he knew full well that many of the fundamental values over which men are divided are not reconcilable. Indeed, even though one might get John Dewey, Robert Maynard Hutchins, and Jacques Maritain to agree on a specific educational practice, one could not expect them to agree on the nature of man or the nature of the good society. These, then, are not very useful questions, as Conant recognized, in achieving a consensus for action. On the other hand, they are extremely useful for understanding the pluralism underlying American thought. In fact, it is this pluralism which causes much of the educational conflict and which creates the need for consensus in the first place.

Contrary to considerable popular opinion, which holds that educational criticism began with Russia's successful launch of Sputnik, American education had been persistently criticized throughout the twentieth century. To be sure, many in education seemed to ignore the criticism until after Sputnik; nevertheless, many of the more effective arguments heard in the fifties were also heard in the twenties and thirties. Among those who consistently registered pointed and effective criticism from the vantage point of a well-defined philosophic position were the humanists.

From Isocrates on, the humanists have functioned as the schoolmasters as well as the social critics of Western culture. In American education, they held their own—especially in the colleges—until the latter half of the nineteenth century. With the rise of Darwinian naturalism, which suggested the continuity of man and animal, the humanist's assumption as to the dualistic nature of man was challenged; with the rise of science, specialization, research, and the explosion in human knowledge, the humanist educational ideal of the well-rounded man was laid waste; and with the increasing democratization of American culture, the humanist ideal of an ordered aristocratic society was devastated. The humanists, then, were struggling against some of the main currents of twentieth-century educational and social thought. As they continued the struggle, they were true to their tradition and soon became leading critics of American society and education.

Even though there were broad general areas of agreement within the humanist position, there still remained considerable differences. While all found eternal verities in tradition, not all found the same truths. Although all would agree that man's nature is divided, not all could agree as to a precise definition of his dualistic nature. In general, the humanists believed in a well-ordered, stable society, but again, not all found refuge in the classical ideal of an aristocratic social order. Indeed, some became exponents of a democratic society. One reason for these differences is that some humanists seemed more sensitive to the realities of the twentieth century and thereby moderated their traditional position, while others seemed quite content to rest their case on eternal truths. The marked differences among various humanists might further be accounted for by the fact that even though all relied on the unchanging aspects of tradition to define man's nature and his education, each group's center of interest was on a different aspect of the Western tradition. In one way or another, at least three major currents of Western thought—the rhetorical, the philosophical, and the religious—were reflected in twentieth-century American humanism. Although Irving Babbitt and Paul Elmer More reflected a narrow, classical, literary humanism, and Jacques Barzun and Gilbert Highet held a more modern, urbane, literary humanist's perspective, both groups were essentially part of the rhetorical humanist tradition. Rooted in the thought of Isocrates, Cicero, and Erasmus, this was a formidable educational tradition. Although Robert M. Hutchins and Jacques Maritain both went back to Thomas Aquinas and Aristotle for their philosophic bases, Maritain's religious humanism relied more on the revealed truths of Christianity, while Hutchins' rational humanism was based more on an Aristotelian conception of man. In spite of these differences, the common grounds of agreement among all humanists should not be overlooked. All humanists found eternal verities in tradition, spoke of the unchanging elements of human nature, emphasized the unchangeable in a rapidly changing society, and were intimately concerned with education and the growth of scientific naturalism.

Rhetorical Humanism

Neohumanism
     In the first two decades of the twentieth century, Paul Elmer More (1864-1937) as the stylist and Irving Babbitt (1865-1933) as the inquiring scholar joined forces to present neohumanism to the world as an alternative to the scientific naturalist perspective of man,

education, and society. From the serenity of Harvard Yard, Babbitt poured forth the *Weltanschauung* of neohumanism in *Literature and the American College* (1908), *New Laokoön* (1910), *The Masters of Modern French Criticism* (1912), *Rousseau and Romanticism* (1919), and *Democracy and Leadership* (1924). From the marketplace, Paul Elmer More, as literary editor of *The Independent* (1901-1903) and *The Evening Post* (1903-1909) and as editor-in-chief of *The Nation* (1909-1914), took up the cudgel against the romantic and naturalist writers. Together, they presented a united front against the humanitarian values of the pragmatists in philosophy as well as against the Darwinian naturalism implicit in the thought of most psychologists, sociologists, and educators in the twentieth century.

From Babbitt's point of view, America was rapidly becoming hopelessly caught in the grip of a relativistic naturalism. The cause was to be found in the growth of humanitarianism, which consisted of romantic naturalism on the one side and scientific naturalism on the other. The romantic tradition as epitomized by Rousseau and the scientific tradition as epitomized by Bacon were viewed as corrupting the civilized standards of the West. Science and romanticism together fed the Frankenstein of mass culture, the myth of progress, and the idea of the perfectibility of man.

Babbitt asserted that men have a choice of living on one of three levels. At one extreme, they may accept the discipline of supernatural religion and thereby become subject to restraints that are "exterior and anterior" to man himself; or they may go to the other extreme and live as naturalists in a confused state without standards, taste, or restraint, becoming puppets of their naturalistic passions. If there were only these two choices, Babbitt insisted, he would take the supernaturalist way of life.

There was another position, however, which he defined as humanistic. The humanists would develop an internal discipline that would free man from his naturalistic instability and yet not subject him to the external discipline of the religious life. The history of the West, Babbitt surmised, had been largely a history of humanism providing ethical standards of taste and judgment for the leadership class and supernatural religion providing the necessary restraints for the great masses of people. From the Enlightenment on, however, man had espoused the new religion of humanitarianism, which ran roughshod over orthodox religious restraints as well as humanistic discipline. Modern Western man, as he intellectually rejected Christianity, still lived unconsciously off the moral capital of the past, a moral capital that was rapidly being eroded by the growth of humanitarianism. In this sense, Western man was heading straight for the abyss of naturalistic destruction. The religious as well as the humanistic sanctions for restraint were simply disappearing from Western culture.

During the eighteenth and nineteenth centuries, in an attempt to find standards in the natural world as the myths of Christianity lost their credibility, the pseudo-classicists, empiricists, and rationalists placed their faith in reason to the exclusion of feeling and imagination. As a consequence of this intellectual debacle, the doctrine of knowledge as power earlier promulgated by Francis Bacon was given realistic expression in the form of scientific naturalism. However, unable to hold feeling in check for very long, reason implicit in scientific naturalism gave way to a surge of romantic naturalism, and the imagination was released to wander freely under the guise of native genius. Jean-Jacques Rousseau epitomized (for Babbitt) the romantic sentimentalism which, when worshiping the "noble savage," could as readily turn to the primitivism of G. Stanley Hall as it could to the permissive child-centered education of Margaret Naumburg.[2]

Man could only oscillate between the extremes of unbridled reason and undisciplined imagination. What eventually followed, Babbitt surmised, was a complete disillusionment with both reason and imagination, to the extent that all civilized standards were lost in a world of nihilism. Neither the romantic who viewed his fleeting imagination as genius nor the utilitarian scientist who specialized to know more and more about less and less could be relied upon to preserve standards so necessary for a humane culture. Baconian science and Rousseauian romanticism were the two pillars which supported the humanitarian lintel under which modern man walked to his own self-destruction. Although at times these two strains of naturalism seemed antagonistic, the utilitarian idea of knowledge as power nicely complemented the romantic's cry for service to a highly sentimentalized notion of the brotherhood of humanity. Science, in the service of unrestrained sentiment, was corrupting the house of intellect.

The solution to all this rested not in a return to supernaturalism but in a revival of the standards and taste of classical humanism. The humanist, as Babbitt defined him, was one who "moved between an extreme of sympathy and an extreme of discipline and selection, and became humane in proportion as he mediated between these extremes."[3] Reason, imagination, emotions, and sense experience must all be subservient to a higher ethical "will to refrain." "A person who has sympathy for mankind in the lump, faith in its future progress, and desire to serve the great cause of this progress,"[4] and is committed to either the utilitarian ideal of knowledge for power or the romantic goal of service to humanity should be called a humanitarian, not a humanist.[5]

At the center of Babbitt's and More's conception of human nature was the ethical "will to refrain." This will "eludes all attempts at analysis" and exists as a "residuum of pure and abstract liberty, not to be expressed in terms of time and space."[6] The neohumanist's quest for certainty ended with the universal, superrational will of man, based not on *a priori* assumptions but rather on what they termed the experience of man. As Babbitt said:

... the opposite of the subrational is not merely the rational but the superrational, and ... this superrational and transcendent element in man is a certain quality of will. This quality of will may prove to be alone capable of supplying a sufficient counterpoise to the various 'lusts,' including the lust of feeling, that result from the free unfolding of man's natural will.[7]

Unlike Henri Bergson's concern with the *élan vital,* Babbitt's interest was in a *frein vital.* The truly educated man was one who had developed and disciplined his ethical will not to act but to refrain from action. Such a discipline could be developed only through a serious study of the ancient classics in the original languages. Translations would not suffice. While the logic of the ancients may survive translations, the finer esthetic shades of meaning so necessary for the disciplining of the ethical will do not survive. Since Hutchins and Adler assumed a universal logic to be at the center of man's nature, they could accept translations in their Great Books curriculum, but Babbitt and More could not. The difference in their educational recommendations is largely due to a difference in the way they defined human nature.

Since the kind of knowledge best designed to develop and strengthen one's "will to refrain" is known, then the question remains: Can the great mass of men rise to the heights of self-discipline necessary to taste the fruits of classical virtue? In a resounding chorus, almost as an echo out of the dead ruins of classical antiquity, the neohumanists answered "No!" The great masses were trainable in the humanitarian sense but uneducable in the humanist sense. As Babbitt put it:

Some persons will remain spiritually anarchical in spite of educational opportunity, others will acquire at least the rudiments of ethical discipline, whereas still
others, a small minority, if we are to judge by past experience, will show
themselves capable of more difficult stages of self-conquest that will fit them for
leadership.[8]

Babbitt's and More's classical view of human nature and knowledge
culminated in a classical aristocratic view of the good society. Both
were fully convinced that the great mass of men were incapable of
rising to the heights of excellence necessary for self-rule. Since most
men will remain intemperate, it follows that most men neither
deserve nor are capable of freedom. "It is ordained in the eternal
constitution of things, that men of intemperate minds cannot be
free. Their passions forge their fetters."[9]

Interest in mankind must begin at the top and progress downward.
The gifted must not only be the exemplars of culture worthy of
emulation but must be allowed to exercise economic, political, and
social power if civilization is to survive.[10] These leaders must learn
that the main purpose of the machinery of government is not to raise
the material welfare of the masses but to create advantages for the
upward striving of the exceptional.[11] Harking back to Aristotle's
Politics, which intellectually justified slavery on the basis of a
dualistic conception of human nature, More found equality only
among equals. Majority rule, he concluded, is nothing more than a
conceit on the part of the mass man. In every social institution there
are leaders and followers, and it behooves the American people to
realize that what really rules is not a nebulous will of the people nor
a popular majority but a small leadership minority.[12] It is the
education of that small leadership minority which will determine the
standards of a just society. As Babbitt suggested, "Our real hope of
safety lies in our being able to induce our future Harrimans and
Rockefellers to liberalize their own souls, in other words to get
themselves rightly educated."[13]

American education had been so thoroughly corrupted by romantic naturalism at the elementary school level and by scientific
utilitarianism at the graduate level, said Babbitt, that there was
serious danger that the liberal arts college, so necessary to train the
elite, would itself be overrun by the spirit of humanitarian naturalism. The humanitarianism of Charles W. Eliot, John Dewey, George
Herbert Mead, Edward L. Thorndike, and many others had thoroughly corrupted American education. The only hope for the
survival of civilized standards rested in the recall of the liberal arts
college to the discipline and content of the classics.

Not only the education of the young but the entire society, Babbitt and More asserted, showed signs of being afflicted by cancerous humanitarianism. From Jefferson on, America had been led down the primrose path of naturalism. Under the false ideal of progress, Americans had come to believe in mass social meliorism. As More said, "The works of Miss Jane Addams and a host of other modern writers [are] in fact only one aspect of the slow drift from medieval religion to humanitarianism."[14] Such a drift was from personal integrity to communal chairty and collective socialism. In a similar vein Babbitt argued that

We may be sure that stalwart believers like St. Paul or St. Augustine or Pascal would look upon our modern humanitarians with their talk of social problems and their tendency to reduce religion to a phase of the tenement-house question as weaklings and degenerates.[15]

The just society was a hierarchical society which distributed its rewards of power, privilege, and property according to the superiority of persons. The humanitarians, however, had encouraged the inferior to utilize the power of government to dip their hands into the pockets of the superior in the name of mass philanthropy and social justice. Under such conditions, Babbitt believed that:

It is not yet clear that it is going to be possible to combine universal suffrage with the degree of safety for the institution of property that genuine justice and genuine civilization both require.[16]

The rights of property must be ensured not only for the sake of social justice but also because inequalities of wealth based on the superiority of persons is essential in maintenance of the hierarchical nature of the good society. Indeed, "to the civilized man *the rights of property are more important than the right to life.*"[17] Since, to More, the main purpose of government was to create advantages for the exceptional, and since property was more important than life, the humanitarians with their gospel of social reform via social and educational meliorism were viewed as the deadly foe of civilization. The critical error of humanitarianism was faith in progress and humanity. Science had reinforced this myth as the mass of men confused material progress with moral progress. Because men collectively could create better automobiles, they were deluded into thinking they could collectively create a better man and a better society.

The ancients, together with the Christian theologians, knew that moral striving was always an individual affair. Salvation could not be made a collective affair. The humanitarians not only offered salvation in this world, but they proposed to save men collectively through urban renewal projects, settlement houses, and mass philanthropy. All the advocates of these efforts ignored the ancient wisdom that virtue begins and ends with the individual and has relatively little to do with the workings of a bureaucratic agency. This delusion of progress was a part of the modern mind not found in the classical world. The ancients, Babbitt argued, appreciated the tragic nature of man too well to be caught up in such mass delusions.

Men have always dreamed of the Golden Age, but it is only with the triumphs of modern science that they have begun to put the Golden Age in the future instead of the past. The great line that separates the new era from the old is, as Renan remarks, the idea of humanity and the cult of its collective achievements.[18]

This naïve faith in progress and the perfectibility of man, supported by science, served to break down the old Ciceronian idea of beneficence. Cicero had clearly warned against the dangerous effects of indiscriminate giving. Beneficence, he cautioned, must always be judged in terms of its possible consequence for individual virtue.[19]

The old philanthropy, as we have said, has been profoundly modified and converted into humanitarianism by being more closely connected with this idea of progress; and the idea of progress in turn rests mainly on a belief in the benefits that are to come to mankind in the mass as the results of a closer cooperation with nature.[20]

The neohumanists' disdain for mass philanthropy turned on the classical ideal of social justice and social order. Mass philanthropy, they believed, tended to destroy personal integrity and responsibility as it emphasized the nebulous needs of humanity in mass. Since true charity begins at home, the personal touch—the real character-building attributes of giving and receiving—are lost in the impersonal characteristics of a bureaucratic agency.

"Am I my brother's keeper?" The whole American people had replied in an 'ecstatic affirmative.' One should note in passing the intolerable dilution of obligation that is implied in extending to men indiscriminately what one owes to one's own brother. At all events, no small issues are involved in the question whether one should start with an expansive eagerness to do something for humanity or with loyalty to one's self. There may be something after all in the Confucian idea that if a man only sets himself right, the rightness will extend to his family first of all, and finally in widening circles to the whole community.[21]

The classical virtue of beneficence had been perverted not by science alone but also by the "religion of humanity" missionaries who insisted on carrying the Christian gospel of brotherhood into the realm of social reform. These reformers had repeatedly failed to make a correct distinction between religious and secular virtues.[22] This error was further compounded when, under the guise of the good Samaritan, these missionaries substituted the second command-ment for the first[23] and replaced the Bible with the tenement house as a center of religious interest.[24] This kind of perversion of the religious sentiment to humanitarian ends would eventually lead to nothing more than communal socialism in which individual integrity would be but a meaningless term.

Consistently, the literary humanists in the twentieth century, from Irving Babbitt in *Literature and the American College* (1908) to Jacques Barzun in *The House of Intellect* (1959), have warned of the corrupting influence of mass philanthropy on society and education. In 1908, Babbitt's protest was a lonely protest, but by mid-century the more moderately liberal voice of Jacques Barzun, arguing essentially the same point with respect to philanthropy, reached a much larger receptive audience. As masses of people appeared as second- and third-generation recipients of welfare, it was clear to most that something was wrong. While urban renewal projects and public housing failed in many cases to produce a more responsible humanity, Russell Kirk and other conservatives were quick to point out not only that philanthropy can corrupt but that you cannot really change human nature. Increasingly, men of more conservative temper were saying that the thorny bush—which Edward Bellamy in *Looking Backward* suggested might bloom as a beautiful rose bush if transplanted from the bog to a more healthy environment—was, after all, nothing more than just another thorny bush. The humanitarians, on the other hand, insisted that we have not controlled the environment and handled the transplant with enough scientific care to warrant such conclusions.[25] By the sixties, amidst racial conflict and considerable economic, social, and educational deterioration in America's major urban centers, many voices reflecting a Sumner-Babbitt point of view could be heard; but when action was taken, it usually followed the humanitarian tradition of Bellamy and Ward.

The neohumanist attack on social reform was only one side of the attack on humanitarianism. The other side of the attack focused on educators who were corrupted by the same ideas. The progressive educators who believed in the progress of humanity by way of education and who assumed, like Rousseau, that the child's nature was good, were "impressionistic" educationists. Those who viewed human nature as neither good nor bad but subject to learning experience and who proposed a science of education were viewed as Baconian specialists or "intellectual fractions," interested in the dissemination, not of knowledge, but of bits and pieces of information. In 1924, Babbitt warned: "We have been permitting Professor Dewey and his kind to have an influence on our education that amounts in the aggregate to a national calamity."[26]

Because Babbitt and More were chiefly concerned with the education of the elite and were willing to write off the masses as only capable of being humanitarianly trained, their educational interests were primarily at the college level. At that level they reserved their bitterest invectives for the social sciences or, as they termed them, the "pseudo-sciences," which presumed to be developing a science of man and society. Departments of anthropology, sociology, psychology, and education came under fire not only because they were the most recent departments to gain university status but because these fields presumed to be seeking answers for questions already answered by the humanists. In this respect, the social sciences were poaching on humanist preserves. Referring to the social sciences, More suggested, "Better the frank unreason of mythology than this labyrinth of intellectual deception."[27] Indeed, dragging the student

... through the slums of sociology, instead of making him at home in the society of the noble dead, debauches his mind with a flabby, or inflames it with a fanatic, humanitarianism.... He is narrow and unbalanced, a prey to the prevailing passion of the hour, with no feeling for the majestic claims of that within us which is unchanged from the beginning.[28]

The pseudo-sciences, from sociology to education, were permeated with Darwinian naturalism. While a student trained solely in science is likely to be left in "a state of relative imbecility,"[29] the student trained solely in the social sciences is likely to be left with a more dangerous, inflamed, flabby conceit. The psychologists, whether they were connectionist, behaviorist, or Freudian, were equally rebuked for their rejection of dualism and for their naturalistic assumptions.[30] Responding to the psychologists who had undercut the humanistic tradition, Babbitt argued that "the behaviorists and other naturalist psychologists ... are to be accounted at present among the chief enemies of human nature."[31] So, also, More suggested: "Certainly the afterclap of that orgy of illicit science, the thing called behaviorism in this country, is no better than a lifeless bogey dressed up to frighten college boys and to delight illiterate psychologists."[32]

The neohumanists attacked modern psychologies not only because they as humanists placed their faith in a competing faculty psychology, but because modern psychologies had undercut the humanist's dualistic view of human nature which, in turn, undermined their learing theory. This theory was based on the assumption that a liberal education was concerned with the discipline of the mind while a vocational education was concerned with training in physical skills. The one education dealt with ideas and the other with things. Although discipline was held to be a vital part of a liberal education, the neohumanist passed beyond this point to emphasize the process of "imitation." "The very essence of education is . . . to set before [youth] the stirring examples of those who have found their joy and consolation in higher things."[33] As one comes to imitate the excellence of the great minds of the past, a catharsis occurs which unifies his being and frees him for truly creative work.

The neohumanist was careful to distinguish between rote Ciceronianism, the curse of the classical tradition, and true imitation. True imitation involved an element of creativity. "The imitation of models, it is well to remember, is not necessarily barren. Many of the neo-classics showed that this type of imitation is compatible with genuine creation."[34] By imitating the excellence of the classical authors, one transcends the limits of self to the higher universal life and at the same time gains in self-knowledge, which is the only virtue achievable by man. In rejecting the Baconian doctrine of knowledge as power, Babbitt and More revived the ancient doctrine of knowledge as virtue. Obviously, not everyone could reach this stage of purification. "Those who can receive the higher initiation into the Hellenic spirit will doubtless remain few in number, but those few will yield a potent influence for good, each in his own circle."[35]

While in a Thorndikean view of education, one might "stamp in" all kinds of information, and in the Skinnerian sense train men in a scientific way, to the humanists the real education of man was fundamentally an art. The art of educating man takes as its chief goal the shaping and creating of the amateur, the man of taste and self-discipline—in short, the man who thinks for himself. Babbitt's and More's man of taste, capable of judging eloquence, was very much akin to Cicero's orator whose "power will never be able to effect its object by eloquence, unless in him who has obtained a thorough insight into the nature of mankind, and all the passions of humanity, and those causes by which our minds are either impelled or restrained."[36] To Cicero it was the *orator* and to Babbitt it was the *man of taste* who needed vigorous training in many fields of knowledge and who must guard himself against sheer specialization. Their educational ideal was a universal man, a man whose knowledge was not encyclopedic but selective and eminently useful for a well-rounded amateur. In the course of his education, he must have developed a disciplined, intuitive sensitivity for the beautiful, the good, and the true.

In many ways the educational ideal of Babbitt and More was very similar to that held for the orator by both Cicero and Quintilian. The difference in educational ideals, however, lies mainly in the fact that Cicero's orator would be a speaker, and Babbitt's man of taste would be a writer. The sacred ground of the rhetorical tradition has always been the art of communication, both written and spoken. Whether one emphasizes the one or the other, the educational rationale for both remains very similar. In this respect, the neohumanists attempted to reconstruct the classical rhetorical ideal in twentieth-century American education.[37]

In an age which was becoming increasingly uncertain, the neohumanists presented an educational rationale that featured as its chief virtues stability, order, and certainty. Their educational views maintained such internal and external consistency that their attitude toward various educational problems was predictable with almost scientific accuracy. With respect to internal consistency, their aristocratic views of the good society were supported by an aristocratic view of education. The belief in a universal, unchanging essence of man, complemented by insistence upon the unchanging essence of education and the concept of knowledge as virtue, was realized in their learning theory of imitation. With respect to external consistency, it can readily be seen that when facing educational problems, they were extremely consistent with the "noble dead." As Babbitt and More spun their classical rationale into social and educational ideas, it became apparent that neohumanism was mainly a rigorous, classical protest against modern thought.

During the first two decades of the century, Babbitt and More presented a stern, united front against the humanitarian currents of American society. After 1915, when More retired as editor of *The Nation* to live the life of a scholar on the Princeton campus, his views began to drift away from those of Irving Babbitt. Unable to find satisfaction in Babbitt's humanism, which cut between naturalism and supernaturalism, More moved to a Christian humanism just as another student of Irving Babbitt, T. S. Eliot, had done.[38] The dilemma for More was that Babbitt's humanism did not seem to lead to any secure haven.

And so I ask myself, reluctantly, almost wishing my answer were mistaken, whether those who advocate humanism, as an isolated movement, are not doomed to disappointment. It is not that the direction in itself is wrong; every step in the program is right, and only by this path can we escape from the waste land of naturalism. But can we stop here in security? For purpose that will not end in bitter defeat; for values that will not mock us like empty masks, must we not look for happiness based on something beyond the swaying tides of mortal success and failure? Will not the humanist, unless he adds to his creed the faith and the hope of religion, find himself at the last, despite his protest, dragged back into the camp of the naturalist?[39]

Unlike T. S. Eliot, who joined the Anglican Church, More, though he moved to a religious humanism,[40] remained outside the church. More's religious experience led him to conclude that good and evil had real existence. The orthodox Christian explanation for evil—i.e., the absence of good—left More unsatisfied. Therefore, he was unwilling to close the dualism of good and evil in an all-perfect, all-powerful God. Like the traditional Christian, he was sure that evil existed as an active force which limits the power of God. Too unorthodox to enter and too orthodox to leave, More ended his quest of certainty on the very steps of the Anglican Church.

Neohumanism Recast

During the 1930's, there appeared in the neohumanist constellation, alongside the bright shining stars of Babbitt and More, such lesser stars as John Jay Chapman, W. C. Brownell, G. R. Elliott, Stuart P. Sherman, George E. Woodberry, and Norman Foerster.[41] Of these lesser stars, it was Norman Foerster who carried the neohumanist ideology to mid-century.[42]

As a student and close disciple of Irving Babbitt, as a teacher of American literature in the state universities of Wisconsin and North Carolina, and as director of the School of Letters at the State University of Iowa, Norman Foerster was in a unique position to carry the neohumanist gospel to foreign parts, the state university. To Foerster, the state universities "were the expression in terms of higher education, of Jacksonian democracy and the humanitarian movement."[43]

How close was Norman Foerster's conception of neohumanism to that held by Irving Babbitt and Paul Elmer More? In most respects Foerster's formulation appears to be an exact replica of Babbitt's and More's rationale. Nevertheless, Foerster introduced certain critical changes. Unlike his mentor, who understood Jefferson's humanitarianism, Foerster, at the price of considerable distortion of historical evidence, changed Jefferson to qualify as a precursor of the

neohumanist tradition. Implicit in Foerster's work is a great eagerness to sell the neohumanist rationale even at the expense of some
contraditions, which neither Babbitt nor More tolerated in their own
thinking. Babbitt and More found the modern foreign languages
unsuitable either as an instrument of discipline or as a medium of
communing with the great ideas of the "noble dead," whereas
Norman Foerster allowed French or German as a substitute for
Greek and Latin in his new liberal education.[44] What prompted
Foerster to make this shift remains unknown. Undoubtedly, one
factor of considerable importance was the apparent decline in the
percentage of students taking classical languages in the American
public secondary schools.[45] Greek had virtually disappeared from
the curriculum, and Latin was diminishing as a major study.

When Foerster abandoned classicism for modern literary humanism, it became apparent that his humanism would be more acceptable to the rational humanism of Hutchins and Adler. If the
neohumanists and the rational humanists disagreed in theory, at least
in practice a major obstruction had been removed. Given Babbitt's
and More's conception of human nature and education, their insistence on the ancient languages was eminently logical. Foerster broke
the neohumanist's logic by allowing modern foreign languages to
substitute for the ancient languages. There was something approaching contradiction when, on the one hand, he insisted, "While it may
suffice to read works of science and philosophy in translations, it
does not suffice so to read works of imaginative literature";[46] and
on the other hand, he proceeded to accept French and German as
substitutes for the classical languages. Foerster was aware of this
discrepancy and admitted, "Eventually the logic of the situation
might well send us back to the despised classical languages, for Greek
especially."[47] Nevertheless, the rational humanists and the neohumanists could now talk about the Great Books curriculum as if
they meant the same thing.

The rational humanism of Hutchins and Adler, which emphasized
the logical syllogism, a metaphysics, and the universal reason of man,
was theoretically closer to the neo-Thomism of Maritain than to the
classical-literary humanism of Babbitt and More. In contrast with the
rational humanists, Babbitt, More, and Foerster rejected any absolute
metaphysics and placed their faith not in "reason" but in the "will to
refrain," the higher intuitive imagination. As Foerster put it, "Unlike
the conceptions of life that grow out of science, humanism seeks to
press beyond reason by the *use of intuition or imagination.*"[48] The
difference might be further demonstrated by recalling the frequent

contests in the late medieval and Renaissance periods between those who emphasized rhetoric at the expense of logic and those who emphasized logic at the expense of rhetoric. The one was part of a literary tradition and the other was part of a philosophic tradition. Although Foerster could not bring himself to accept a reasoned metaphysics, he flirted with the rational humanists when he said:

Our Occidental love of reason might drive us to the last step, the formulation of the metaphysics or the theology latent in this humanistic philosophy. Admittedly, this would give us more order than we easygoing Americans are ready for today. On the other hand we do yearn, in our bewilderment, in our empty aimlessness, for order. We are weary of the chaos within our minds.[49]

It is clear that Foerster was more interested in closing ranks with the rational humanists than in refuting them. Once humanitarianism was laid low, there would be time enough to resume the age-old conflict between the logical and the rhetorical traditions.

Foerster also sought an alliance with orthodox religion as he insisted that humanism and religion could work together in stemming the tide of naturalism. On the one hand, Foerster had to admit that "pure humanism is incompatible with a dogmatic, revealed religion"[50] and that "old religious solutions are inadequate"[51] for the neohumanist; but on the other hand, he was quick to point out that "humanism may be regarded as auxiliary to religion. It attracts, not only those seeking order as critical individualists, but also those who feel the need of order as members of a visible Church."[52]

One might go further, Foerster surmised, and emphasize the common grounds of humanism and Christianity by recognizing that both conceive of reality in dualistic terms.

Of the trend of past experience there can be no doubt; both of the old guiding traditions, the Greek and the Christian, however different outwardly, were absolutely at one in their sharp contrast between the human and the natural.[53]

Although it is difficult to view the worldly temper of the Christian as a mere outward difference, it becomes clear that Foerster, for the sake of harmony, was emphasizing the very point that made it possible for the early Church fathers to blend classical dualism into Christian dualism, even though the Christian dualism was fundamentally very different from the classical. While Foerster recognized that "pure humanism was incompatible with a dogmatic revealed religion," he sought the support of orthodox religion as an ally against the common enemy, naturalism.

Neohumanism, as recast by Norman Foerster, took on many of

the characteristics of an opposition party willing to minimize basic differences between itself and possible supporters in order to dislodge a common foe. Behind this façade of rapprochement, which evoked a limited degree of flexibility, remained the rigid dualistic humanism of Irving Babbitt. Babbitt's and More's conception of human nature, the good society, the purpose of knowledge, and the nature of a liberal education are all aptly paraphrased in most of the work of Norman Foerster. As Foerster himself said, "I know of nothing better than the dualistic humanism which Irving Babbitt set forth with great learning and critical power."[54] Foerster, like his mentor before him, squared off against Darwinian naturalism, which assumed a continuity of man and animal, by asserting that man is forever separate from nature, not in degree, but in kind. The world of man is a world of moral values, the world of nature "amoral, blind, and pitiless." One must recognize that "human nature is in all times and places of recorded history fundamentally the same and that it will not be changed tomorrow."[55] Just as Babbitt and More had earlier argued, Foerster thundered against Baconian science and Rousseauian naturalism. The true humanist function of knowledge is virtue, and virtue, in the end, is being true to oneself, true to what one ought to be in the higher sense.

The philosophy of humanism finds its master truth, not in men as they are (realism) or in men as worse than they are (naturalism) or in men as they 'wish' to be (romanticism), but in men as they 'ought' to be—'ought,' of course, not in the usual restrictedly moral sense, but with reference to the perfection of the human type.[56]

Foerster's educational ideal was the same as Babbitt's, and so was his belief in the ideal society as a stable aristocratic society. Just as Irving Babbitt had found that "in substituting the love of man for the love of God the humanitarian is working in a vicious circle,"[57] so Foerster argued that "humanitarianism found no meaning in the primary law, *Love the Lord thy God,* and therefore perverted the meaning of the secondary, *Love thy neighbor as thyself."*[58] "Christian love," Foerster insisted, "was metamorphosed into natural sympathy, and the old faith in personal immorality yielded to the new faith in social progress."[59]

Once again a neohumanist attacked the social meliorists largely, one would suspect, because a society predicated on a "slave class,"[60] as Aristotle viewed it, or an "indoctrinated class,"[61] as Foerster saw it, or a class "compelled by fear or blind obedience,"[62] as Paul Elmer More saw it, was not possible so long as men persisted in viewing mankind as perfectible and insisted on being their brother's keepers. Most of organized philanthropy was, Foerster insisted, "nothing but a form of communal materialism,"[63] which administered to the needs of the body but rigorously failed to minister to the needs of the soul. "Freedom from physical suffering is a good thing, but it is not the best. Relatively [sic] to ethical and spiritual values it is not important."[64] Physical suffering has not increased but actually decreased; humanitarianism has increased man's sensitivity to physical pain to the extent that the very moral fibers of civilization are threatened with deterioration. In the Middle Ages, when charity was under proper controls, Foerster concluded,

... there was none of the instinctive repugnance to *bodily* suffering that is so marked in the eighteenth century and later. On the contrary, the mortification of the flesh was held to be praiseworthy, torture was allowed by common consent, and burning at the stake was regarded with positive satisfaction. Not that such things are desirable. But it is clear that when humane and enlightened men could endure and approve such sights the valuation of physical pain in the Middle Ages, the great age of Christianity, was quite different from our own.[65]

The fact that humane and enlightened men could view human sacrifice on the altar of religious unity with "positive satisfaction" seemed, to Foerster, *prima facie* evidence that theirs was an age which at least had its values straight. This age had not confused the second commandment with the first. Foerster believed that humanitarianism had made us a soft, flabby people.

We are a coddled people. . . . Certainly people used to make little of bodily suffering which they could not stand at all today, such as floggings of five hundred lashes, or operations without anaesthetics. I do not recommend such suffering, for myself or others; I am simply affirming that a civilization based upon the avoidance of suffering is an empty and hollow affair.[66]

Although at times Foerster may seem extreme, he was only making more explicit the neohumanist social idealogy. The classical concept of charity invariably carried with it the corollary virtue of stoic fortitude. Fortitude, the ability to withstand pain and suffering, was viewed as a positive good. The humanitarian attempt to reduce pain to a minimum deprived people of the opportunity to develop virtue.

At this point, many of the conservative social ideas of William Graham Sumner and Edward L. Thorndike seemed to merge with those of the neohumanists. Although each arrived at his conclusions from a radically different set of conceptions of human nature, they all saw the ideal society as inevitably hierarchical and therefore rested their hopes for the future in the education of the gifted child. All argued against the social meliorists, who assumed that their human nature as well as society was capable of intelligent collective change, and all viewed the masses as trainable but not educable. While Sumner arrived at his conclusions by way of social Darwinism, and Thorndike by way of testing and measuring society as it exists, Babbitt and More arrived at what they thought society ought to be by way of ancient models. However, neither Foerster nor Babbitt was content to amass the classical evidence to support his case but each used humanitarian evidence whenever it seemed useful. It should be recalled that Paul Shorey, Irving Babbitt, and Paul Elmer More had attacked Edward L. Thorndike on the grounds that he was a pseudo-scientist who failed to recognize the duality of human nature and therefore his research amounted to nothing more than a compendium of errors. Although Foerster rejected the connectionist school of psychology, he looked with great favor on Thorndike's social views. Since Foerster insisted that the growth of the state universities, as well as our secondary schools, had been a waste of taxpayers' money in a foolish philanthropic venture to educate the uneducables, he was delighted to find Thorndike saying the same thing.

Unimpressed by pseudo-idealism, Professor Thorndike boldly opposes the growing tendency to keep youth in school and college as long as possible. 'Indiscriminate advances in the compulsory school age beyond sixteen seem, in view of the facts, a weak and wasteful procedure. . . . We need laws to prevent greedy or perverse parents from depriving gifted children of schooling, not laws to force them to keep in school children who have neither the ability nor the interest to profit thereby.'[67]

Obviously, Thorndike and Foerster were both interested in education of the gifted child. They were both interested in developing and maintaining a conservative social order, and they arrived at their common conclusion from opposing traditions. Both Babbitt and Foerster frequently pointed with satisfaction to the fact that the intelligence testers in World War I had confirmed what the humanists had been saying all the time; namely, that our society cannot afford to be governed by the average since "the average mental age of our male voter is about fourteen."[68] While Babbitt was quick to point out the social implications of the tests and measurement movement, Foerster was even more apt at seeing the implications for educational practice.

If we are prepared to take the psychologists' word for it most pupils may at that age [12] be divided into three groups. The first is composed of pupils who have reached, or already passed, their natural limits of educability. They are so low in endowment that further instruction would involve definite waste. The second group is composed of pupils who can be trained in preparation for some activities of citizenship and some types of vocation. Receptive of authoritative instruction, they can be indoctrinated. . . . The third group is composed of pupils who can do more than passively learn items of fact, thought, and habit, who are capable of active assimilation and expression of mind and personality.[69]

The American school might best be concerned with "indoctrination" for the masses and "education" for the gifted children. A concept of a democracy of the people, by the people, and for the people, and an education compatible with this conception were untenable. Interestingly enough, they were made untenably by the humanitarian social scientists themselves. "Even the intellectual turned against democracy, Old Style, partly because it had not worked, and partly because its dogmas could not endure the facts being amassed against them by political scientists, psychologists, and biologists."[70] Indeed,

. . . if psychology proved anything, it seemed to prove not only that people differed in intelligence but that in the aggregate they had very little of it—that, if not a great beast, as Hamilton had opined, the people were certainly a great fool.[71]

The neohumanism of Norman Foerster had reached some kind of ultimate in sophistry when he denied the validity of certain knowledge and then used that same knowledge to support his own position.

While Irving Babbitt, in the first two decades of the twentieth century, had written about the deterioration of the ideas of equalitarian democracy, social progress, and optimistic faith in the moral improvement of humanity as if this was something to be expected in the near future, Norman Foerster, writing in the next two decades, marshaled with considerable satisfaction evidence to show that this deterioration had already come to pass. John Dewey[72] and Norman Foerster both recognized the disillusionment of the American intellectual, and both saw it as an opportunity to introduce their own ideas. The disillusionment, to Dewey, was caused by a rejection of traditional values, whereas, to Foerster, the disillusionment was caused by a rejection of naturalistic values and the eroding of Enlightenment concepts. To Dewey, the opportunity lay in the development of a science of man based on the reconstruction of

Enlightenment values; to Foerster, the opportunity lay in the renaissance of humanism. Both men, however, sensed certain features in this crisis in American values which Daniel Bell aptly described some decades later as a profound distrust on the part of the younger generation for any neat, systematic philosophy of human nature or the good society.[73]

As Foerster carried the neohumanist ideology to mid-century, certain subtle changes in his attitude may be noted. He himself did not report any major changes in his thought, nor did his last important educational work, *The Humanities and the Common Man* (1946), indicate any fundamental change in his concept of the nature of man, the function of knowledge, the nature of the good curriculum, or the nature of the teaching-learning process. Nevertheless, there was an explicit shift from a more aristocratic to a more equalitarian view of the function of the humanities. Less emphasis was given to the evils of mass education and "indoctrination" for the masses, and more emphasis was given to the ideal of a liberal education for all men. The humanities, he commented, "are not exclusive, not for any class, not for an artificial aristocracy of birth or wealth, not for a natural aristocracy of intelligence, but for all men and women."[74] He further suggested that:

To say that what is great is for the few is to insult the common man, to deny the element of greatness in his nature. He has a stake in spiritual as well as material wealth. The century of the common man calls for a better distribution of material wealth; it needs, no less, a better distribution of spiritual wealth.[75]

This, indeed, was not neohumanism as Babbitt or More developed it, nor was it the same as Foerster's own ideas as expressed in his earlier works. One can only speculate as to why this shift occurred. Perhaps Foerster was pragmatically sensitive to the postwar atmosphere which had little tolerance for elitist systems and felt it necessary to redirect neohumanism toward a more democratic view of the good society. One thing was clear, however. As Norman Foerster began to write about the humanities for all men, without making distinctions between the freemen (the liberally educable) and the slave class (the uneducable), he brought neohumanism more closely in line with the more liberal ideas of such literary humanists as Mark Van Doren and Jacques Barzun and the rational humanism of Hutchins and Adler, who insisted that liberal education in a democratic society must be for all.

By mid-century, neohumanism had been redefined by Norman Foerster to mean something very different from what Babbitt and More had envisioned at the beginning of the century. Foerster, sensitive to the trends of the times, displayed a greater willingness to modify his position than had any of his predecessors. In his attempt to make Jefferson the precursor of neohumanism, and in his later, more explicit concern for the "greatness" of the common man's nature, he demonstrated a sensitivity to the major trend of the twentieth century, the democratization of American culture. It is important to recognize, however, that at no time did Foerster explicitly recognize a conflict between the American concept of democracy and the classical conception. Nor did he change his conception of human nature. Whether Foerster's change from aristocratic to democratic emphasis was sophistical, superficial, or sincere remains an unanswered question.

In his willingness to substitute the modern for the classical languages, Foerster represented a sharp break with the educational tradition in which both Babbitt and More placed their faith. While neohumanism, under Foerster, continued to bear the marks of the classical tradition, the classical languages no longer were held to be an absolute requirement for a liberal education. The terms *classical humanism* and *neohumanism* ceased to be interchangeable. Although Foerster in his earlier works carried the neohumanist's conception of charity to its logical conclusions, there is a distinct absence of the suffering wisdom of Parzival in his later works. Here again, Foerster may have been sensitive to the social thought of the American citizenry, as the American public increasingly came to look at poverty and physical suffering as an evil breeding vice and delinquency, and less as a human condition which would enable the moral athlete to vault to spiritual virtue.

Although Babbitt's and More's neohumanism ceased with Norman Foerster, much of the classical rationale of Babbitt and More resounded in the great debate in American education at mid-century. Voices calling for discipline, community of values, narrow and prescribed curriculum, elimination of electives, elimination of educational frills, separation of utilitarian from liberal studies, education for the leadership class, and education as transmission of our cultural heritage could be heard with increasing vigor. Though the exact formulation of neohumanism changed with Norman Foerster, the educational values inherent in this tradition remained very much alive.

New Conservatism

No sooner had Norman Foerster begun to find a place for the humanities in the education of the common man than others took up the cudgel against humanitarianism in the interest of the conservative

society as Babbitt and More defined that society. Peter Viereck in
Conservatism: From John Adams to Churchill (1956), Russell Kirk
in *A Program for Conservatives* (1954), and Gordon Keith Chalmers
in *The Republic and the Person* (1952) clearly resurrected Irving
Babbitt's view of the good society. As an editor of *Modern Age* and a
frequent contributor to the *National Review,* Russell Kirk led the
attack on social and educational humanitarianism. Although there
are differences between the neohumanists and the neoconservatives,
their conception of the good society as aristocratic, their scathing
denunciation of democratic values, their abhorrence of mass culture,
their retreat into tradition, and their attack on education are all
common characteristics. Thus, Russell Kirk said:

A truly conservative system of learning, aimed at some restoration of the ideal of
the unbought grace of life, cannot breathe until the stifling empire of the doctrinaire Deweyites is overthrown. For no one in our time is more old-fashioned
than a hard-and-fast pupil of John Dewey; the weight of this being upon our
schools and colleges and universities is the weight of an intellectual corpse.[76]

Very much in line with Norman Foerster's view, Kirk went on to
attack the naïve democratic notion of majority rule. The masses are
not going to save civilized culture from destruction, Kirk pointed
out, for "no mysterious wisdom abides in the bosom of the people."
Only through the education of the gifted will humanity find stability
enough to survive in the twentieth century. The steps required were
clearly pointed out by Kirk:

The *public* is not going to save us from the decay of reason; we must save
ourselves, and thereby society. The first step is to confess that any society, no
matter how democratic politically, requires leaders of opinion and taste and
serious thought, and that the primary purpose of any system of education is to
encourage and instruct those leaders, the guardians of the World and unbought
grace of life. The second step is to resuscitate that liberal learning which teaches
men the meaning of time and duty, and which nurtures the idea of a gentleman.[77]

The liberal learning that Kirk proposed to resuscitate bore the
familiar marks of neohumanism. When it came to education, however, the new conservatives proposed a greater militancy against the
doctrinaire Deweyites. As Kirk put it, "the modern thinking conservative [when dealing with education] must employ some of the
methods of revolutionaries, and echo the Jacobin cry of Danton,
'audacity, and again audacity and always audacity.' "[78] Repeatedly,
the neohumanists provided the ammunition with which the neocon-

servatives attacked education with audacity. Since the neohumanists were the disfranchised educationists of the twentieth century, their arsenal was well stocked with educational criticism. By mid-century, such neoconservatives as Russell Kirk, Gordon Keith Chalmers, and such leaders in the Council for Basic Education as James D. Koerner, Harold Clapp, and Douglas Bush seemed to find the neohumanists' ammunition extremely useful for attacking humanitarians in education. In Koerner's *The Case for Basic Education,* [79] and Clapp's and Bush's frequent essays in the Council for Basic Education *Bulletin,* the educational views of Babbitt and More reached a wider audience. [80] In general, most neoconservatives not only sympathized with the educational views of Babbitt but also found considerable grounds for agreement with his conception of human nature and the good society. By 1956, in the twilight of the McCarthy era, amid growing attacks on the schools, Russell Kirk felt that things were looking up for the neohumanists:

... nowadays their number is increasing rapidly. University and college presidents like Dr. Nathan Pusey and Dr. Gordon Keith Chalmers have been his disciples; some of the best-known Catholic writers and some of the most able Protestant clergymen acknowledge their debt to him and the rising generation is rallying round the memory of Irving Babbitt who died in 1933. [81]

Kirk went on to say: "The Marxist, Freudian, instrumentalist, and naturalist schools of opinion against which Babbitt and Paul Elmer More and their friends contended so stoutly are now in their marked decline." [82] Babbitt, according to Kirk, had won the battle after all. One is inclined to wonder if, again, Kirk might have mistaken the end of the Marxist, Freudian, instrumentalist, and naturalist schools for what was really the end of ideology, and the end of systematic schools, including humanism, in which the younger generation could no longer place their faith.

Literary Humanism

While neoconservatism was, in a very real sense, the authentic heir of neohumanism as Babbitt defined it, there were other humanists who rejected Babbitt's narrow, aristocratic social and educational views and yet were a significant part of the literary humanist tradition. This group, represented by such men as Mark Van Doren, Gilbert Highet, and Jacques Barzun, reflected far more liberal humanitarian social views. In many ways, this group was more akin to the sweetness and light of Matthew Arnold than to the narrowed stoicism of Irving Babbitt.

These literary humanists kept alive the role of the well-rounded amateur whose function it was to act as an influential social and educational critic. Just as it was the orator's function to use the spoken word artistically to persuade, so it was the function of the man of literature, the man of taste, to use the written word to persuade. One might well ask: Persuade humanity to what? The answer was clear: To persuade humanity toward those truths which the disciplined, well-rounded amateur senses are true. As word artists, these men exerted a powerful influence on the literate population.[83] They could, in a sense, paint a picture of American education and society as bright or as dark as they felt it warranted.

As heirs of the rhetorical tradition, the literary humanists were the modern-day orators who employed their talents not on the public platform of oral debate but on that of written debate. Thus, when Jacques Barzun in *Teacher in America* (1945) painted with verve and humor the picture of the "Ph.D. octopus," one could not help but sense the ideal of the well-rounded gentleman lurking in the shadows. One could also recall that it was that same Ph.D. specialist who advanced the cause of technological and theoretical science at the expense of the humanist's well-rounded man. The ideal of the Ph.D. was not to know all the best that was thought and said in the past, but rather to create new knowledge. As the Ph.D. replaced the amateur at the head place of the table of culture, many humanists such as Barzun were seriously concerned about the humanist's loss. When Barzun further suggested that the "three great forces of mind and will—Art, Science, and Philanthropy—have, it is clear, become enemies of Intellect,"[84] one could detect strong overtones of Babbitt's concern with Rousseauian art, Baconian science, and humanitarian philanthropy. In Barzun's attack on Philanthropy, one could not help but sense a reflection of Cicero's attitude toward benevolence as dangerously corrupting, if not discriminately controlled. As Barzun pictured "education without instruction" and "instruction without authority"[85] as characteristic of the American school, he portrayed the failings and excesses of mass education in a humanitarian society as a modern humanist sees them.

The humanists, as schoolmasters, represented the oldest educational tradition in the history of the West. As such, their central focus was on the education of the well-rounded man. Aside from the educational ideal of the orator-courtier-gentleman, there remained the consistent recognition that the teaching process is fundamentally an art. Whether it was Quintilian, concerned with the education of the orator, Erasmus with the Christian prince, Matthew Arnold with the English gentleman, or Gilbert Highet with the liberally educated man, all viewed teaching as an art which involved discipline, discrimination, emotion, and imitation. While the teaching process involved orderly planning and some degree of precision, it could not be made scientific.[86] As Gilbert Highet aptly put it:

Teaching is not like inducing a chemical reaction: it is much more like painting a picture or making a piece of music, or on a lower level like planting a garden or writing a friendly letter. You must throw your heart into it, you must realize that it cannot all be done by formulas, or you spoil your work, and your pupils, and yourself.[87]

In a narrower, more conservative, polemical fashion, A. Whitney Griswold lamented the decline of liberal education in America. The cause of this decline he attributed not only to the elective system espoused by Charles W. Eliot, the instrumentalism of John Dewey, and the rise of departments of education on university campuses, but, more important, to the influence on American education of the immigrant, whose children filled the classrooms of the twentieth-century educational frontier. The parents of such children did not "comprehend" the meaning of a liberal education, and consequently they failed to support it.[88] However, what Griswold failed to realize was that much of the classical conception of a liberal education was premised on the assumption that only the few were educable and that many of the staunchest defenders of the tradition, such as Paul Shorey, Irving Babbitt, Paul Elmer More, Norman Foerster, and Albert Jay Nock,[89] had failed to heed Matthew Arnold's warning that the age of the common man was about to dawn.

Considerably more sensitive to this advent, Mark Van Doren insisted: "The notion of Nock is that only a few are educable, whereas the thesis of this book is that many are and indeed all men."[90] In the fifties, many literary humanists took a similar position and attempted to define a liberal education for all men in terms of a democratic society. Few, however, were optimistic that a future American culture would be any more receptive to their educational ideas than had been the case in the immediate past. The flood of new knowledge had inundated virtually all the humanist's hallowed ground. It was symptomatic of the times that, more often than not, the literary humanist spoke of re-creating the educational ideal rather than preserving it. If Joseph Wood Krutch was correct when he said, "The modern novels most discussed in advanced circles during the fifties are nihilistic. . . . They preach despair rather than, as Lewis did, the benefits of a culture accessible to all who want it,"[91] then the literary humanists, in re-creating their educational ideal, would have to contend not only with the naturalistic pragmatism of James or Dewey but, more important, with the nihilism of a Nietzschean view of reality. Such a view had become increasingly popular with the *avant-garde* of the younger generation.

Philosophic Humanism

The rational humanism of Hutchins and Adler relied heavily on St. Thomas Aquinas and Aristotle for its definition of man. Rational humanism was to the Middle Ages what literary humanism was to the Renaissance; i.e., where the Renaissance emphasized rhetoric and esthetic taste, the Middle Ages emphasized logic and scholastic reasoning. Hutchins and Adler defined man's nature as divided between his reason and his passions in basically Aristotelian terms. The essence of man's nature that distinguishes him from the animal world was his ability to reason. This was viewed as a universal characteristic of man in every time and place. It followed, then, that a truly liberal education was that education which liberates man's mind from his passions, an education which teaches men to think rationally; a vocational education, on the other hand, teaches men to use their hands. As a result of American pragmatism and many other materialistic and naturalistic influences, this innate dualism has been ignored, and American education has become permeated from the early grades through the university with a confused vocationalism. Very much in the rationalistic tradition, Hutchins assumed universal truths, a universal metaphysics as well as a universal nature of man. Just as Aristotle was concerned with the essence of man but not his accidents and Aquinas was concerned with the unity of truth, so Hutchins argued that the essence of man, truth, and education were everywhere the same. As he put it:

One purpose of education is to draw out the elements of our common nature. These elements are the same in any time or place. The notion of educating a man to live in any particular time or place, to adjust him to any particular environment is therefore foreign to a true conception of education.[92]

What follows, then, is an oft-quoted but questionable syllogism. "Education implies teaching. Teaching implies knowledge. Knowledge is truth. The truth is everywhere the same. Hence education should be everywhere the same."[93] If education is rightly understood, it will inevitably be "the same at any time, in any place, under any political, social, or economic conditions."[94]

Starting with a universal conception of human nature and a

universal conception of education, Hutchins went on to sketch a blueprint of higher education in terms of the trivium and quadrivium as he understood them. Ultimately, the aim of higher education was wisdom. "Wisdom is knowledge of principles and causes. Metaphysics deals with the highest principles and causes. Therefore metaphysics is the highest wisdom."[95] Metaphysics became for Hutchins and Adler the highest science. Herein lies one of the major differences between the religious humanism of Jacques Maritain and the rational humanism of Hutchins and Adler. While Hutchins and Adler stopped at metaphysics, Maritain completed the Thomist system with theology as the "queen of science" and the ultimate source of wisdom.

From Hutchins' and Adler's point of view, the disintegration of American education was of such a nature that this was no time to quibble about theology. What was needed was a clear definition of man as a rational animal and a clear set of educational aims that proceed from first principles. The education which follows must be that kind of education which develops men's intellectual virtues.

I suggest that the cultivation of the intellectual virtues can be accomplished through the communication of our intellectual tradition and through training in the intellectual disciplines. This means understanding the great thinkers of the past and present, scientific, historical, and philosophical. It means a grasp of the disciplines of grammar, rhetoric, logic, and mathematics; reading, writing, and figuring. It does not, of course, mean the exclusion of contemporary materials. They should be brought in daily to illustrate, confirm, or deny the ideas held by the writers under discussion.[96]

At St. John's College in Annapolis, Maryland, under the presidency of Stringfellow Barr, Hutchins had his chance to test his ideas in action. With the trivium and quadrivium as loose guidelines, the four-year college curriculum was designed around the one hundred "great books" of Western civilization.[97] Such a reconstruction of the liberal arts curriculum was designed to develop those intellectual powers necessary for a rational man. Neither Hutchins nor Barr nor Adler was concerned with vocational, technical, or professional education, but rather that education which is necessary for developing those characteristics common to all men's nature. Once one was liberally educated, he could then proceed to apply himself to whatever specialty he selected. Thorndike had not convinced everyone that mental discipline did not work. This was most clearly illustrated when Stringfellow Barr argued:

The man who has learned to practice these arts successfully, can 'concentrate' on anything, can 'apply himself' to anything, can quickly learn any specialty, any profession, any business. That man can deliberate, can make practical decisions by other means than tossing a coin, can understand his failures, can recognize his obligations as well as his opportunities. He is in short what an earlier generation eloquently termed 'an educated man.'[98]

Although few institutions at the college level followed the direction of St. John's, Hutchins and Adler went on to argue that a similar curriculum should be organized at the high school level. They both believed that if all men have a common nature and there is a common content best designed to develop this common nature, then a democratic society which has equalized the right to vote must be primarily concerned with the development of the intellectual arts in *all* children, and not just the gifted few.[99] What is needed is not, as Thorndike would have it, one kind of content for the slow learner and another kind of content for the gifted, nor, as Babbitt would have it, a humanistic education for the few and humanitarian education for the many, but rather the same content for all children. "I insist, however, that the education I shall outline is the kind that everybody should have, that the answer to it is not that some people should not have it, but that we should find out how to give it to those whom we do not know how to teach at present."[100] Hutchins and Alder consistently pressed their point that any educational system which presumes to take as its goal critical thinking for the gifted and something less than this for the average or less-than-average student is an educational system designed for something less than a free democratic society. Under the guise of meeting individual needs, Hutchins charged, American educators avoided the tougher problem of how to liberally educate the common man.[101]

Hutchins' and Adler's good society was the democratic society where all men were equipped to carry on the "great conversation." Such a society was predicated not on a slave class as in ancient Greece, nor on a serf class as in the Middle Ages, but on the idea that all men can be free. The rational humanists were selective with respect to what aspects of the historic tradition they chose to espouse. Aristotle, for instance, had made a mistake when he concluded that some men are by nature slaves. As Hutchins said, "Aristotle's views on the natural slave are refuted by a simple reference to his basic proposition that man is a political animal. If all men are men, none of them can by nature be a slave."[102]

Aristotle had come to his conclusions from a study of man within Greek society, which depended on slavery; and Robert Hutchins derived his view of human nature within a society that rejected slavery. If, in one social context, one can conclude natural slavery, and in another, rational freedom for all, either human nature or our perspective of that nature has changed. There was something in the rational humanist's position approaching contradiction. If neither human nature nor education had changed, then the social system had changed our conception of that nature. As much as Hutchins and Adler universalized education and human nature outside of society, many of their views on human nature, as well as on education, were conditioned by their own conception of the good society—which was neither ancient nor medieval, but very modern indeed.

While Hutchins and Adler proved to be formidable educational critics who prepared the way for other critics by mid-twentieth century, the direction they attempted to push American education was not followed. The multiplicity of purposes of education in a pluralistic society were not easily rationalized into a single purpose, nor in actual practice was it as easy to distinguish the liberal from the technical as both Hutchins and Adler had argued. To a considerable extent, both men were voices crying in the wilderness of a technocracy. A technological society which valued change and relied on specialists in many fields of human knowledge for its very survival was neither able nor, indeed, willing to trust its educational fortunes to the idea of Stringfellow Barr that a St. John's type of education adequately educates one for "any specialty, any profession, any business." The age when John Milton could define a liberal education as that education "which fits a man to perform justly, skillfully, and magnanimously all the offices, both private and public, of peace and war" had passed.

Religious Humanism

Throughout the history of the West, there has existed a dynamic tension between supernaturalism and naturalism. From Darwin on, however, the major thrust of Western culture has been toward a naturalistic definition of man and culture. So much has this been true that men have frequently described the modern era as the "post-Christian era." Paralleling this trend in Europe at the beginning of the century and in America by mid-twentieth century has been the decline of certain key Enlightenment ideas which seem to undermine man's confidence not only in God but also in himself. Not only the gods of the supernaturalists had come under question but also the gods of reason, nature, and science. In the midst of this transvaluation emerged both a nihilistic and an existential view of reality.

In the context of this *Zeitgeist* of disillusionment, there also emerged various reassertions of older traditional religious values in terms of Protestant neo-orthodoxy and neo-Thomism. While the neo-orthodoxy of Karl Barth, Reinhold Niebuhr, and Paul Tillich evolved from an existential base, the Thomism of Jacques Maritain was clearly a reconstruction of St. Thomas Aquinas' thirteenth-century synthesis of faith and reason, naturalism and supernatural-ism, cast in terms of the twentieth century. Although Thomism cannot be judged an influential philosophy outside of Roman Catholic education in America, within that faith it is a vitally significant philosophy. In American education, however, it not only nicely illustrates a tightly reasoned position with respect to the problem of defining human nature and its implications for educational practice but also clearly illuminates those areas where beliefs in supernatural revelation do make a difference in practice.

For American educators, Jacques Maritain (b. 1882) was among the more influential leaders in the revival of the philosophy of St. Thomas Aquinas in the twentieth century. For almost fifty years as a teacher and writer at the Collège Stanislas and the Institut Catholique in Paris, at the Institute of Mediaeval Studies in Toronto, and at Princeton University, Maritain reworked and reconstructed Thomistic philosophy. As had Aquinas, Maritain insisted that there was no conflict between the natural and the supernatural if they were rightly understood. There was a place for philosophy and a place for theology within a unified cosmology. While man's nature is divided between a spiritual soul and a natural body, the two are integrally a part of the unified man. Although neither Maritain nor Aquinas could accept a strict Cartesian dualism, on close analysis there always remained a functional dualism of body and soul, matter and spirit.

Just as Aquinas conceived of universal Christendom with one body politic and one church, Maritain conceived of the good society as a democratic Christian world society. If there was a universal natural law, which Aquinas thought he had arrived at through Aristotelian reasoning, and a universal divine law revealed in Christian scripture and tradition, then the ideal society was not to be found in the national state but in a universal world state. In the post-World War II period, both Hutchins and Maritain argued for an international world order based on a Thomistic model.[103] Such a society would be permeated by the "Christian spirit." As Maritain put it:

Well, those Christians who are turned toward the future and who hope—be it a long range hope—for a new Christendom, a new Christianly inspired civilization, know that 'the world has done with neutrality. Willingly or unwillingly, states will be obliged to make a choice for or against the Gospel. They will be shaped either by the totalitarian spirit or by the Christian spirit.' They know that a new Christianly inspired civilization, if and when it evolves in history, will by no means be a return to the Middle Ages, but a typically different attempt to make the leaven of the Gospel quicken the depths of temporal existence.[104]

The possibility of the development of the world state as a purely Christian civilization was recognized by Maritain as remote. But he retained the possibility that men could arrive at the idea of natural law through the use of their natural reason, as Aquinas had suggested. Perhaps Hutchins and Adler were more realistic on this point. Humanity with its many faiths might be expected to use its natural reason to arrive at a universal metaphysics more readily than it could come to accept a universal theology. Nevertheless, Maritain stayed with the synthesis of Aquinas and insisted that theology was functionally related to a correct definition of man, society, and education.

Jacques Maritain shared Paul Elmer More's concern, late in life, that an educational humanism without a theology seems to lead back to the humanitarian camp in the end, and if not there, nowhere. Fundamentally, Maritain argued that the education of man today suffers from a false definition of the ends of education. The sociologist who conceives of man in terms of his social needs, the psychologist who conceives of man in terms of psychological needs, and the pragmatist who insists on reconstructing ends as well as means give, at best, a partial view of man's nature and the appropriate education, and at worst, a very false conception. The true education of man must be based on the Christian idea of man if it is to be well grounded. Such an idea incorporates and assumes the divine destiny of man. Man is defined

. . . as an animal endowed with reason, whose supreme dignity is in the intellect; and man as a free individual in personal relation with God, whose supreme righteousness consists in voluntarily obeying the law of God; and man as a sinful and wounded creature called to divine life and to the freedom of grace, whose supreme perfection consists of love.[105]

Maritain never lost sight of this end. Education is an art, an artistic endeavor in the creation of the Christian man who uses all his faculties for the ultimate glory of God.[106]

While Hutchins separated the vocational from the liberal in a very rigorous fashion, Maritain viewed the technical as an integral part of a liberally educated man. Maritain had far more confidence that the technical could be humanized as part of a unified educational experience. On this point, interestingly, there is a greater consensus between John Dewey and Maritain than there is between Maritain and Hutchins. In fact, when Maritain left the "aims of education" and discussed the "dynamics of education," there were numerous points upon which pragmatic and naturalistic educators were in hearty agreement with him.[107] Nevertheless, the fundamentally supernaturalist view of man held by Maritain remained irreconcilable with the fundamentally naturalistic philosophy of John Dewey. If, however, those on the naturalistic side found it difficult to reach consensus as to the nature of man or the good society, those on the supernaturalist side were just as divided. Once one got beyond the definition of the Christian man and Christian civilization to its meaning in action, the pluralistic religious character of American society came into play. American society reflected a fundamental secular as well as religious pluralism by mid-twentieth century. In view of this pluralism, perhaps Conant was correct in not asking the ultimate questions but rather directing attention to those educational practices upon which a greater consensus could be reached.

Humanism itself could not be characterized as an educational philosophy which defined man's nature, the good society, and educational practice with complete unanimity. While the narrow classicism of Babbitt and More might be favorable compared with the neoconservatism of Russell Kirk, neither position would fit well with the urbane literary humanism of Jacques Barzun or Gilbert Highet, nor would Hutchins' and Adler's emphasis on a universal metaphysics set well within the literary humanist tradition. More important was the fact that the rational and literary humanists were divided in their conception of the good society all the way from a very elitist position on the one hand to a great concern for a democratic society on the other.

There were, however, broad areas of agreement. All found eternal verities in tradition and, more often than not, conceived of human nature as unchanged by time and place and of education as a changeless art. If pragmatists were concerned with a scientific view of man in a universe of change, the humanists were concerned with the literature and philosophy of man in a universe of stability and eternal truths. On the surface, most humanists would agree with Dewey's suggestion that educators must learn "to make acquaintance with the past a *means* for understanding the present" and with Whitehead's assertion that "the only use of a knowledge of the past is to equip us for the present."[108] Most humanists found in their past more certitude to explain their present than either Dewey or Whitehead had found. The humanist quest for present certainty was satisfied by their study of the past. The eternal truths were not only revealed in the past, but the past explained how humanity had gone astray. Repeatedly, it was scientific naturalism, the idea of progress, social meliorism, mass philanthropy, and romantic art which had corrupted American society, which in turn had corrupted American education. The humanists, then, provided some of the main social and educational criticism in twentieth-century American education. As such, they disagreed at times with each other as to the nature of the good society and at various points as to the meaning of a liberal education, as well as the nature of man. Nevertheless, all would firmly agree with Emerson when he said:

> There are two laws discrete,
> Not reconciled—
> Law for man, and law for thing;
> The last builds town and fleet,
> But it runs wild,
> And doth the man unking.

FOOTNOTES

1. Edward Waldo Emerson, ed., *The Complete Works of Ralph Waldo Emerson*, (Cambridge, Mass.: Riverside Press, 1904), 9:78.

2. Lawrence A. Cremin, *The Transformation of the School* (New York: Alfred A. Knopf, Inc., 1961).

3. Irving Babbitt, *Literature and the American College* (Boston: Houghton Mifflin Company, 1908), p. 22.

4. *Ibid.*, p. 7.

5. For a similar conception of humanism, see Paul Elmer More, *Shelburne Essays*, (Boston: Houghton Mifflin Company, 1913), vol. I.

6. Irving Babbitt, *The Masters of Modern French Criticism* (Boston: Houghton Mifflin Company, 1912), p. 247.

7. Irving Babbitt, *On Being Creative* (Boston: Houghton Mifflin Company, 1932), p. 199.

8. Irving Babbitt, *Democracy and Leadership* (Boston: Houghton Mifflin Company, 1924), p. 310.

9. More, *Shelburne Essays*, 9:26. This is a quotation from Burke which More used to express his own sentiment.

10. For More's concept of aristocracy see "Natural Aristocracy," *Shelburne Essays*, 9:3-38.

11. See More, *Shelburne Essays*, 9:31.

12. See Babbitt, *Democracy and Leadership*, p. 16. Babbitt's and More's distrust of the people is much like that of Emile Faguet who expressed his ideas in *The Cult of Incompetence*.

13. Babbitt, *Literature and the American College*, p. 71.

14. More, *Shelburne Essays*, 9:197.

15. Babbitt, *Literature and the American College*, pp. 10-11.

16. Babbitt, *Democracy and Leadership*, p. 207.

17. More, *Shelburne Essays*, 9:136. The attitude of Babbitt and More toward property and social meliorism is very much akin to that of another decided opponent of social meliorism, William Graham Sumner.

18. Babbitt, *Literature and the American College*, p. 34.

19. See Moses Hadas, ed., *The Basic Works of Cicero* (New York: The Modern Library, 1951).

20. Babbitt, *Literature and the American College*, p. 34.

21. Babbitt, *Democracy and Leadership*, p. 201.

22. See More, *Shelburne Essays*, 1:251.

23. *Ibid.*, 9:288.

24. *Ibid.*, 1:250-251. One would suspect that both Babbitt and More, if alive today, would view the current activities of various churches in the civil rights movement as a continuation of the same humanitarian sentiment. The recent "War on Poverty" would probably also be viewed as another humanitarian venture which fattens the budgets of the bureaucracy and collectively alleviates the guilt and anxiety of people escaping their individual responsibility.

25. Some even suggested that the solution to the educational problems of the urban centers lay in the creation of public boarding schools, much as Robert Dale Owen had proposed earlier in the nineteenth century.

26. Babbitt, *Democracy and Leadership*, p. 313.

27. More, *Shelburne Essays*, 1:300.

28. *Ibid.*, 9:37.

29. *Ibid.*, p. 47.

30. It is interesting that neither Babbitt nor More recognized the classical dualism of Freud and consistently typed him as a Rousseauian romantic. It seems clear that Babbitt did not get the same insights into human nature as Freud from Sophocles' *Antigone* and *Oedipus Rex*. See Edmund Wilson, "Sophocles, Babbitt, and Freud," *New Republic*, 65 (Dec. 3, 1930): 68-71.

31. Irving Babbitt, "What I Believe," *The Forum* (Feb. 1930), p. 83.

32. Paul Elmer More, *The Skeptical Approach to Religion*, 5th ed. (Princeton, N. J.: Princeton University Press, 1958), p. 100.

33. Paul Elmer More, *The Demon of the Absolute* (Princeton, N. J.: Princeton University Press, 1928), p. 26.

34. Irving Babbitt, *On Being Creative* (Boston: Houghton Mifflin Company, 1932), p. 14.

35. Babbitt, *Literature and the American College*, p. 180.

36. J. S. Watson, trans., *Cicero on Oratory and Orators* (New York: Harper & Brothers, 1860), p. 19.

37. One might, however, recognize that Cicero's orator was more a man of action, whereas the neohumanist man of taste tended more toward the contemplative life.

38. See Robert M. Davies, *The Humanism of Paul Elmer More* (New York: Bookman Associates, Inc., 1958).

39. Paul Elmer More, *On Being Human* (Princeton N. J.: Princeton University Press, 1936), p. 20.

40. The direction of More's thought is clearly portrayed in the titles of his books: *Platonism* (1917), *The Religion of Plato* (1921), *The Christ of the New Testament* (1924), *Christ the Word* (1927), *The Catholic Faith* (1931), *Anglicanism* (1935).

41. See Norman Foerster, *Toward Standards* (New York: Farrar & Rinehart,

Inc., 1930), p. 157. See also Norman Foerster, ed., *Humanism and America* (New York: Farrar & Rinehart, Inc., 1930), p. ix. To be sure, all these men did not exactly duplicate the thought of Babbitt and More. There were minor differences, and some defected from the neohumanists' ranks early. Thus, Stuart P. Sherman was viewed by other neohumanists as a renegade. As Foerster put it, "He drifted from his humanistic position into an ever vaguer faith in the common man, and at length as a literary journalist in New York, into a rather indulgent impressionism."

42. As Louis J. A. Mercier put it, "But Foerster alone developed a systematic and prolonged exploitation of Babbitt's humanism." Louis J. A. Mercier, *American Humanism and the New Age* (Milwaukee: Bruce Publishing Company, 1948), p. 166.

43. Norman Foerster, *The American State University* (Chapel Hill: University of North Carolina Press, 1937), p. 59.

44. *Ibid.*, pp. 261-263.

45. By 1934 the number of students in public high school taking Greek was so small that Greek was no longer listed as a subject of study in the public secondary school. See *The Biennial Survey of Education in the United States, 1934-1936* (Bulletin 1937, No. 2, U. S. Printing Office, 1939), vol. 2, chap. 1, "Statistical Summary of Education, 1935-1936," p. 20.

46. Foerster, *American State University*, p. 261.

47. *Ibid.*, p. 262.

48. Foerster, *Toward Standards*, p. 167.

49. Norman Foerster, *The Future of the Liberal College* (New York: D. Appleton-Century Company, 1938), p. 77.

50. Foerster, *Toward Standards*, p. 205.

51. *Ibid.*, p. 202.

52. *Ibid.*, p. 204. One might also consider the practical support the churches gave to neohumanism through their emphasis on the classical languages. It was the private schools which persistently held Latin and Greek in the curriculum of the secondary schools. In 1934, the percentage of students taking Latin in public secondary schools had dropped to 16.04 percent and Greek to almost nothing. In 1933, the private high schools reported 56.0 percent in Latin and 1.6 percent in Greek. In spite of the fact that the enrollment of the private schools more than doubled between 1900 and 1933, one can note a rise in the percentage of students taking Latin from 46.9 percent in 1900 to 56.0 percent in 1933. The great bulk of these private high schools were church-affiliated schools; 2113 were reported sectarian and 522 nonsectarian. See *The Biennial Survey of Education in the United States, 1934-1936*, "Statistical Summary of Education," pp. 23-24.

53. *Ibid.*, p. 161.

54. Foerster, *Future of the Liberal College*, p. 17.

55. *Ibid.*, p. 75.

56. Foerster, *Toward Standards*, p. 188.

57. Babbitt, *Democracy and Leadership*, p. 283.

58. Foerster, *American State University*, p. 32.

59. *Ibid.*, p. 32.

60. See Benjamin Jowett, trans. and ed., *The Politics of Aristotle* (Oxford: The Clarendon Press, 1885).

61. Foerster, *American State University*, p. 179.

62. More, *On Being Human*, pp. 154-155.

63. Foerster, *Future of the Liberal College*, p. 19.

64. *Ibid.*, p. 9.

65. *Ibid.*, p. 8.

66. Norman Foerster, "The College, the Individual, and Society," *The American Review* 4, no. 2 (December 1934): 139.

67. Foerster, *American State University*, p. 176.

68. Babbitt, *Democracy and Leadership*, p. 264. Also see Foerster, *American State University*, p. 171.

69. Foerster, quoting a *New York Times* excerpt (March 20, 1932) of an address by Thorndike; *American State University*, p. 179.

70. Foerster, *American State University*, p. 137.

71. *Ibid.*, p. 138.

72. See John Dewey, "What I Believe," *Forum* 83, no. 3 (March 1930): 176-182.

73. See Daniel Bell, *The End of Ideology* (New York: The Free Press of Glencoe, Inc., 1960).

74. Norman Foerster, *The Humanities and the Common Man* (Chapel Hill: University of North Carolina Press, 1946), p. vii.

75. *Ibid.*, p. viii.

76. Russell Kirk, *A Program for Conservatives* (Chicago: Henry Regnery Company, 1954), p. 63.

77. *Ibid.*, p. 76.

78. *Ibid.*, p. 63.

79. See also James D. Koerner, *The Miseducation of American Teachers* (Boston: Houghton Mifflin Company, 1963). For a more detailed study of neohumanism, see unpublished dissertation (University of Wisconsin, 1960) by Clarence J. Karier, "The Neo-Humanist Protest in American Education, 1890-1933." For the relationship between the neohumanists and the Council for Basic Education, see Robert H. Beck, "The New Conservatism and the New Humanism," *Teachers College Record* 63 (May 1962): 435-444.

80. To be sure, not all who sympathized with the Council's position were neohumanists or neoconservatives. For example, when the Council sponsored Admiral H. G. Rickover's book, *Swiss Schools and Ours: Why Theirs Are Better* (Boston: Little, Brown and Company, 1962), they were supporting not a humanist who looked to the past for the eternal verities but a scientist whose main concern was with the present development of academic talent for a scientific technological age. Both Rickover and the Council called for a radical reconstruction of American education, but for very different reasons.

81. Russell Kirk's introduction to Babbitt's *Literature and the American College* (Los Angeles: Gateway Editions, Inc., 1956), p. vii.

82. *Ibid.*, p. viii.

83. Perhaps the best example of this occurred when William H. Whyte, trained in literature, attacked the social scientist's methodology and then went on to verbally paint a picture of what the Organization Man really looked like: *The Organization Man* (New York: Simon and Schuster, Inc., 1956). As an amateur, disciplined in literature, Whyte carried on the great dialog with many people as he intuitively sensed what was taking place. He, then, verbally painted the picture of the "new suburbia." It is interesting that some social scientists mistook a literary approach to social criticism for social science research!

84. Jacques Barzun, *The House of Intellect* (New York: Harper & Brothers, 1959), p. 27.

85. *Ibid.*, pp. 88-144.

86. It is interesting that on this point John Dewey could agree with the humanists. While much scientific work could be done with respect to education, Dewey believed the teaching process itself was an art. See John Dewey, *The Sources of a Science of Education* (New York: Liveright Publishing Corporation, 1929).

87. Gilbert Highet, *The Art of Teaching* (New York: Vintage Books, 1954), p. viii.

88. A. Whitney Griswold, *Liberal Education and the Democratic Ideal*, rev. ed. (New Haven: Yale University Press, 1962), p. 25.

89. See Albert Jay Nock, *The Theory of Education in the United States* (New York: Harcourt, Brace and Company, 1932).

90. Mark Van Doren, *Liberal Education* (Boston: The Beacon Press, 1959), p. 70.

91. Joseph Wood Krutch, "Reflections on the Fifties," *Saturday Review* (January 2, 1960), p. 9.

92. Robert Maynard Hutchins, *The Higher Learning in America* (New Haven: Yale University Press, 1962), p. 66.

93. *Ibid.*, p. 66.

94. *Ibid.* Adler said essentially the same thing: "The *ultimate* ends of education are the same for all men at all times and everywhere." Mortimer J. Adler, "In Defense of the Philosophy of Education," *The Forty-First Yearbook of the National Society for the Study of Education* (Chicago: University in Chicago Press, 1942)

95. Hutchins, *Higher Learning in America*, p. 98.

96. Robert M. Hutchins, *Education for Freedom* (Baton Rouge: Louisiana State University Press, 1943), p. 60.

97. See "A Report on a Project of Self-study," *Bulletin of St. John's College in Annapolis* 7, no. 2 (April 1955). Also see Russell Thomas, *The Search for a Common Learning: General Education, 1800-1960* (New York: McGraw-Hill Book Company, 1962), pp. 230-243.

98. Quoted in V. T. Thayer, *Formative Ideas in American Education* (New York: Dodd, Mead & Company, 1965), p. 341.

99. It is interesting that although many high schools do seem to follow a modified Great Books approach in their special education of the gifted, few seem to entertain the idea that such courses should be open to the so-called average learner.

100. Hutchins, *Higher Learning in America*, p. 61.

101. By mid-century the question of what is the appropriate education of a free man in a free society was a critical question for many both in and out of the humanist fold. See, for example, the report of the Harvard Committee, *General Education in a Free Society* (Cambridge, Mass.: Harvard University Press, 1945).

102. Robert M. Hutchins, *The Democratic Dilemma* (Uppsala, Sweden: Almquist and Wirsells Boktryceri AB, 1952), p. 36.

103. See Robert M. Hutchins, *St. Thomas and the World State* (Milwaukee: Marquette University Press, 1949). Also see Jacques Maritain, *Man and the State* (Chicago: University of Chicago Press, 1951).

104. Maritain, *Man and the State*, p. 159.

105. Jacques Maritain, *Education at the Crossroads* (New Haven: Yale University Press, 1943), p. 7.

106. As Maritain put it, "May I confess at this point that, although I believe in natural morality, I feel little trust in the educational efficacy of any merely rational moral teaching abstractly detached from its religious environment." Maritain, *Education at the Crossroads* p. 68.

107. Maritain, *Education at the Crossroads*, pp. 29-57.

108. Quoted in Mortimer J. Adler and Milton Mayer, *The Revolution in Education* (Chicago: University of Chicago Press, 1958), pp. 155-156.

REFERENCES

Adler, Mortimer J., and Milton Mayer. *The Revolution in Education.* Chicago, University of Chicago Press, 1958.

Babbitt, Irving, *Democracy and Leadership.* Boston, Houghton Mifflin Company, 1924.

————. *Literature and the American College.* Boston, Houghton Mifflin Company, 1908.

————. *On Being Creative.* Boston, Houghton Mifflin Company, 1932.

Barzun, Jacques. *The House of Intellect.* New York, Harper & Brothers, 1959.

Beck, Robert H. "The New Conservatism and the New Humanism," *Teachers College Record,* 63 (May 1962): 435.

Davies, Robert M. *The Humanism of Paul Elmer More.* New York, Bookman Associates, Inc., 1958.

Foerster, Norman. *The American State University.* Chapel Hill, University of North Carolina Press, 1937.

————. *The Future of the Liberal College.* New York, D. Appleton-Century Company, 1938.

————. *The Humanities and the Common Man.* Chapel Hill, University of North Carolina Press, 1946.

————. *Toward Standards.* New, Farrar & Rinehart, 1930.

Griswold, A. Whitney. *Liberal Education and the Democratic Ideal,* rev. ed. New Haven, Yale University Press, 1962.

Highet, Gilbert. *The Art of Teaching.* New York, Vintage Books, 1954.

Hutchins, Robert M. *The Democratic Dilemma.* Uppsala, Sweden, Almquist and Wirsells Boktryceri AB, 1952.

————. *The Higher Learning in America.* New Haven, Yale University Press, 1962.

————. *St. Thomas and the World State.* Milwaukee, Marquette University Press, 1949.

Kirk, Russell. *A Program for Conservatives.* Chicago, Henry Regnery Company, 1954.

Krutch, Joseph Wood. "Reflections on the Fifties," *Saturday Review* (January 2, 1960), p. 9.

Maritain, Jacques. *Education at the Crossroads.* New Haven, Yale University Press, 1943.

Mercier, Louis J. A. *American Humanism and the New Age.* Milwaukee, Bruce Publishing Company, 1948.

More, Paul Elmer. *The Demon of the Absolute.* Princeton, N. J., Princeton University Press, 1928.

————. *On Being Human*. Princeton, N. J., Princeton University, 1936.

————. *The Skeptical Approach to Religion*, 5th ed. Princeton, N. J., Princeton University Press, 1958.

Nock, Albert Jay. *The Theory of Education in the United States*. New York, Harcourt, Brace and Company, 1932.

Van Doren, Mark. *Liberal Education*. Boston, The Beacon Press, 1959.

HUMANISTIC EXISTENTIALISM
AND THE SCHOOL ADMINISTRATOR

Harry J. Hartley

Introduction

The primary purpose of this essay is to formulate a complement, or perhaps an alternative, to the present scientific-empirical-systemic approach to administrative conduct. More specifically, subsequent paragraphs describe *existential humanism* and show how it may be an appropriate philosophical basis for contemporary urban school administration. Major sections include: (1) underlying assumptions; (2) existential philosophy; (3) four major existential writers; (4) existential implications for urban administration; and (5) behavioral manifestations of an existential administrator. Advocacy of an alternative approach, such as existential humanism, should not be misconstrued as a rejection of current management science techniques and strategies.

There is no quarrel between the humanities and the sciences. There is only a need, common to them both, to put the idea of man back where it once stood, at the focus of our lives; to make the end of education the preparation of men to be men, and so to restore to mankind—and above all to this nation of mankind—a conception of humanity with which humanity can live.[1]

We are moving into an age where, it seems, nearly any man can be replaced by a machine. The worth of human beings is decreasing in direct proportion to our technological progress. Deeper values have given way to material strength, and the result is urban wastelands.

"Humanistic Existentialism and the School Administrator," by Harry J. Hartley from *Toward Improved Urban Education*, Frank W. Lutz, editor, Worthington, Ohio: Charles A. Jones Publishing Company, 1970. Reprinted by permission.

Underlying Assumptions

The contemporary urban school administrator who espouses humanistic values is a spiritual leader in an age of disbelief. However, he may be part of an advance guard that is capable of creating new life styles for the urban school leader of tomorrow. It is an exaggeration to relate current urban wastelands and the decay of cities to public policy made by short-sighted technocrats. But it is fairly obvious that the present administrative era is one in which we venerate scientism while barely tolerating humanism. Urban education no longer exists to produce men prepared for life in a society of men. It exists to prepare men as specialized experts who can readily gain professional or industrial employment. The latter can provide specialized answers, whereas the former can formulate liberating questions. The danger in overemphasizing the latter is that it may lead to the congealing and eventual self-destruction of urban society. Our cities have been built and rebuilt not with human purposes in mind but with technological means at hand. "A curious automatism, human in origin but not human in action, seems to be taking over."[2]

Administration is on the threshold of a systems era in which policies are being developed by means of techniques such as PPBS, PERT, input-output analysis, operations research, cost-effectiveness analysis, and so forth.[3] The intricate problems of our time can be analyzed immediately with computers, but what to do with these analyses is a persistent dilemma. Recent advances in technology and science far outspace any comparable advances in human wisdom. Systems analysis, as a derivative of general systems theory, is a substantial improvement over previous administrative methodologies. However, systems analysis is more a mode of thought than a mechanical tool. Too often, urban analysts focus upon efficient means (such as program budgeting) rather than noble ends (such as human purposes) as they plan school programs for city children.

There *is* a wisdom lag. Unfortunately, some of the urban schools that use systems analysis have tended to emphasize *saving* at the expense of *accomplishing*. The need exists in ghetto schools, for example, for *uneconomic* allocations of resources. It is necessary to "waste" money on noneconomic values that reflect our social conscience. Social conscience in the arena of urban polity is intertwined with existential humanism.

Educational administration has many philosophical dimensions and it is possible to relate contemporary schools of thought to urban school officials. Philosophy involves the study of questions, and the individual who assumes the awful burden of responsibility of providing educational leadership is confronted with questions arising from seemingly insoluble problems.

Any attempt to link existentialism with educational administration is based upon the premise that the former may be conceived as an educational philosophy. It is sufficient to assert that existentialism is one of the competing theories in education, and thus little attempt is made here to repeat what readily can be found elsewhere in foundation texts and journals.

Professionally-oriented administrators occasionally may be criticized for studying academic philosophy in a somewhat nontechnical manner. However, a characteristic of existential philosophy that distinguishes it from analytical schools of thought is that ". . . the existentialist has not relinquished philosophy's traditional audience —namely, everybody, regardless of any technical competence, philosophical or other. . . ."[4] Furthermore, any question pursued to its beginning or its end becomes a philosophic question, even though the individuals involved may not be aware they are engaged in philosophic dialogues. Thus, the administrator who rejects philosophical inquiry and the humanistic side of education may ultimately discover that his position is not unlike that of the French Revolutionist who proclaimed, "The mobs are in the street. I must find out where they are going, for I am their leader."

The phenomenon of administration may be viewed as the product of a particular school of philosophy, namely, realism, which is based upon the Aristotelian doctrine of forms. Administration is principally an attempt to order and regulate some process, and the goal of a realist is a fixed, orderly, and regular cosmic process. As a field of study, administration has not yet reached the level of reflection. It is still in a pre-reflective era inasmuch as there have been relatively few attempts to include the humanities in the preparation programs of future administrators. Admittedly, administration is becoming much more sophisticated, as attested by the incorporation of knowledge contributed by the behavioral sciences and by the fairly recent development of conceptual frameworks in the area of administrative theory; but it is still more closely related to custom than to thought. The role of the educational administrator is not unlike that of Plato's ruler of the state, because both are leaders of the human community. Many of the moral and social problems unresolved by our society are being delegated to the public school, i.e., integration, social justice, societal goals, educational equality, intellectual freedom, religious affairs, moral ideals, etc. The ultimate responsibility for solutions to such problems frequently resides with the administrator, who being short of divinity, requires many of the intellectual qualities which were necessary for the philosopher-king.

If the school administrator of today is pursuing ideals of clarity, simplicity, sincerity, and goodness, he must deliberately examine alternative propositions before engaging in practical courses of action. One such set of propositions is the philosophy of existentialism.

Existential Philosophy: An Historical Consciousness

Existential thought is frequently designated under the rubric of existentialism, but most philosophers are careful not to interchange the two expressions. Existential thought is the broader term and suggests the lack of a systematic, unified doctrine or school. For purposes of simplicity, the term existentialism will be used herein, but it might be argued that this label ought to be abandoned altogether. Existentialism is not easily reducible to any simple set of tenets because it contains several widely different revolts against traditional philosophy; it represents a basic divergence from analytical and logico-rational philosophy in terms of the nature of reality and in the approach philosophy should employ in discerning reality. More a mood than a systematic theory, it is characterized by a great faith in human intentness and potentiality.

Existentialism questions the very presence of a fixed, immutable reality, and it is staunchly opposed to the tradition of classical philosophy—from Plato to Hegel—which seeks eternal, universal truths primarily by means of the objectivistic rational intellect of man. The rejection of conventional values by existentialists has led many critics to call it a philosophy of complete nihilism and utter despair. On the other hand, existentialism is perhaps the most humanistic and appealing movement in modern philosophy. At one time or another almost everyone has reflected upon such major existential themes as the sources of agony, despair, suffering, detachment, dread, anxiety, neuroses, guilt, anguish, care, pain, freedom, absurdity, injustice, cruelty, love, kindness, abandonment, alienation, suicide, death, authenticity, the nature and limits of reason, existence and essence, the triumph over adversity, self-realization, God, and the relationship between the individual and society.

Because existentialism contains a distrust of reason, it is frequently accused of being anti-intellectual and irrational. It stands in opposition to the scientific conception of the world which presently dominates the United States in our Age of Analysis. In fact, existentialists appear to be unequivocal in their rejection of the method science; their basis is that we have stopped *living* our lives in favor of *knowing* our lives. They consider existence a mystery and something exclusively human; truth is regarded as subjectivity and priority is given to the categories of the irrational.[5]

Existentialism differs from other schools of philosophy because it is based on the belief that human existence precedes essence. Traditional philosophies have always assumed the priority in time of the essence (unique qualities; blueprint) of man over his existence (act of being). The existentialist reverses this assumption by affirming: "We first are; then we attempt to define ourselves. Man is the great contingency; his essence is not given. His very specialness lies in his ungivenness."[6]

Man is a builder, whose life is spent in the project of constructing himself and achieving liberation from his self-imposed slavery. He is an unfinished product and he is ultimately responsible for each of the choices made in his lifetime. The highest good is individuality, even though it is somehow wretched, revolting, and miserable. Existential man is thrown into the world, and although he is abandoned to a life that ends in death, he strives for authenticity by becoming an ascetic of the spirit. The Idea of Man is not yet completed, for we help formulate this Idea with our lives and with our freely-made choices. In fashioning myself, I am fashioning MAN, although there is no absolute conception of man. I invent my own morality, for I have freedom of choice and am not coerced by others. Life is viewed as its own reward. This value theory emphasizes free-expression through such things as painting, dialogue, sculpture, literature, and music; and it is based upon emotional sources.

Four Major Existential Writers

It is interesting to observe that most of the living "existentialists" have repudiated this label, and it has been suggested that the only feature these writers have in common is a marked aversion for each other. The intellectual ancestry of existentialism is usually traced to Soren *Kierkegaard* (1813-55) of Denmark, who was a Protestant of sorts. He regarded it as his mission in life to defend true Christian life against its distortion by the church, and he was concerned with how one can advance from unauthentic being to authentic being. He stressed the morbid aspects of human life and implied that individual man is being engulfed in the mass of men. Kierkegaard rejected ". . . the senseless accumulation of knowledge. He wanted to discard the superfluity of knowledge, in order that we may again learn what it means to live as a human being."[7] His dislike of rational thought is illustrated in two statements: "Whoever wants to be a Christian should tear the eyes out of his reason," and "Reason is a whore."

Friederich Wilhelm *Nietzsche* (1844-1900) of Germany, related metaphysics and ethics to the moral crisis of Western civilization. He concluded that belief in God is no longer tenable in the modern world: "God is dead and we have killed him." He opposed the maxims of bourgeois society and believed that in society, man loses his authentic self and sinks into a general mediocrity. He developed the popular concept of a "Superman," or Overman, who represented something of a man-god. When man acts "morally," he is only following the precepts of society and thus remains at the herd level. To be truly an individual, man must dare to be immoral, like Nature. He rejected the notion that man is made in the image of God and asserted that man is essentially free in defining himself. The freedom to produce possibilities is creativity, the highest form of which is self-creativity.

Martin *Heidegger* (born in 1889) is a German who believes that the whole history of human thought and existence has been dominated and characterized by man's understanding of *being*. His writings are based upon the consideration of such metaphysical concerns as "Why is there anything at all, rather than nothing?" and "What does it mean to be?"[8] Methodically, Heidegger analyzes the concept of *dasein* (similar to human existence) in respect to its temporal and historical character. He attempts to penetrate the origins of being and pleads for a return of metaphysical considerations.

Probably the most influential and best-known existentialist is Jean-Paul *Sartre* (born in 1905), who has contributed greatly to French philosophy and literature and who rejected the 1964 Nobel Prize for literature. Both he and Heidegger have been greatly influenced by Edmund *Husserl* (German, 1859-1938), who provided them with the phenomenological method (descriptive analysis of subjective processes). Sartre distinguishes between the two major divisions within existentialism, Christian and Atheistic, and he states: "Atheistic Existentialism, of which I am representative, declares with greater consistency that if God does not exist there is at least one being whose existence comes before its essence, a being which exists before it can be defined by any conception of it. That being is man or, as Heidegger has it, the human reality."[9]

Sartre's many philosophical essays and books, novels, plays, literary criticisms, and autobiography (*The Words*) have made him a kind of conscience in modern French thought. In his autobiography, Sartre attacks the roots of self-deception and hypocrisy and lashes out at the very elements that contributed to his character—heredity, religion, family, and the bourgeois confidence in culture. As was the case with the other writers discussed above, the dialectical development of Sartre's thinking makes it easy to describe him briefly but difficult to represent him adequately. Because paradox and irony constitute intrinsic elements of existential methodology, there is little sacrosanctity in some of the writings.

Others who might be classified as existentialists are Martin Buber, Gabriel Marcel, Miguel de Unamuno, Simone de Beauvoir, Albert Camus, Maurice Merleau-Ponty, Franz Kafka, and Paul Tillich. Some writers have interpreted by means of existentialist themes the writings of Dostoevsky, Freud, Goethe, Shakespeare, Rilke, Toynbee, G. Allport, Maritain, and others.

Because existentialism is philosophy in its most subjective and individualized form, one might assume that it would find favor in our modern world. Many writers, artists, intellectuals, and professional educators (G. Kneller, V. C. Morris, and T. Brameld, among others) have been influenced by, and contributed to, existential thought. [10] Even the so-called "hippie movement" has been defined as a somewhat degenerate form of existentialism for the weak-minded and weak-willed, although it differs from continent existentialism. Recent university student revolts and the "New Politics" certainly have existential overtones.

Existential Implications for Urban Administration

The educational administrator is *not* a philosopher. He is a philosophizing person of practical affairs who transforms the theoretical elements of his thinking into an operational context. For the existential urban administrator, this transformation might be more easily observed by describing characteristics *not* associated with him. This is not unexpected, for he is the embodiment of a non-systematized philosophy which rejects much of the traditionalism of American education. His leadership style represents deviant behavior, for he is providing spiritual leadership (humanistic roots) during an age of disbelief (positivistic influence). The existential leader sustains a strong moral paradox, a fervent belief both in legitimate human hope and in the limitations that existence places implacably upon every human hope. As such, he is an existent self who reflects upon the most extraordinary, intense emotional experiences involved in expanding the selfhood of others through education.

A basic principle of Sartre states that as a man chooses he is choosing for humanity. Applying this to the administrator, we can easily see his burden, for in choosing and making decisions he is choosing for all. He reflects the human predicament and the anguish of freedom. He must base decisions on intuition and finite knowledge within which human lives are enclosed. There is a denial of universals and formal categories and the choices must be formulated singularly. His intuitive insight results from affective experiences such as anguish and from an understanding of the human condition; 'to be' means to be engaged in choosing and personal appropriation, and existential knowledge provides the basis for authentic choice. Assuming that man's freedom is the foundation of ethics, the "good" decision is one which the administrator makes freely on behalf of self-fulfillment.

The existential administrator is the counterpart of the Persian prophet Zarathustra, whom Nietzsche described in *Thus Spoke Zarathustra* as a liberator of mankind. Nietzsche's prophet aided men in freeing themselves from their self-imposed tyranny and attempted a restructuring of the world out of chaotic ruins.

In reflecting upon the fundamental presuppositions of his work, Zarathustra underwent an existential transformation and became a higher man (Overman). His existence, his life in solitude, and his creation of new values were the result of an assessment of old values; he created a new essence on the basis of a prior existence that was justified by the inner necessities of the life of the overman that he was. Zarathustra, as a leader, provided for man's possibility to overcome himself by asserting that man will be nothing else but what he makes of himself. The price that this leader pays for his beliefs may be isolation, but since human existence involves abandonment anyhow, this voluntary isolation may be a cheap price for the results obtained.

Educational administrators are frequently depicted as organizational change-agents who incorporate meaningful innovations into the social processes of education. If they are influenced by existentialism, they must begin their consideration of betterment with critical reassessment of the basic present structure. Schools are formally organized along the Weberian pure-type models of rational bureaucracy. The curriculum is also formally structured and priority is given to the method of science in presenting the content of the behavioral, social, and natural sciences. There is a trend toward increased objectification of students in regard to the importance attached to such things as class rankings, grade point averages, intelligence quotients, standardized exams, automated teaching methodology, and even educational research which dehumanizes the subjective nature of man. *Man is becoming merely a datum.*

The existential administrator is the faint beacon of light which flickers in the darkness of educational scientism. He is a sometimes misunderstood provocateur of humanism resisting the growing tide of educators who have turned upon man as an object of knowledge (*en-soi*). If positivism succeeds in knowing about the self completely, it will drive out *pour-soi*, or selfhood. Men will merely exist as objects, like chairs, rather than as subjects possessing emotions, feelings, and passions which defy rational analysis. Granted that knowledge has objective, social aspects, but thought is subjective and individualized, and the school should encourage both knowledge and thought.

The administrator, like Zarathustra, must create new humanistic values out of old, and define a new educational essence. Sallust once remarked, "Every man is the architect of his own fortune." The individual who administers an urban educational institution is the architect of each of the persons assigned to his organization. His power is commensurate with his responsibility.

Education represents a form of power, ". . . more powerful than any other agency on earth, . . . the one generative force potentially great enough to combat all degenerative human forces."[11] This statement and one to follow by Professor Brameld are significant for students of administration. It was Brameld, in 1950, who provided the foundations of social reconstructionism (a form of modern progressivism) in education. In 1965, he modified his position in view of contemporary influences. After analyzing such patterns of thought as scientific humanism, objective idealism, dialectical materialism, supernaturalism, and existentialism, Brameld chose to identify himself with the latter: "The reconstructionist philosophy of education . . . is the philosophy of existential humanism."[12]

Underlying the existential leader is the concept of irrationality which provided the foundation for George Bernard Shaw's contention that all progress depends on the unreasonable man. In a description of leadership qualities, Shaw once remarked that a true leader is an unreasonable man who persists in trying to adapt the world to himself while the reasonable man adapts himself to the world. Such a person is the existential school superintendent.

A list delineating some of the behavioral elements of an existential educational administrator is presented here. This outline is both tentative and exploratory in nature. Not only do the elements overlap, but their framework contains intentional leaps from pre- to pro-scription and from area to area (teaching, curriculum, organizational structure, student counseling, etc.). The import of this approach is to be found in the totality of the 20 components rather than in the isolated items.

Behavioral Manifestations of an Existential Administrator

1. Resist positivistic methodology which formulates decisions solely on the basis of quantitative analysis. Management science, including such techniques as operations research, statistical decision theory, systems analysis, and linear programming, assists the human decision-making process, but is in no sense a substitute for it.
2. Use intuition as a major basis for decision-making. Recognize the positive role of intuition which implies self-knowledge and familiarity with the area involved. This might be a form of "romantic rationalism."
3. Emphasize the humanistic tradition insofar as this contributes to the expansion of an individual's selfhood. Reject absolute nihilism and lead the organization in such a manner that human freedoms are implemented and expanded.
4. Reject the senseless accumulation or superfluity of knowledge that attempts to describe MAN (universal conception) rather than men as particularistic individuals. The concrete, diverse aspects of human separateness are stressed.
5. Encourage the Socratic method of teaching, in which the instructor serves primarily as a midwife in eliciting knowledge from the learner.
6. Advocate a curriculum related to social and personal reality which includes such humanistic elements as the arts, moral philosophy, great books, and individualized programs of study.
7. Liberate students and teachers from restrictions upon learning imposed by the doctrines of traditional educational philosophies.
8. Encourage liberal "free-thinking" in which each person assumes responsibility for his choices, feelings, emotions, and entire life. Unconstrained emotional responses for each person are sought. The choices must be meaningful —something important and "real" for the student.
9. Show concern for the extraordinary—for the most intense emotional experiences related to administering an educational organization.
10. Avoid sources of impersonality and alienation in student-faculty-administrator-community relationships. In contrast to the detached form of analysis by the linguistic philosophers is the emphasis on involvement and participation in the concrete concerns of human life found among the existential practitioners.
11. Encourage interpersonal confrontation of professional and nonprofessional personnel. Individuals work in a social environment which should be an expression of community (not merely collectivism). The individual cannot become human by himself, for self-being is only real in communication with other self-beings.
12. Refute supervision and coercion of personnel by external standards. Supervision criteria should be formulated from within the organization by its members.
13. Promote education as a source of freedom. Freedom is a necessary basis for

human creativity and intellectual growth. Education, including history, should be used by students to change the course of history away from Cacotopia towards something more human.

14. Express a commitment to openness rather than to teleological closed-ended systems and procedures. Man is always what he is yet to be; his acts are contingent upon his decisions, which should be freely made.

15. Oppose organizational patterns of bureaucracy, which are based almost solely upon the Weberian element of rationality. A purely rational social organization such as a school is undesirable because it ignores the nonrational aspects of social conduct. Neo-Weberian models, such as Blau's "other-face of bureaucracy," are more suitable for schools than Weber's pure-types.

16. Develop a unique leadership style which, in terms of one well-known social system model, might be described as more idiographic (emphasis on individual need-dispositions of subordinates) than nomothetic (emphasis on institutional sanctions and role-expectations of subordinates).

17. Promote an attitude of "fallibilism" in the school. Individuals and human knowledge are never absolute but exist on a continuum of uncertainty and of indeterminacy.

18. Resist the scientific temper of pragmatism which permeates American public education. Science unites us only as intellectual beings, not as human beings. Existential truth is infinitely more than scientific correctness.

19. Initiate existential counseling techniques into the school program. These are related to existential psychoanalysis and psychotherapy techniques from psychology; they emphasize nondirective approaches to the counseling of students rather than behavioristic, client-centered methods.

20. Oppose selected elements of control by the various levels of government which tend to increase the constraints upon individual decision-making. This is not a plea for the "local control" concept as such, but it does imply a need for some autonomy of local districts.

These 20 existential dimensions might be summarized by formulating four dominant themes and relating each item to one of these themes:

A. Emphasize self-expression for each individual (items 2, 3, 5, 6, 8, 9, 13).
B. Oppose externally based determinants and sanctions (7, 12, 14, 15, 16, 20).
C. Resist quantitative assumptions that deny human separateness (1, 17, 18).
D. Create conditions in which interpersonal communication and social selfhood are encouraged (4, 10, 11, 19).

Conclusion

A major difficulty with transposing existentialism into practice is that our culture tends to extol the worth of social intercourse, group activity, group norms, and socially acceptable behavior. Our conceived values may include a desire for individuality, but our operative values generally do not reflect such a belief. Those who advocate the extreme individuality of existentialism in the schools could easily become the objects of severe criticism.

Many educators are characterized by their adherence to tradition and fear of change. If one were to construct a continuum with traditional values at one end and emergent values at the other, the educators who are in a positon to bring about change (such as administrators and boards of education) probably would be located on the side of the traditional values. This is unfortunate, for the mutual impact of school and society is so profound that these unimaginative administrators can wield an influence far beyond their immediate confines. The burden of proof is upon those who would introduce existentialism into public education. It must be shown that this is an improvement over present dominant patterns of thought.

The acceptance by an individual of the position of school administrator might appear to preclude the possibility of existential thought. However, the broad restrictions of the role can be accepted by the occupant if his choice is uncoerced and he is given the freedom to administer in a meaningful and creative manner. He brings with him a unique personality, particular need-dispositions, emotions, and an individualized style of leadership. Education is characterized by fixed ends and varying means. It is this premise that enables one to conceive that the restrictions that limit an organizational leader are broad enough to permit individual discretion to operate.

In the vanished past of not too many years, the power of urban school administrators was nearly as unlimited as an absolute monarch. Today, with demands for decentralization, community-operated schools, increasing teacher activism in policy eras, and other issues, the urban administrator is a much-harried man with an increasing sense of powerlessness. Some claim that it is an ungrateful job for which the duties, sacrifices, risks, and anguish seem altogether disproportionate to the rewards. One is tempted to describe city school officials as the fallen women of Europe have been described: ". . . the eternal priestesses of humanity blasted for the sins of their people." School officials are no longer priests, but whenever a crisis arises, they are certain to be criticized by all sides. Perhaps a greater concern for humanity will restore administrative prestige in the eyes of an extremely sensitive, discontented, and demanding public constituency.

Existentialism was included in several recent examinations of the relationship of philosophy to educational administration[13], and it may someday exert more influence upon this professional field. Student demands may transform administative values. The seeds of existentialism that were present in the 1950's on college campuses grew to new proportions in the 1960's and are likely to mushroom in the 1970's. Students at Berkeley, Columbia, and other campuses brought about administrative reforms that will also affect lower education. Students today are trying to be genuine, authentic people freely choosing their own behavior, attitude, and mode of living. "Existentialism means, to students, being different and it offers them a change from the morass of conformity, boredom and the meaningless competitiveness in which they see so many of their elders caught."[14]

Compassion and intellectual curiosity are essential ingredients in the makeup of the men who lead our urban schools. In education, the chief school officer is the ultimate chooser and he stands alone in assuming responsibility for specified areas of the human condition. Existential humanism helps to make man more human, and this is the true vocation of a school administrator.

FOOTNOTES

1. Archibald MacLeish, "The Great American Frustration," *Saturday Review*, July 13, 1968, p. 16.

2. Ibid., p. 14.

3. For my interpretation of the systems perspective, see Harry J. Hartley, *Educational Planning-Programming—Budgeting: A Systems Approach* (Englewood Cliffs, N.J.: Prentice-Hall, Inc., 1968), 304 pp.; "Twelve Hurdles to Clear Before You Take on System Analysis," *American School Board Journal*, Vol. 156, No. 1 (July 1968); "PPBS: The Emergence of a Systemic Concept for Public Governance," *General Systems*, XIII (1968).

4. Stanley Cavell, "Existentialism and Analytical Philosophy," *Daedalus*, 93, No. 3 (Summer 1964), 947.

5. For an interesting treatment of traditional rationalism examined in the context of existential phenomenology, see John A. Mourant, "Thomistic Existentialism," *Essays in Philosophy*, ed. J. M. Anderson (University Park, Pa.: Penn State University Press, 1962).

6. Van Cleve Morris, *Philosophy and the American School* (Boston: Houghton Mifflin Company, 1961), p. 74.

7. F. H. Heinemann, *Existentialism and the Modern Predicament* (New York: Harper Torchbook, 1958), p. 40.

8. Martin Heidegger, *An Introduction to Metaphysics* (Garden City, N.Y.: Anchor Books, 1961), chap. 1.

9. Walter Kaufmann, *Existentialism from Dostoevsky to Sartre* (Cleveland: The World Publishing Company, 1956), p. 290.

10. The three existentialist classics are probably Soren Kierkegaard, *Concluding Unscientific Postscript*, Martin Heidegger, *Being and Time*, Jean-Paul Sartre, *Being and Nothingness*.

11. Theodore Brameld, *Education As Power* (New York: Holt, Rinehart and Winston, Inc., 1965), p. 8.

12. Ibid., p. 80.

13. Robert E. Ohm and William G. Monahan, *Educational Administration— Philosophy in Action* (Norman, Oklahoma: University Council for Educational Administration, University of Oklahoma, 1965), pp. 70 and 75; Orin B. Graff et al., *Philosophic Theory and Practice in Educational Administration* (Belmont, Calif.: Wadsworth Publishing Company, Inc., 1966), chap. 10.

14. Robert Baust, "The Inner World of Today's College Student," *Education Synopsis*, XIII, No. 1 (Winter 1967-68), 39.

END OF THE IMPOSSIBLE DREAM

Peter Schrag

It is ten years later, and the great dream has come to an end. We thought we had solutions to everything—poverty, racism, injustice, ignorance; it was supposed to be only a matter of time, of money, of proper programs, of massive assaults. Perhaps nothing was ever tried without restraint or dilution, perhaps we were never willing to exert enough effort or spend enough money, but it is not clear that the confidence is gone, that many of the things we *knew* no longer seem sure or even probable. What we believed about schools and society and the possibilities of socially manageable perfection has been reduced to belying statistics and to open conflict in the street and the classroom.

Twenty years ago we took as fact the idea that American public schools—that *the school system*—could be reformed, first to make the education enterprise more intellectually rigorous and selective, and then to make it more democratic. Thus we had our decade with the Rickovers, the Bestors, the Conants, and the Zachariases; men who believed that students did not know enough physics or French or English, and that through new programs, or a return to "the fundamentals," or through adjustments in teacher training, students could become superior academic operators and, above all, better qualified candidates for the university. And then, beginning in about 1960, we had our decade with the democrats, the integrationists, and the apostles of universal opportunity: Kenneth B. Clark, Thomas

Schrag, Peter, "The End of the Impossible Dream," *Saturday Review*, September 19, 1970. Copyright 1970 Saturday Review, Inc.

Pettigrew, Francis Keppel, and John Gardner, who believed that by changing teacher attitudes, or through busing, or through fiscal and geographical rezoning, all children could have equal educational opportunities.

In the first instance the reformers represented the aspirations of the enfranchised, the suburban parents of affluence who once sent their children to Harvard by right of birth and now had to do it by right of achievement. In the second, the reformers demanded for the deprived what they thought the advantaged were getting, believing in the magic of the good school and accepting the rhetoric of individual accomplishment. Now, suddenly, the optimism is gone, and the declining faith in educational institutions is threatening the idea of education itself.

If we want to understand why the schools have "failed," we have only to state the criteria of success. The schools achieved their reputation when they did not have to succeed, when there were educational alternatives—the farm, the shop, the apprenticeship—and when there were other routes to economic and social advancement. Every poor little boy who became a doctor represented a victory. Poor little boys who became ditch diggers disappeared from the record. As soon as we demanded success for everyone—once there were no alternatives—failure was inevitable, not only because the demands were too great, but because they were repressive and contradictory. No other nation, wrote Henry Steele Commager in a representative flight of self-congratulation, "ever demanded so much of schools and of education . . . none other was ever so well served by its schools and its educators." We expected the schools to teach order, discipline, and democracy, the virtues of thrift, cleanliness, and hard work, the evils of alcohol, tobacco, and later of sex and communism; we wanted them to acculturate the immigrants, to provide vocational skills, to foster patriotism and tolerance, and, above all, to produce a high standard of literacy throughout the population. All this they sometimes did and still do.

The impossible demand was enshrined in the mythology of the American dream itself: that the schools constitute the ultimate promise of equality and opportunity; that they enable American society to remain somehow immune from the economic inequities and social afflictions that plague the rest of mankind; that they, in short guarantee an open society. In 1848, Horace Mann, in one of his annual reports as secretary of the Massachusetts Board of Education, described his vision of the common school—the school for children of all classes and backgrounds—as "a great equalizer of the conditions of men, the balance wheel of the social machinery. . . . It does better than disarm the poor of their hostility toward the rich: It prevents being poor. . . ." The school is our answer to Karl Marx—and to everything else. With the closing of the frontier, which once was regarded as a safety valve and from which the schools inherited many of their mythological functions (if you're not born rich you can go west, can, that is, go to school), and with the rise of a certificated, schooled meritocracy, the educational system has become the central institution of the American dream. Education, it has often been said, is the American religion. Thus, if the school system fails, so does the promise of equality, so does the dream of the classless society, so does our security against the inequalities of society. The school system has failed.

Evidence? Is it necessary again to cite statistics, dropout rates, figures on black and white children who go to college (or finish high school), comparisons of academic success between rich and poor kids, college attendance figures for slums and suburbs? The most comprehensive data on hand indicate that, in the final analysis, nothing in school makes as much difference as the economic background of the student and the social and economic backgrounds of his peers. There is no evidence that increasing educational expenditures in a particular district will produce greater achievement, and a fair amount of evidence that it will not. But this sort of argument is still misleading and, in the final analysis, rather useless, because it presumes that we agree on what constitutes success. Failure to complete high school is regarded as some sort of cosmic failure, a form of personal and social death. Dropout becomes synonymous with delinquent. Yet the evidence indicates that in some school systems the smart ones drop out and the dumb ones continue. Self-educated men used to be heroes; now they are prejudged unfit, or, more likely, they just don't appear in the social telescope at all.

Then why have the schools failed? Why boycotts and strikes, why the high school SDS, why the battles over long hair, underground newspapers, and expressions of independent student opinion? Why are there cops in the corridors and marijuana in the gym lockers? Why is it that most students panic when they're invited to work on their own, to study independently? Why is it that most students are more interested in what the teacher wants or what's going to be on the test than they are in understanding the subject that's ostensibly under study? Why bells, monitors, grades, credits, and requirements? Why do most students learn to cheat long before they learn how to learn? Yes, there are exceptions—there are teachers who ask real questions and schools that honor real intellectual distinction and practice real democracy. But a system that requires all children (except the very rich who can buy their way out) to attend a particular school for a specified period—that, in other words, sentences everyone to twelve years of schooling—such a system can and must be judged by its failures.

Everything that we could not, or would not, do somewhere else we expected to be done in the schools. And in the process we thought we saw what in fact does not exist. The greatest failure of American educational journalism in the last decade is that its practitioners refused to believe what they saw, and reported instead what they were supposed to see. Thus we have been inundated with millions of words about the new math, the new physics, and the compensatory this and advanced that, about BSCS and PSSC, about IPI and SMSG, about individual progress and head start, upward bound, and forward march. And thus also we have read, with increasing incomprehension, about student uprisings, protests and boycotts and strikes. But few of us ever described the boredom, the emptiness, the brutality, the stupidity, the sheer waste of the average classroom.

What choices does a fifteen-year-old have in the average high school? Choices as to courses, teacher, or physical presence? What does he do most of the day? He sits—and maybe listens. Follow him, not for a few minutes, but for six hours a day, 180 days a year. What goes on in the class? What is it about, what questions are asked? Is it about the real world? Is it about an intellectually honest discipline? Is it about the feelings, passions, interests, hopes, and fears of those who are present? No. It is a world all of its own. It is mostly about nothing.

It worked as long as the promise of schooling itself appeared credible, that is, as long as the proffered reward looked more like a rainbow and less like a mirage, before the end of the road was crowded with people reporting back that the trip wasn't worth it. It is not necessary again to describe the travesties of the average classroom or the average school. But it is important to point out the nothingness of schooling because nothingness (or conformity and repression and boredom) is necessary to the system. Which is not to suggest an Establishment conspiracy to keep children docile so they will become satisfactory candidates for the military-industrial complex. No one planned schools this way, nor have teachers and principals betrayed them: The schools do what they do out of a structural necessity, because we don't know enough about learning, and because social mythology permits very little else.

Any single, universal public institution—and especially one as sensitive as the public school—is the product of a social quotient verdict. It elevates the lowest common denominator of desires, pressures, and demands into the highest public virtue. It cannot afford to offend any sizable community group, be it the American Legion, the B'nai B'rith, or the NAACP. Nor can it become a subversive enterprise that is designed to encourage children to ask real questions about race or sex or social justice or the emptiness and joys of life. Occasionally, of course, it does do these things, but rarely in a significant and consistent manner. Students who ask real questions tend to be threatening to teachers, parents, and the system. They destroy the orderliness of the management procedure, upset routines, and question prejudices. The textbook, the syllabus, the lesson plan are required not only because most teachers are lost without them, but because they represent an inventory for the community, can be inspected to ascertain the purity of the goods delivered. Open-ended programs, responsive to the choices and interests of students, are dangerous not only because all real questions are dangerous, but because they cannot be preinspected or certified for safety. The schools are not unresponsive to the immediate demands of the society. They are doing precisely what most Americans expect.

Earlier, I spoke about contradictory objectives. One is the objective of "equality of educational opportunity"; the other is to reinforce and legitimize distinctions. For many years, these objectives were, in fact, consistent. They share certain behavioral values that are honored and enforced in the average classroom: discipline, order, certain kinds of manners, styles of speech and dress, punctuality, cleanliness, and so on. Kids who do not meet these standards are ridiculed, punished, and demeaned. The two sets of values also share a declared commitment to certain skills: reading, writing, the skills of the average intelligence test—and a disdain for other attributes: originality, curiosity, diversity. They share, in other words, a linear standard of success and failure. Slow and bright, average and retarded, all fall on one scale, one straight line that runs from zero to one hundred, from A to F. Any teacher in any school can tell any other teacher in any other school about his good, average, and slow students, about his difficult students, and about his cooperative ones, and both will know precisely who and what is being described. (Occasionally, of course, some school or teacher honors a "difficult" child, or a genuinely curious one, or one who has skills—in music or dance, for example—which are outside the normal scale of classroom success. But those are rare instances.)

About a decade ago, something began to change. Until then "equality of educational opportunity" was understood in simple (and misleading) terms. It was the equality inherited from social Darwinism: Everyone in the jungle (or in society, or in school) was to be treated equally: one standard, one set of books, one fiscal formula for children everywhere, regardless of race, creed, or color. Success went to the resourceful, the ambitious, the bright, the strong. Those who failed were stupid or shiftless, but whatever the reason, failure was the responsibility of the individual (or perhaps of his parents, poor fellow), but certainly not that of the school or the society. It was this premise that fired the drive for school integration. Negro schools, we believed, were older, more poorly equipped, badly financed. By equalizing resources, and perhaps throwing in a little compensation to offset differences deriving from "cultural disadvantage," everybody would be competing in the same race. Thus Head Start and "counterpoise" and "early enrichment." Every program launched in the past decade assumed a linear standard of success; each took for granted that schooling was a competitive enterprise and that life was a jungle where only the fit survive. Integration was, more than anything else, a political attempt to win white hostages to black education: Where white kids went to school with black there would be better resources and teachers. Apparently it never occurred to anyone that as long as we operated by a linear standard (bright, average, slow, or whatever) the system would, by definition, have to fail at least some kids. Every race has a loser. Failure is structured into the American system of public education. Losers are essential to the success of the winners.

In the process of compensating and adjusting, of head starting and upward bounding, the burden of responsibility shifted subtly from the individual to the school and the society. Failure used to be the kid's fault; now, increasingly, it seems, at least in part to be the fault of the system. And thus all was thrown into confusion. Do we measure equality by what goes in or what comes out? That is, do we measure it in terms of resources provided, efforts made, or by achievement? Assuming, for example that certain groups in the society are not merely "disadvantaged" but culturally distinct, and that those distinctions are valuable—assuming these things, what does equality mean when it comes to education? Equality before the law, yes; equality in medical treatment, yes; equality in the hiring of plumbers and mechanics, yes. But equality in education? James Coleman, who directed the huge federal study called "Equality of Educational Opportunity," subsequently wrestled with the question (in an article in *Public Interest*) and concluded that "equality of educational opportunity implies not merely 'equal' schools but equally effective schools, whose influences will overcome the differences in starting point of children from different social groups." This is the statement of a homogenizer, hardly different from that of the DAR lady who, sixty years ago, gave the schools a similar mission. "What kind of American consciousness can grow," she asked, "in the atmosphere of sauerkraut and limburger cheese?" The differences, in these views, should be equalized away: All comers should be transformed into mainstream, middle-class competitors (or consumers?) who are equally able to run the race.

There was nothing insidious or sinister about these things; they are as American as the flag. Our dream, as a society, was in the possibilities of transformation: frogs into princes, immigrants into Americans, poor children into affluent adults. And now, with other options closed, the schools, which always have received a major share of the credit for such accomplishments, are expected to do it all. But the schools never did what they were praised for doing; many immigrant groups, for example, did not achieve economic and social success through the public school, but through an open market for unskilled and semi-skilled labor, through sweatshops and factories, through political organizations and civil service jobs. There are more poor whites in America than poor blacks, and if the schools can be credited with the success of those who made it, they also have to be blamed for the failure of those who did not. But to say all this is not to say very much, because in the definition of making it, in a competitive race with one set of criteria, one man's success is defined by another's failure.

Then what do the schools actually do? More than anything else they certify and legitimize success and failure. "Equality of educational opportunity," even if it has no meaning, is necessary because it says to the loser, "You had your chance." Therefore equality remains a significant political and moral imperative, a tune that has to be sung by politicians, guidance counselors, and other apologists of the status quo. (Increasingly it also becomes a rallying cry of liberal intellectuals, who now ascribe their personal triumphs in the brain business to the same ego-flattering virtues as the self-made enterpreneurs of another age: opportunity, hard work, ingenuity. I have made it, son, and so can you.) But there is, as Mr. Conant once said in another context, social dynamite in this propaganda.

The common school, quite simply, no longer exists, except as public rhetoric. With the large-scale movement to the suburbs after World War II, much of the American middle class seceded from the common school by physically removing its children to what it regarded as a more salubrious educational environment. For the successful in the suburbs the schools became contractual partners in a bargain that trades economic support (higher taxes, teacher salaries, bond issues) for academic credentials and some guarantee of advancement in the form of college admission. They went there seeking not equality but advantage, a head start for the rich. And who can blame them? We all "want the best for our children." Education, and especially higher education, is regarded as the sine qua non of position and power in this society. The "new class" of managers and technicians, as David Bazelon has said, is not based on birth or social standing but on educational skills (or at least on credentials). Cash and power, in other words, can be converted into more cash and power. The suburban school, the current demands for community control, and the concomitant failure of integration are all massive testimonials to the end of the common school.

What is being ignored is that the suburban schools don't actually do anything for most kids, other than bore them. Their prime function (aside from baby sitting) is to certify skills and reinforce characteristics and attitudes that are produced somewhere else. The money, in other words, did not buy much learning. But it did buy exclusiveness. They come in at this end, bright and shiny, and come out at that one, ready for Harvard or Cornell. The schools are, in brief, selective mechanisms, and through their selections they appear to justify (and are, in turn, justified by) the distinctions the society wants to make.

This is why we are fighting about schools and why we are in such serious trouble. Part of the fight—in the cities at least—is over a share of political power, over jobs and patronage and control. But the ideology that gives that battle energy, the ideas that help rally the troops, is the belief in the schools and in what remains of the dream of opportunity. But if *the* school system is the only mode of access to social and economic salvation, and if there is only one officially honored definition of such salvation (house in the suburbs, job at IBM, life insurance, and a certain set of manners), and if the school excludes any sizeable minority from such salvation, then we have obviously defined ourselves into a choice between revolution and repression. The great dream of universal opportunity originated in an era of social alternatives, when schooling was one of several options for advancement: the school therefore could demand certain kinds of conformity. Individuality and pluralism could take refuge and sustenance elsewhere. But for the moment all advancement (we are told, are indeed required, to believe) begins in school, and we are, for this reason if for no other, no longer an open society. By definition, no society with but one avenue of approved entry into the mainstream of dignity can be fully open. When that single instrument of entry is charged with selecting people out, and when there are no honorable alternatives for those who are selected out, we are promising to all men things that we cannot deliver.

Inevitably, there are questions about the demands of a technological society and the necessity for universal literacy. Haven't many schools succeeded; don't we have one of the highest standards of literacy in the world? Don't schools make selections according to the demands that the technology and the culture impose? The answer is complicated, but there is nothing in it that makes the existing system of schooling imperative or even desirable, except—as always—the maintenance of the status quo. Which is to say that the system is necessary if the system is to be preserved.

Obviously, the society, as organized, makes certain demands—sometimes irrelevant, but often not—for employment and acceptability. Computers impose a rigid discipline on programmers, and heart transplants are better performed by people who have learned what they are doing. A dishwasher with the soul of a poet (or even the skills of a poet) may be more valuable than one without, but he is still a dishwasher. But for every flight of romantic nonsense there are a hundred statements about the rigors and demands of technology and about the complexities of this world. We have hitched the deities of complexity and technology to the rhetoric of success. Technology is not the curriculum (nor, needless to say, is complexity); it is the liturgy of motivation.

Even if the school system were proficient in traning people to deal with a world defined as technological (which it is not), it would still be guilty of the worst sort of parochialism and idolatry. Part of the significance of technology, we are told, is to free man from all those boring, menial tasks, maybe even to free him from the necessity of working at all. To prepare for this, the school system imposes boring, menial tasks. The very propaganda of technology would suggest other worlds, other options, time for other concerns. It suggests more, not less, pluralism, more leisure time, more lonely moments, and the necessity for more personal resources for recreation, satisfaction, and human encounter. But what actually happens is that by deifying technology, or by joining the rest of us in so doing, the schools are reinforcing the existing linear standards of judgment and selection—are, in other words, employing the rhetoric of the brave new world to coerce kids and parents rather than to free them.

What the technology argument does is to lock the schools into one definition of complexity, one version of education, and hence only one honorable way of becoming a full human being. It perpetuates and updates an essentially vocational view of schooling. Technological complexity, yes; inner, human complexity, no. We are always—all of us—asked to understand the world by studying the transistor and the laser. All arguments to the contrary notwithstanding, the message comes out backwards: Technology is given; people are dependent variables who must be trained to use and control it.

Mathematics and history and literature thus become tokens of acquiescence rather than instruments of liberation. They are used by teachers to maintain order, reinforce distinctions, and intimidate or embarrass students. Complexity becomes a club and technology a prison. We are training a generation of people who regard the disciplines of the intellect as instruments of oppression.

One of the things we learned in the past decade is that we don't know very much. We don't know much about kids, about learning, or about motivation. One of the more fundamental assumptions of ten years ago was that curriculum planners sitting in some university, a foundation, or a central school office could invent programs (for teachers and students) and thereby engineer pedagogical success. What we discovered is that most of the time it couldn't be done, which may well be a good thing. If our pedagogical instruments were really powerful, we would have in hand one of the most totalitarian instruments imaginable. It is by now patently clear that not only history and politics but the very way that people think can be loaded with cultural and social presumptions, and that "reason" itself is often, if not always, political. Teaching inevitable assumes a form of control; it may be directed toward independence, but there is no assurance of it: The more centralized our school systems and our social agencies become, the greater the danger of creating pressures for the production of socially and technologically acceptable people. Fortunately, we don't yet know how to do these things.

What we do know is that children are different, and that different people learn different things in different ways, that some people think better in numbers than in words, that certain groups perceive and understand mathematical relationships more easily than verbal relationships, and that still others are particularly skillful in manipulating spatial problems but relatively incompetent with literature. Most of all, we know that personalities, backgrounds, and interests differ. It may well be that certain levels of literacy and ability in arithmetic constitute "fundamentals" for survival in America or anywhere in the Western world. But it does not follow that learning these things can be achieved by a single set of techniques, or that any teacher can be trained to them. More defensible is the assumption that, while drill, order, and tight discipline may be suitable for some students and teachers, they may be destructive for others; that "permissive" classes or Deweyan practices may work well with certain personalities but not with everyone. It is even possible to assume that the "fundamentals" should not always precede music or auto mechanics, but may, in many cases, grow naturally from other activities and from curiosity stimulated in other ways. We know that illiterate adults, properly motivated, have learned to read and write in a few months, and that recruits who almost failed Selective Service intelligence tests can be trained to operate computers and maintain radar equipment.

More important, we should have learned in the last decade that there is no magic in the single school system or in any set of curricular prescriptions, and that the most successful motivating device may simply be the sense that one has chosen what one wants to learn and under what conditions: In urban areas there is no reason why children in one neighborhood should be forced to attend one particular school for a specified period of time; why there should not be choice as to place, subject, style of teaching, and hours; why, for all children, French and history and algebra should have absolutely equal value; why, for some, art or dance or music should not be given more time than history; why reading a book is more of a humanistic activity than making a film or playing an instrument; why children should not be allowed to choose between permissive and highly structured situations (many would choose the latter); why parents and children should not have the economic power to punish unsuccessful schools (by leaving them) and reward effective ones; or why single, self-serving bureaucracies should continue to hold monopoly power in what is probably the most crucial, and certainly the most universal, public enterprise in America. Wealthy children and middle-class parents have some options about schools; lower-class children have none.

What I am arguing for, obviously, is a restoration of multiple options and, as much as possible, multiple values. Christopher Jencks and others have proposed a system whereby parents are given educational vouchers that they can spend in any school or educational activity of their choice. The voucher would be roughly equal in cash value to the amount that the local school system spends each year on the education of one child, and it could be spent in any school that does not charge more in tuition than the voucher is worth. With support from the Office of Economic Opportunity, Jencks will try the system over a period of eight years in a place yet to be chosen. No one claims that this is the only way of restoring choice, options, and multiple values. It is conceivable that single public school systems might, on their own initiative, introduce the kind of pluralism that the voucher system is designed to achieve. Clearly, many have become more "flexible" and more cognizant of individual choice. And yet the pressure within a single system is likely to be the other way; it is likely, always, to demand a certain caution. Separate schools, accountable not to public vote and citizen support but only to their clients, may be immune to such pressure; they will have to make their way on the basis of performance. Ideally, moreover, vouchers would be usable in apprenticeships, in community-operated schools, in projects of independent study, travel (for older kids), or simply for learning resources to be used at home.

There is, obviously, no certainty that changes in the structure or financing of public education will generate a situation in which individuality is honored and where the system does not impose the fearful price it now extracts from the young in the name of "growing up." But such changes may, at least, remove some obstacles. They may, if nothing else, represent a social declaration by the system—by the state and the citizen—that education is not simply the acceptance of impersonality and conformity, and that schooling is not merely the training and selection of candidates for corporate life. The practice of encouraging, through a new structure, the idea that personal fulfillment is the first responsibility of an educational system, and that human dignity is not founded on a single standard, may do more than anything else to mitigate the alienation and hostility of the angry young. What the ideal system would do—not in rhetoric nor with slogans from the principal, but in practice—would be to declare itself unequivocally to be the ally of difference, of individuals, and of the tolerant against the invidious: it would recognize its own limitations in choosing for people and recognize their ability to choose for themselves, and it would, in all cases, stand at their side against the imperious collective demands of crowds, machines, and bureaucrats. All of that may be a vain hope, but given the impossible and possibly destructive hopes of social engineering that we entertained in the Sixties, it is, at least, a hope worth hoping.

THE FULLY FUNCTIONING SELF

Earl C. Kelley

In a discussion of the self, it will perhaps be helpful to attempt to say as well as we can what it is we are trying to discuss. This is done at the risk of using the conversation stopper, "Let's define it." Many a fine discussion has ended at this point.

The self consists, in part at least, of the accumulated experiential background, or backlog, of the individual. It is what has been built, since his life began, through unique experience and unique purpose, on the individual's unique biological structure. The self is therefore unique to the individual.

This self is built almost entirely, if not entirely, in relationship to others. While the newborn babe has the equipment for the development of the self, there is ample evidence to show that nothing resembling a self can be built in the absence of others. Having a cortex is not enough; there must be continuous interchange between the individual and others. Language, for example, would not be possible without social relationships. Thus, it is seen that man is necessarily a social being.

The self has to be achieved; it is not given. All that is given is the equipment and at least the minimal (mother and child) social environment. Since the self is achieved through social contact, it has to be understood in terms of others. "Self and other" is not a duality, because they go so together that separation is quite impossible.

From *Perceiving, Behaving, Becoming: A New Focus for Education*, Yearbook 1962, Chapter 2, pp. 9-20. Copyright © 1962 by the Association for Supervision and Curriculum Development.

The self consists of an organization of accumulated experience over a whole lifetime. It is easy to see, therefore, that a great deal of the self has been relegated to the unconscious, or has been "forgotten." This does not mean that these early experiences have been lost. It merely means that they cannot readily be brought into consciousness. We must recognize the fact that the unconscious part of the self functions, for weal or woe, depending on the quality of the experiences.

It is intended here, however, to deal with the conscious self. The unconscious self (not a separation but a continuum) is difficult to deal with for the very reason that it is below the level of consciousness. We want here to look especially at how the individual sees himself. This is indeed the critical point, because it is what the person *sees* that is enabling or disabling. The crucial matter is not so much what you are, but what you think you are. And all of this is always in relationship to others.

The fully functioning personality (self) needs to have certain characteristics. Here, perhaps, is as good a place as any to discuss word trouble. We live in a moving, changing, becoming-but-never-arriving world, yet our language was built by people who believed this to be a static world. I have often spoken of the adequate self, but "adequate" will not do, because it is static. In fact, "inadequate" is a more useful word than "adequate." If there were a word that combines "aspiring-becoming," it would come closer to our needs. I have chosen "fully functioning," which I think I learned from Carl Rogers, as the best I can do. This expression at least implies movement.

In order for a person to be fully functioning, when he looks at his self, as he must, he must see that it is enough—enough to perform the task at hand. He must see in his experiential background some history of success. He needs to see process, the building and becoming nature of himself. This being so, he will see that today has no meaning in the absence of yesterdays and tomorrows. In fact, there could be no today except for both yesterday and tomorrow. He must like what he sees, at least well enough for it to be operational.

Many People Do Not Like Their Selves

Unfortunately, many people in the world today suffer from inadequate concepts of self, which naturally lead to mistaken notions of others. Perhaps everybody is afflicted thus to some degree. There may be some rare spirits who are not, but they are few indeed.

We see evidence of this all around us. We see people ridden by unreasonable fears. The fearful person looks at his self and sees that it is not sufficient to meet what he fears. Middle-aged graduate students are afriad to stick their necks out. They are afraid to write; they suffer from stage fright. The question uppermost in their minds is, "What will people think?" Their selves are veritable skeletons in their closets, and if one has a skeleton in his closet, it is best not to do anything except to keep quiet. Any move may reveal it. So they try to sit tight so that they may not be revealed to others. This is a great loss to others—to mankind—for new paths are forbidding and exploration is fraught with terrors.

This is Crippling

An inadequate concept of self, so common in our culture, is crippling to the individual. Our psychological selves may become crippled in much the same way as our physical selves may be crippled by disease or by an accident. They are the same, in effect, because each limits what we can do. When we see ourselves as inadequate, we lose our "can-ness." There becomes less and less that we can do.

Perhaps it is unfortunate that we cannot see the psychological self in the same way that we see the physical self. Our hearts go out to the physical cripple—we do not enter him in a foot race—but we expect the psychological cripple to step lively and meet all of the vicissitudes of life as though he were whole. Both kinds of cripples need therapy, though of different sorts. Many benefit by therapy, though all do not.

How Do We Get That Way?

Now we come to the question, "How do we get that way?" We get that way in the same way that a physical cripple does—by the lives we lead. Of course there are some cases of congenital defect, but if these were the only cripples we had, we would be fortunate indeed.

The newborn babe has enormous potential for health, but this health has to be built out of his experience with others. It has to be achieved, and it has to be achieved in relationship to others. The health potential then lies strictly in the quality of the people around him, since the infant, for many years to come, has, himself, no control over whom he will associate with.

Damage to the self, so disabling to so many of us, comes from the fact that we grow up in an authoritarian culture. While it is true that this is a democracy in governmental form, we have not achieved democracy in the home, the school or the church. The fact that we have a democratically chosen president or governor has no effect upon the developing child. He is built by the people close to him, and he does not elect them. The people close to him, having themselves been crippled, know no better than to continue the process.

The evils of authoritarianism are more extensive than is ordinarily understood. It is easy to see on a grand scale, as when a Hitler gains power. We all abhor a Hitler, but we seem to think that tyranny in small doses or on a small scale is somehow good. All in all, it appears that small tyrants do more harm than grand ones. The small tyrant operates on the growing edge of the personality of the young.

The trouble with the tyrant is basically that he does not have any faith in anyone except himself. He gets that way by living with people who never had any faith in him. Of course he does not really have any faith in himself either, but he has longed for and striven for a position of power over others weaker than himself. Getting his concept of others from his concept of himself, he believes that nothing worthwhile will happen unless he forces it to happen.

Lack of faith in others—the feeling that one has to see to it that others, who are perverse by nature, do what they should—starts a chain reaction of evils, one piled upon another. The burden one bears when he feels that he must watch others and coerce them must be unbearable. And so it turns out to be, for the tyrant deprives himself of others, and grows in the direction of more loneliness and hostility.

From this we can see what happens to the newborn babe as he faces the tyrant. Of course, the tyrant loves his baby in such manner as he is able to love. But he still regards the infant as a "thing," naturally in need of correction. One might think that the very young would not know the difference. But there are ample data to show that even in the first few days after birth, the child knows the difference between being loved and being viewed as in need of coercion. He knows whether the parent is doing things *with* him or *to* him. And the personality at that stage must be tender.

After five or six years of the authoritarian home, the child goes to school. The school is a place inhabited by adults, and too often these adults hold adult concepts of what a child ought to be. These concepts are unverified by the study of children. Here he meets preconceived standards, grade levels, and all of the other paraphernalia of the adult-centered school. If he does not measure up to these standards, then obviously he is perverse and in need of coercion. The fact that these standards are not derived from the child, that there is nothing about them in the Bible, that they arise and reside only in the minds of adults, bothers the adults not at all. Thus, coercion and criticism become the daily fare, while the deviations in behavior brought about by the uniqueness of the personality are stopped. Conformity is the way to the good life, and the best way to conform is to withdraw. One cannot be unique and extend himself and still conform. His uniqueness will show. Shells look a great deal alike, and so if one crawls into his shell, his differences will not be so apparent.

In our authoritarian culture, many forces converge upon the young individual which have the effect of making him think less of himself. The church is one of these forces. The concept of guilt, with its imaginary burden of sin, cannot help one to think well of himself. Of course one can acquire these damaging concepts without getting them at church. But those who have salvation to dispense hold a powerful weapon. When one is made to feel unworthy, he is crippled in some degree, because he cannot do what he otherwise might.

There is a distinction here between the effects of religion and the effects of the church as often administered. It is not religion per se which makes one think ill of himself. It is the representatives of religion who use authoritarian methods to gain their ends. Likewise schooling or education can be expanding in their nature. It is that the representatives of the school—teachers and administrators—often have their own ends to be served, not those of their learners. They act from their own fears which cause them to dampen and delimit the expanding personalities of their young, thus defeating the very purpose for their being.

Nor is it intended here to deny the need for standards. A fully functioning personality cannot operate without standards. Such standards are the basis for aspiration, the basis for the hope for tomorrow. But it is doubtful that extrinsic, materialistic standards can be successfully applied. Standards have to be the product of values held, and of the life that has been led. The better the quality of the life that has been experienced, the better the values held and the standards which result from these values. Standards will be unique—not the same for everyone—even as the experience from which they are derived has been unique. They will be in terms of other human beings.

Basis for Healthy Growth

The dynamic which changes a speck of protoplasm into a fully functioning human being is growth. The questions, then, are: What does he grow on? What are the environmental conditions which feed him?

We need to consider that in growing up one is developing both his physical structure and his psychological structure. We are most familiar with the physical structure and are apt to think of that as growth. We know what the body needs to develop and that lack of development will result in physical crippling. We can identify the diseases of malnutrition and know that a man will not become truly a man in the best sense without an adequate supply of the required stuff of physical growth.

All of the time that the physical body is being developed, so also is the psychological self. The physical body fortunately stops growing after about 20 years. The psychological self, however, continues to grow throughout life. As the physical body has its own unique food requirements, so does the psychological self. This is a different kind of stuff, however, with a different point of intake. We feed the psychological self through the perceptive process. This is what comes into consciousness when stimuli from the environment impinge on the organism. It is the stuff of growth for the personality, and it builds attitudes, habits and knowledge. The perceptive stuff of growth provides the experiential background from which we operate. This controls what we do with the body. The quality of the perceptive stuff of growth therefore determines the quality of the behavior of the individual.

It is necessary here to make clear the fact that the physical body and the psychological self do not constitute a duality, even though it is necessary to speak of them one at a time. The organism is unitary in its operation. There is no body apart from personality, no psychological self without a body to inhabit. What affects one affects all. But that does not prevent speaking of a part. Although we know that hand and foot, attitude, emotion and habit are all one, we still can talk of the hand as having certain characteristics while the foot has others. Speaking of parts does not deny the unitary nature of the individual.

We Select What We Will Perceive

Since in this paper we are primarily concerned with the development of the fully functioning self, we will discuss what feeds the self and how it is fed. As we have noted, perception is the stuff of growth for the psychological self. The perceptive process is the only avenue by which the self can be fed. Recent understandings as to the nature of this process have enabled us to see more clearly than before how the self is built.

One of the most revealing facts about perception is that it is *selective*. We do not see everything in our surroundings. There are thousands of coincidences in the situation in which we find ourselves at any point of time. To perceive them all would cause pandemonium. We therefore *choose* that which the self feeds upon. The direction of the growth of the self depends upon those choices.

The choices seem to be on the basis of experience and unique purpose. We all have a background of experience upon which perception is in part based. We cannot see that which we have no experience to see. But experience is not enough to account for what happens, for there are many objects in our surroundings with which we have had experience, but which we do not perceive.

The additional element which appears to determine perceptive intake is purpose. There is ample evidence now to show that all living tissue is purposive, and, of course, in man this purpose is partly, but only partly, on the conscious level. In perception, purpose operates automatically most of the time. And so, just as we do not eat everything, our psychological selves are particular as to what they feed on. What they take in has to suit their purposes, and has to fit onto their past experiences.

Enhancement and Defense

The self "looks out" upon the surrounding scene largely in terms of its own enhancement or defense. It tends to extend in the direction of that which promises to make it better off. It withdraws from that which seems likely to endanger it. This is largely true throughout life and entirely true in the early stages when the self is being established—when "self" and "other" first come into being. Altruism is a highly sophisticated concept, and, if it is achieved at all, it comes late. It is the result of great understanding of the self-other interdependency.

The Self Needs Boundaries

If the self is going to reach out toward facilitating factors and withdraw from endangering ones, it has to have something to reach out from, something to hide behind. It helps to understand this if we assume that the self has to have boundaries in much the same sense that the physical self has to have a skin. The self has certain things that it will let in, others that it will keep out. The boundaries are not, of course, physical—to be seen—but neither is the self. A physical concept, however, helps us to comprehend it. So if we can imagine a physical shell, or armor, necessary for the confinement of the self, we then can imagine how it functions.

Some kind of boundary—a selective screen—is therefore essential to the maintenance of the self. We could not manage the affairs of living without something of this kind. It follows that the nature of the environment, whether it is seen to be facilitating or endangering, will determine the permeability of this screen. That is, the more facilitating the environment, the less need for protection. The more endangering the environment, the greater need for protection. Thus, under adverse conditions, the screen develops into a shell, so that very little is admitted. When this process is continued over a long period of time, that which enabled us to be selective in our perception becomes almost impermeable.

Boundaries then become barriers. Protection becomes isolation. The self becomes a prisoner in its own fort. We have all seen persons off whom words or ideas seemed to bounce. They have built their barriers against other people so strong that they have become inaccessible. Since fear feeds on itself, especially when a person is in isolation, it has a tendency to extend itself beyond the people who are endangering, to include all people.

When the fearful person withdraws within his psychological shell, communication is shut off. It is just as difficult for such a person to give as it is for him to receive. The self then is denied that which it feeds on. The psychological self feeds on ideas, which come from other people. Without the stuff of growth, the self becomes less adequate, and the whole person loses its ability to do, to venture, to create. The individual comes to see himself as impoverished, but he is not able to do much about it by himself.

The Life Good To Live

Such a person, however, by having enhancing relationships with others, can break down some of the barriers which separate him from others. By good experiences, he can become less fearful and more open. This process, too, feeds on itself, and confidence can be built by the quality of his experience with others. Confidence opens the barriers so that the perceptive stuff of growth can again be received. He has to learn not to see others as threats, but as assets. Of course, this will not happen unless others cease to act toward him as threats. The parent or teacher who depends upon threats or other techniques of fear will not be able to open the self of one who is in his power.

Fortunate indeed, and not too common in this authoritarian culture, is the person who has had the opportunity to grow up with people whom he can see as facilitating. Most of us have to build our shell against others, and if we are to have fully functioning selves, we have to have experiences which will open these shells.

For the development of a fully functioning self, a person needs to have opportunity to live the life good to live. This life, or his world, needs to be populated by people whom he can view as facilitating. It is almost entirely a matter of people, not things. Facilitating people can be poor in material things. In fact, some of the happiest and most open people are found in poor material circumstances. The most closed and fearful people, the most authoritarian people, may be surfeited by the material goods of the earth. While this is no plea for poverty and privation, it seems that the very possession of great quantities of material goods is apt by its very nature to make the holder fearful that he will lose his goods to others. Vague fear always causes the personality to close up and to become less accessible.

The life good to live does not depend upon the material status of the person. It depends upon the quality of the people around him. He needs people who are open, so that he can feel their quality. He needs people who respect him as a person from the very beginning. It is paradoxical that many parents love their young, but do not respect them. Parents and teachers often say that the child is, of course, too young to be able to make any decisions for himself. It is true that the newborn infant cannot make decisions. But the babe can feel the difference between being held in respect and being regarded as though he had no personality. Respect for the budding self brings it out. Disrespect starts the process of closing up, which in some of our older children and adults is often so complete.

The life good to live is a cooperative one. No child is too young to sense whether or not he lives in a cooperative relation with the people around him. The reason that cooperation is so important is that the cooperative atmosphere is one of involvement. The growing self must feel that it is involved, that it is really part of what is going on, that in some degree it is helping shape its own destiny, together with the destiny of all. Perhaps there is no one quality more important for the developing self than this feeling of involvement in what is taking place. This is what gives a person a "reason to be." The lack of consultation and involvement is the cause of the continuing war between parents and their children, between teachers and learners, between teachers and administrators, employers and employees, ad infinitum. When the person is a part of something, then be becomes responsible.

Whenever the cooperative life is proposed, the authoritarians say, "Oh yes, you want children (or workers or teachers) to do just as they please!" This is a gross misunderstanding of the cooperative way of life, and the shell on such people is so thick that we are baffled in our efforts to reach them. The fact is that in the cooperative life there is much less freedom "to do just as they please" than there is under the surveillance of the autocrat. For the obligation is owed, and the responsibility is felt, to ourselves and to those who facilitate us. The obligation is with us 24 hours a day, rather than just when the autocrat is looking. We do not neglect or sabotage our own projects. This happens to the other's project, particularly if he has met us with threat or fear.

The cooperative life, where everyone from his beginning receives the respect due to a person, and, as he is able, becomes involved in and responsible for what goes on, is not an easy life. The obligation is continuous and pressing. But the difficulties of such a life are inherent in the living, and they cause the self to extend and stretch and grow. These difficulties have quite the opposite effect from those thought up by and inflicted on us by someone else. The latter, not having meaning to the person, cause him to withdraw and begin to calculate how he can protect himself.

The Fully Functioning Person

What is a person with a fully functioning self like? This can be answered only in terms of his behavior. Conclusions can be drawn from this behavior. The temptation here is to vest this person, like Rose Aylmer, with "every virtue, every grace." Rather than simply listing virtues, there are some characteristics not necessarily cherished in our culture, which such a person would logically have. From what has been stated here, it might be inferred that nobody has escaped with a fully functioning self. And it seems to be likely that very few survive home, church and school without damage to the self.

Yet there are a good many people who, through contact with facilitating persons, have been reopened and whose selves function well. To argue otherwise would be to deny the potential for change and improvement on which life itself depends. In fact, it can be considered that no one can experience elation who has never known despair; no one can be courageous without having known fear. So the human personality is not doomed to endure its present state, but can be brought into flower by enhancing experiences. As Karen Horney has said, "My own belief is that man has the capacity as well as the desire to develop his potentialities and become a decent human being, and that these deteriorate if his relationship to others and hence to himself is, and continues to be, disturbed. I believe that man can change and keep on changing as long as he lives."*

---

* Karen Horney, *Our Inner Conflicts* (New York: W. W. Norton & Co., 1945.) p. 19.

The fully functioning personality thinks well of himself. He looks at himself and likes what he sees well enough so that he can accept it. This is essential to doing, to "can-ness." He does not see himself as able to do anything and everything, but he sees himself as able in terms of his experience. He feels he can do what is reasonable to expect on the basis of his experience.

Those who do not like what they see when they look at themselves are the fearful ones—not just afraid of present danger, but taking a fearful view of everything in general. Fear renders them helpless, and this leads to alienation from others and hostility toward others, thus shutting themselves off from the stuff they feed upon. The harmful ramifications of not accepting self are endless, because one attitude leads to another.

He thinks well of others. This comes about automatically because of the one-ness of the self-other relationship. It is doubtful that there can be a self except in relation to others, and to accept one implies the acceptance of the other. The acceptance of others opens a whole world with which to relate. It is the opposite of the hostility which results from nonacceptance of self.

He therefore sees his stake in others. He sees that other people are the stuff out of which he is built. He has a selfish interest then in the quality of those around him and has responsibility in some degree for that quality. The whole matter of selfishness and altruism disappears when he realizes that self and other are interdependent—that we are indeed our brother's keeper, and he is ours. Coming into the awareness of mutual need modifies human behavior. He comes to see other people as opportunities, not for exploitation, but for the building of self. He becomes a loving person, so that he can get closer to the real source of his power.

He sees himself as a part of a world in movement—in process of becoming. This follows from the whole notion of self and others and the acceptance that they can feed off each other and hence can improve. When one looks outward rather than inward, the idea of change—in self, in others, in things—becomes apparent. The acceptance of change as a universal phenomenon brings about modifications of personality. The person who accepts change and expects it behaves differently from the person who seeks to get everything organized so that it will be fixed from now on. He will not search for the firm foundation on which he can stand for the rest of his life. He will realize that the only thing he knows for sure about the future is that tomorrow will be different from today and that he can anticipate this difference with hopeful expectation.

Optimism is the natural outcome of an accepting view of self and hence of others. Such a person is a doer, a mobile person, one who relates himself in an active way with others. Such activity would be meaningless unless the person had hopes for improvement. As has been stated, today has no meaning except in relation to an expected tomorrow. This is the basis for hope, without which no one can thrive. Improvement is that which enhances and enriches self and others. Neither can be enhanced by itself.

The fully functioning personality, having accepted the ongoing nature of life and the dynamic of change, *sees the value of mistakes.* He knows he will be treading new paths at all times, and that, therefore, he cannot always be right. Rigid personalities suffer much from their need to be always right. The fully functioning personality will not only see that mistakes are inevitable in constantly breaking new ground, but will come to realize that these unprofitable paths show the way to better ones. Thus, a mistake, which no one would make if he could foresee it, can be profitable. In fact, much of what we know that is workable comes from trying that which is not. In our culture, it seems that most of our moral code is based on the values of rigid people who cannot bear to be wrong, and so, making a mistake is almost sinful. The effective person cannot afford to have his spirit of adventure thus hampered. He knows that the only way to find out is to go forward and to profit from experience—to make experience an asset.

The fully functioning self, seeing the importance of people, *develops and holds human values.* There is no one, of course, who does not come to hold values. Values come about through the life one lives, which determines what one comes to care about. The better the life, the better the values accumulated. The one who sees human beings as essential to his own enhancement develops values related to the welfare of people. Holding these values in a world which most people consider to be static, he encounters problems in meeting static mores. He is, therefore, on the creative edge of the generally accepted mores or morals. Values in terms of what is good for all people are continuously in conflict with materialistic values held by the majority.

He knows no other way to live except in keeping with his values. He has no need continuously to shift behavior, depending upon the kind of people nearest him. He has no need for subterfuge or deceit, because he is motivated by the value of facilitating self and others. While treading new paths is fraught with risk, he does not have to engage in a continuous guessing game to make his behavior match new people and also be consistent with what he has done before. A fully functioning person, holding human values, does not have to ask himself constantly what it was he said last week.

We are tempted to call this courage and integrity. This is another way of saying that one has what it takes to live as life really exists and to do it all in one piece. Can we call it courage when there is no alternative?

Since life is ever-moving and ever-becoming, *the fully functioning person is cast in a creative role.* But more than simply accepting this role, he sees creation going on all around him. He sees that creation is not something which occurred long ago and is finished, but that it is now going on and that he is part of it. He sees the evil of the static personality because it seeks to stop the process of creation to which we owe our world and our being. He exults in being a part of this great process and in having an opportunity to facilitate it. Life to him means discovery and adventure, flourishing because it is in tune with the universe.

FOSTERING SELF-DIRECTION

Arthur W. Combs

Schools which do not produce self-directed citizens have failed everyone—the student, the profession, and the society they are designed to serve. The goals of modern education cannot be achieved without self-direction. We have created a world in which there is no longer a common body of information which everyone must have. The information explosion has blasted for all time the notion that we can feed all students the same diet. Instead, we have to adopt a cafeteria principle in which we help each student select what he most needs to fulfill his potentialities. This calls for student cooperation and acceptance of major responsibility for his own learning.

As Earl Kelley has suggested, the goal of education in the modern world must be the production of increasing uniqueness. This cannot be achieved in autocratic atmospheres where all decisions are made by the teachers and administration while students are reduced to passive followers of the established patterns. Authoritarian schools are as out of date in the world we live in as the horse and buggy. Such schools cannot hope to achieve our purposes. Worse yet, their existence will almost certainly defeat us.

The world we live in demands self-starting, self-directing citizens capable of independent action. The world is changing so fast we cannot hope to teach each person what he will need to know in twenty years. Our only hope to meet the demands of the future is

From *Educational Leadership*, Vol. 23, No. 5, February 1966, pp. 373-376. Reprinted by permission of the Association for Supervision and Curriculum Development and Arthur Combs.

the production of intelligent, independent people. Even our military establishment, historically the most authoritarian of all, has long since discovered that fact. For twenty years the armed forces have been steadily increasing the degree of responsibility and initiative it expects of even its lowest echelons. The modern war machine cannot be run by automatons. It must be run by *thinking* men.

Much of the curriculum of our current schools is predicated on a concept of learning conceived as the acquisition of right answers and many of our practices mirror this belief. Almost anyone can pick them out. Here are a few which occur to me: Preoccupation with right answers; insistence upon conformity; cookbook approaches to learning; overconcern for rules and regulations; preoccupation with materials and things instead of people; the solitary approach to learning; the delusion that mistakes are sinful; emphasis on memory rather than learning; emphasis on grades rather than understanding and content details rather than principles.

Meanwhile, psychologists are telling us that learning is a *personal* matter; individual and unique. It is not controlled by the teacher. It can only be accomplished with the cooperation and involvement of the student in the process. Providing students with information is not enough. People rarely misbehave because they do not know any better. The effectiveness of learning must be measured in behavior change: whether students *behave differently* as a consequence of their learning experience. This requires active participation by the student. So learning itself is dependent upon the capacity for self-direction.

Toward Self-Direction

What is needed of us? How can we produce students who are more self-directed?

1. *We Need To Believe This Is Important.* If we do not think self-direction is important, this will not get done. People are too pressed these days to pay much attention to things that are not important. Everyone does what seems to him to be crucial and urgent. It seems self-evident that independence and self-direction are necessary for our kind of world. Why then has self-direction been given such inadequate attention? It is strange we should have to convince ourselves of its importance.

Unfortunately, because a matter is self-evident is no guarantee that people will really put it into practice. It must somehow be brought into clear figure in the forefront of our striving if it is to affect behavior. Everyone knows it is important to vote, too, yet millions regularly fail to vote. To be effective as an objective, each of us must hold the goal of self-direction clear in our thinking and high in our values whenever we are engaged in planning or teaching of any kind.

This is often not easy to do because self-direction is one of those goals which *everyone* is supposed to be working for. As a result, almost no one regards it as urgent! For each person, his own special duties are so much clearer, so much more pressing and his derelictions so much more glaring if he fails to produce. The goals we hold in common do not redound so immediately to our credit or discredit. They are therefore set aside while we devote our energies to the things that *really* matter to us.

To begin doing something about self-direction we must, therefore, begin by declaring its importance; not as a lofty sentiment, but as an absolute essential. It must be given a place of greater concern than subject matter itself, for a very simple reason: It is far more important than subject matter. Without self-direction no content matters much. It is not enough that it be published in the handbook as a "Goal of Education." Each of us at every level must ask himself: Do I really think self-direction is important and what am I doing about it?

2. *Trust in the Human Organism.* Many of us grew up in a tradition which conceived of man as basically evil and certain to revert to bestial ways if someone did not control him. Modern psychologists tell us this view is no longer tenable. From everything we can observe in humans and animals the basic striving of the organism is inexorably toward health both physical and mental. It is this growth principle on which doctors and psychotherapists depend to make the person well again. If an organism is free to do so—it can, will, it *must* move in positive ways. The organism is not our enemy. It wants the same things we do, the achievement of adequacy. Yet alas, how few believe this and how timid we are to trust our students with self-direction.

A recent best selling book, *Summerhill*, by A. S. Neill has fascinated many educators. In it Neill describes the absolute trust he placed in the children under his care. Many teachers are shocked by his unorthodox procedures and the extreme behavior of some of the children. But whether one approves of Neill's school or not, the thing which impressed me most was this: Here was a man who dared to trust children far beyond what most of us would be willing to risk. Yet, all the things we are so afraid might happen if we did give them such freedom, never happened! For forty years the school continued to turn out happy, effective citizens as well as, or better than, its competitors. It is time we give up fearing the human organism and learn to trust and use its built-in drives toward self-fulfillment. After all, the organism has had to be pretty tough to survive what we have done to it through the ages.

Responsibility and self-direction are learned. They must be acquired from experiences, from being given opportunities to be self-directing and responsible. You cannot learn to be self-directing if no one permits you to try. Human capacities are strengthened by use but atrophy with disuse. If young people are going to learn self-direction, then it must be through being *given* many opportunities to exercise such self-direction throughout the years they are in school. Someone has observed that our schools are operated on a directly contrary principle. Children are allowed more freedom of choice and self-direction in kindergarten (when they are presumably least able to handle it) and each year thereafter are given less and less, until by the time they reach college, they are permitted practically no choice at all! This overdraws the case, to be sure, but there is enough truth in the statement to make one uncomfortable. If we are to produce independent, self-starting people we must do a great deal more to produce the kinds of experiences which will lead to these ends.

3. *The Experimental Attitude.* If we are going to provide young people with increased opportunity for self-direction, we must do it with our eyes open *expecting* them to make mistakes. This is not easy, for the importance of "being right" is in our blood. Education is built on right answers. Wrong ones are regarded as failures to be avoided like the plague. Unfortunately, such attitudes stand squarely in the way of progress toward self-direction and independence.

People too fearful of mistakes cannot risk trying. Without trying, self-direction, creativity and independence cannot be discovered. To be so afraid of mistakes that we kill the desire to try is a tragedy. Autonomy, independence and creativity are the products of being willing to look and eager to try. If we discourage these elements we do so at our peril. In the world we live in, victory is reserved only for the courageous and inventive. It is possible we may lose the game by making mistakes. We will not even get in the game if we are afraid to try.

Experimentation and innovation must be encouraged everywhere in our schools, in teachers as well as students. Each of us needs to be engaged in a continuous process of trying something new. The kind of experimentation which will make the difference to education in the long run is not that produced by the professional researcher with the aid of giant computers but by the everyday changes in goals and processes brought about by the individual teacher in the classroom.

To achieve this, teachers need to be freed of pressures and details by the administration for the exercise of self-direction and creativity. In addition, each of us must accept the challenge and set about a systematic search for the barriers we place in the path of self-direction for ourselves, our colleagues and our students. This should suggest all kinds of places for experimentation where we can begin the encouragement of self-direction. One of the nice things about self-direction is that it does not have to be taught. It only needs to be encouraged and set free to operate.

4. *The Provision of Opportunity*. The basic principle is clear. To produce more self-directed people it is necessary to give more opportunity to practice self-direction. This means some of us must be willing to give up our traditional prerogatives to make all the decisions. Education must be seen, not as providing right answers, but as confrontation with problems; not imaginary play problems either, but *real* ones in which decisions count.

Experiences calling for decision, independence and self-direction must be the daily diet of children, including such little decisions as what kinds of headings and margins a paper should have and big ones like the courses to be taken next year. They must also include decisions about goals, techniques, time, people, money, meals, rules, and subject matter.

If we are to achieve the objective of greater self-direction, I see no alternative to the fuller acceptance of students into partnership in the educative endeavor. Our modern goal for education, "the optimal development of the individual," cannot be achieved without this. Such an aim requires participation of the student and his whole-hearted cooperation in the process. This is not likely to be accomplished unless students have the feeling they matter and their decisions count. Few of us are deeply committed to tasks imposed upon us; and students are not much different. Self-direction is learned from experience. What better, more meaningful experience could be provided than participation in the decisions about one's own life and learning?

The basic belief of democracy is that when people are free they can find their own best ways. Though all of us profess our acceptance of this credo, it is distressing how few of us dare to put it to work. Whatever limits the capacity of our young people to accept both the challenge and the responsibilities of that belief is destructive to all of us. It is time we put this belief to work and to expression in the education of our young as though we really meant it.

SELF-DISCLOSURE:
THE SCIENTIST'S PORTAL TO MAN'S SOUL

Sidney M. Jourard

The soul of which poets speak, and which philosophers and theologians concern themselves with, is now operationally defined by psychologists and called the Self. That the soul, or self, is real, in the sense of existing, few can doubt. At least few would doubt its reality when we define the self as the subjective side of man—that which is private and personal, which he experiences immediately and spontaneously. Of course, what we term "self" has correlates—neurophysiological correlates and environmental stimuli. Doubtless too, the self—feelings, wishes, memories, thoughts, dreams, etc.—is lawful as well. But the self is unique in all of nature, though it is a part of nature. It is unique in this respect: Any other part of nature passively submits to the inquiry of the investigator who is after the facts. Man's self, as near as we now know, can never be known to any save the experiencing individual unless the individual man unequivocally co-operates and *makes his self known.* In short, man must consent; if we would know his self, he must *want* to tell us. If he doesn't wish to tell us of his self, we can torture him, browbeat him, tempt him, even make incisive psychoanalytic guesses; but unless he wishes to make his self known, we will of course never know it. However shrewd our guesses might be about a man's self, when we guess about a man's self, we never know whether we are correct until he says, and means it, "You're right." Moreover, we don't know for a certainty whether he means it.

This line of thinking should make us despair of ever subjecting man's soul to scientific scrutiny, except for one thing. It is likely that the *act* of self-disclosure follows laws—perhaps the laws of reinforcement (cf. Skinner, 1953). I believe that I may have stumbled upon a key to the lock of the portal to man's soul. So far, the key barely fits the lock; it doesn't always work; it needs to be made more precise, of course. But it is such an obvious kind of key, and it has been lying around unnoticed for such a long time, that I wonder why no one ever picked it up to try it out for size.

What is this key? It is the study of what information a person will tell another person about himself, or, more technically, about his *self.* I call the key—or portal, it doesn't really matter, since we are mixing metaphors—self-disclosure. Through my self-disclosure, I let others know my soul. They can know it, really know it, only as I make it known. In fact, I am beginning to suspect that I can't even know *my own soul* except as I disclose it. I suspect that I will know myself "for real" at the exact moment that I have succeeded in making it known through my disclosure to another person.

Let us look for a moment at the act of disclosing something about one's self to another person, a simple statement such as one's name, age, weight, height, what one did with whom yesterday, or the relating of a dream. A little introspection will verify that even simple, factual disclosures of this sort can often be matters that are fraught with anxiety. Whence the anxiety? Cameron and Magaret (1951) have a section in their excellent treatise on *Behavior Pathology* which is concerned with what they call behavioral duplicity. They point out that dissemblance is learned early in life by all of us. As children we *are,* and we *act,* our real selves. We say what we think, we scream for what we want, we tell what we did. These spontaneous disclosures meet variable consequences—some disclosures are ignored, some rewarded, and some punished. Doubtless in accordance with the laws of reinforcement, we learn early to withhold certain disclosures because of the painful consequences to which they lead. We are punished, in our society, not only for what we actually do, but also for what we think, feel, or want. Very soon, then, the growing child learns to display a highly expurgated version of his self to others. ¹ have coined the term "public self" (Jourard, 1958) to refer to the concept of oneself which one *wants* others to believe. We monitor, censor our behavior and disclosures in order to construct in the mind of the other person a concept of ourselves which we want him to have. Obviously, our assorted public selves are not always accurate portrayals of our real selves. In fact, it often comes to pass—perhaps as a socially patterned defect (Fromm, 1955)—that our public selves become so estranged from our real selves that the net consequence is self-alienation: we no longer know our real selves. Our disclosures reflect, not our spontaneous feelings, thoughts, and wishes, but rather pretended experience which will avoid punishment and win unearned approval. We say that we feel things we do not feel. We say that we did things we did not do. We say that we believe things we do not believe. When self-alienation, which I believe is the consequence of what I call pseudo-self-disclosure, has proceeded far enough, the individual loses his soul, literally. Or, we may say he has sold his soul, his real self, in order to purchase popularity, his mother's affection, or a promotion in the firm.

Self-disclosure, then, entails courage—the kind of courage that Paul Tillich (1952) had in mind in writing his book *The Courage to Be*. I would paraphrase that title to read, *The Courage to Be Known*, since Being always occurs in a social context. Since I seem to be in a paraphrasing frame of mind, let me modify some other well-known sayings. The Delphic Oracle advised, "Know Thyself"; I would say "Make Thyself Known, and then Thou wilt Know Thyself." Shakespeare is the source of, "And this above all, to thine own self be true, and . . . thou cans't not then be false to any man." Let me re-state it, "And this above all, to any other man be true, and thou cans't not then be false to thyself."

What, after all, is the situation called psychotherapy, but a situation wherein one person, the patient—alienated from himself, troubled—starts to disclose his self to the other person, the therapist. Then he "blocks," he resists. The therapist uses his skill to overcome the resistance, thus promoting more self-disclosure. Whether or not psychotherapy works as well as nothing or anything, as Eysenck (1952) seems to believe (I do not really believe he really believes this), of one thing we can be sure: At the conclusion of a series of psychotherapeutic sessions, the therapist knows more about his patient's self than he knew at the beginning. Possibly, too, the patient knows more about his own self at that time too. What he does with this knowledge is of course another cup of tea.

Does it come as a shock that, in the studies conducted at Chicago by Rogers (1954) into the effects of psychotherapy, that after umpteen hours of therapy, the therapist could guess the self-description of his patient better than he could at the outset of therapy? It is a case of the therapist being taught by the patient's self-disclosures of what manner of a man the patient believes he is. Should we assert that empathy is facilitated by self-disclosure? Let's ask the question,

"How do we obtain an accurate concept of another man's experiencing?" We can guess his experience on the basis of interpretations of such things as facial cues; we can indulge in assimilative projection, imagine how we could feel in that situation, and then assume that that in fact is what the other man *is* at the moment. A more effective way of obtaining an accurate concept of the man's experiencing is to ask him what he is thinking and feeling. If he tells us honestly, there we have it: the basis for perfect empathy.

I could go on in this vein, but I had better not. I have some data that I would like to share with you. Let me tell you of a method we have been using to study self-disclosure, and some findings. Then, I shall conclude with some plans, or rather hopes that I have for further investigation.

A few years ago, I was puzzling about Karen Horney's (1950) concept of the "real self." I wondered how to adapt this concept for purposes of research. Out of this thinking came the idea that the kind of personal data we all put down on an application form when we are applying for a job might have the makings of a research tool. Some application forms, labeled "confidential," ask for amazingly detailed data about oneself. I asked myself, "Whom would an applicant tell these things to besides his prospective employer, or teacher?" And then I was off. I started itemizing classes of information about oneself which could only be known by another person through direct verbal telling. After much fiddling this way and that, I wound up with a 60-item questionnaire listing 10 items of information in each of 6 categories, which I called Aspects of Self. I devised an answer sheet with rows corresponding to the items, and columns headed by Target-Persons. To start with I arbitrarily selected Mother, Father, Male Friend, and Female Friend and/or Spouse as Target-Persons. Subjects were asked to indicate whether or not they had made information about each item known to each of the Target-Persons. Those devotees of analysis of variance can see the makings of a colossal pot of data to be unscrambled with that method. After all, we had four of five Target-Persons and six Aspects of Self; our subjects could be classified endlessly (male-female, Negro-white, good-bad, etc.); and not the least, we had individual differences to look into.

My colleague Paul Lasakow and I tested several hundred subjects with this simple instrument, and we selected smaller subsamples for particular analyses. Here are some of the things that we found. Men do not disclose as much about themselves, generally, as women. White subjects of both sexes disclose more, generally, than Negro subjects of comparable social class and educational level. For the age range we studied: white females disclose most to mother and girl friend, and least to father and boy friend; Negro females follow a similar pattern. White males disclose in about equivalent amount to both parents and male friend, and significantly less to female friend. Negro males disclose most to their mothers, and comparatively little, if at all, to father, male friend, or female friend.

Married subjects, of course, disclose most to their spouse. With regard to other target-persons, such as both parents, and the same-sex friend, female married subjects disclose more than male married subjects, though there is no sex difference in disclosure to the spouse. I am led to suspect that males are relatively unknown to and by anyone until they marry, while women are better known. In fact, it seems that women are both the givers and the receivers of subjective data. Women know more, and tell more, about people's selves than men do. This, doubtless, is part of their "expressive role" in social systems, in contrast with the male "instrumental role." It staggers me a little when I think of the stupendous amount of private and personal "self-data" that women have at their disposal. Men know the facts of nature, but women know the facts about men and women!

In connection with the theme of marriage, we are led, of course, to love. Married subjects, male and female, disclose less to their parents and friends than unmarried subjects of comparable age. What they have taken away from these folks, in the way of self-disclosure, they give unto their spouses. In this respect, they more or less follow the biblical injunction which holds that in marriage one should forsake all others. However, while our young married females obeyed the spirit of this injunction, they did not obey its letter—Momma was still disclosed to quite a bit by these young wives. Presumably, there is love in marriage. The loved spouse is disclosed to more than other target-persons. But we have more direct data than this, concerned with the relation between love and self-disclosure. Questionnaires measuring the feelings of a group of young female subjects toward their mothers and fathers produced scores that correlated substantially with self-disclosure to mother and father. In other words, when one loves or likes one's parents, one will make oneself known to them; not otherwise. Of course, psychotherapists are familiar with this fact; self-disclosure gets dammed up in their patients with every twinge of negative transference. And it is influenced by both positive and negative *counter*transference. But I am led to propose that when poets speak of love as a case of giving one's heart and soul to another, they are speaking, among other things of this prosaic thing, self-disclosure.

Here is an interesting finding. Married police officers were compared with young married college males on self-disclosure to Wife and to Closest Male Friend. Compared with the college boys, the police officers were tight-lipped. Their wives and friends knew virtually nothing about them. Is this paranoia? An occupational pattern?

I am beginning to formulate a rather crude hypothesis about self-disclosure, one which is strongly suggested by certain patterns in our data. Let me state it rather dogmatically, so that it can be more readily tested. Speaking generally, we see in our data that our subjects disclose more to their family than to non-family members, and excepting the married subjects, more to their own sex than to the opposite sex; and they disclose more to their age-peers than to their elders or youngers. In other words, the subjects tended to disclose more about themselves to people who *resembled them in various ways* than to people who differed from them. This leads me to propose that disclosure of self is a byproduct, among other things, of the perception or belief that the other, the target-person, is similar to the self. Probably the similarity which is crucial is similarity in *values*. We disclose ourselves when we are pretty sure that the target-person will evaluate our disclosures and react to them as we do ourselves (within certain limits).

Another finding of a general nature is obvious and was expected. The aspects of self were differentially disclosed. Obviously, some kinds of information about ourselves are easier to disclose than others. Psychotherapists are familiar with this fact, as were Kurt Lewin (1948) and, more recently, Maria Rickers-Ovsiankina (1956).

Where to follow this self-disclosure next? There are many avenues, not the least in importance being efforts to refine our instrument, which at present is very crude. But we can explore many general hypotheses in a broad spade-work operation—age-changes, social class, many and many group comparisons. We can explore content systematically for its varying ease of disclosure. We can investigate, even map, interpersonal relationships, lending a depth dimension to sociometry. I'm of course interested in the mental health implications of self-disclosure.

Let me comment a little about self-disclosure and mental health. I really don't know which is cause and which is effect here; perhaps it doesn't matter. I have some evidence that the relationship between the two variables is curvilinear—too much or too little self-disclosure betokens disturbance in self and in interpersonal relationships, while some as yet undetermined amount under specified conditions is synonymous with mental health. I believe that self-disclosure is the obverse of repression and self-alienation. The man who is alientated from his fellows is alienated from himself. Alienated man is not known by his fellows, he doesn't know himself, and he doesn't know his fellows. Self-disclosure appears to be one means, perhaps the most direct, by which self-alienation is transformed into self-realization. Man hides much of his real self—his experience—behind an iron curtain. Our evidence shows that this iron curtain melts like wax when it is exposed to the warm breath of love.

    I will conclude by sharing with you some less scientific aspects of the study of self-disclosure. Another man's self is an utterly fascinating datum. We spend much of our time in our daily life speculating about the other person's self; we have to in order to interact with him. Our purposes in securing knowledge of the other man's self vary, of course, but it is not difficult to see how one could become a student of others' selves for the love of the game. If I seem repetitious, enthusiastic, or both, I am like the guitar-player who, daily, for 20 years, sat with a one-string guitar, holding the same fret, plucking the same sound. One day his wife said, with surprise, "Dear, I noticed on TV today that a man was playing a guitar, but it had six strings, and the man kept moving his hands around, and making lots of different sounds—not like you." Her husband said, "Don't worry about him, dear. He's still huntin' the right note, and I already found it."

MANIPULATION OF HUMAN BEHAVIOR:
AN ETHICAL DILEMMA

Herbert C. Kelman

The social scientist today—and particularly the practitioner and investigator of behavior change—finds himself in a situation that has many parallels to that of the nuclear physicist. The knowledge about the control and manipulation of human behavior that he is producing or applying is beset with enormous ethical ambiguities, and he must accept responsibility for its social consequences. Even the pure researcher cannot withdraw into the comforting assurance that knowledge is ethically neutral. While this is true as far as it goes, he must concern himself with the question of how his knowledge is *likely* to be used, given the particular historical context of the society in which it is produced. Nor can the practitioner find ultimate comfort in the assurance that he is helping others and doing good. For, not only is the goodness of doing good in itself a matter of ethical ambiguity—a point to which I shall return shortly—but he also confronts the question of the wider social context in which a given action is taken. The production of change may meet the momentary needs of the client—whether it be an individual, an organization, or a community—yet its long-range consequences and its effects on other units of the system of which this client is a part may be less clearly constructive.

There are several reasons why the ethical problems surrounding the study of behavior change are of increasing concern. First, our

Herbert C. Kelman, *A Time to Speak: On Human Values and Social Research*, (San Francisco: Jossey-Bass, 1968) "Manipulation of Human Behavior: An Ethical Dilemma," pp. 13-31. Reprinted by permission.

knowledge about the control of human behavior is increasing steadily and systematically. Relevant information is being developed in various areas within psychology—clinical, social, and experimental—as well as in sociology and anthropology. There is reason to question whether the dangers from that direction are imminent. I have the feeling that the power and sensitivity of scientifically based techniques for controlling and shaping complex human behaviors are often exaggerated. Nevertheless, we are constantly working toward a systematization of this knowledge and we must at least anticipate the day when it will have developed to a point where the conditions necessary for producing a particular change in behavior can be specified with relative precision. Second, there is an increasing readiness and eagerness within our society to use whatever systematic information (or misinformation) about the control of human behavior [that] can be made available. This readiness can be found in different quarters and in response to different motivations. It can be found among therapists and pedagogues, among idealists and agitators, among hucksters and image-makers. Third, social scientists are becoming increasingly respectable, and many agencies within government, industry, the military, and the fields of public health and social welfare are becoming interested in our potential contributions. Here too there is no imminent danger. We still have a long way to go before becoming truly influential and we may find the road rather bumpy. Nevertheless, we must anticipate the possibility that social scientists will meet with a serious interest in their ideas about behavior control and have an opportunity to put them to the test on a large scale.

For all of these reasons, concern about the implications of our knowledge of behavior control is less and less a matter of hypothetical philosophical speculation. The possibilities are quite real that this knowledge will be used to control human behavior—with varying degrees of legitimacy, effectiveness, and scope. Moreover, this knowledge is being produced in a socio-historical context in which its use on a large scale, for the control of vast populations, is particularly likely. Ours is an age of mass societies, in which the requirements of urbanization and industrialization, together with the availability of powerful media of communication, provide all the necessary conditions for extensive manipulation and control of the behavior of masses. An interest in controlling the behavior of its population is, of course, a characteristic of every society and by no means unique to our age. What *is* unique is that this is done on a mass scale, in a systematic way, and under the aegis of specialized institutions deliberately assigned to this task. Like the nuclear physicist, then, the social scientist is responsible for knowledge that, in the light of the world situation in which it is being produced, has decided explosive possibilities. It behooves us, therefore, to be concerned with the nature of the product that we are creating and the social process to which we are contributing.

The Social Scientist's Dilemma

In their attempts to come to grips with this problem, it seems to me, the practitioner and investigator of behavior change are confronted with a basic dilemma. On the one hand, for those of us who hold the enhancement of man's freedom of choice to be a fundamental value, any manipulation of the behavior of others constitutes a violation of their essential humanity. This would be true regardless of the form the manipulation takes—whether, for example, it be based on threat of punishment or positive reinforcement. Moreover, it would be true regardless of the "goodness" of the cause that this manipulation is designed to serve. Thus, an ethical problem arises not simply from the ends for which behavior control is being used (although this, too, is a major problem in its own right), but from the very fact that we are using it. On the other hand, effective behavior change inevitably involves some degree of manipulation and control, and at least an implicit imposition of the change agent's values on the client or the person he is influencing. There are many situations in which all of us—depending on our particular values—would consider behavior change desirable: for example, childhood socialization, education, psychotherapy, racial integration, and so on. The two horns of the dilemma, then, are represented by the view that any manipulation of human behavior inherently violates a fundamental value, but that there exists no formula for so structuring an effective change situation that such manipulation is totally absent.

In calling attention to the inevitability of behavior control whenever influence is being exerted, I am not suggesting that we should avoid influence under all circumstances. This is not only impossible if there is to be any social life, but it is also undesirable from the point of view of many important social values. Nor am I suggesting that we need not worry about the manipulation inherent in all influence attempts, simply because it is inevitable. The view that we can forget about this problem, because there is nothing we can do about it anyway, ignores the fact that there are important differences in degree and kind of manipulation and that there are ways of mitigating the manipulative effect of various influence attempts even if the effect cannot be eliminated entirely.

This leads me to another very crucial qualification with respect to the first horn of the dilemma that I have presented. In stating that all manipulation of behavior, regardless of its form or of the purpose it is designed to serve, as a violation of the person's essential humanity, I am not suggesting that differences between different types of manipulation are ethically insignificant. The extent to which the influence attempt, despite its manipulative component, allows for or even enhances the person's freedom of choice, the extent to which the relationship between influencer and influencee is reciprocal, the extent to which the situation is oriented toward the welfare of the influencee rather than the welfare of the influencing agent—all of these are matters of great moment from an ethical point of view. In fact, these differences are the major concern of the present analysis. But I consider it essential, as a prophylactic measure, to keep in mind that even under the most favorable conditions manipulation of the behavior of others is an ethically ambiguous act.

It is this first horn of the dilemma that Skinner seems to ignore, as can be seen from his debate with Rogers, several years ago, on issues concerning the control of human behavior (C. R. Rogers and B. F. Skinner, "Some Issues Concerning the Control of Human Behavior," *Science*, 1956, 124: 1057-1066) Rogers, on the other hand, tends to minimize the second horn of the dilemma.

Skinner is well aware of the inevitability of control in human affairs, and urges for a type of control that is based on intelligent planning and positive reinforcement and is not "exercised for the selfish purposes of the controller" (p. 1057). He makes a number of telling points in responding to his critics. For example, he reminds us that, while we object to external controls, we often ignore psychological constraints that limit freedom of choice to the same or an even greater extent. He asks why a state of affairs that would otherwise seem admirable becomes objectionable simply because someone planned it that way. He points out that control based on the threat and exercise of punishment, which is built into our political and legal institutions, is fully accepted, but that use of positive reinforcement by government is regarded with suspicion. I find these and other points useful because they help us to focus on forms of control that often remain unrecognized and to consider forms of control that may be ethically superior to current ones but that we tend to reject because of their unorthodox nature. But Skinner fails to see the basis of many of the criticisms directed at him, because he is concerned about the control of human behavior only when that control is aversive, and when it is misused, that is,

when it is used for the benefit of the controller and to the detriment
of the controllee. He seems unable to see any problem in the mere
use of control, regardless of technique or purpose. This inability is
consistent with his value position, which does not recognize the
exercise of choice as a good per se.*

My own statement of the first horn of the dilemma is predicated
on the assumption that the freedom and opportunity to choose is a
fundamental value. To be fully human means to choose. Complete
freedom of choice is, of course, a meaningless concept. But the
purpose of education and of the social order, as I see it, is to enable
men to live in society while at the same time enhancing their
freedom to choose and widening their areas of choice. I therefore
regard as ethically ambiguous any action that limits freedom of
choice, whether it be through punishment or reward or even through
so perfect an arrangement of society that people do not care to
choose. I cannot defend this value because it is not logically derived
from anything else. I can, of course, offer supporting arguments for
it. First, I can try to show that the desire to choose represents a
universal human need, which manifests itself under different historical circumstances (not only under conditions of oppression). Second,
I can point out that freedom of choice is an inescapable component
of other valued states, such as love, creativity, mastery over the
environment, or maximization of one's capacities. Third, I can try to
argue that valuing free individual choice is a vital protection against
tyranny: Quite aside from the notion that power corrupts its user,
even the well-motivated, unselfish controlling agent will be tempted
to ignore human variability and to do what *he* thinks is good for
others rather than what they think is good for themselves—and thus
in essence become tyrannical—if he is unhampered by the right to
choose as a basic human value. While I can offer these supporting
arguments, I recognize that freedom of choice is, in the final analysis,
a rock-bottom value for me. Skinner is not concerned with the
dilemma presented here because apparently he does not share this
fundamental value, even though he is strongly committed to certain
other related values, such as the rejection of aversive control and
selfish exploitation (albeit without recognizing their status as values).

With Rogers on the other hand, I feel a complete affinity at the
value level. He values "man as a self-actualizing process of becoming"
and in general proposes that "we select a set of values that focuses on

---

*This in turn is related to a point stressed by Rogers, namely Skinner's
underestimation of the role of value choices in human affairs in general and in
the application of science to social problems in particular.

fluid elements of process rather than static attributes" (p. 1063). He favors a society "where individuals carry responsibility for personal decisions" (p. 1064). He regards "responsible personal choice" as "the most essential element in being a person" (p. 1064). But, as I have pointed out, Rogers tends to minimize the second horn of the dilemma presented here: the inevitability of some degree of manipulation in any influence attempt. He makes what appears to me the unrealistic assumption that by choosing the proper goals and the proper techniques in an influence situation one can completely sidestep the problem of manipulation and control. He seems to argue that, when an influencing agent is dedicated to the value of man as a self-actualizing process and selects techniques that are designed to promote this value, he can abrogate his power over the influencee and maintain a relationship untainted by behavior control. This ignores, in my opinion, the dynamics of the influence situation itself. I fully agree that influence attempts designed to enhance the client's freedom of choice and techniques that are consistant with this goal are ethically superior, and that we should continue to push and explore in this direction. But we must remain aware that the nature of the relationship between influencing agent and influencee is such that inevitably, even in these influence situations, a certain degree of control will be exercised. The assumption that we can set up an influence situation in which the problem of manipulation of behavior is removed, because of the stated purpose and formal structure of the situation, is a dangerous one. It makes us blind to the continuities between all types of influence situations and to the subtle ways in which others can be manipulated. It lulls us into the reassuring certainty that what we are doing is, by definition, good. I would regard it as more in keeping with both the realities of behavior change, and the ethical requirements of minimizing manipulation, to accept the inevitability of a certain amount of control as part of our dilemma and to find a *modus vivendi* in the face of the ethical ambiguities thus created.

Manipulative Uses of Knowledge

Let me proceed to examine briefly the implications of this general dilemma for each of three roles involving social science knowledge about behavior change: the practitioner, as exemplified by the psychotherapist and the group leader or group process trainer; the applied researcher, such as the social scientist in industry or the public opinion pollster; and the basic researcher, such as the investigator of attitude change. These roles are, of course, highly overlapping, but separating them may help us focus on different nuances of the general dilemma.

The practitioner. The practitioner must remain alert to the possibility that he is imposing his own values on the client; that in the course of helping the client he is actually shaping his behavior in directions that he, the practitioner, has set for him. Thus, psychotherapy, even though it is devoted to what I would consider a highly valuable end—enabling the patient to live more comfortably and achieve his own goals more effectively—is definitely open to the possibility of manipulation. Psychotherapy (at least "good" psychotherapy) is markedly different from brainwashing: the client enters into the relationship voluntarily; the therapist is concerned with helping the patient, rather than with furthering his own ends or the ends of some institution that he represents. Influence techniques are designed to free the patient, to enhance his ability to make choices, rather than to narrow his scope. Yet there are some striking similarities between the methods of therapy and those of brainwashing to which the therapist must always remain alert, lest he overstep what is sometimes a rather thin line. The therapist cannot avoid introducing his own values into the therapeutic process. He cannot be helpful to the patient unless he deliberately tries to influence him in the direction of abandoning some behaviors and trying out others. But in doing so he must beware of two types of dangers. One is the failure to recognize that he is engaged in the control of the client's behavior. The other is intoxication with the goodness of what he is doing for and to the client, which in turn leads to a failure to recognize the ambiguity of the control that he exercises. Only if he recognizes these two conditions is he able to take steps to counteract them.

Similar considerations hold for the group leader. Some of the principles of group leadership developed by social psychologists and variously called applied group dynamics, human relations skills, or group process sensitivity are highly congenial to democratic values. They are designed to involve the group in the decision-making process and to foster self-expression on the part of the individual member. Yet the possibilities for manipulation abound. A skillful group leader may be able not only to manipulate the group into making the decision that he desires, but also to create the feeling that this decision reflects the will of the group discovered through the workings of the democratic process. This need not involve a deliberate Machiavellian deception on the part of the group leader; the leader himself may share the illusion that a group product has emerged over which he has exercised no influence. It is essential, therefore, to be fully aware of the leader's control implicit in these techniques. Some of their proponents argue that, by their very nature, these techniques can be used only for democratic ends. I would question this assumption and, in fact, consider it dangerous because it exempts the group leader from asking those questions that any practitioner of behavior change should keep before his eyes: What am I doing in my relationship to the client? Am I creating a situation in which he can make choices in line with his own values, or am I structuring the situation so that my values dominate?

When the group leader is involved in training others in human relations skills or sensitivity to group process, he is confronted with a further problem. Typically, the trainee is a member of some organization—industrial, governmental, military, educational, religious—in which he will apply the skills he is now learning. The human relations trainer is, thus, in a sense improving the trainee's ability to manipulate others in the service of the organization that he represents. Of course, this is not the goal of the training effort, and trainers always try to communicate the value of the democratic process in group life. But the fact remains that they are training a wide variety of people who will be using these skills for a wide variety of ends. It can certainly be argued that the widespread introduction of human relations skills is likely to have more positive than negative effects from the point of view of a democratic ideology. Perhaps this is true. But it is dangerous to assume that these skills carry their own built-in protection. There is no substitute for a continued attention, on the trainer's part, to questions such as these: Whom am I training? To what uses will they put the skills that I am placing at their disposal? What are the organizational processes in which I am now becoming a partner?

The applied researcher. It is essentially these same questions to which the applied social researcher in the broad field of behavior change must address himself. I am here thinking specifically of applied research in the sense that it is done for a client. While the researcher is merely gathering facts, he is nonetheless participating quite directly in the operations of the organization that employs him. If his work is successful, then his findings will be applied to the formulation and execution of the organization's policies. There is thus the real possibility that the investigator is directly helping the organization in its attempts to manipulate the behavior of others—workers in an industry, consumers, or the voting public.

Let us take, for example, the industrial social scientist who studies

factors affecting worker morale. On the basis of his recommendations, and often with his direct assistance, management may become
more aware of human relations aspects of industrial work and
introduce methods designed to improve morale. Ideally, these methods would consist of increased involvement and participation of
workers in decisions relating to their jobs. Critics of this type of
approach argue that the social scientist is working for management,
providing them with information and introducing procedures that are
designed to increase productivity at the worker's expense. The
assumption in this criticism, to which I think there is some validity,
is that the worker is being manipulated so that he experiences a sense
of participation and involvement which is not reflected in the reality
of his position within the industrial organization. In response to this
criticism it can be argued that, considering the over-all lack of
satisfaction in industrial work, it is a net good to give the worker
some sense of participation and involvement in the work situation, to
give him at least a limited opportunity to make choices and thus find
some meaning in the job. To be sure, management is interested in
these innovations because they expect the changes to increase
productivity, but does that necessarily vitiate the advantages from
the worker's point of view? This is a rather convincing defense, but
in evaluating the pros and cons we must also take into account the
social context in which these changes are introduced. What effect
does the human relations approach have on unions, which represent
the only source of independent power of the industrial worker? Does
it sidestep them, and will it eventually weaken them? What are the
general implications of helping the worker adjust to a situation in
which he has no real freedom of choice, in any ultimate sense? These
questions are not easy to answer, and every social scientist has to
decide for himself whether his work in industry is doing more good
than harm. In deciding whether or not, and in what way, to do
applied social research in industry or elsewhere, the social scientist
must ask himself: Whom am I doing this work for? How are my
findings likely to be used? Will they increase or decrease the freedom
of choice of the people whose behavior will be influenced? What are
the social processes, both short-run and long-run, in which I am
participating through my research?

Another example of applied social research that raises questions
about manipulation of the population is public opinion polling, when
used in connection with political campaigns or the political process
in general. For instance, in a recent presidential election, computer
simulating was used—based on data derived from numerous opinion

polls—to predict the responses of various segments of the population to different campaign issues. Information generated by this process was made available to one of the political parties. This type of social research has some troubling implications. It raises the possibility that a candidate might use this information to manipulate the voters by presenting a desirable image, that is, saying what the public presumably wants to hear. In defense against such criticisms, the originators of this technique have pointed out that it represents a systematic way of providing the candidate with relevant information about the interests and concerns of the public, or of particular publics. He can then address himself to those issues with which the public is deeply concerned, thus making his campaign more relevant and meaningful and enhancing the democratic political process. They point out further that this is what candidates try to do anyway—and properly so; all the social scientist does is to help them base their campaigns on more adequate information, rather than on the usually unreliable estimates of politicians. Of course, what assurance do we have that opinion polls and computer simulations based on them will, in fact, be used in this ideal manner to bolster the democratic process, rather than to short-circuit it? The information can be used both to widen and to restrict the citizen's freedom of choice. But, as long as it is information that can help political organizations to manipulate the public more effectively, the researcher must concern himself actively with the question of how it is going to be used and to what kind of process it is going to contribute.

The basic researcher. For the man engaged in "basic" research on one or another aspect of behavior change—in contrast to the man who does research for a specific client—it is much easier to take the position that the knowledge he produces is neutral. Yet, since there is a possibility that his product will be used by others for purposes of manipulation, he cannot be completely absolved from responsibility. He must consider the relative probabilities, given the existing socio-historical context, that this knowledge will be used to enhance or to restrict people's freedom of choice. These considerations must enter into his decision whether or not to carry out a given piece of research, and how to proceed with it.

Take, for example, the area of attitude change, with which I myself am strongly identified. Much of the research in this area is clearly dedicated to the discovery of general principles, which can presumably be applied to many situations with differing goals. Yet, because of the nature of the principles and the experimental settings from which they are derived, they can probably be applied most

readily, most directly, and most systematically to mass communications. And, because of the nature of our social order, they are
particularly likely to be used for purposes of advertising, public
relations, and propaganda, forms of mass communication that are
least oriented toward enhancing the listener's freedom of choice.
There are, cf course, many reasons for continuing this line of
research, despite the probability that its findings will be used for
manipulative purposes. First, one can argue that extending our
general knowledge about processes of attitude change and increasing
our understanding of the nature of influence are in themselves
liberating forces whose value outweighs the possibility that this
knowledge will be used for undesirable ends. Second, such research
may not only increase the knowledge of the potential manipulator,
but also help in finding ways to counteract manipulative forces, by
providing the information needed for effective resistance to manipulation, or by developing knowledge about forms of influence that
enhance freedom of choice. Third, one might argue that information
about attitude change, despite its potential for manipulative uses, is
important for the achievement of certain socially desirable goals,
such as racial integration or international understanding.

I obviously find these arguments convincing enough to continue
this line of research. But the nagging thought remains that the
knowledge I am producing, if it has any scientific merit, may come
to be used for ever more effective manipulation of human behavior.
Thus, even the basic researcher in the domain of behavior change
must always ask himself: Given the realities of our present society,
what are the probable uses to which the products of my research are
going to be put? What are the social processes to which I am
contributing by the knowledge that I feed into them?

Mitigating the Manipulative Aspects of Behavior Change

The very fact that I have presented my position in the form of a
dilemma should make it clear that I do not see an ultimate
"solution," a way of completely avoiding the ethical ambiguity with
which practitioners and researchers in the field of behavior change
are confronted. I do feel, however, that there are ways of mitigating
the dehumanizing effects of new developments in the field of
behavior change. I would like to propose three steps designed to
contribute to this end. Stated in their most general form, they would
involve: (1) increasing our own and others' active awareness of the
manipulative aspects of our work and the ethical ambiguities inherent therein; (2) deliberately building protection against manipula-

tion or resistance to it into the processes we use or study; and (3) setting the enhancement of freedom of choice as a central positive goal for our practice and research. To spell out in somewhat greater detail what these three steps might imply, I would like to examine them from the point of view of each of the three separate (though overlapping) roles that have already been differentiated: the role of the practitioner, of the applied researcher, and of the "basic" researcher in the field of behavior change. The argument that follows is summarized in Figure 1.

The practitioner. I have already stressed how essential it is for the practitioner of behavior change to be aware of the fact that he is introducing his own values both in the definition of the situation and in the setting of standards. Thus, in the therapeutic situation, it is not only inevitable but also useful for the therapist to have certain values about what needs to be done in the situation itself and what are desirable directions in which the patient might move, and to

Figure 1. Steps Designed to Mitigate the Manipulative Aspects of
Behavior Change in Each of Three Social Science Roles

Desirable Steps	*Practitioner*	*Applied Researcher*	*Basic Researcher*
(1) Increasing awareness of manipulation	Labeling own values to self and clients; allowing client to "talk back"	Evaluating organization that will use findings; considering how, on whom, and in what context they will be used	Predicting probabilities of different uses of research product, given existing socio-historical context
(2) Building protection against or resistance to manipulation into the process	Minimizing own values and maximizing client's values as dominant criteria for change	Helping target group to protect its interests and resist encroachments on its freedom	Studying processes of resistance to control, and communicating findings to the public
(3) Setting enhancement of freedom of choice as a positive goal	Using professional skills and relationship to increase client's range of choices and ability to choose	Promoting opportunities for increased choice on part of target group as integral features of the planned change	Studying conditions for enhancement of freedom of choice and maximization of individual values

communicate these values to the patient. But he must be clear in his own mind that he is bringing these values into the relationship, and he must label them properly for the patient. By recognizing himself that he is engaged in a certain degree of control—and that this is an ethically ambiguous act, even though his role as therapist requires it—and by making the patient aware of this fact, he provides some safeguards against this control. Among other things, such a recognition would allow the patient, to a limited extent, to "talk back" to the therapist, to argue about the appropriateness of the values that the therapist is introducing. A therapeutic situation is, of course, not a mutual influence situation in the true sense of the word. By definition, it is designed to examine only the patient's values and not those of the therapist. But, from the point of view of reducing the manipulativeness of the situation, it would be important to encourage mutuality at least to the extent of acknowledging that what the therapist introduces into the situation is not entirely based on objective reality, but on an alternative set of values which are open to question. There may be particular therapeutic relationships in which a therapist finds it difficult to acknowledge the values that he brings to them, because his own motivations have become too deeply involved. There may also be institutional settings in which the therapist is required to present the institutional values as the "right" ones, in contrast to the patient's own "wrong" values. These are danger signals, and the therapist may well consider refraining from entering a therapeutic relationship or working in an institutional setting in which he is not free to acknowledge the contribution of his own values.

Second, in addition to increasing awareness of the manipulative aspects of the situation, it is important to build into the change process itself procedures that will provide protection and resistance against manipulation. For the practitioner of behavior change this means structuring the influence situation in such a way that the client will be encouraged to explore his own values and to relate new learnings and new behavioral possibilities to his own value system. At the same time, it is important that the practitioner, be he therapist or group leader, keep to a minimum the direct and indirect constraints that he sets on the influencee. Constraints are, of course, necessary to varying degrees, both for the protection of clients and for keeping the process moving in useful directions. Insofar as possible, however, the situation should be so structured that the influencee determines the direction of the process to a maximal extent. It should be noted that what I am suggesting here is not the same as the use of nondirective techniques. In and of themselves these merely represent a set of formal techniques which may or may not have the desired effect. The crucial point is that the client's own values should be at the center of attention when change is under consideration and should be readily available as criteria against which any induced behavior can be measured. To the extent to which this is true, the patient or the group will be in a better position to resist manipulation in the service of alien values. Often, however, this will require much more than noninterference on the part of the practitioner. It may require active efforts on his part to encourage the client to bring his values to the fore and measure the induced changes against them.

Third, it is important to go beyond providing protection and resistance against manipulation that would encroach on the client's freedom of choice. The actual *enhancement* of freedom of choice should, ideally, be one of the positive goals of any influence attempt. Thus, the therapist should use his professional skills and his relationship to the patient to provide him with new experiences that enhance his ability to choose (and thus to maximize his own values) and with new information that widens his range of choices. Similarly, the group leader should attempt to bring the group to a point where members can make more effective and creative choices, conducive to the achievement of individual and group goals. The enhancement of freedom and creativity as the positive value toward which behavior change should be directed has been discussed most eloquently by Rogers (for example, Rogers and Skinner, 1956).

Needless to say, it would be essential to include in the training of practitioners of behavior change and in their professional standards some consideration of these three desiderata for mitigating the manipulative aspects of their activities. If they learn to acknowledge the role of their own values in the situation, to make active efforts at keeping the client's values in the foreground, and to regard increased freedom of choice as a primary goal, they are less likely to make full use, either unwittingly or by design, of the potential for manipulation that they possess.

The applied researcher. In deciding whether to take on a particular piece of research, the applied researcher must keep in mind that the information he is being asked to supply may be used for the manipulation of others, for example, workers in an industry for whom he is doing a morale survey or the voting public if he is working with poll data. The question of *who* is employing him becomes crucial, therefore. He must evaluate the organizations that will be using his findings, and consider how they are likely to use them, whose behavior they will attempt to influence, and in what context this influence will occur. He must consider the probable uses of these findings not only in the short run but also in the long run. Thus, for example, he cannot simply rely on the fact that his contact man in an organization is someone he trusts. If this man is in a peripheral position within the organization, and if the organization is generally undemocratic and exploitative in its orientation, then the long-run prospects are not too reassuring. There is, of course, the possibility that the research itself will have a liberalizing effect on the organization; the probability that this will, in fact, happen must also be estimated. In the final analysis, there can be no foolproof guarantees, but the investigator must at least feel reasonably certain that the net effect of his research will not be a reduction in the freedom of choice of a segment of the population. Each investigator has to draw his own line, with respect to both the probability and the amount of manipulation that he is willing to tolerate. If they are likely to go beyond this line, then he must consider turning down the assignment. Once a researcher has decided to take on an assignment, he must continue to keep the manipulative potential of his findings in mind, and try to counteract it by the way he communicates his findings and the recommendations he bases on them. If his research is, indeed, to have a liberalizing effect on the organization, then he will have to take active steps in this direction.

In order to build some protection against manipulation into the change procedures based on his findings, the researcher should make it a rule to communicate directly with the target group—the group that is to be influenced—and to involve it in the research, and in the change process insofar as he has charge of it. Thus, an industrial social scientist employed by management might insist on informing the workers in detail about the purposes and findings of the research and the attempted changes that are likely to result from it. In giving them this information, he would try to help them protect their interests against undue attempts at manipulation and to offer them specific recommendations for resisting encroachments on their freedom of choice. Furthermore, in order to promote freedom of choice as a positive goal, he should make a concerted effort to influence the planned change that will be based on his research so that it will actually leave the target group with greater choice than it had before. In submitting his findings and recommendations to the organization that contracted for the research, he should actively seek and point up opportunities for enhancing freedom of choice on the part of the target group that can be integrated into the planned change.

The two last points both imply a rather active role for the researcher in the planning of change based on his research. I would not want to say that the researcher must always participate directly in the change process itself; there are many times when this would be impossible or inappropriate. But since he is providing information that will, at least in principle, be directly translated into action, it is his responsibility to take some stand with respect to this action. The uses to which the information is put are not only the problem of the contracting organization, but also very much the problem of the man who supplied the information. The researcher should be clear about this, and he should have the support of his profession when he takes an active part in expressing his point of view.

The basic researcher. Let me finally, and more briefly, turn to the basic researcher. I have already stated my position that, even though the products of pure research are in a sense neutral, the investigator cannot escape responsibility for their probable consequences. The student of attitude change, for example, must keep in mind that his findings can be used for the systematic manipulation of the population, in ways and for purposes that would produce a net constriction in freedom of choice. In deciding whether or not to proceed with his research, he must try to make some estimate of the probabilities of different uses of his research product, in the light of existing social forces. If he expects restrictive uses to outweigh constuctive ones, he would be bound to refrain from engaging in this research. If, on balance, he decides to undertake the research—and there are, of course, many good reasons for doing so—then he must continue to remain alert to its manipulative potential, and must constantly review his decision, particularly as his research emphases shift or as social conditions change.

Researchers in this area also have a special responsibility to be actively concerned with the ways in which the knowledge they produce is used by various agencies in their society. Eternal vigilance to the possibilities of manipulation is, of course, the duty of every citizen. But, as producers of knowledge about manipulation, social scientists are in a position similar to that of the many nuclear physicists who feel a *special* sense of responsibility for the ways in which their knowledge is being used.

Earlier, I suggested that research on attitude change may not only increase the knowledge of the potential manipulator, but also help in finding ways to counteract manipulative forces. So far, research along these lines has been rather limited. If investigators of attitude change and related problems are to mitigate the manipulative potential of their research, they will have to focus more deliberately and more actively on this other line of work. Thus, in order to build some protection against manipulation into the social structure, we will have to extend our research on processes of resistance to control and make a special effort to communicate relevant findings to the public. Such an emphasis will contribute to the development of knowledge about manipulation itself. From a scientific point of view, such work will be highly germane to the study of attitude change, since it represents an exploration of its limiting conditions.

In order to promote the enhancement of freedom of choice as a positive goal, research will have to focus on the conditions favoring a person's ability to exercise choice and to maximize his individual values. Admittedly, this is a rather value-laden way of stating a problem for basic research. However, if we want our science to contribute to the liberation of man rather than to his dehumanization, this is the kind of problem to which we will have to turn our attention.

A THEORY OF HUMAN MOTIVATION

A. H. Maslow

Introduction

In a previous paper (13)* various propositions were presented which would have to be included in any theory of human motivation that could lay claim to being definitive. These conclusions may be briefly summarized as follows:

1. The integrated wholeness of the organism must be one of the foundation stones of motivation theory.

2. The hunger drive (or any other physiological drive) was rejected as a centering point or model for a definitive theory of motivation. Any drive that is somatically based and localizable was shown to be atypical rather than typical in human motivation.

3. Such a theory should stress and center itself upon ultimate or basic goals rather than partial or superficial ones, upon ends rather than means to these ends. Such a stress would imply a more central place for unconscious than for conscious motivations.

4. There are usually available various cultural paths to the same goal. Therefore conscious, specific, local-cultural desires are not as fundamental in motivation theory as the more basic, unconscious goals.

5. Any motivated behavior, either preparatory or consummatory, must be understood to be a channel through which many basic needs may be simultaneously expressed or satisfied. Typically an act has *more* than one motivation.

6. Practically all organismic states are to be understood as motivated and as motivating.

7. Human needs arrange themselves in hierarchies of pre-potency. That is to say, the appearance of one need usually rests on the prior satisfaction of

---

*See References printed at end of article.—Ed.

Maslow, A. H., "A Theory of Human Motivation," *Psychological Review*, Vol. 59, No. 4, July 1943, pp. 370-396. Copyright 1943 by the American Psychological Association, and reproduced by permission.

another, more pre-potent need. Man is a perpetually wanting animal. Also no need or drive can be treated as if it were isolated or discrete; every drive is related to the state of satisfaction or dissatisfaction of other drives.

8. *Lists* of drives will get us nowhere for various theoretical and practical reasons. Furthermore any classification of motivations must deal with the problem of levels of specificity or generalization of the motives to be classified.

9. Classifications of motivations must be based upon goals rather than upon instigating drives or motivated behavior.

10. Motivation theory should be human-centered rather than animal-centered.

11. The situation or the field in which the organism reacts must be taken into account but the field alone can rarely serve as an exclusive explanation for behavior. Furthermore the field itself must be interpreted in terms of the organism. Field theory cannot be a substitute for motivation theory.

12. Not only the integration of the organism must be taken into account, but also the possibility of isolated, specific, partial or segmental reactions.

It has since become necessary to add to these another affirmation.

13. Motivation theory is not synonymous with behavior theory. The motivations are only one class of determinants of behavior. While behavior is almost always motivated, it is also almost always biologically, culturally and situationally determined as well.

The present paper is an attempt to formulate a positive theory of motivation which will satisfy these theoretical demands and at the same time conform to the known facts, clinical and observational as well as experimental. It derives most directly, however, from clinical experience. This theory is, I think, in the functionalist tradition of James and Dewey, and is fused with the holism of Wertheimer (19), Goldstein (6), and Gestalt Psychology, and with the dynamicism of Freud (4) and Adler (1). This fusion or synthesis may arbitrarily be called a "general-dynamic" theory.

It is far easier to perceive and to criticize the aspects in motivation theory than to remedy them. Mostly this is because of the very serious lack of sound data in this area. I conceive this lack of sound facts to be due primarily to the absence of a valid theory of motivation. The present theory then must be considered to be a suggested program or framework for future research and must stand or fall, not so much on facts available or evidence presented, as upon researches yet to be done, researches suggested perhaps, by the questions raised in this paper.

The Basic Needs

The "Physiological" Needs
The needs that are usually taken as the starting point for motivation theory are the so-called physiological drives. Two recent lines of research make it necessary to revise our customary notions about

these needs, first, the development of the concept of homeostasis, and second, the finding that appetites (preferential choices among foods) are a fairly efficient indication of actual needs or lacks in the body.

Homeostasis refers to the body's automatic efforts to maintain a constant, normal state of the blood stream. Cannon (2) has described this process for (1) the water content of the blood, (2) salt content, (3) sugar content, (4) protein content, (5) fat content, (6) calcium content, (7) oxygen content, (8) constant hydrogen-ion level (acid-base balance) and (9) constant temperature of the blood. Obviously this list can be extended to include other minerals, the hormones, vitamins, etc.

Young in a recent article (21) has summarized the work on appetite in its relation to body needs. If the body lacks some chemical, the individual will tend to develop a specific appetite or partial hunger for that food element.

Thus it seems impossible as well as useless to make any list of fundamental physiological needs for they can come to almost any number one might wish, depending on the degree of specificity of description. We can not identify all physiological needs as homeostatic. That sexual desire, sleepiness, sheer activity and maternal behavior in animals, are homeostatic, has not yet been demonstrated. Furthermore, this list would not include the various sensory pleasures (tastes, smells, tickling, stroking) which are probably physiological and which may become the goals of motivated behavior.

In a previous paper (13) it has been pointed out that these physiological drives or needs are to be considered unusual rather than typical because they are isolable, and because they are localizable somatically. That is to say, they are relatively independent of each other, of other motivations and of the organism as a whole, and secondly, in many cases, it is possible to demonstrate a localized, underlying somatic base for the drive. This is true less generally than has been thought (exceptions are fatigue, sleepiness, maternal responses) but it is still true in the classic instances of hunger, sex, and thirst.

It should be pointed out again that any of the physiological needs and the consummatory behavior involved with them serve as channels for all sorts of other needs as well. That is to say, the person who thinks he is hungry may actually be seeking more for comfort, or dependence, than for vitamins or proteins. Conversely, it is possible to satisfy the hunger need in part by other activities such as drinking water or smoking cigarettes. In other words, relatively isolable as these physiological needs are, they are not completely so.

Undoubtedly these physiological needs are the most pre-potent of all needs. What this means specifically is, that in the human being who is missing everything in life in an extreme fashion, it is most likely that the major motivation would be the physiological needs rather than any others. A person who is lacking food, safety, love, and esteem would most probably hunger for food more strongly than for anything else.

If all the needs are unsatisfied, and the organism is then dominated by the physiological needs, all other needs may become simply non-existent or be pushed into the background. It is then fair to characterize the whole organism by saying simply that it is hungry, for consciousness is almost completely preempted by hunger. All capacities are put into the service of hunger-satisfaction, and the organization of these capacities is almost entirely determined by the one purpose of satisfying hunger. The receptors and effectors, the intelligence, memory, habits, all may now be defined simply as hunger-gratifying tools. Capacities that are not useful for this purpose lie dormant, or are pushed into the background. The urge to write poetry, the desire to acquire an automobile, the interest in American history, the desire for a new pair of shoes are, in the extreme case, forgotten or become of secondary importance. For the man who is extremely and dangerously hungry, no other interests exist but food. He dreams food, he remembers food, he thinks about food, he emotes only about food, he perceives only food and he wants only food. The more subtle determinants that ordinarily fuse with the physiological drives in organizing even feeding, drinking or sexual behavior, may now be so completely overwhelmed as to allow us to speak at this time (but *only* at this time) of pure hunger drive and behavior, with the one unqualified aim of relief.

Another peculiar characteristic of the human organism when it is dominated by a certain need is that the whole philosophy of the future tends also to change. For our chronically and extremely hungry man, Utopia can be defined very simply as a place where there is plenty of food. He tends to think that, if only he is guaranteed food for the rest of his life, he will be perfectly happy and will never want anything more. Life itself tends to be defined in terms of eating. Anything else will be defined as unimportant. Freedom, love, community feeling, respect, philosophy, may all be waved aside as fripperies which are useless since they fail to fill the stomach. Such a man may fairly be said to live by bread alone.

It cannot possibly be denied that such things are true but their *generality* can be denied. Emergency conditions are, almost by defi-nition, rare in the normally functioning peaceful society. That this truism can be forgotten is due mainly to two reasons. First, rats have few motivations other than physiological ones, and since so much of the research upon motivation has been made with these animals, it is easy to carry the rat-picture over to the human being. Secondly, it is too often not realized that culture itself is an adaptive tool, one of whose main functions is to make the physiological emergencies come less and less often. In most of the known societies, chronic extreme hunger of the emergency type is rare, rather than common. In any case, this is still true in the United States. The average American citizen is experiencing appetite rather than hunger when he says "I am hungry." He is apt to experience sheer life-and-death hunger only by accident and then only a few times through his entire life.

Obviously a good way to obscure the "higher" motivations, and to get a lopsided view of human capacities and human nature, is to make the organism extremely and chronically hungry or thirsty. Anyone who attempts to make an emergency picture into a typical one, and who will measure all of man's goals and desires by his behavior during extreme physiological deprivation is certainly being blind to many things. It is quite true that man lives by bread alone—when there is no bread. But what happens to man's desires when there *is* plenty of bread and when his belly is chronically filled?

At once other (and "higher") needs emerge and these, rather than physiological hungers, dominate the organism. And when these in turn are satisfied, again new (and still "higher") needs emerge and so on. This is what we mean by saying that the basic human needs are organized into a hierarchy of relative prepotency.

One main implication of this phrasing is that gratification becomes as important a concept as deprivation in motivation theory, for it releases the organism from the domination of a relatively more physiological need, permitting thereby the emergence of other more social goals. The physiological needs, along with their partial goals, when chronically gratified cease to exist as active determinants or organizers of behavior. They now exist only in a potential fashion in the sense that they may emerge again to dominate the organism if they are thwarted. (But a want that is satisfied is no longer a want. The organism is dominated and its behavior organized only by unsatisfied needs.) If hunger is satisfied, it becomes unimportant in the current dynamics of the individual.

This statement is somewhat qualified by a hypothesis to be dis-cussed more fully later, namely that it is precisely those individuals in whom a certain need has always been satisfied who are best equipped to tolerate deprivation of that need in the future, and that furthermore, those who have been deprived in the past will react differently to current satisfactions than the one who has never been deprived.

The Safety Needs

If the physiological needs are relatively well gratified, there then emerges a new set of needs, which we may categorize roughly as the safety needs. All that has been said of the physiological needs is equally true, although in lesser degree, of these desires. The organism may equally well be wholly dominated by them. They may serve as the almost exclusive organizers of behavior, recruiting all the capacities of the organism in their service, and we may then fairly describe the whole organism as a safety-seeking mechanism. Again we may say of the receptors, the effectors, of the intellect and the other capacities that they are primarily safety-seeking tools. Again, as in the hungry man, we find that the dominating goal is a strong determinant not only of his current world-outlook and philosophy but also of his philosophy of the future. Practically everything looks less important than safety, (even sometimes the physiological needs which being satisfied, are now underestimated). A man, in this state, if it is extreme enough and chronic enough, may be characterized as living almost for safety alone.

Although in this paper we are interested primarily in the needs of the adult, we can approach an understanding of his safety needs perhaps more efficiently by observation of infants and children, in whom these needs are much more simple and obvious. One reason for the clearer appearance of the threat or danger reaction in infants, is that they do not inhibit this reaction at all, whereas adults in our society have been taught to inhibit it at all costs. Thus even when adults do feel their safety to be threatened we may not be able to see this on the surface. Infants will react in a total fashion and as if they were endangered, if they are disturbed or dropped suddenly, startled by loud noises, flashing light, or other unusual sensory stimulation, by rough handling, by general loss of support in the mother's arms, or by inadequate support.[1]

In infants we can also see a much more direct reaction to bodily illnesses of various kinds. Sometimes these illnesses seem to be immediately and *per se* threatening and seem to make the child feel unsafe. For instance, vomiting, colic or other sharp pains seem to make the child look at the whole world in a different way. At such a moment of pain, it may be postulated that, for the child, the appearance of the whole world suddenly changes from sunniness to darkness, so to speak, and becomes a place in which anything at all might happen, in which previously stable things have suddenly become unstable. Thus a child who because of some bad food is taken ill may, for a day or two, develop fear, nightmares, and a need for protection and reassurance never seen in him before his illness.

Another indication of the child's need for safety is his preference for some kind of undisrupted routine or rhythm. He seems to want a predictable, orderly world. For instance, injustice, unfairness, or inconsistency in the parents seems to make a child feel anxious and unsafe. This attitude may be not so much because of the injustice *per se* or any particular pains involved, but rather because this treatment threatens to make the world look unreliable, or unsafe, or unpredictable. Young children seem to thrive better under a system which has at least a skeletal outline of rigidity, in which there is a schedule of a kind, some sort of routine, something that can be counted upon, not only for the present but also far into the future. Perhaps one could express this more accurately by saying that the child needs an organized world rather than an unorganized or unstructured one.

The central role of the parents and the normal family setup are indisputable. Quarreling, physical assault, separation, divorce or death within the family may be particularly terrifying. Also parental outbursts of rage or threats of punishment directed to the child, calling him names, speaking to him harshly, shaking him, handling him roughly, or actual physical punishment sometimes elicit such total panic and terror in the child that we must assume more is involved than the physical pain alone. While it is true that in some children this terror may represent also a fear of loss of parental love, it can also occur in completely rejected children, who seem to cling to the hating parents more for sheer safety and protection than because of hope of love.

Confronting the average child with new, unfamiliar, strange, unmanageable stimuli or situations will too frequently elicit the danger or terror reaction, as for example, getting lost or even being separated from the parents for a short time, being confronted with new faces, new situations or new tasks, the sight of strange, unfamiliar or uncontrollable objects, illness or death. Particularly at such times, the child's frantic clinging to his parents is eloquent testimony to their role as protectors (quite apart from their roles as food-givers and love-givers).

From these and similar observations, we may generalize and say that the average child in our society generally prefers a safe, orderly, predictable, organized world, which he can count on, and in which unexpected, unmanageable or other dangerous things do not happen, and in which, in any case, he has all-powerful parents who protect and shield him from harm.

That these reactions may so easily be observed in children is in a way a proof of the fact that children in our society, feel too unsafe (or, in a word, are badly brought up). Children who are reared in an unthreatening, loving family do *not* ordinarily react as we have described above (17). In such children the danger reactions are apt to come mostly to objects or situations that adults too would consider dangerous.[2]

The healthy, normal, fortunate adult in our culture is largely satisfied in his safety needs. The peaceful, smoothly running, "good" society ordinarily makes its members feel safe enough from wild animals, extremes of temperature, criminals, assault and murder, tyranny, etc. Therefore, in a very real sense, he no longer has any safety needs as active motivators. Just as a sated man no longer feels hungry, a safe man no longer feels endangered. If we wish to see these needs directly and clearly we must turn to neurotic or near-neurotic individuals, and to the economic and social underdogs. In between these extremes, we can perceive the expressions of safety needs only in such phenomena as, for instance, the common preference for a job with tenure and protection, the desire for a savings account, and for insurance of various kinds (medical, dental, unemployment, disability, old age).

Other broader aspects of the attempt to seek safety and stability in the world are seen in the very common preference for familiar rather than unfamiliar things, or for the known rather than the unknown. The tendency to have some religion or world-philosophy that organizes the universe and the men in it into some sort of satisfactorily coherent, meaningful whole is also in part motivated by safety-seeking. Here too we may list science and philosophy in general as partially motivated by the safety needs (we shall see later that there are also other motivations to scientific, philosophical or religious endeavor).

Otherwise the need for safety is seen as an active and dominant mobilizer of the organism's resources only in emergencies, *e.g.*, war, disease, natural catastrophes, crime waves, societal disorganization, neurosis, brain injury, chronically bad situation.

Some neurotic adults in our society are, in many ways, like the unsafe child in their desire for safety, although in the former it takes on a somewhat special appearance. Their reaction is often to un-known, psychological dangers in a world that is perceived to be hostile, overwhelming and threatening. Such a person behaves as if a great catastrophe were almost always impending, *i.e.,* he is usually responding as if to an emergency. His safety needs often find specific expression in a search for a protector, or a stronger person on whom he may depend, or perhaps, a Fuehrer.

The neurotic individual may be described in a slightly different way with some usefulness as a grown-up person who retains his childish attitudes toward the world. That is to say a neurotic adult may be said to behave "as if" he were actually afraid of a spanking, or of his mother's disapproval, or of being abandoned by his parents, or having his food taken away from him. It is as if his childish attitudes of fear and threat reaction to a dangerous world had gone underground, and untouched by the growing up and learning pro-cesses, were now ready to be called out by any stimulus that would make a child feel endangered and threatened.[3]

The neurosis in which the search for safety takes its clearest form is in the compulsive-obsessive neurosis. Compulsive-obsessives try frantically to order and stabilize the world so that no unmanageable, unexpected or unfamiliar dangers will ever appear (14). They hedge themselves about with all sorts of ceremonials, rules and formulas so that every possible contingency may be provided for and so that no new contingencies may appear. They are much like the brain injured cases, described by Goldstein (6), who manage to maintain their equilibrium by avoiding everything unfamiliar and strange and by ordering their restricted world in such a neat, disciplined, orderly fashion that everything in the world can be counted upon. They try to arrange the world so that anything unexpected (dangers) cannot possibly occur. If, through no fault of their own, something unex-pected does occur, they go into a panic reaction as if this unexpected occurrence constituted a grave danger. What we can see only as a none-too-strong preference in the healthy person, *e.g.,* preference for the familiar, becomes a life-and-death necessity in abnormal cases.

The Love Needs

If both the physiological and the safety needs are fairly well gratified, then there will emerge the love and affection and belong-ingness needs, and the whole cycle already described will repeat itself with this new center. Now the person will feel keenly, as never before, the absence of friends, or a sweetheart, or a wife, or children. He will hunger for affectionate relations with people in general, namely, for a place in his group, and he will strive with great intensity to achieve this goal. He will want to attain such a place more than anything else in the world and may even forget that once, when he was hungry, he sneered at love.

In our society the thwarting of these needs is the most commonly found core in cases of maladjustment and more severe psychopathology. Love and affection, as well as their possible expression in sexuality, are generally looked upon with ambivalence and are customarily hedged about with many restrictions and inhibitions. Practically all theorists of psychopathology have stressed thwarting of the love needs as basic in the picture of maladjustment. Many clinical studies have therefore been made of this need and we know more about it perhaps than any of the other needs except the physiological ones (14).

One thing that must be stressed at this point is that love is not synonymous with sex. Sex may be studied as a purely physiological need. Ordinarily sexual behavior is multi-determined, that is to say, determined not only by sexual but also by other needs, chief among which are the love and affection needs. Also not to be overlooked is the fact that the love needs involve both giving *and* receiving love.[4]

The Esteem Needs

All people in our society (with a few pathological exceptions) have a need or desire for a stable, firmly based, (usually) high evaluation of themselves, for self-respect, or self-esteem, and for the esteem of others. By firmly based self-esteem, we mean that which is soundly based upon real capacity, achievement and respect from others. These needs may be classified into two subsidiary sets. These are, first, the desire for strength, for achievement, for adequacy, for confidence in the face of the world, and for independence and freedom.[5] Secondly, we have what we may call the desire for reputation or prestige (defining it as respect or esteem from other people), recognition, attention, importance or appreciation.[6] These needs have been relatively stressed by Alfred Adler and his followers, and have been relatively neglected by Freud and the psychoanalysts. More and more today however there is appearing widespread appreciation of their central importance.

Satisfaction of the self-esteem need leads to feelings of self-confidence, worth, strength, capability and adequacy of being useful and necessary in the world. But thwarting of these needs produces feelings of inferiority, of weakness and of helplessness. These feelings in turn give rise to either basic discouragement or else compensatory or neurotic trends. An appreciation of the necessity of basic self-confidence and an understanding of how helpless people are without it, can be easily gained from a study of severe traumatic neurosis (8).[7]

The Need for Self-Actualization

Even if all these needs are satisfied, we may still often (if not always) expect that a new discontent and restlessness will soon develop, unless the individual is doing what he is fitted for. A musician must make music, an artist must paint, a poet must write, if he is to be ultimately happy. What a man *can* be, he *must* be. This need we may call self-actualization.

This term, first coined by Kurt Goldstein, is being used in this paper in a much more specific and limited fashion. It refers to the desire for self-fulfillment, namely, to the tendency for him to become actualized in what he is potentially. This tendency might be phrased as the desire to become more and more what one is, to become everything that one is capable of becoming.

The specific form that these needs will take will of course vary greatly from person to person. In one individual it may take the form of the desire to be an ideal mother, in another it may be expressed athletically, and in still another it may be expressed in painting pictures or in inventions. It is not necessarily a creative urge although in people who have any capacities for creation it will take this form.

The clear emergence of these needs rests upon prior satisfaction of the physiological, safety, love and esteem needs. We shall call people who are satisfied in these needs, basically satisfied people, and it is from these that we may expect the fullest (and healthiest) creativeness.[8] Since, in our society, basically satisfied people are the exception, we do not know much about self-actualization, either experimentally or clinically. It remains a challenging problem for research.

The Preconditions for the Basic Need Satisfactions

There are certain conditions which are immediate prerequisites for the basic need satisfactions. Danger to these is reacted to almost as if it were a direct danger to the basic needs themselves. Such conditions as freedom to speak, freedom to do what one wishes so long as no harm is done to others, freedom to express one's self, freedom to investigate and seek for information, freedom to defend one's self, justice, fairness, honesty, orderliness in the group are examples of such preconditions for basic need satisfactions. Thwarting in these freedoms will be reacted to with a threat or emergency response.

These conditions are not ends in themselves but they are *almost* so since they are so closely related to the basic needs, which are apparently the only ends in themselves. These conditions are defended because without them the basic satisfactions are quite impossible, or at least, very severely endangered.

If we remember that the cognitive capacities (perceptual, intellectual, learning) are a set of adjustive tools, which have, among other functions, that of satisfaction of our basic needs, then it is clear that any danger to them, any deprivation or blocking of their free use, must also be indirectly threatening to the basic needs themselves. Such a statement is a partial solution of the general problems of curiosity, the search for knowledge, truth and wisdom, and the ever-persistent urge to solve the cosmic mysteries.

We must therefore introduce another hypothesis and speak of degrees of closeness to the basic needs, for we have already pointed out that *any* conscious desires (partial goals) are more or less important as they are more or less close to the basic needs. The same statement may be made for various behavior acts. An act is psychologically important if it contributes directly to satisfaction of basic needs. The less directly it so contributes, or the weaker this contribution is, the less important this act must be conceived to be from the point of view of dynamic psychology. A similar statement may be made for the various defense or coping mechanisms. Some are very directly related to the protection or attainment of the basic needs, others are only weakly and distantly related. Indeed if we wished, we could speak of more basic and less basic defense mechanisms, and then affirm that danger to the more basic defenses is more threatening than danger to less basic defenses (always remembering that this is so only because of their relationship to the basic needs).

The Desires To Know and To Understand

So far, we have mentioned the cognitive needs only in passing. Acquiring knowledge and systematizing the universe have been considered as, in part, techniques for the achievement of basic safety in the world, or, for the intelligent man, expressions of self-actualization. Also freedom of inquiry and expression have been discussed as preconditions of satisfactions of the basic needs. True though these formulations may be, they do not constitute definitive answers to the question as to the motivation role of curiosity, learning, philosophizing, experimenting, etc. They are, at best, no more than partial answers.

This question is especially difficult because we know so little about the facts. Curiosity, exploration, desire for the facts, desire to know may certainly be observed easily enough. The fact that they often are pursued even at great cost to the individual's safety is an earnest of the partial character of our previous discussion. In addition, the writer must admit that, though he has sufficient clinical evidence to postulate the desire to know as a very strong drive in intelligent people, no data are available for unintelligent people. It may then be largely a function of relatively high intelligence. Rather tentatively, then, and largely in the hope of stimulating discussion and research, we shall postulate a basic desire to know, to be aware of reality, to get the facts, to satisfy curiosity, or as Wertheimer phrases it, to see rather than to be blind.

This postulation, however, is not enough. Even after we know, we are impelled to know more and more minutely and miscroscopically on the one hand, and on the other, more and more extensively in the direction of a world philosophy, religion, etc. The facts that we acquire, if they are isolated or atomistic, inevitably get theorized about, and either analyzed or organized or both. This process has been phrased by some as the search for "meaning." We shall then postulate a desire to understand, to systematize, to organize, to analyze, to look for relations and meanings.

Once these desires are accepted for discussion, we see that they too form themselves into a small hierarchy in which the desire to know is prepotent over the desire to understand. All the characteristics of a hierarchy of prepotency that we have described above, seem to hold for this one as well.

We must guard ourselves against the too easy tendency to separate these desires from the basic needs we have discussed above, *i.e.,* to make a sharp dichotomy between "cognitive" and "conative" needs. The desire to know and to understand are themselves conative, *i.e.,* have a striving character, and are as much personality needs as the 'basic needs' we have already discussed (19).

Further Characteristics of the Basic Needs

The Degree of Fixity of the Hierarchy of Basic Needs
We have spoken so far as if this hierarchy were a fixed order but actually it is not nearly as rigid as we may have implied. It is true that most of the people with whom we have worked have seemed to have these basic needs in about the order that has been indicated. However, there have been a number of exceptions.

1. There are some people in whom, for instance, self-esteem seems

to be more important than love. This most common reversal in the hierarchy is usually due to the development of the notion that the person who is most likely to be loved is a strong or powerful person, one who inspires respect or fear, and who is self confident or aggressive. Therefore such people who lack love and seek it, may try hard to put on a front of aggressive, confident behavior. But essentially they seek high self-esteem and its behavior expressions more as a means-to-an-end than for its own sake; they seek self-assertion for the sake of love rather than for self-esteem itself.

2. There are other, apparently innately creative people in whom the drive to creativeness seems to be more important than any other counter-determinant. Their creativeness might appear not as self-actualization released by basic satisfaction, but in spite of lack of basic satisfaction.

3. In certain people the level of aspiration may be permanently deadened or lowered. That is to say, the less prepotent goals may simply be lost, and may disappear forever, so that the person who has experienced life at a very low level, *i.e.*, chronic unemployment, may continue to be satisfied for the rest of his life if only he can get enough food.

4. The so-called "psychopathic personality" is another example of permanent loss of the love needs. These are people who, according to the best data available (9), have been starved for love in the earliest months of their lives and have simply lost forever the desire and the ability to give and receive affection (as animals lose sucking or pecking reflexes that are not exercised soon enough after birth).

5. Another cause of reversal of the hierarchy is that when a need has been satisfied for a long time, this need may be underevaluated. People who have never experienced chronic hunger are apt to under-estimate its effects and to look upon food as a rather unimportant thing. If they are dominated by a higher need, this higher need will seem to be the most important of all. It then becomes possible, and indeed does actually happen, that they may, for the sake of this higher need, put themselves into the position of being deprived in a more basic need. We may expect that after a long-time deprivation of the more basic need there will be a tendency to reevaluate both needs so that the more prepotent need will actually become con-sciously prepotent for the individual who may have given it up very lightly. Thus, a man who has given up his job rather than lose his self-respect, and who then starves for six months or so, may be willing to take his job back even at the price of losing his self-respect.

6. Another partial explanation of *apparent* reversals is seen in the

fact that we have been talking about the hierarchy of prepotency in terms of consciously felt wants or desires rather than of behavior. Looking at behavior itself may give us the wrong impression. What we have claimed is that the person will *want* the more basic of two needs when deprived in both. There is no necessary implication here that he will act upon his desires. Let us say again that there are many determinants of behavior other than the needs and desires.

7. Perhaps more important than all these exceptions are the ones that involve ideals, high social standards, high values and the like. With such values people become martyrs; they will give up everything for the sake of a particular ideal, or value. These people may be understood, at least in part, by reference to one basic concept (or hypothesis) which may be called "increased frustration-tolerance through early gratification." People who have been satisfied in their basic needs throughout their lives, particularly in their earlier years, seem to develop exceptional power to withstand present or future thwarting of these needs simply because they have strong, healthy character structure as a result of basic satisfaction. They are the "strong" people who can easily weather disagreement or opposition, who can swim against the stream of public opinion and who can stand up for the truth at great personal cost. It is just the ones who have loved and been well loved, and who have had many deep friendships who can hold out against hatred, rejection or persecution.

I say all this in spite of the fact that there is a certain amount of sheer habituation which is also involved in any full discussion of frustration tolerance. For instance, it is likely that those persons who have been accustomed to relative starvation for a long time, are partially enabled thereby to withstand food deprivation. What sort of balance must be made between these two tendencies of habituation on the one hand, and of past satisfaction breeding present frustration tolerance on the other hand, remains to be worked out by further research. Meanwhile we may assume that they are both operative, side by side, since they do not contradict each other. In respect to this phenomenon of increased frustration tolerance, it seems probable that the most important gratifications come in the first two years of life. That is to say, people who have been made secure and strong in the earliest years, tend to remain secure and strong thereafter in the face of whatever threatens.

Degrees of Relative Satisfaction

So far, our theoretical discussion may have given the impression that these five sets of needs are somehow in a step-wise, all-or-none relationships to each other. We have spoken in such terms as the following: "If one need is satisfied, then another emerges." This statement might give the false impression that a need must be satisfied 100 percent before the next need emerges. In actual fact, most members of our society who are normal, are partially satisfied in all their basic needs and partially unsatisfied in all their basic needs at the same time. A more realistic description of the hierarchy would be in terms of decreasing percentages of satisfaction as we go up the hierarchy of prepotency. For instance, if I may assign arbitrary figures for the sake of illustration, it is as if the average citizen is satisfied perhaps 85 percent in his physiological needs, 70 percent in his safety needs, 50 percent in his love needs, 40 percent in his self-esteem needs, and 10 percent in his self-actualization needs.

As for the concept of emergence of a new need after satisfaction of the prepotent need, this emergence is not a sudden, saltatory phenomenon but rather a gradual emergence by slow degrees from nothingness. For instance, if prepotent need A is satisfied only 10 percent then need B may not be visible at all. However, as this need A becomes satisfied 25 percent, need B may emerge 5 percent, as need A becomes satisfied 75 percent need B may emerge 90 percent, and so on.

Unconscious character of Needs

These needs are neither necessarily conscious nor unconscious. On the whole, however, in the average person, they are more often unconscious rather than conscious. It is not necessary at this point to overhaul the tremendous mass of evidence which indicates the crucial importance of unconscious motivation. It would by now be expected, on a priori grounds alone, that unconscious motivations would on the whole be rather more important than the conscious motivations. What we have called the basic needs are very often largely unconscious although they may, with suitable techniques, and with sophisticated people become conscious.

Cultural Specificity and Generality of Needs

This classification of basic needs makes some attempt to take account of the relative unity behind the superficial differences in specific desires from one culture to another. Certainly in any particular culture an individual's conscious motivational content will usually be extremely different from the conscious motivational content of an individual in another society. However, it is the common experience of anthropologists that people, even in different societies, are much more alike than we would think from our first contact with them, and that as we know them better we seem to find more and more of this commonness. We then recognize the most startling differences to be superficial rather than basic, *e.g.*, differences in style of hair-dress, clothes, tastes in food, etc. Our classification of basic needs is in part an attempt to account for this unity behind the apparent diversity from culture to culture. No claim is made that it is ultimate or universal for all cultures. The claim is made only that it is relatively *more* ultimate, more universal, more basic, than the superficial conscious desires from culture to culture, and makes a somewhat closer approach to common-human characteristics. Basic needs are *more* common-human than superficial desires or behaviors.

Multiple Motivations of Behavior

These needs must be understood *not* to be *exclusive* or single determiners of certain kinds of behavior. An example may be found in any behavior that seems to be physiologically motivated, such as eating, or sexual play or the like. The clinical psychologists have long since found that any behavior may be a channel through which flow various determinants. Or to say it in another way, most behavior is multi-motivated. Within the sphere of motivational determinants any behavior tends to be determined by several or *all* of the basic needs simultaneously rather than by only one of them. The latter would be more an exception than the former. Eating may be partially for the sake of filling the stomach, and partially for the sake of comfort and amelioration of other needs. One may make love not only for pure sexual release, but also to convince one's self of one's masculinity, or to make a conquest, to feel powerful, or to win more basic affection. As an illustration, I may point out that it would be possible (theoretically if not practically) to analyze a single act of an individual and see in it the expression of his physiological needs, his safety needs, his love needs, his esteem needs and self-actualization. This contrasts sharply with the more naive brand of trait psychology in which one trait or one motive accounts for a certain kind of act, *i.e.*, an aggressive act is traced solely to a trait of aggressiveness.

Multiple Determinants of Behavior

Not all behavior is determined by the basic needs. We might even say that not all behavior is motivated. There are many determinants of behavior other than motives.[9] For instance, one other important class of determinants is the so-called "field" determinants. Theoretically, at least, behavior may be determined completely by the field, or even by specific isolated external stimuli, as in association of ideas, or certain conditioned reflexes. If in response to the stimulus word 'table,' I immediately perceive a memory image of a table, this response certainly has nothing to do with my basic needs.

Secondly, we may call attention again to the concept of 'degree of closeness to the basic needs' or 'degree of motivation.' Some behavior is highly motivated, other behavior is only weakly motivated. Some is not motivated at all (but all behavior is determined).

Another important point[10] is that there is a basic difference between expressive behavior and coping behavior (functional striving, purposive goal seeking). An expressive behavior does not try to do anything; it is simply a reflection of the personality. A stupid man behaves stupidly, not because he wants to, or tries to, or is motivated to, but simply because he *is* what he is. The same is true when I speak in a bass voice rather than tenor or soprano. The random movements of a healthy child, the smile on the face of a happy man even when he is alone, the springiness of the healthy man's walk, and the erectness of his carriage are other examples of expressive, non-functional behavior. Also the *style* in which a man carries out almost all his behavior, motivated as well as unmotivated, is often expressive.

We may then ask, is *all* behavior expressive or reflective of the character structure? The answer is 'No.' Rote, habitual, automatized, or conventional behavior may or may not be expressive. The same is true for most 'stimulus-bound' behaviors.

It is finally necessary to stress that expressiveness of behavior, and goal-directedness of behavior are not mutually exclusive categories. Average behavior is usually both.

Goals as Centering Principle in Motivation Theory

It will be observed that the basic principle in our classification has been neither the instigation nor the motivated behavior but rather the functions, effects, purposes, or goals of the behavior. It has been proven sufficiently by various people that this is the most suitable point for centering in any motivation theory.[11]

Animal- and Human-Centering

This theory starts with the human being rather than any lower and presumably "simpler" animal. Too many of the findings that have been made in animals have been proven to be true for animals but not for the human being. There is no reason whatsoever why we should start with animals in order to study human motivation. The logic or rather illogic behind this general fallacy of "pseudo-simplicity" has been exposed often enough by philosophers and logicians as well as by scientists in each of the various fields. It is no more necessary to study animals before one can study man than it is to study mathematics before one can study geology or psychology or biology.

We may also reject the old, naive, behaviorism which assumed that it was somehow necessary, or at least more "scientific" to judge human beings by animal standards. One consequence of this belief was that the whole notion of purpose and goal was excluded from motivational psychology simply because one could not ask a white rat about his purposes. Tolman (18) has long since proven in animal studies themselves that this exclusion was not necessary.

Motivation and the Theory of Psychopathogenesis

The conscious motivational content of everyday life has, according to the foregoing, been conceived to be relatively important or unimportant accordingly as it is more or less closely related to the basic goals. A desire for an ice cream cone might actually be an indirect expression of a desire for love. If it is, then this desire for the ice cream cone becomes extremely important motivation. If however the ice cream is simply something to cool the mouth with, or a casual appetitive reaction, then the desire is relatively unimportant. Everyday conscious desires are to be regarded as symptoms, as *surface indicators of more basic needs*. If we were to take these superficial desires at their face value we would find ourselves in a state of complete confusion which could never be resolved, since we would be dealing seriously with symptoms rather than with what lay behind the symptoms.

Thwarting of unimportant desires produces no psychopathological results; thwarting of a basically important need does produce such results. Any theory of psychopathogenesis must then be based on a sound theory of motivation. A conflict or a frustration is not necessarily pathogenic. It becomes so only when it threatens or thwarts the basic needs, or partial needs that are closely related to the basic needs (10).

The Role of Gratified Needs

It has been pointed out above several times that our needs usually emerge only when more prepotent needs have been gratified. Thus gratification has an important role in motivation theory. Apart from this, however, needs cease to play an active determining or organizing role as soon as they are gratified.

What this means is that, *e.g.*, a basically satisfied person no longer has the needs for esteem, love, safety, etc. The only sense in which he might be said to have them is in the almost metaphysical sense that a sated man has hunger, or a filled bottle has emptiness. If we are interested in what *actually* motivates us, and not in what has, will, or might motivate us, then a satisfied need is not a motivator. It must be considered for all practical purposes simply not to exist, to have disappeared. This point should be emphasized because it has been either overlooked or contradicted in every theory of motivation I know.[12] The perfectly healthy, normal, fortunate man has no sex needs or hunger needs, or needs for safety, or for love, or for prestige, or self-esteem, except in stray moments of quickly passing threat. If we were to say otherwise, we should also have to aver that every man had all the pathological reflexes, *e.g.*, Babinski, etc., because if his nervous system were damaged, these would appear.

It is such considerations as these that suggest the bold postulation that a man who is thwarted in any of his basic needs may fairly be envisaged simply as sick man. This is a fair parallel to our designation as "sick" of the man who lacks vitamins or minerals. Who is to say that a lack of love is less important than a lack of vitamins? Since we know the pathogenic effects of love starvation, who is to say that we are invoking value-questions in an unscientific or illegitimate way, any more than the physician does who diagnoses and treats pellagra or scurvy? If I were permitted this usage, I should then say simply that a healthy man is primarily motivated by his needs to develop and actualize his fullest potentialities and capacities. If a man has any other basic needs in any active, chronic sense, then he is simply an unhealthy man. He is as surely sick as if he had suddenly developed a strong salt-hunger or calcium hunger.[13]

If this statement seems unusual or paradoxical the reader may be assured that this is only one among many such paradoxes that will appear as we revise our ways of looking at man's deeper motivations. When we ask that man wants of life, we deal with his very essence.

Summary

1. There are at least five sets of goals, which we may call basic needs. These are briefly physiological, safety, love, esteem, and self-actualization. In addition, we are motivated by the desire to achieve or maintain the various conditions upon which these basic

satisfactions rest and by certain more intellectual desires.

2. These basic goals are related to each other, being arranged in a hierarchy of prepotency. This means that the most prepotent goal will monopolize consciousness and will tend of itself to organize the recruitment of the various capacities of the organism. The less prepotent needs are minimized, even forgotten or denied. But when a need is fairly well satisfied, the next prepotent ("higher") need emerges, in turn to dominate the conscious life and to serve as the center of organization of behavior, since gratified needs are not active motivators.

Thus man is a perpetually wanting animal. Ordinarily the satisfaction of these wants is not altogether mutually exclusive, but only tends to be. The average member of our society is most often partially satisfied and partially unsatisfied in all of his wants. The hierarchy principle is usually empirically observed in terms of increasing percentages of non-satisfaction as we go up the hierarchy. Reversals of the average order of the hierarchy are sometimes observed. Also it has been observed that an individual may permanently lose the higher wants in the hierarchy under special conditions. There are not only ordinarily multiple motivations for usual behavior, but in addition many determinants other than motives.

3. Any thwarting or possibility of thwarting of these basic human goals, or danger to the defenses which protect them, or to the conditions upon which they rest, is considered to be a psychological threat. With a few exceptions, all psychopathology may be partially traced to such threats. A basically thwarted man may actually be defined as a 'sick' man, if we wish.

4. It is such basic threats which bring about the general emergency reactions.

5. Certain other basic problems have not been dealt with because of limitations of space. Among these are (a) the problem of values in any definitive motivation theory, (b) the relation between appetites, desires, needs and what is 'good' for the organism, (c) the etiology of the basic needs and their possible derivation in early childhood, (d) redefinition of motivational concepts, i.e., drive, desire, wish, need, goal, (e) implication of our theory for hedonistic theory, (f) the nature of the uncompleted act, of success and failure, and of aspiration-level, (g) the role of association, habit and conditioning, (h) relation to the theory of inter-personal relations, (i) implications for psychotherapy, (j) implication for theory of society, (k) the theory of selfishness, (l) the relation between needs and cultural patterns,

(m) the relation between this theory and Allport's theory of functional autonomy. These as well as certain other less important questions must be considered as motivation theory attempts to become definitive.

FOOTNOTES

1. As the child grows up, sheer knowledge and familiarity as well as better motor development make these "dangers" less and less dangerous and more and more manageable. Throughout life it may be said that one of the main conative functions of education is this neutralizing of apparent dangers through knowledge, *e.g.*, I am not afraid of thunder because I know something about it.

2. A "test battery" for safety might be confronting the child with a small exploding firecracker, or with a bewhiskered face, having the mother leave the room, putting him upon a high ladder, a hypodermic injection, having a mouse crawl up to him, etc. Of course I cannot seriously recommend the deliberate use of such "tests" for they might very well harm the child being tested. But these and similar situations come up by the score in the child's ordinary day-to-day living and may be observed. There is no reason why these stimuli should not be used with, for example, young chimpanzees.

3. Not all neurotic individuals feel unsafe. Neurosis may have at its core a thwarting of the affection and esteem needs in a person who is generally safe.

4. For further details see (12) and (16, Chap. 5).

5. Whether or not this particular desire is universal we do not know. The crucial question, especially important today, is "Will men who are enslaved and dominated, inevitably feel dissatisfied and rebellious?" We may assume on the basis of commonly known clinical data that a man who has known true freedom (not paid for by giving up safety and security but rather built on the basis of adequate safety and security) will not willingly or easily allow his freedom to be taken away from him. But we do not know that this is true for the person born into slavery. The events of the next decade should give us our answer. See discussion of this problem in (5).

6. Perhaps the desire for prestige and respect from others is subsidiary to the desire for self-esteem or confidence in oneself. Observation of children seems to indicate that this is so, but clinical data give no clear support for such a conclusion.

7. For more extensive discussion of normal self-esteem, as well as for reports of various researches, see (11).

8. Clearly creative behavior, like painting, is like any other behavior in having multiple determinants. It may be seen in 'innately creative' people whether they are satisfied or not, happy or unhappy, hungry or sated. Also it is clear that creative activity may be compensatory, ameliorative or purely economic. It is my impression (as yet unconfirmed) that it is possible to distinguish the artistic and intellectual products of basically satisfied people from those of basically unsatisfied people by inspection alone. In any case, here too we must distinguish, in a dynamic fashion, the overt behavior itself from its various motivations or purposes.

9. I am aware that many psychologists and psychoanalysts use the term "motivated" and "determined" synonymously, *e.g.,* Freud. But I consider this an obfuscating usage. Sharp distinctions are necessary for clarity of thought, and precision in experimentation.

10. To be discussed fully in a subsequent publication.

11. The interested reader is referred to the very excellent discussion of this point in Murray's *Explorations in Personality* (15).

12. Note that acceptance of this theory necessitates basic revision of the Freudian theory.

13. If we were to use the word 'sick' in this way, we should then also have to face squarely the relations of man to his society. One clear implication of our definition would be that (1) since a man is to be called sick who is basically thwarted, and (2) since such basic thwarting is made possible ultimately only by forces outside the individual, then (3) sickness in the individual must come ultimately from a sickness in the society. The "good" or healthy society would then be defined as one that permitted man's highest purposes to emerge by satisfying all his prepotent basic needs.

REFERENCES

1. Adler, A. *Social interest,* London: Faber & Faber, 1938.

2. Cannon, W. B. *Wisdom of the body.* New York: Norton, 1932.

3. Freud, A. *The ego and the mechanisms of defense.* London: Hogarth, 1937.

4. Freud, S. *New introductory lectures on psychoanalysis.* New York: Norton, 1933.

5. Fromm, E. *Escape from freedom.* New York: Farrar and Rinehart, 1941.

6. Goldstein, K. *The organism.* New York: American Book Co., 1939.

7. Horney, K. *The neurotic personality of our time.* New York: Norton, 1937.

8. Kardiner, A. *The traumatic neuroses of war.* New York: Hoeber, 1941.

9. Levy, D. M. Primary affect hunger. *Amer. J. Psychiat.,* 1937, 94, 643-652.

10. Maslow, A. H. Conflict, frustration, and the theory of threat. *J. abnorm. (soc.) Psychol.,* 1943, 38, 81-86.

11. ————. Dominance, personality and social behavior in women. *J. soc. Psychol.,* 1939, 10, 3-39.

12. ————. The dynamics of psychological security-insecurity. *Character & Pers.,* 1942, 10, 331-344.

13. ————. A preface to motivation theory. *Psychosomatic Med.,* 1943, 5, 85-92.

14. ————, & Mittelmann, B. *Principles of abnormal psychology.* New York: Harper & Bros., 1941.

15. Murray, H. A., *et al. Explorations in personality.* New York: Oxford University Press, 1938.

16. Plant, J. *Personality and the cultural pattern.* New York: Commonwealth Fund, 1937.

17. Shirley, M. Children's adjustments to a strange situation. *J. abnorm. (soc.) Psychol.,* 1942, 37, 201-217.

18. Tolman, E. C. *Purposive behavior in animals and men.* New York: Century, 1932.

19. Wertheimer, M. Unpublished lectures at the New School for Social Research.
20. Young, P. T. *Motivation of behavior*. New York: John Wiley & Sons, 1936.
21. ————. The experimental analysis of appetite. *Psychol. Bull.*, 1941, 38, 129-164.

TOWARD A MODERN APPROACH TO VALUES:
THE VALUING PROCESS IN THE MATURE PERSON

Carl R. Rogers

There is a great deal of concern today with the problem of values. Youth, in almost every country, is deeply uncertain of its value orientation; the values associated with various religions have lost much of their influence; sophisticated individuals in every culture seem unsure and troubled as to the goals they hold in esteem. The reasons are not far to seek. The world culture, in all its aspects, seems increasingly scientific and relativistic, and the rigid, absolute views on values which come to us from the past appear anachronistic. Even more important, perhaps, is the fact that the modern individual is assailed from every angle by divergent and contradictory value claims. It is no longer possible, as it was in the not too distant historical past, to settle comfortably into the value system of one's forebears or one's community and live out one's life without ever examining the nature and the assumptions of that system.

In this situation it is not surprising that value orientations from the past appear to be in a state of disintegration or collapse. Men question whether there are, or can be, any universal values. It is often felt that we may have lost, in our modern world, all possibility of any general or cross-cultural basis for values. One natural result of this uncertainty and confusion is that there is an increasing concern

Rogers, Carl R., "Toward a Modern Approach to Values: The Valuing Process in the Mature Person," *Journal of Abnormal and Social Psychology*, Vol. 68, No. 2, February 1964, pp. 160-167. Copyright 1964 by the American Psychological Association, and reproduced by permission.

about, interest in, and a searching for, a sound or meaningful value approach which can hold its own in today's world.

I share this general concern. As with other issues the general problem faced by the culture is painfully and specifically evident in the cultural microcosm which is called the therapeutic relationship, which is my sphere of experience.

As a consequence of this experience I should like to attempt a modest theoretical approach to this whole problem. I have observed changes in the approach to values as the individual grows from infancy to adulthood. I observe further changes when, if he is fortunate, he continues to grow toward true psychological maturity. Many of these observations grow out of my experience as therapist, where I have had the mind stretching opportunity of seeing the ways in which individuals move toward a richer life. From these observations I believe I see some directional threads emerging which might offer a new concept of the valuing process, more tenable in the modern world. I have made a beginning by presenting some of these ideas partially in previous writings (Rogers, 1951, 1959); I would like now to voice them more clearly and more fully.

Some Definitions

Charles Morris (1956, pp. 9-12) has made some useful distinctions in regard to values. There are "operative values," which are the behaviors of organisms in which they show preference for one subject or objective rather than another. The lowly earthworm, selecting the smooth arm of a Y maze rather than the arm which is paved with sandpaper, is giving an indication of an operative value.

There are also "conceived values," the preference of an individual for a symbolized object. "Honesty is the best policy" is such a conceived value.

There is also the term "objective value," to refer to what is objectively preferable, whether or not it is sensed or conceived of as desirable. I will be concerned primarily with operative or conceptualized values.

Infant's Way of Valuing

Let me first speak about the infant. The living human being has, at the outset, a clear approach to values. We can infer from studying his behavior that he prefers those experiences which maintain, enhance, or actualize his organism, and rejects whose which do not serve this end. Watch him for a bit:

Hunger is negatively valued. His expression of this often comes through loud and clear.

Food is positively valued. But when he is satisfied, food is negatively valued, and the same milk he responded to so eagerly is now spit out, or the breast which seemed so satisfying is now rejected as he turns his head away from the nipple with an amusing facial expression of disgust and revulsion.

He values security, and the holding and caressing which seem to communicate security.

He values new experience for its own sake, and we observe this in his obvious pleasure in discovering his toes, in his searching movements, in his endless curiosity.

He shows a clear negative valuing of pain, bitter tastes, sudden loud sounds.

All of this is commonplace, but let us look at these facts in terms of what they tell us about the infant's approach to values. It is first of all a flexible, changing, valuing *process*, not a fixed system. He likes food and dislikes the same food. He values security and rest, and rejects it for new experience. What is going on seems best described as an organismic valuing process, in which each element, each moment of what he is experiencing is somehow weighed, and selected or rejected, depending on whether, at that moment, it tends to actualize the organism or not. This complicated weighing of experience is clearly an organismic, not a conscious or symbolic function. These are operative, not conceived values. But this process can nonetheless deal with complex value problems. I would remind you of the experiment in which young infants had spread in front of them a score or more of dishes of natural (that is, unflavored) foods. Over a period of time they clearly tended to value the foods which enhanced their own survival, growth, and development. If for a time a child gorged himself on starches, this would soon be balanced by a protein "binge." If at times he chose a diet deficient in some vitamin, he would later seek out foods rich in this very vitamin. The physiological wisdom of his body guided his behavioral movements, resulting in what we might think of as objectively sound value choices.

Another aspect of the infant's approach to values is that the source or locus of the evaluating process is clearly within himself. Unlike many of us, he *knows* what he likes and dislikes, and the origin of these value choices lies strictly within himself. He is the center of the valuing process, the evidence for his choices being supplied by his own senses. He is not at this point influenced by what his parents think he should prefer, or by the persuasive talents of an advertising firm. It is from within his own experiencing that his organism is saying in nonverbal terms, "This is good for me." "That is bad for me." "I like this." "I strongly dislike that." He would laugh at our concern over values, if he could understand it.

Change in the Valuing Process

What happens to this efficient, soundly based valuing process? By what sequence of events do we exchange it for the more rigid uncertain, inefficient approach to values which characterizes most of us as adults? Let me try to state briefly one of the major ways in which I think this happens.

The infant needs love, wants it, tends to behave in ways which will bring a repetition of this wanted experience. But this brings complications. He pulls baby sister's hair, and finds it satisfying to hear her wails and protests. He then hears that he is "a naughty, bad boy," and this may be reinforced by a slap on the hand. He is cut off from affection. As this experience is repeated, and many, many others like it, he gradually learns that what "feels good" is often "bad" in the eyes of significant others. Then the next step occurs, in which he comes to take the same attitude toward himself which these others have taken. Now, as he pulls his sister's hair, he solemnly intones, "Bad, bad boy." He is introjecting the value judgment of another, taking it in as his own. To that degree he loses touch with his own organismic valuing process. He has deserted the wisdom of his organism, giving up the locus of evaluation, and is trying to behave in terms of values set by another, in order to hold love.

Or take another example at an older level. A boy senses, though perhaps not consciously, that he is more loved and prized by his parents when he thinks of being a doctor than when he thinks of being an artist. Gradually he introjects the values attached to being a doctor. He comes to want, above all, to be a doctor. Then in college he is baffled by the fact that he repeatedly fails in chemistry, which is absolutely necessary to becoming a physician, in spite of the fact that the guidance counselor assures him he has the ability to pass the course. Only in counseling interviews does he begin to realize how completely he has lost touch with his organismic reactions, how out of touch he is with his own valuing process.

Perhaps these illustrations will indicate that in an attempt to gain or hold love, approval, esteem, the individual relinquishes the locus of evaluation which was his in infancy, and places it in others. He learns to have a basic *dis*trust for his own experiencing as a guide to his behavior. He learns from others a large number of conceived values, and adopts them as his own, even though they may be widely discrepant from what he is experiencing.

Some Introjected Patterns

, It is in this fashion, I believe, that most of us accumulate the introjected value patterns by which we live. In the fantastically complex culture of today, the patterns we introject as desirable or undesirable come from a variety of sources and are often highly contradictory. Let me list a few of the introjections which are commonly held.

Sexual desires and behaviors are mostly bad. The sources of this construct are many—parents, church, teachers.

Disobedience is bad. Here parents and teachers combine with the military to emphasize this concept. To obey is good. To obey without question is even better.

Making money is the highest good. The sources of this conceived value are too numerous to mention.

Learning as accumulation of scholarly facts is highly desirable. Education is the source.

Communism is utterly bad. Here the government is a major source.

To love thy neighbor is the highest good. This concept comes from the church, perhaps from the parents.

Cooperation and teamwork are preferable to acting alone. Here companions are an important source.

Cheating is clever and desirable. The peer group again is the origin.

Coca-Colas, chewing gum, electric refrigerators, and automobiles are all utterly desirable. From Jamaica to Japan, from Copenhagen to Kowloon, the "Coca-Cola culture" has come to be regarded as the acme of desirability.

This is a small and diversified sample of the myriads of conceived values which individuals often introject, and hold as their own, without ever having considered their inner organismic reactions to these patterns and objects.

Common Characteristics of Adult Valuing

I believe it will be clear from the foregoing that the usual adult—I feel I am speaking for most of us—has an approach to values which has these characteristics:

The majority of his values are introjected from other individuals or groups significant to him, but are regarded by him as his own.

The source or locus of evaluation on most matters lies outside of himself.

The criterion by which his values are set is the degree to which they will cause him to be loved, accepted, or esteemed.

These conceived preferences are either not related at all, or not clearly related, to his own process of experiencing.

Often there is a wide and unrecognized discrepancy between the evidence supplied by his own experience, and these conceived values.

Because these conceptions are not open to testing in experience, he must hold them in a rigid and unchanging fashion. The alternative would be a collapse of his values. Hence his values are "right."

Because they are untestable, there is no ready way of solving contradictions. If he has taken in from the community the conception that money is the *summum bonum* and from the church the conception that love of one's neighbor is the highest value, he has no way of discovering which has more value for *him*. Hence a common aspect of modern life is living with absolutely contradictory values. We calmly discuss the possibility of dropping a hydrogen bomb on Russia, but find tears in our eyes when we see headlines about the suffering of one small child.

Because he has relinquished the locus of evaluation to others, and has lost touch with his own valuing process, he feels profoundly insecure and easily threatened in his values. If some of these conceptions were destroyed, what would take their place? This threatening possibility makes him hold his value conceptions more rigidly or more confusedly, or both.

Fundamental Discrepancy

I believe that this picture of the individual, with values mostly introjected, held as fixed concepts, rarely examined or tested, is the picture of most of us. By taking over the conceptions of others as our own, we lose contact with the potential wisdom of our own functioning, and lose confidence in ourselves. Since these value constructs are often sharply at variance with what is going on in our own experiencing, we have in a very basic way divorced ourselves from ourselves, and this accounts for much of modern strain and insecurity. This fundamental discrepancy between the individual's concept and what he is actually experiencing, between the intellectual structure of his values and the valuing process going on unrecognized within—this is a part of the fundamental estrangement of modern man from himself.

Restoring Contact with Experience

Some individuals are fortunate in going beyond the picture I have just given, developing further in the direction of psychological maturity. We see this happen in psychotherapy where we endeavor to provide a climate favorable to the growth of the person. We also see it happen in life, whenever life provides a therapeutic climate for the individual. Let me concentrate on this further maturing of a value approach as I have seen it in therapy.

As the client senses and realizes that he is prized as a person* he can slowly begin to value the different aspects of himself. Most

---

*The therapeutic relationship is not devoid of values. When it is most effective it is, I believe, marked by one primary value, namely, that this person (the client) has *worth*.

importantly, he can begin, with much difficulty at first, to sense and to feel what is going on within him, what he is feeling, what he is experiencing, how he is reacting. He uses his experiencing as a direct referent to which he can turn in forming accurate conceptualizations and as a guide to his behavior. Gendlin (1961, 1962) has elaborated the way in which this occurs. As his experiencing becomes more and more open to him, as he is able to live more freely in the process of his feelings, then significant changes begin to occur in his approach to values. It begins to assume many of the characteristics it had in infancy.

Introjected Values in Relation to Experiencing

Perhaps I can indicate this by reviewing a few of the brief examples of introjected values which I have given, and suggesting what happens to them as the individual comes closer to what is going on within him.

The individual in therapy looks back and realizes, "But I *enjoyed* pulling my sister's hair—and that doesn't make me a bad person."

The student failing chemistry realizes, as he gets close to his own experiencing, "I don't like chemistry; I don't value being a doctor, even though my parents do; and I am not a failure for having these feelings."

The adult recognizes that sexual desires and behavior may be richly satisfying and permanently enriching in their consequences or shallow and temporary and less than satisfying. He goes by his own experiencing, which does not always coincide with social norms.

He recognizes freely that this communist book or person expresses attitudes and goals which he shares as well as ideas and values which he does not share.

He realizes that at times he experiences cooperation as meaningful and valuable to him, and that at other times he wishes to be alone and act alone.

Valuing in the Mature Person

The valuing process which seems to develop in this more mature person is in some ways very much like that in the infant, and in some ways quite different. It is fluid, flexible, based on this particular moment, and the degree to which this moment is experienced as enhancing and actualizing. Values are not held rigidly, but are continually changing. The painting which last year seemed meaningful now appears uninteresting, the way of working with individuals which was formerly experienced as good now seems inadequate, the belief which then seemed true is now experienced as only partly true, or perhaps false.

Another characteristic of the way this person values experience is that it is highly differentiated, or as the semanticists would say, extensional. The examples in the preceding section indicate that what were previously rather solid monolithic introjected values now become differentiated, tied to a particular time and experience. It is his own experience which provides the value information or feedback. This does not mean that he is not open to all the evidence he can obtain from other sources. But it means that this is taken for what it is—outside evidence—and is not as significant as his own reactions. Thus he may be told by a friend that a new book is very disappointing. He reads two unfavorable reviews of the book. Thus his tentative hypothesis is that he will not value the book. Yet if he reads the book his valuing will be based upon the reactions it stirs in *him*, not on what he has been told by others.

There is also involved in this valuing process a letting oneself down into the immediacy of what one is experiencing, endeavoring to sense and to clarify all its complex meanings. I think of a client who, toward the close of therapy, when puzzled about an issue, would put his head in his hands and say, "Now what *is* it that I'm feeling? I want to get next to it. I want to learn what it is." Then he would wait, quietly and patiently, trying to listen to himself, until he could discern the exact flavor of the feelings he was experiencing. He, like others, was trying to get close to himself.

In getting close to what is going on within himself, the process is much more complex than it is in the infant. In the mature person it has much more scope and sweep. For there is involved in the present moment of experiencing the memory traces of all the relevant learnings from the past. This moment has not only its immediate sensory impact, but it has meaning growing out of similar experiences in the past (Gendlin, 1962). It has both the new and the old in it. So when I experience a painting or a person, my experiencing contains within it the learnings I have accumulated from past meetings with paintings or persons, as well as the new impact of this particular encounter. Likewise the moment of experiencing contains, for the mature adult, hypotheses about consequences. "It is not pleasant to express forthrightly my negative feelings to this person, but past experience indicates that in a continuing relationship it will be helpful in the long run." Past and future are both in this moment and enter into the valuing.

I find that in the person I am speaking of (and here again we see a similarity to the infant), the criterion of the valuing process is the degree to which the object of the experience actualizes the individual himself. Does it make him a richer, more complete, more fully developed person? This may sound as though it were a selfish or unsocial criterion, but it does not prove to be so, since deep and helpful relationships with others are experienced as actualizing.

Like the infant, too, the psychologically mature adult trusts and uses the wisdom of his organism, with the difference that he is able to do so knowingly. He realizes that if he can trust all of himself, his feelings and his intuitions may be wiser than his mind, that as a total person he can be more sensitive and accurate than his thoughts alone. Hence he is not afraid to say, "I feel that this experience [or this thing, or this direction] is good. Later I will probably know *why* I feel it is good." He trusts the totality of himself, having moved toward becoming what Lancelot Whyte (1950) regards as "the unitary man."

It should be evident from what I have been saying that this valuing process in the mature individual is not an easy or simple thing. The process is complex, the choices often very perplexing and difficult, and there is no guarantee that the choice which is made will in fact prove to be self-actualizing. But because whatever evidence exists is available to the individual, and because he is open to his experiencing, errors are correctable. If this chosen course of action is not self-enhancing this will be sensed and he can make an adjustment or revision. He thrives on a maximum feedback interchange, and thus, like the gyroscopic compass on a ship, can continually correct his course toward his true goal of self-fulfillment.

Some Propositions Regarding the Valuing Process

Let me sharpen the meaning of what I have been saying by stating two propositions which contain the essential elements of this viewpoint. While it may not be possible to devise empirical tests of each proposition in its entirety, yet each is to some degree capable of being tested through the methods of psychological science. I would also state that though the following propositions are stated firmly in order to give them clarity, I am actually advancing them as decidedly tentative hypotheses.

Hypothesis I. There is an organismic base for an organized valuing process within the human individual.

It is hypothesized that this base is something the human being shares with the rest of the animate world. It is part of the functioning life process of any healthy organism. It is the capacity for receiving feedback information which enables the organism continually to adjust its behavior and reactions so as to achieve the maximum possible self-enhancement.

Hypothesis II. This valuing process in the human being is effective in achieving self-enhancement to the degree that the individual is open to the experiencing which is going on within himself.

I have tried to give two examples of individuals who are close to their own experiencing: the tiny infant who has not yet learned to deny in his awareness the processes going on within; and the psychologically mature person who has relearned the advantages of this open state.

There is a corollary to this second proposition which might be put in the following terms. One way of assisting the individual to move toward openness to experience is through a relationship in which he is prized as a separate person, in which the experiencing going on within him is empathically understood and valued, and in which he is given the freedom to experience his own feelings and those of others without being threatened in doing so.

This corollary obviously grows out of therapeutic experience. It is a brief statement of the essential qualities in the therapeutic relationship. There are already some empirical studies, of which the one by Barrett-Lennard (1962) is a good example, which give support to such a statement.

Propositions Regarding the Outcomes of the Valuing Process

I come now to the nub of any theory of values or valuing. What are its consequences? I should like to more into this new ground by stating bluntly two propositions as to the qualities of behavior which emerge from this valuing process. I shall then give some of the evidence from my experience as a therapist in support of these propositions.

Hypothesis III. In persons who are moving toward greater openness to their experiencing, there is an organismic commonality of value directions.

Hypothesis IV. These common value directions are of such kinds as to enhance the development of the individual himself, of others in his community, and to make for the survival and evolution of his species.

It has been a striking fact of my experience that in therapy, where individuals are valued, where there is greater freedom to feel and to be, certain value directions seem to emerge. These are not chaotic directions but instead exhibit a surprising commonality. This commonality is not dependent on the personality of the therapist, for I have seen these trends emerge in the clients of therapists sharply different in personality. This commonality does not seem to be due to the influences of any one culture, for I have found evidence of these directions in cultures as divergent as those of the United States, Holland, France, and Japan. I like to think that this commonality of value directions is due to the fact that we all belong to the same species—that just as a human infant tends, individually, to select a diet similar to that selected by other human infants, so a client in therapy tends, individually, to choose value directions similar to those chosen by other clients. As a species there may be certain elements of experience which tend to make for inner development and which would be chosen by all individuals if they were genuinely free to choose.

Let me indicate a few of these value directions as I see them in my clients as they move in the direction of personal growth and maturity.

They tend to move away from façades. Pretense, defensiveness, putting up a front, tend to be negatively valued.

They tend to move away from "oughts." The compelling feeling of "I ought to do or be thus and so" is negatively valued. The client moves away from being what he "ought to be," no matter who has set that imperative.

They tend to move away from meeting the expectations of others. Pleasing others, as a goal in itself, is negatively valued.

Being real is positively valued. The client tends to move toward being himself, being his real feelings, being what he is. This seems to be a very deep preference.

Self-direction is positively valued. The client discovers an increasing pride and confidence in making his own choices, guiding his own life.

One's self, one's own feelings come to be positively valued. From a point where he looks upon himself with contempt and despair, the client comes to value himself and his reactions as being of worth.

Being a process is positively valued. From desiring some fixed goal, clients come to prefer the excitement of being a process of potentialities being born.

Sensitivity to others and acceptance of others is positively valued. The client comes to appreciate others for what they are, just as he has come to appreciate himself for what he is.

Deep relationships are positively valued. To achieve a close, intimate, real, fully communicative relationship with another person seems to meet a deep need in every individual, and is very highly valued.

Perhaps more than all else, the client comes to value an openness to all of his inner and outer experience. To be open to and sensitive to his own *inner* reactions and feelings, the reactions and feelings of others, and the realities of the objective world—this is a direction which he clearly prefers. This openness becomes the client's most valued resource.

These then are some of the preferred directions which I have observed in individuals moving toward personal maturity. Though I am sure that the list I have given is inadequate and perhaps to some degree inaccurate, it holds for me exciting possibilities. Let me try to explain why.

I find it significant that when individuals are prized as persons, the values they select do not run the full gamut of possibilities. I do not find, in such a climate of freedom, that one person comes to value fraud and murder and thievery, while another values a life of self-sacrifice, and another values only money. Instead there seems to be a deep and underlying thread of commonality. I believe that when the human being is inwardly free to choose whatever he deeply values, he tends to value those objects, experiences, and goals which make for his own survival, growth, and development, and for the survival and development of others. I hypothesize that it is *character-istic* of the human organism to prefer such actualizing and socialized goals when he is exposed to a growth promoting climate.

A corollary of what I have been saying is that in *any* culture, given a climate of respect and freedom in which he is valued as a person, the mature individual would tend to choose and prefer these same value directions. This is a significant hypothesis which could be tested. It means that though the individual of whom I am speaking would not have a consistent or even a stable system of conceived values, the valuing process within him would lead to emerging value directions which would be constant across cultures and across time.

Another implication I see is that individuals who exhibit the fluid valuing process I have tried to describe, whose value directions are generally those I have listed, would be highly effective in the ongoing process of human evolution. If the human species is to survive at all on this globe, the human being must become more readily adaptive to new problems and situations, must be able to select that which is valuable for development and survival out of new and complex situations, must be accurate in his appreciation of reality if he is to make such selections. The psychologically mature person as I have described him has, I believe, the qualities which would cause him to value those experiences which would make for the survival and enhancement of the human race. He would be a worthy participant and guide in the process of human evolution.

Finally, it appears that we have returned to the issue of univer-sality of values, but by a different route. Instead of universal values "out there," or a universal value system imposed by some group—philosophers, rulers, priests, or psychologists—we have the possibility of universal human value directions *emerging* from the experiencing of the human organism. Evidence from therapy indicates that both personal and social values emerge as natural, and experienced, when the individual is close to his own organismic valuing process. The suggestion is that though modern man no longer trusts religion or science or philosophy nor any system of beliefs to *give* him values, he may find an organismic valuing base within himself which, if he can learn again to be in touch with it, will prove to be an organized, adaptive, and social approach to the perplexing value issues which face all of us.

REFERENCES

Barrett-Lennard, G. T. Dimensions of therapist response as causal factors in therapeutic change. *Psychol. Monogr.*, 1962, 76, (43, Whole No. 562).

Gendlin, E. T. Experiencing: A variable in the process of therapeutic change. *Amer, J. Psychother.*, 1961, 15, 233-245.

Gendlin, E. T. *Experiencing and the creation of meaning.* Glencoe, Ill.: Free Press, 1962.

Morris, C. W. *Varieties of human value.* Chicago: Univer. Chicago Press, 1956.

Rogers, C. R. *Client-centered therapy.* Boston: Houghton Mifflin, 1951.

Rogers, C. R. A theory of therapy, personality and interpersonal relationships. In S. Koch (Ed.), *Psychology: A study of a science.* Vol. 3. *Formulations of the person and the social context.* New York: McGraw-Hill, 1959. pp. 185-256.

Whyte, L. L. *The next development in man.* New York: Mentor Books, 1950.

2

Administrative Functions
and
Human Behavior

This part of the book focuses on the individual administrator in an organizational setting. The O'Brien and Gibb articles relate to the question of leadership and how it best functions in an organizational setting. They explore the dimensions of leadership, including what leadership is not. Gross' article deals with hierarchical authority in educational institutions. It challenges a basic premise long valued by administrators, and the concept of authority is set in a new perspective. It explores the question of leadership and its characteristics. Sigband suggests that the nonverbal behavior of administrators is important and that listening as an important administrative activity has been undervalued.

A new function of administrators is accepting and understanding the nature of controversy. Developing competence to handle controversy effectively is a needed skill. Attention is devoted by Albrook, Tannenbaum, and Argyris to the individual administrator's behavior in organizations. The nature of both organizational and interpersonal controversy is explored in the articles by Full and Sherif.

The well known Theory X and Theory Y postulates of McGregor are explored more fully in the Morse and Lorsch article, "Beyond Theory Y."

LEADERSHIP IN ORGANIZATIONAL SETTINGS

Gordon E. O'Brien

Aside from problems of economics such as markets or depressions an organization's success or failure depends on the quality of its management. Modern organization theory has thus given special attention to the problem of organizational leadership. While a number of principles of effective leadership have been stated, not all of them are consistent. For example, some principles advocate that company leaders should be task-oriented, directive, and distant in their relations with subordinates; other principles recommend a leadership style which is person-oriented, participative, and nondirective.

An executive who wishes to apply such principles to his own workgroup and organization is faced with a problem of choice, which is made more difficult in that each theorist supports his leadership principles with research results which appear to confirm his particular position. This difficulty in applying leadership theory then is largely attributable to theorists and researchers who devote their efforts to establishing the superiority of one out of a number of alternative styles.

To date relatively little work has been devoted to the problem of defining the conditions under which different leadership styles are effective. The leadership style which is most effective for a supervisor dealing with workers on an assembly line is probably not the most effective style for an executive dealing with his departmental managers. The importance of situational factors as determinants of

Reproduced by special permission from the *Journal of Applied Behavioral Science*, "Leadership in Organizational Settings," Gordon E. O'Brien, pp. 45-63, copyright 1969, published by NTL Institute for Applied Behavioral Science.

effective leadership style is generally accepted by writers on organization theory, but lack of research data has prevented them from describing the manner in which these situational variables affect leadership effectiveness. A particularly clear statement on this issue was made by McGregor (18)* when he recognized that managerial leadership was related not only to the personal characteristics of leaders and followers but also to the characteristics of the organization (such as its purpose and structure) and the social, economic, and political milieu. However, in his main contributions to leadership theory he has considered the significance of only one subset of situational variables for effective leadership. His principle of integration described the way in which managers should take account of personal needs and motives of workers when setting and achieving organizational objectives. Unfortunately he did not consider so fully how managerial behavior should be affected by other features of the total situation, such as organizational power and task structures.

A logical extension of McGregor's theory would show how organizational features such as power and task structures interact with personality structures to form organizational settings which require differential leadership styles or functions.

The purpose of this article is to consider how effective leadership can be related to situational factors. The criteria of effective leadership will be measures of productivity and efficiency and measures of worker satisfaction, personal growth, or "self-actualization." First, research relevant to this problem will be reviewed briefly before considering the main difficulties facing further conceptual and empirical progress. Second, a way of describing organizational settings will be considered and the usefulness of this conceptual scheme for guiding leadership research and leadership practice will be discussed.

Situational Factors in Theory and Research

Situational factors may be divided into two types. The first includes structural features of the organization such as power structure, task structure, and patterns of interpersonal relationships. These factors will be termed organizational variables. The second type refers to personality variables used to describe persons who interact within the organizational structures. The total set of situational factors then will include both organizational and personality variables.

Theories of organizational leadership are alike in asserting that

---

*See References at end of article—Ed.

both organizational and personality variables are important. However, most of them fail to define specifically the set of organizational and personality variables they deal with and so are unable to describe fully the way in which such variables interact in determining organizational productivity and worker satisfaction.[1] This lack of specificity is attributable to emphasis on *types* of variables and dimensions rather than on *specific* variables. Basically, this kind of approach is due to the theorist's attempt to show that one set of variables, the personality, human, or "psychological" set, is just as important as organizational variables in planning organizational growth, if not more so. Theorists who stress the importance of the leader's achieving an "integration" of these variable types by use of participative, supportive procedures (2; 17; 18) belong to this category.

The definition of specific organizational and personality dimensions, together with a description of the manner in which these dimensions interact to affect productivity and satisfaction, characterizes theories of group leadership which are likely to be more useful for research and application than theories of the kind discussed above. The theories of Bennis (4), Fiedler (5; 6), and Schutz (29) are of this second, and more specific, kind.

Although relatively few research studies show how certain situational variables affect leadership effectiveness, many studies show how these variables may under certain conditions determine the success of particular leadership styles. Guest (10), Likert (17) and Pelz (25) have shown that leadership effectiveness is influenced not only by the relation of the leader to his subordinates but also by his relation to his superiors. The total pattern of authority within an organization may prevent the leader from being successful, however much he tries to use the principles of integration, interdependence, and supportiveness. Training in human relations or sensitivity does not improve a leader's performance when he has to work in an organization which utilizes contrary principles of leader-worker relationships (7).

Other studies have shown that task variables determine group productivity and morale. Under these conditions effective leadership practice requires the leader to initiate changes in the task system rather than in his personal relationships. Studies in the restaurant industry (36), the coal-mining industry (34), and in textile factories (27) all show how changes in the task structure may have to be introduced by management if both organizational and personal objectives are to be met satisfactorily.

In some situations a leader may have to change his behavior

toward employees because of task requirements. Vroom and Mann (35) found that the task characteristics in a trucking company were related to different kinds of supervisory behavior. Workers engaged on tasks requiring a large amount of group cooperation (e.g., package-handlers) preferred employee-centered supervision, while directive, production-centered supervision was preferred by workers whose tasks did not require group cooperation (e.g., truck-drivers). The task cooperation requirements were also considered in a study of Schutz (29) with small groups engaged in problem solving. By varying both the tasks and the distribution of personality types within groups, he was able to show that personal compatibility had an increasing effect on group productivity as the amount of cooperation required by the group task increased. This particular study is one of the few available which investigates systematically the interactive effects of personality structure and group structure upon group productivity.

The significance of this interaction for effective leadership is demonstrated very clearly by Fiedler (5; 6). Analysis of data obtained from his own researches on leadership effectiveness in a variety of organizational settings showed that group productivity could not be consistently related to leader attitudes and behavior without taking into account the total "group task situation."

His earlier studies with military, industrial, and experimental groups indicated that the leader's attitudes toward his co-workers significantly affected the group's productivity. Leaders who sharply distinguished between most preferred and least preferred co-workers on a set of descriptive categories tended to have more effective groups than those who made little distinction between most and least preferred co-workers. The behavior of the more effective leaders tended to be distant, authoritative, and task-oriented, whereas the less effective leaders were less distant and remained permissive and person-oriented.

Because some of the results obtained with different groups were inconsistent, Fiedler was led to consider the relationship of leadership effectiveness to situational factors. Three organizational dimensions were specified as important factors: first, the "group atmosphere," or pattern of informal relationships between leaders and workers; second, the authority pattern, or the amount of power held by the leader; third, the amount of structuring in the group task. Variations in these organizational dimensions make the group conditions more or less favorable for a leader with a given attitudinal structure. For instance, a leader who rates least and most preferred co-workers quite differently is likely to be most effective in groups where he is accepted and has high power and where the group task is well structured. When the task is unstructured, leader power is low, and the group is accepting, then the leader whose cognitions of co-workers are less differentiated is likely to be the more successful. Reaching beyond the typical situational approach which stresses the importance of a loosely defined "situation," Fiedler first defines relatively precisely what are significant group dimensions, and second, specifies the possible ways in which these organizational and personality traits are related to leader effectiveness. Fiedler's research has concentrated largely on small groups and has dealt with a limited number of the variables known to affect organizational development.

The effect on productivity and morale of the personality structures of the workers exemplifies one set of problems which Fiedler has not so far investigated. Further research is therefore needed in order to achieve a comprehensive account of leadership effectiveness within organizational settings.

Difficulties of Situational Analysis

Further advances in leadership theory appear to depend largely on the solution of certain conceptual problems. Further empirical research is needed but this research must be guided by significant abstractions and appropriate strategies. Conceptual problems which stand in need of solution are here listed briefly.

1. *Definition of sets of organizational and personality dimensions which are comprehensive, economical, and precise.* It is inevitable that some selection of organizational dimensions has to be made. Compiling lists of known or possible variables will not automatically guarantee the discovery of the most useful variables, although it may facilitate the abstraction process.

Consideration of theory and research suggests that four types of structural elements or entities are necessary in any comprehensive set. These types are associated with personality structure (intrapersonal structure), interpersonal structure, positional structure, and task structure.

2. *Precise methods of representing relationships between sets of structural dimensions must be constructed.* A large part of the difficulty in developing theories of organizational behavior is attributable to inadequate methods of describing the types and patterns of relationships which are able to order the organizational dimensions.

3. *Structural variables must be distinguished from, yet be related to, process variables.* Concepts which may be used to describe pro-

cess or change are logically different from those used to describe structure.

4. *A systematic analysis of types of organizational and group tasks must be devised.* Much research has been devoted to conceptualizing types of personality structure and types of power structure, but practically no work has been devoted to task analysis. Labeling tasks as problem-solving, creative, or mechanical, for example, does not help us to understand the abstract dimensions which differentiate one task type from another. There are few articles that deliberately consider the problems of group task analysis (20; 21; 24; 28; 31), and these are of a preliminary nature.

Leadership Functions and Structural Analysis

So far the significance and difficulties of conceptualizing situational factors have been discussed. A number of studies have shown that these factors may determine effective leadership, as measured through group productivity and worker morale or satisfaction. Ideally, theory and research should provide guidance for a leader of a specific workgroup and organization so that maximum productivity and personal growth could be achieved. A leader would be able to (a) describe his situation, identifying those aspects which are capable of change and those which are not; (b) obtain information about the conditions required for goal achievement for a group of this kind; and finally, (c) change the situation as far as possible in order to maximize both productivity and the degree of congruence between organizational structure and personality structure. Thus a leader is projected as one who performs diagnostic, change, and command functions. His goal is, first, to describe his workgroup situation and its potentialities for change and second, to implement change in organizational variables in order to achieve an optimal balance between productivity and the satisfaction, happiness, or self-actualization of his workers. The set of variable types with which the leader deals is schematically represented in Figure 1.

In order to perform these functions, a leader requires (a) a useful method of describing the structure of the total situation (which includes both organizational and personality structure); (b) a procedure for defining congruence between organizational and personality structure; and (c) a set of principles for maximizing productivity and happiness for situations of various types.

In the following paragraphs an outline will be given of one way in which "the situation" and "congruence" could be understood. Also an attempt will be made to specify a set of principles, inevitably

Figure 1. Variable Types in the Organizational Setting

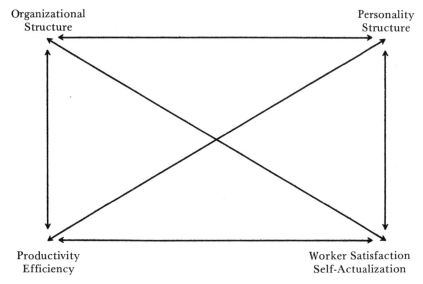

| Organizational Structure | Personality Structure |

| Productivity Efficiency | Worker Satisfaction Self-Actualization |

incomplete, which could guide the leader in promoting organizational development.

Structural Role Theory and Organizational Structure

The structural role approach (22; 23; 24) provides a relatively simple set of concepts which are intended to describe organizational and group structure. The concepts are of two types: elements and relations. The three elements defined are person (H), position (P), and task (T); the set of relations includes power, task precedence, person assignment, task allocation, and interpersonal relations. The terminology used in structural role theory is summarized schematically in Figure 2 (after 22). The terminology of digraph theory (11) is used to illustrate and describe how any given sets of these three elements may be logically interrelated.

The elements of the theory are defined in an abstract fashion but may readily be given empirical interpretation. The three elements are defined in the following way:

Task— a primitive term meaning something that has to be done.

Person— defined as a human being who has no relationships to other human beings except for those laid down by the rules of his office, and no

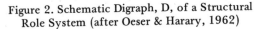

Figure 2. Schematic Digraph, D, of a Structural
Role System (after Oeser & Harary, 1962)

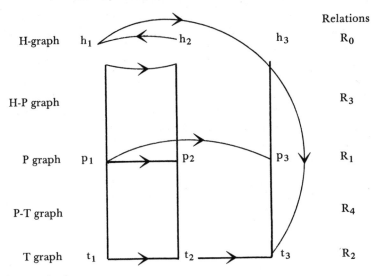

Terminology

D = the digraph of the role system
$H = (h_1 \ldots h_n)$ = the set of persons
$P = (p_1 \ldots p_n)$ = the set of positions
$T = (t_1 \ldots t_n)$ = the set of tasks
$R_0 = (R_{00} \ldots R_{0n})$ = the set of informal social relations
R_1 = the power relation
R_2 = the task precedence relation
R_3 = the person assignment relation
R_4 = the task allocation relation
R_5 = the induced relation, person to tasks

characteristics other than those prescribed for assigning him to the
occupancy of a given position.

Position— defined as a location on an organization chart, a concept which gains
its meaning through being connected to (a) persons by the assignment
relation, (b) tasks by the allocation relation, and (c) positions by the
power relation.

Contributions of the Model

The author argued earlier that advances in leadership theory were
largely dependent on the solution of a number of difficult conceptual problems. Structural role formulations appear to contribute to
the solution of these problems in a number of ways. First, a set of

organizational elements and relations is defined which is comprehensive, economical, and precise. The elements *person, position,* and *task* are comprehensive in scope because most organizational variables considered in the literature may be related to one or more of these elements. The conceptual scheme gains economy of expression and precision through its use of mathematical terminology. More complex organizational variables may be defined in terms of a fixed number of elements and relationships. For example, syncratic (or "democratic") and autocratic power or influence structures within an organization may be defined simply in terms of a specific pattern of influence relationships on a fixed number of positions. For a four-position group, autocratic and syncratic influence structures are depicted in Figure 3.

Figure 3. Representation of (a) Formal Autocratic, (b) Syncratic
Power or Influence Structures in a Four-Position Group,
(c) One of Many Intermediate Patterns

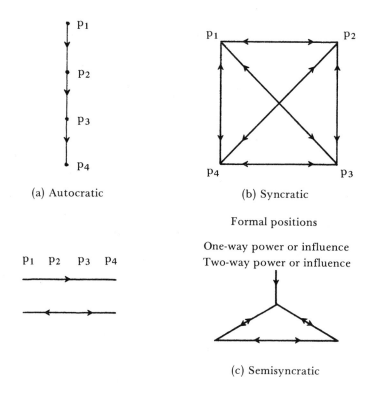

(a) Autocratic   (b) Syncratic

Formal positions

P₁   P₂   P₃   P₄   One-way power or influence
                                     Two-way power or influence

(c) Semisyncratic

Besides providing precise and economical terminology, this method of description provides ways of representing a range of variables which are not easily described using natural language. For instance, many intermediate patterns of influence structure could be represented in Figure 3 by varying the pattern of influence relationships.

The second contribution of this structural role model to the solution of the conceptual problems of organizational analysis is through its provision of a set of relationships which can be used to describe the complex pattern of relationships which may obtain among persons, positions, and tasks.

A third conceptual problem which faces organizational analysis is the provision of an adequate formal definition of "structure." Structural role theory provides such a definition through its use of a mathematical theory of structure.

A final contribution with more direct practical application is made through providing a basis for the analysis of group task structure.[2] In structural role theory, the analysis of group tasks is carried out by considering the possible ways in which the group goal can be related to the total set of elements and relations. Hence, a major advantage of this conceptualization is its ability to relate a part of the group structure (the task system) to the total structure. Content and precision can thus be given to the "field" or "system" character of group structure. In any task analysis it is necessary to distinguish among (a) the formal analysis of the task, which consists initially of specifying the number of subtasks and the set of precedence or connectivity relationships which may be used to order the subtasks; (b) the group organization required by the task, which includes descriptions of how tasks are allocated to positions and the types of power structures needed for task completion; (c) the skills and knowledge required to do the task; and (d) the attitudes which the individual members may have toward the task. These distinctions can be made easily and precisely within structural role theory and so provide the basis for a complete and clear description of group task properties (20; 24).

Besides a method for description, there is also the potentiality for defining and measuring complicated task properties like cooperation requirements and goal path multiplicity. Consider the cooperation concept. Cooperation is basically related to the degree of interdependence of a set of tasks. For a simple two-position group, there are two types of cooperation—illustrated in Figure 4. Cooperation may occur through positions which share the same tasks or through the sequencing of tasks which are allocated to different positions.

Figure 4. Types of Cooperation

Interposition Collaboration occurs when more than one position
performs the same task.
Interposition Coordination occurs when tasks allocated to different positions are ordered by precedence relationships.

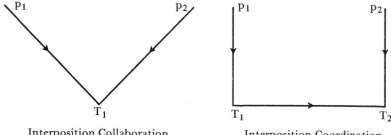

Interposition Collaboration   Interposition Coordination

Structural role theory can then provide a group leader with a
method of describing his organization's structure. This step is one of
his diagnostic functions. The description of the organizationally
relevant personality structures of organization members is another
step, but structural role theory cannot help here for it considers only
interpersonal or person-position structures. Before considering the
description of personality structure and the interactive effects of
personality and organizational structure on organizational goals, the
primacy of the task system must be emphasized.

The major task of a leader is the maintenance of maximum
productivity of his workgroup. With productivity as his main objective, the task system must always be his major concern. The task or
goals of an organization determine largely what type of power
structure is used and the kinds of people that are employed. The task
system and the pattern of position-task allocation often influence the
quality of personal relationships within the workgroup.

Leadership Functions Related to Task Structure

On the basis of some of the research findings, it is possible to
specify a few principles which help the leader to define and establish
an appropriate task system.

1. The goal must be defined. A group without a clear idea of its
task will decrease in productivity due to self-oriented and competi-

tive behavior on the part of its members (16.)

2. Once set, the goal should be split into subtasks. This is necessary for analyzing task characteristics and for specifying worker roles. Lack of clear specification contributes to role conflict and organizational stress (9; 12).

3. If the group task is well structured, then the task system should be arranged for efficient work flow. This can be done by applying critical path procedures to the task graph. Although this is a relatively technical function, it may be important for the social relations and productivity of the group. For example, Guest (10) observed that poor productivity and negative relationships in an automobile factory were due partly to inappropriate task sequencing on the assembly line. In this case, management contributed to organizational and personal harmony by attending first to the task system rather than to interpersonal tensions.

4. The authority or power structure should be matched to the cooperation requirements of the task. Little research has been performed on the consequences of lack of matching between the power and task structures. However, it seems probable that "power equalization" is appropriate for tasks which require a great deal of cooperation (especially interposition collaboration). High power differentials within a group are unlikely, for example, to lead to high productivity on creative, planning, or problem-solving tasks.

workers may not have been met (1; 15). A number of general motives or needs are known to be important (economic, autonomy, affiliation, understanding), but how these motives may influence the work behavior of persons is still a matter for systematic investigation.

Personality Structure and Organizational Structure

It is generally agreed that efficient organization of a workgroup does not guarantee its success since the personality needs of the workers may not have been met (1; 15). A number of general motives or needs are known to be important (economic, autonomy, affiliation, understanding), but how these motives may influence the work behavior of persons is still a matter for systematic investigation.

What knowledge we have about the cross-organization between personality and group settings is largely based on case studies involving the responses of a particular set of persons to a particular environmental change. In a systematic approach to the study of person-group congruence and its relation to productivity and personality change, two stages may be distinguished. First, both organiza-

tional and personality structure must be described. Second, systematic variation of both types of variables must be brought about in
order to trace the effect of their interaction upon organizational and
personality development.

Research of this kind is difficult to find, but the studies by Mann
and Mann (19), Schutz (29), Tannenbaum and Allport (33) and
Tannenbaum (32) are of this type. Tannenbaum (32) found that
when workers were engaged in an organization with a hierarchical
control structure certain personality traits ("autonomous" traits)
decreased in strength or potency. On the other hand, in a more
syncratic structure a different set of traits decreased in their strength.
Furthermore, he found that the closer that the workers' trait structures fitted the organizational climate, the more they were satisfied
with their work and liked the organization.[3]

The result suggests that there may be different "facilitative" traits
for different organizations and for different roles within the same
organization. Persons who possessed "facilitative" traits for a particular role would be likely to experience rewards due to (a) increased
opportunities for expressing their personalities and (b) direct rewards
associated with efficient performance. It is a general postulate, then,
that persons will positively evaluate the organization if it provides a
means of achieving "rewards," whereas persons will negatively evaluate the organization if it does not provide these means.

In order to test this prediction, it is necessary to specify for any
given organization the facilitative traits for each role type under the
following headings:

1. Person-Person Traits (e.g., sociability)
2. Position-Position Traits (e.g., dependence, status needs)
3. Position-Task Traits (e.g., likes to know exactly what he has to
do)
4. Task-Task Traits (e.g., likes to understand how organization
works).

In order to predict the degree of satisfaction achieved by workers
about to operate in a given organization, it is necessary to measure
them on the set of group relevant traits. Predicted job satisfaction
can then be treated as a function of the discrepancy between the
required and actual trait strength, summed over all persons and all
traits.

This approach could also be used to study the variation of productivity with the degree of fit between personality and organization. In

the absence of extensive data of this type, it is not possible at present to enunciate principles of personality-organization interaction which could be confidently applied by organizational leaders. However, further research within this conceptual framework should yield detailed information on this question. The main advantage of this approach is derived from the definition of categories of organizational and personality structure and a means of precisely describing their interrelationship.

Summary

Besides providing a way of thinking about the problems of leadership in an organizational setting, this article has indicated some specific examples of how this approach could be useful in a practical situation. First, the set of concepts discussed provides a simple yet comprehensive way of describing organizational settings. The description of the setting is important for at least two reasons. The description enables a leader to evaluate or place in perspective the findings from research reports on leadership and to accurately pinpoint the situation or setting which is the object of his concern. Using the categories of structural role theory, it is possible to identify the elements and relationships dealt with by a particular study. From the evaluation of the research findings and the definition of the immediate situation, it is possible to make a reasonable estimate of the applicability of these findings.

This approach also derives its usefulness from the notion of task analysis. Not only does task analysis force the leader to consider the specific role structure of workgroups; it also suggests that different organizations (and leadership practices) will be required for different tasks and for different stages of the same task. It is conceivable that such an analysis by a supervisor, for example, would lead him to realize that, in a particular group task, there were two main subtasks —planning and actual operations on materials. Effective leadership would involve recognizing the types of subtasks and dividing the labor accordingly. Often supervisors fail to be as effective as they might be because they define their own role inadequately and attempt to perform both types of tasks themselves. Also, from a consideration of the tasks themselves, it is possible that the supervisor would decide to use participative leadership for planning tasks and directive leadership for tasks involving repetitive operations on materials.

A strategy for initiating change has been suggested. Once the analysis of the actual situation has been compared with the desired situation, the leader is faced with the problem of restructuring. Sometimes the course of action required is fairly obvious (e.g., hiring more staff, replacing inadequate machinery), but sometimes the decision is made more difficult when it is not immediately apparent what element or elements of the situation need to be changed. Earlier sections have argued for the primacy of the task and therefore the importance of concentrating first on the task system when group productivity is low or worker dissatisfaction high. If the major determinants cannot be found in the task system, then it is necessary to consider systematically the set of relationships between the task and every other element in the situation.

FOOTNOTES

1. These general theories have been criticized on both methodological grounds (8) and on the basis of evidence showing the large modifying effects of specific organizational variables on group behavior (8; 26). Unless these theories become more specific in defining how organizational and personality structure are interrelated, their application in human relations training and T Groups will not be so effective as the theorists desire.

2. There are many types of work analyses, such as those discussed by Baldamus (3) and Lafitte (14), but these apply to individual rather than group tasks.

3. The design did not allow Tannenbaum to consider the effects of personality structure on productivity.

REFERENCES

1. Argyris, C. *Personality and organization.* New York: Harper, 1957.
2. ————. Organizational leadership. In L. Petrello & B. Bass (Eds.), *Leadership and interpersonal behavior.* New York: Holt, Rinehart & Winston, 1961.
3. Baldamus, W. *Efficiency and effort.* London: Tavistock, 1961.
4. Bennis, W. G. Leadership theory and administrative behavior: The problem of authority. *Admin. Sci. Quart.,* 1959-60, 4, 259-301.
5. Fiedler, F. E. A contingency model of leadership effectiveness. In L. Berkowitz (Ed.), *Advances in experimental social psychology.* New York: Academic Press, 1964, Pp, 150-191.
6. ————. Engineer the job to fit the manager. *Harvard bus. Rev.,* 1965, 43, 115-122.
7. Fleishman, E. A., Harris, E. F., & Burtt, H. E. *Leadership and supervision in industry.* Columbus, Ohio: Ohio State Univer., 1955.
8. Forehand, G. A., & Gilmer, B. H. Environmental variation in studies of organizational behavior. *Psychol. Bull.,* 1964, 62, 361-382.
9. Gross, N., Mason, W. S., & McEachern, A. W. *Explorations in role analysis.* New York: Wiley, 1958.

10. Guest, R. H. *Organizational change: The effect of successful leadership.* London: Tavistock, 1962.
11. Harary, F., Norman, R. Z., & Cartwright, D. *Structural models: An introduction to the theory of directed graphs.* New York: Wiley, 1965.
12. Kahn, R., Wolfe, D., Quinn, R., Snoek, J. D., & Rosenthal, R. *Organizational stress.* New York: Wiley, 1964.
13. Katzell, R. A. Contrasting systems of work organization. *Amer. Psychologist,* 1962, 17, 102-108.
14. Lafitte, P. *Social structure and personality in the factory.* London: Routledge & Kegan Paul, 1958.
15. Levinson, D. J. Role, personality and social structure in the organizational setting. *J. abnorm. soc. Psychol.,* 1959, 58, 170-180.
16. Lewin, K., Lippitt, R., & Wight, R. Patterns of aggressive behavior in experimentally created social climates. *J. soc. Psychol.,* 1939, 10, 271-299.
17. Likert, R. *New patterns of management.* New York: McGraw-Hill, 1961.
18. McGregor, D., *The human side of enterprise.* New York: McGraw-Hill, 1960.
19. Mann, J. H., & Mann, Carola H. The importance of a group task in producing group-member personality and behavior changes. *Human Relat.,* 1959, 12, 75-80.
20. O'Brien, G. E. Methods of analyzing group tasks. Technical Report No. 46, ONR. Urbana, Ill.: Group Effectiveness Research Laboratory, Univer. of Illinois, 1967.
21. ————. The measurement of cooperation. *Org. Behav. human Performance,* 1968, 3, 427-439.
22. Oeser, O. A., & Harary, F. A mathematical model for structural role theory, I. *Human Relat.,* 1962, 15, 89-109.
23. ————. A mathematical model for structural role theory, II. *Human Relat.,* 1964, 17, 3-17.
24. Oeser, O. A., & O'Brien, G. E. A mathematical model for structural role theory, III. *Human Relat.,* 1967, 20, 83-97.
25. Pelz, D. C. Influence a key to effective leadership in the first line supervisor. *Personnel,* 1952, 29, 3-11.
26. Porter, L. W., & Lawler, E. E. Properties of organization structure in relation to job attitudes and job behavior. *Psychol. Bull.,* 1965, 61, 23-51.
27. Rice, A. K. *Productivity and social organization.* London: Tavistock, 1958.
28. Roby, T. B., & Lanzetta, J. T. Considerations in the analysis of group tasks. *Psychol. Bull.,* 1958, 55, 88-101.
29. Schutz, W. C. What makes groups productive? *Human Relat.,* 1955, 8, 429-465.
30. ————. The ego, FIRO theory and the leader as completer. In L. Petrullo & B. Bass (Eds.), *Leadership and interpersonal behavior.* New York: Holt, Rinehart & Winston, 1961.
31. Shaw, M. Scaling group tasks: A method for dimensional analysis. Technical Report No. 1. Gainesville, Fla.: Univer. of Florida, 1963.
32. Tannenbaum, A. S. Personality change as a result of experimental change of environmental conditions. *J. abnorm. soc. Psychol.,* 1957, 55, 404-406.
33. Tannenbaum, A. S., & Allport, F. Personality structure and group structure: An interpretative study of their relationship through an event-structured hypothesis. *J. abnorm. soc. Psychol.,* 1956, 53, 272-280.

34. Trist, E. L,. & Bamforth, K. W. Some social and psychological consequences of the long-wall method of coal-getting. *Human Relat.*, 1951, 4, 3-38.

35. Vroom, V. H., & Mann, F. C. Leader authoritarianism and employee attitudes. *Personnel Psychol.*, 1960, 13, 125-140.

36. Whyte, W. F. *Human relations in the restaurant industry.* New York: McGraw-Hill, 1948.

DYNAMICS OF LEADERSHIP

Jack R. Gibb

People must be led. People perform best under leaders who are creative, imaginative, and aggressive—under leaders who lead. It is the responsibility of the leader to marshall the forces of the organization, to stimulate effort, to capture the imagination, to inspire people, to coordinate efforts, and to serve as a model of sustained effort.

The leader should keep an appropriate social distance, show no favorites, control his emotions, command respect, and be objective and fair. He must know what he is doing and where he wants to go. He must set clear goals for himself and for the group or institution, and then communicate these goals well to all members of the organization. He must listen for advice and counsel before making decisions. But it is his responsibility to make decisions and to set up mechanisms for seeing that the decisions are implemented. After weighing the facts and seeking expert counsel, he must make policy and rules, set reasonable boundaries, and see that these are administered with justice and wisdom, even compassion.

The leader should reward good performance and learn effective ways of showing appreciation. He must be equally ready to give negative criticism where warranted and to appraise performance frequently, fairly, and unequivocally. He must command strong discipline, not only because people respect a strong leader, but because strength and firmness communicate care and concern. Good leadership requires good fellowship. People tend to follow good

From *In Search of Leaders,* American Association for Higher Education, National Education Association, 1967, pp. 55-66. Reprinted by permission.

leaders. Leaders are born. Methods of election and selection are thus very important. Finding the right chairman or president is the success of a program or an institution. The quality of an organization is often judged by the perceived quality of the leadership.

The above is an oversimplified statement of one view of leadership theory and practice. A similarly oversimplified statement of an alternative viewpoint follows below.

People grow, produce, and learn best when they set their own goals, choose activities that they see as related to these goals, and have a wide range of freedom of choice in all parts of their lives. Under most conditions persons are highly motivated, like to take responsibilities, can be trusted to put out a great deal of effort toward organizational goals, are creative and imaginative, and tend to want to cooperate with others.

Leadership is only one of several significant variables in the life of the group or the institution. Leaders can be helpful and often are. The most effective leader is one who acts as a catalyst, a consultant, and a resource to the group. His job is to help the group to grow, to emerge, and to become more free. He serves the group best when he is a whole person, is direct, real, open, spontaneous, permissive, emotional, and highly personal. The leader at his best is an effective member. He acts in such a way as to facilitate group strength, individual responsibility, diversity, nonconformity, and aggressiveness. The leader is thus not necessary to the group and quickly becomes replaceable, dispensable, and independent. The good leader tends not to lead. He permits, feels, acts, relates, fights, talks—acts human as do other members of the group and the institution. The leader is present, available, and with the group *as a person*, not as a role.

We find many shades and variations of each of these two oversimplified statements of the theory and practice of leadership in our society. Several years of consulting and research in representative organizations make it very clear to me that attitudes toward leadership tend to cluster around these two poles. This bifurcation has analogues in current educational theory, politics, religion, philosophy, and administration.

The first view, described variously as authoritarian, paternalistic, or conservative, I classify as defensive because dynamically the view defends the administrator against his own fears and distrusts and against perceived or anticipated attack from the outside.

This authoritarian or defensive view is particularly appropriate to some viable aspects of the culture we live in to organizational forms inherited from the medieval church and military; to a life of vertical hierarchy, prescribed role responsibilities, and delegated authority; to a highly competitive economic and educational system; to the current dominant values of efficiency, excellence, productivity, task performance, and perfectionism; to the impersonality, alienation, loneliness, impotence, and indifference in our people; to a world of automation, programming, data processing, and engineering; to a forensic, persuasive, public relations, and marketing mode of interpersonal commerce; to a world continually at war, threatened by war, or preparing for war; in short, to a world of machines. It is not accidental that all around the country when administrators administer the ultimate forensic weapon in arguing against participative forms of leadership they say, "But it would never work in the military or on the production line." Actually, research indicates that this point is probably not true, but in any event the image of the leaders of our educational and governmental institutions using as a reference point for administrative theory the demands of the military organization and the production line is at least disconcerting.

It seems to me equally clear that defensive leadership is highly inappropriate and perhaps even fundamentally dissonate with another viable side of the world we live in: with education for growth, intimacy, authenticity, humanness, and creativity; with the Judeo-Christian ethics of love, honesty, intimacy, faith, cheek-turning and brotherhood; with a climate for research, inquiry, scholarship, contemplation, and learning; with cooperation, group planning, team building, and various successful forms of group effort; with the new emerging models of industrial organization and manufacturing productivity; with what might be thought of as the behavioral science approach to organizational productivity and organizational change; with the world of ambiguity, feeling, conflict, sorrow, creativity, and diversity; with many new and exciting developments in education, architecture, the creative arts, economics, management, and all phases of modern life; in short, with the world of human beings, with people.

I have deliberately drawn sharp and oversimplified distinctions in a problem area which is very complex and legitimately polemic. It is essential today that those who are administratively responsible for the colleges and universities of America see clearly this conflict and its implications for all facets of American life. It is my observation that much of the dysfunctional disturbance that the papers report daily from the college campuses is created as unintended but inevitable effects of defensive leadership practices among administrators of American colleges.

Let us look at the dynamics of defensive leadership. The major dynamic of the defensive model is fear and distrust. Observations indicate that people who have mild or more serious fears tend to do several things: distrust the people being led; filter the data that are given to the followers and develop strategies for such filtering and programming of data dissemination; attempt to control and manipulate the motivations of the followers; and attempt to control their behavior. The incidence and degree of low trust, strategic, persuasional, and controlling behavior varies directly with the amount of fear. Most of us who are leaders or are placed in leadership roles have varying degrees of fear about our own adequacy, how we are seen by others, the effectiveness of our leadership strategies, the effects of rebellion, the anxieties about insubordination and other unfollower-like behavior. I guess that our major fear has to do with anxiety about being followed!

The behavior of leaders tends to camouflage, perhaps even to themselves, the underlying fears which support the strategic, manipulative, and controlling behavior. For images of fear on assuming leadership roles one has but to think of the new teacher in the schoolroom, the new mother bringing back her first baby from the hospital, the new lieutenant guiding a patrol into action, or the newly appointed administrative official handling a student riot. The fears that we all have are quelled and softened by various adaptive, self-deceptive, and façade-building mechanisms for presenting ourselves to ourselves and to others.

Some educational leaders are today more fearful than ever. In reaction to student strikes, riots, demonstrations, and protests, as well as to the more normal vicissitudes of campus life, college and university leaders utilize defensive practices that generate unintended byproducts of fear, distrust, hostility, and counter-defensive behavior. The classical models of leadership are time and again proved to be ineffective. Why does defensive leadership arise and persist among educational leaders?

A reciprocal or circular process seems to be operating. Normal fears of life are exacerbated by the ambiguity, high control, and threat of the group or organization. However necessary this ambiguity and control is thought to be, it serves to create fears and hostilities which in turn call forth still more restrictive ambiguity and controlling behavior. This reciprocal fear-distrust cycle sustains the defensive behavior of leadership. The fears accompany and reinforce feelings of inadequacy and self-rejection in leaders and other members of the group or organization.

But the fears, hostilities, and distrusts are so successfully camouflaged in the social defenses that the casual observer might well think the above discription of educational life to be strangely out of touch with reality as he sees it. Certainly it is not the conscious intent of educational leaders to create such a state of affairs.

Why is it then that we get in the university so many unintended effects? These unintended effects seem to result from a kind of self-fulfilling prophecy: low-trust, high-fear theories, when put into practice, actually generate distrust and fears that not only confirm the assumptions underlying the theories, but also provide emotional support and strong motivation to continue the low-trust, high-fear behavior. An interactive and self-preserving cycle is thus set in motion, supported in depth by latent fear-distrusts and by rationalized theories which appear to be confirmed. Leadership behavior, thus supported, is exceedingly difficult to change.

Behind the façade of paternalism, politeness, one-big-happy-family-living, heartiness, and the accompanying soft-sell influence and velvet-glove control lie defensive relationships that pervade the colleges. Defensive leadership is characterized by low trust, data distortion, persuasion, and high control. These four aspects of defensive leadership are parallel to four basic dimensions of all group or social behavior: the feeling climate, the flow of data within the system, the formation of goals, and the emergence of control.

The key to defensive leadership is a state of low trust. The defensive leader assumes that the average person cannot be trusted, he is essentially lazy and irresponsible, action must be taken to inspire and motivate him, and he requires supervision and control. The defensive leader can counteract his feelings of inferiority by assuming that his subordinates are less than they actually are; and he can service his hostile feelings by keeping the subordinate in demeaning, dependent, and inferior roles in relation to himself and to leadership as a class.

The defensive leader or administrator rationalizes the service of his needs by developing formal or informal leader theories which both justify and camouflage his fears and hostilities. An essential step in theory and in practice is to manipulate the flow of information and communication within the organization. Information sent down from the top is often deliberately "corrected" to increase morale, to allay fears, to put the best administrative foot forward, and to justify administrative action. "Correction" is achieved by consciously or unconsciously filtering and distorting information to present a good image, to encourage positive thinking, or to build loyalty.

Strategies are devised to improve the administrative image: a worker's name is remembered to make him feel good; a birthday file is kept to demonstrate that the administrator feels the subordinate is important enough to warrant a birthday card. The "good" administrator is especially careful to smile acceptingly at those members of the "family" team towards whom he has temporary or sustained feelings of animosity. Interpersonal cues are thus manipulated and distorted to present a façade of warmth, friendliness, or cohesiveness.

The defensive leader is continually challenged to create new prods, rewards, and gimmicks as the old ones become ineffective. Thus the responsibility for sustaining motivations is thrust upon the administrator or teacher rather than upon the student. The inherent impetus to derive self-satisfaction and self-respect through accomplishment for its own sake becomes atrophied and lost. Self-satisfaction becomes dysfunctional as an incentive system.

The person who is being motivated by others through extrinsic rewards tends either to resist being influenced or to come under the control of the rewarder. He is motivated, not to achieve something, but to gain the approval of the teacher or administrator, to hunt for his satisfactions in status, grade, and social approval rather than to look for his satisfactions *within*, in terms of self-respect, self-approval, and the achievement of personal goals.

Thus the roots of dependence and apathy lie in the reward system, for the person who learns to find his values from without is always at the mercy of other persuaders—teachers, companions, demagogues, groups, or other sources of approval and authority. He becomes dependent, passive, and susceptible to all sorts of external controls.

The reward system may in others foster resistance and rebellion, resentment, cynicism, and a variety of negative and competitive feelings. People who work under competition learn to be competitive, and the extrinsic rewards do not satisfy the deep needs for self-satisfaction and self-respect which are gained by achieving our personal goals as unique individuals.

Both dependence and resistance require controls, and the defensive leader expends a considerable amount of energy devising a variety of controls both for the people and for the processes of the enterprise. The more fearful and anxious he is, the more he feels caught in recurring emergencies and the greater is his need to control. Regulations are put on car-parking, coffee-break duration, channels of reporting, library schedules, methods of work, habits of dress, use of safety devices, more and more complex filing systems, rigid report systems—until all aspects of living in the organization are controlled.

The conscious and official reasons given for the controls usually relate to organization and productive efficiency, but the underlying impulses often spring from, or are reinforced by, the leader's personal needs for rigid order or needs to demonstrate his superiority and strength, express hostility, exercise power, justify his position ("What else would I do if I didn't plan these controls?"), reinforce hierarchy, force people to be orderly or conforming, and keep them in line.

Control systems become functionally autonomous—traditional and conventional elements of the organizational system—and often outlive any practical utility. Indeed, people seem to sense that many regulations actually serve personal needs for punishment or power and bear little relation to the actual needs of the organization itself. In looking at organizations we have often found that many controls are universally violated in the system by common consent. In fact, there is clear indication—and often conscious awareness—that some controls are so dysfunctional that if everyone obeyed them the system would come to a grinding halt.

These defensive techniques of leadership produce certain predictable results. Fear and distrust beget fear and distrust. People who are distrustful tend to see untrustworthy behavior in others. If the relationship between an administrator and his subordinate is basically one of distrust, almost any action on either's part is perceived by the other as untrustworthy. Thus a cycle is created which nurtures self-corroborating leadership hypotheses.

This cycle is well illustrated in connection with communications. Any restriction of the flow of information and any closed strategy arouses energy devoted to circumventing the strategy and fosters counter-strategies that are at least as imaginative and often more effective than the original inducing strategy. A familiar example is the strategy of countering the top brass by distorting the upward-flowing data: feelings of hostility are camouflaged by deferential politeness; reports are "fixed up"; records are doctored or "cooked" to fit administrative goals and directives. Such attempts are augmented by emergency and threat; the greater the fear and distrust, the greater the circumvention, counter-strategy, and counter-distortion.

Defensive leaders use various forms of persuasion to motivate subordinates towards the organization's goals, but often the results are either apathy and passivity or frenetic conformity. Persuasion is a form of control and begets resistance, which may take many subtle forms. Open and aggressive cold war between teachers and administrators, for instance, is an obvious form. More common—and less easy to deal with—is passive, often unconscious resistance such as apathy, apparent obtuseness, dependent demands for further and more minute instructions, bumbling, wheel-spinning, and a whole variety of inefficiences that reduce creative work.

As we have seen, tight control leads to some form of dependency and its accompanying hostility; it may vary from the yes man's deference and conformity to the no man's rebellion against even the most reasonable and normal requests and rules. Deference and rebellion are cut from the same cloth. When unnecessary and arbitrary controls are imposed, or when normal controls are seen as unnecessary or arbitrary, as is the case when there is fear and distrust, then almost all members of the hierarchy become concerned with their feelings about authority. Most of us are ambivalent toward authority figures, and these mixed feelings are augmented in periods of stress and fear. In tightly controlled, disciplining, and disciplined organizations members demand clarity in rules and in boundary demarcations. But rules can never be made completely clear in practical work situations; boundaries are always permeable and inadequately defined. Thus the demands for further clarification are endless, and controls lead to further controls.

We see how the cycle is set up: hostility and its inevitable counterpart, fear, are increased by the distrust, distortion, persuasion-reward, and control systems of defensive leadership; and the continuing cycle is *reinforced* at all stages, for as fear breeds distrust, distrust is rationalized and structured into theories which sanction distrustful leadership practices. The practices reinforce distrust; now the theorist is justified, and latent motivation to continue the cycle is itself reinforced.

Defensive leadership theories and practices permeate our society. We find them in the home, in school, and in the church, as well as in business organizations. Let us see, for instance, how the child-rearing patterns of our culture fit the picture described above. There are so many frightening things in the world that can harm helpless children. The fearful person can, with little effort, find a variety of frightening aspects in the environment of the child—anything from matches and electric outlets to busy roads and unacceptable playmates. Anxiety makes it easy to exaggerate the number of people ready to kidnap and even rape one's child; the fears of the parent embellish natural dangers and provide nourishment and comforting rationalization for defensive practices.

Communications must be managed for the good of the child. Because he might be worried or upset, emotional and financial discord must be camouflaged and a façade of security and serenity maintained. Children are inexperienced and immature, therefore they cannot be trusted to do things on their own. Moreover, since the natural interests of the child are likely to be frivolous, demeaning, or harmful, he should be carefully guided and persuaded to do what is right—to select appropriate playmates, read good books, and generally adopt goals set by the parental culture or aspirations. To protect the child from ubiquitous dangers and to set his feet on the proper path, parents readily learn to use bribes, praise, and deprivation as tools of coercion. And because children are initially dependent and helpless, it is easy for the fearful parent to prolong the period of dependency.

Schools reinforce these patterns. They receive children whose dependency has been created by defensive parental techniques, and they maintain the dependency by continuing these practices. Having been distrusted, children continue to be untrustworthy. The insecure teacher finds it necessary to maintain a protective façade; she rationalizes her behavior by making a number of low-trust, tight-control assumptions about the children under her tutelage. She builds a changing repertoire of tricks to keep them busy, orderly, neat, attentive, and—she hopes—motivated. Impressed by the awesome culture heritage she is charged to transmit, she feels it imperative that she instill in her pupils the goals, ideals, and rules of the culture. As bodies of knowledge become increasingly standardized, pressures towards indoctrination increase. By codifying rules, regulations, and standards, the teachers build internal control systems—in the classroom, and hopefully, in the children themselves. As part of the informal curriculum, children are taught façade-building; they are encouraged to put the best foot forward, to be polite, to be decorous, and to adopt the essentially hypocritical social graces of the dominant middle class.

What is the alternative to defensive leadership? This is not as easy to specify. The key to emergent leadership centers in a high degree of trust and confidence in people. Leaders who trust their colleagues and subordinates and have confidence in them tend to be open and frank, to be permissive in goal setting, and to be noncontrolling in personal style and leadership policy. People with a great deal of self-acceptance and personal security do trust others, do make trust assumptions about their motives and behavior. The self-adequate person tends to assume that others are also adequate and, other things being equal, that they will be responsible, loyal, appropriately work-oriented when work is to be performed, and adequate to carry out jobs that are commensurate with their levels of experience and growth.

Just as we saw that distrust arises from fear and hostility, so we can see that people with little fear and minimal needs to be hostile are ready to trust others. Of course, there is some risk in trusting others, in being open and freedom-giving.

People naturally tend to share their feelings and concerns with those whom they trust, and this is true at the simplest and most direct level of interpersonal relationships as well as at more complex levels of organizational communication. Thus a high-trust system may institute open planning meetings and evaluation meetings; public criteria for promotion; easily available information of salaries, cost figures, and budgets; and easy access to material in the files. There is comparatively little concern with public relations, with the corporate or family image, or with communications programs. Communication in such a system is a *process* rather than a program.

The participative leader is permissive in his relations with subordinates, for he assumes that as people grow they learn to assess their own aptitudes, discover their deep-lying interests, and develop their basic potentials. Therefore he gives his subordinates every opportunity to maximize self-determination and self-assessment, to verbalize their goals, to try new jobs or enlarge the scope of the work they are doing, and he trusts them to make mature judgments about job assignments. Where he is dealing with a work-team or a group, he lets the group make decisions about job allotments and work assignments.

This process of allowing people to be responsible for their own destinies, for setting their own targets, assessing their own development needs, searching out resources to aid in job accomplishment, and participating in setting organizational objectives is basic to high-trust leadership. Instead of using conventional defensive-leadership techniques of skilled persuasion to induce acceptance of leadership goals, the high-trust administration participates in cooperative determination of goals and in cooperative definition of production and staff problems. He knows that goal-formation is a significant skill that must be learned, and that to develop such skill students and adults must exercise a variety of opportunities to make decisions, explore goals, and experiment with many kinds of activities.

The participative administrator joins in creating a climate in which he has no need to impose controls. He knows that in a healthy group controls emerge from group processes as the need is perceived. Then controls are mediated by group or organization objectives and by such relevant data as deadlines and target dates. People or groups who have set their own objectives and have clearly stated their own goals build internal tension-systems which maintain goal orientation and create appropriate boundaries.

Formal and written rules about such things as work space, library use, and stockroom neatness are less and less necessary when people are engaged in a common task with others whose feelings and perceptions they freely share; when there is trust and mutuality, people are inclined to respect the rights and concerns of fellow members. This principle applies to large and small systems alike—in either, the participative administrator reduces as far as practicable all formal controls evidenced by rules, regulations, written memoranda, signs, formal job specification sheets, rigid lines of responsibility and authority, and the like.

The effects of participative leading are diametrically contrary to those of defensive leading. Love begets love. Respect begets respect. Trust produces trust. People who are trusted tend to trust themselves and to trust those in positions of responsibility. Moreover, the feeling that one is trusted encourages exploration, diversity, and innovation, for the person spends little time and energy trying to prove himself. His time and energy are freed to define and solve problems, accomplish work, and create new dimensions of his job. A fearful person uses a great deal of energy in defending himself against present or anticipated threat or attack; a confident and self-assured person can direct his energy towards goals that are significant to him as a person.

Again, openness begets openness. In the long run, at least, one who freely shares data, whether of feelings or of figures, reduces fear and distrust in himself and in others. Defensive administrators build massive communication programs, not to disseminate objective information but to mold attitudes, create favorable and appropriate images, and influence people. Such persuasional and distortive communication produces resistance. Direct and open flow of information, on the other hand, serves to create an atmosphere which encourages people to share information with those above as well as with those below.

In general, openness and information giving improves the deci-sion-making process, for experience in giving information and expres-sing feelings enhances consensus; and the more nearly a group can reach consensus on operational issues, the higher the quality of the decision and the greater the group's commitment to the program.

Moreover, participative goal-formation optimizes self-determina-tion and self-assessment. Intrinsic motivations become increasingly relevant and powerful. People explore their own capacities and interests, and try to find or create work for themselves that is satisfying and fulfilling. They enlarge their own jobs, asking for more responsibility and more creative and interesting work. Such work is fulfilling to the person, and extrinsic rewards are secondary to satisfaction in accomplishing the task. Administrators find that peo-ple like to work; they "own" their jobs and feel great loyalty and responsibility toward the common goals of the group. People feel little need to escape from the work situation, and the "thank goodness it's Friday" clubs become less enticing. Concerns over salary and merit increases are symptomatic of defensive-leading pres-sures.

Participative administration creates interdependence and dimin-ishes the problem of authority. For instance, work is allocated by consensus—people assess their abilities and select or create appropri-ate tasks. Where there is interdependence, conflict and disagreement are openly expressed and can thus be resolved and integrated into productive work. Where people feel they are working together for a common goal, the organization of work can be flexible, diverse, and informal, with a minimum of written job boundaries and rigid role requirements. Channels of communication are free, open, and spon-taneous.

The attainment of emergent leadership on the college campus is a developmental task of awesome proportion. If the above analysis of the leadership problem has some validity, then it is clear where some responsibilities lie.

These concepts particularly are a challenge to the university. The Ohio State studies, particularly, showed how far behind even the military and industry the university administration is in achieving some kind of more participative and less authoritarian administrative relationships. The headlines today are filled with conflicts. The university is in many ways more susceptible to the pressures which produce fear than is industry, government, or business. The univer-sity is at one and the same time vulnerable to attacks from public opinion and also historically inviolate. The products of the university are highly intangible, and it is difficult to apply vigorous controls to the product and to tell if the university is successful in the same way that a business or even the military is with its hard criteria for productivity, profit, or victory. Thus highly vulnerable, the university has preserved a historical isolation from social pressures; and administrative behavior is often strangely medieval and out of touch with the vigorous demands of democratic growth. The university, strangely, is sometimes a citadel for autocratic administrative behavior.

I should say a word about the implications of this model for ethical behavior. In abstract, this model of leadership specifies a theory of ethics. That behavior is more ethical when it is most trusting, most open, most self-determining, and most interdependent. Thus one would look in the university setting for unethical or moral behavior in the areas of distrust, strategic filtering of feelings and ideas (honesty), manipulative abridgement of self-determination, and dependency-producing or rebellion-producing high control behavior.

It seems to me that joint, interdependent, and shared planning is the central concept of the kind of participative, consultative leadership that we are considering. Planning, to be moral, in this framework, to be efficient, and to be growth-producing must be organic to the institution, involve to an optimal degree all of the participants, and must be done interdependently. It is easy to find illustrations on the university campus of buildings in architectural styles that are unrelated to experimental learning theory, fund-raising methods that are planned by a special group of people who are usually collecting funds in ways that would be anathema to other members of the college community, athletic programs that arise from financial need rather than from educational policy, personnel practices that are inherited unabashedly from business institutions that have aims that are incommensurate with university goals, and many other illustrations where planning is a fragmentary, emergency process engaged in by small groups of people who are often out of touch with the university as a community.

Our assumption is that the blocks to innovation and creativity are fear, poor communication, imposition of motivations, and the dependency-rebellion syndrome of forces. People are innovative and creative. The administration of innovation involves freeing the creativity that is always present. The administrative problem of innovation is to remove fear and increase trust, to remove strategic and distortional blocks to open communication, to remove the tight controls on behavior that tend to channel creative efforts to circumvention, counter-strategy, and organizational survival rather than into innovative and creative problem-solving.

Valid, direct, and open communication among all segments of the organic institution is a central process of effective leadership in the model we are examining. Effective leadership grows with communication in depth. Effective leadership is hampered by all forces which inhibit or restrain communication in depth. If emergent or participative leadership were prevalent on the campus, communication programs would become less and less necessary. Defensive administration breeds the conditions that require an increasing escalation of massive communication programs to hopefully alleviate the conditions produced by the defensive leadership.

We are attempting to *become* as a people and as culture. We are in the process of discovering and creating models of interdependent, high trust, self-determining, and open behavior. We are trying to create an interdependent, achieving, free, becoming culture. This has never before been done in the world, and the strains of transition are awesome and somewhat frightening. But for those of us who are dedicated to the university as a way of life, the challenge to the college and university administrator and leader is clear. The challenge is there. The road is unclear. The goal is at one and the same time the preservation of certain concepts we hold dear and the achievement of a more free, a more open, a more self-determining, and a more human environment for learning and growth.

HIERARCHICAL AUTHORITY IN EDUCATIONAL INSTITUTIONS

Llewellyn Gross

The Question of Hierarchical Authority in Educational Institutions

The thesis that every idea must be open to continuous inquiry is not likely to be disputed by those who pursue modern educational aims. But when the thesis is used to question established beliefs it may become too disturbing to receive approval. Nevertheless, this is what we propose to do with the highly respectable concept of authority. We propose to raise the question of whether hierarchical authority as ordinarily understood is usually justified; whether, indeed, reasonable men can support its use in academic institutions.

If what is called authority is always acceptable then there can be no problem of what form of administration, autocratic or democratic is most worthy, no problem of the separtation of force from justice, no problem of the kind of social order men should have. If authority is sometimes acceptable then there is a problem of what it means, of who should hold it, and of the conditions under which it should be held.

Our principal assumption is that authority is never justified when those who exercise it fail to explore its problematic nature. Unless those in authority seriously examine the grounds upon which their position may or may not be defended, they are unfit to hold it. When positions of authority cannot be justified the universal ethical question of why one person rather than another should govern is not confronted. Without such a confrontation authority is irresponsible and irresponsible authority is no authority at all.[1]

From *Focus on Change and the School Administrator,* edited by Hartley and Holloway, published by the School of Education, State University of New York at Buffalo, pp. 23-33. Reprinted by permission.

What is Authority?

Concepts of authority occupy a central place in social organization, political leadership and administrative behavior. Unfortunately their empirical bases are rarely subject to critical analysis. The case for authority as a necessary ingredient in social life appears to follow three distinguishable strands of interpretation.[2] First, there is the "scientific" view that authority is justified by the imperatives of specialization and coordination in large organizations. According to this view, complex forms of organization—industrial, educational, military, etc., are impossible without vesting control in the hands of a select group. Secondly, there is the legal-ethical view that authority is justified by virtue of some universal principle or process rooted in the natural, rational or superhuman orders of existence. According to this view authority is a *right* based on justice, legitimacy, reason or community consensus which individual members of society must recognize regardless of their private wills. Thirdly, there is the view, less often articulated, that authority is the expression of force or power under the subterfuge of an ideological language and ritual. According to this view authority is a psuedo rational or psuedo legitimating concept behind which the strong hide their interest in exploiting the weak. The present discussion is largely restricted to the first viewpoint and excludes the simple descriptive notion, characterizing much operational research in social science, that authority is the *prima facia* fact of command and obedience.

The "Scientific" Viewpoint

As indicated, the "scientific" view claims that coordination by hierarchical authority is required by modern specialization. However, in most colleges, coordination of specialities is achieved by faculty deliberation rather than by administrative decree. In other educational settings departmental operations are unspecialized to the point of performing essentially the same functions. Consider, for instance, the rural elementary school in which all subjects are taught by a single teacher. The ubiquitous use of faculty committees together with performance records, assembly line and other automated procedures for regulating interaction among students and teachers suggests that hierarchical coordination is not always essential. In such situations, coordination must be collaborative rather than hierarchical to realize the ends of education. It may be asked, then, why coordination of specialized roles (allocation of positions and duties) is believed to require a stable hierarchy of authoritative controls? Is it because those who hold authoritative positions make the claim for specialized competence? Is it because inequalities in social power create conditions which require authority to maintain them? Let us take note of some of the arguments, many of which are informed by word of mouth.

(1) It is said that organizational coordination is a competence or skill available only to administrative experts. But is this skill really much different from the clerical and interpersonal competence of many white collar employees with college level education?

(2) It is said that consensus (or homogeneity of outlook) on organizational goals is not characteristic of subordinates, or if it is, it is not a sufficient reason for eliminating authoritative controls. But do not superordinates often prevent subordinates from gaining the information and experience which would develop a strong interest in organizational goals? In other words, which is antecedent and which is consequent; is hierarchical authority the cause of inexperience or inexperience the cause of hierarchical authority?

(3) It is said that the "irrational" needs of subordinates as whole persons (including the pursuit of private interests) run counter to organizational goals which require total commitment; hence authoritative control is necessary. But do rationality and commitment follow more certainly from the privileges attending authoritative positions than they do from the obligations of non-authoritative positions?

(4) It is said that organizational coordination can be achieved only through the leadership of a small group (oligarchy); whoever leads must be invested with legitimate authority. But cannot leadership "be achieved by custom, public meetings or delayed action (societies can tolerate a good deal of chaos),—the gravitation toward a 'natural' balance in which no one decides"?[3]

(5) It is said that participants will contribute to organizational goals only if they receive inducement (some form of payments) in return. Authoritative coordination is believed necessary to define and enforce the required scale of inducements and contributions. But if equity is obtained between inducements and contributions would "authoritative" definitions be necessary? Is not the issue of each man's worth nearly the most difficult in the history of human society—so difficult that everyone should have occasion to persuade and be convinced?

(6) It is said that increase in size and complexity of organizations, following upon technical advance, requires a high degree of integration and this can be achieved only by authoritative controls. But in the larger society, roles are integrated by processes of socialization

and imitation which are largely unconscious. Just as one learns language and acquires habits of interaction without awareness of cultural patterning so one may adapt to organizational processes without benefit of authority. Again it may be asked, is it the special privileges of those in power and the resistance of organizational members to such privileges that accounts for authoritative controls?

A Brief Historical Observation

Perhaps a bit of historical knowledge can be used to illuminate these issues. In the long spectrum of man's development, performance of narrow and routine tasks contributed little to the individual's economic value, his worth to society or his power to make his needs the concern of others.[4] Being easily replaceable he had little opportunity to win either social or self-esteem. However, with the industrialization of society, diversification of skills occurred and the unity of "work and toil" disappeared. The new diversification depended upon opportunities to develop the person's potentialities, upon freely chosen careers in a community which required his contribution and recognized his power to satisfy human needs. As science and technology advanced community status depended increasingly upon technical skills. Thus democratic decision-making was forced upon organizations to assure that abilities would be fully utilized. When contributions to organizational policy became dependent upon technical ability, coordination by authority proved inimical to organizational goals. It tended to destroy the basis of organizational solidarity by reducing the decision-making freedom of specialists and isolating them from one another.

Since the historical aim of hierarchical authority has been individual prestige and privilege it is misleading to contend that the central interest of those in command is the coordination of specialized skill or knowledge. Those who take knowledge and skill as their guiding interest often refuse to occupy offices which remove them from these functions. To be effective, specialists require a rationalized, well ordered environment, assured careers with rewards based on merit, and impersonally defined rights and duties. However, organizational criteria for legitimating hierarchical authority often undermine the bases upon which technical competence is effective. As with other institutionalized arrangements, authority rests in part upon criteria which perpetuate inequalities of sex, class, ethnic membership, nepotism and economic inheritance.[5] Coordination is then achieved in the face of disciplinary problems, competitive failures, lack of consensus on organizational rules, wide disparity in status and wealth, and uneven participation in the determination of organizational policies.

If knowledge and skill are necessary conditons for the realization of organizational goals, a "rational" organization would employ superiors with more knowledge and skill than their subordinates. Otherwise the superiors' directives would be impediments rather than aids to the efficient performance of organizational goals. Since such practices are virtually impossible,[6] attempts to maintain the legitimacy of authority lead to the creation of various myths about superiors and subordinates.[7] Reference has been made to the belief that organizational coordination is a technical competence available only to occupants of authoritative positions. Belief in technical competence becomes the basis for justifying the right of hierarchical authority to make decisions. From the right to make decisions other rights are assumed to follow: (a) the right to obedience; (b) the right to status deference; (c) the right to select personnel and to initiate and assign activities; (d) the right to determine organizational goals and settle conflicts; (e) the right to advance knowledge; (f) the right to special emoluments; and finally, (g) the right to express ideas freely. In some cases these myths presume to be explanations of the necessity for authority; in reality they often amount to ideological devices for maintaining authority.

Applications to Educational Institutions

In education, hierarchical authority is maintained through institutionalized privileges granted to superordinates.[8] These privileges discriminate against subordinates by downgrading their scholarly and teaching contributions to the academic enterprise.

(1) Superordinates are invited to social gatherings of subordinates but not vice versa. Thus a college president will not usually entertain his faculty without inviting the college board, but when he entertains the college board he usually does so without inviting his faculty. Consistent with his practice is the fact that higher administration is frequently granted expense accounts not available to lower administration for entertaining "worthy" guests. The informal network of associations are such that superordinates are regarded as entitled to any information concerning the school or college which is possessed by subordinates. On the other hand, subordinates are not usually entitled to information possessed by superordinates, especially knowledge of salaries, overhead expenses and data on the competence and limitations of administrative boards. Compare, for instance, opportunities to discuss openly the credentials written in

behalf of a professor with those supporting a college president.[9]

(2) Closely related to the unfavorable balance of information provided to the rank and file school or college teacher is the assumption that lay members of a school or college board and other influential citizens are in better position to judge the qualifications of a faculty member in the performance of his role than is the faculty member to judge the qualifications of a board member in the performance of his role. If the performance of a board member depends on common sense and practical experience these would seem to be more available to the teacher than is the accessibility of the teacher's specialized knowledge to the board member. The question here is whether the goals of a school are best realized by vesting decisions in the hands of its faculty or by its lay board, if one must choose. And, if one need not choose, a bipartisan division of power is the only reasonable answer. Of course, the most important single reason why school boards are free to judge the qualifications of faculty, and not vice versa, is that they control the financial resources which keep the institution solvent. In many respects the structure of wealth and influence parallels that found in modern industry. But wealth is not a qualification for anything except possibly to acquire more wealth. By itself it is surely not a qualification for managing schools and performing the functions ordinarily given to board members.[10]

(3) Superordinates are regarded as entitled to wider and more superlative publicity and popular acclaim. Witness, for instance, the larger and more decorative offices given to higher ranking personnel and the location and spread of newspaper accounts of their appointments and promotions. In cases where a subordinate's scholarly or academic achievements are great, worthwhile information concerning him is either omitted or deleted. Not all of this is due to news interest or conscious decision. Much of it reflects an almost unconscious and automatic conformity to popular beliefs about the superior achievements of administators. In many instances an institution's catalogue reflects this form of privilege. The names of administrators appear on the front pages and are set apart from the regular staff. In some cases such blatant favoritism appears as a listing of all university degrees for the administrator but only the terminal degree for the professor. Thus Dean Smith has the degrees B.A., M.A. and Ph.D. after his name while Professor Jones has only a Ph.D. degree. Similarly, honorary degrees are listed without any attempt to separate them from earned degrees or to define the basis upon which they are awarded. No wonder faculty members sometimes suspect collusion

between board members and college presidents to see that the ingroup of which both are members receives an ample supply of honorific symbols.

(4) Superordinates favor procedures of negotiation over rational appraisal when confronted with opposing interests. Since their objective is to maintain the status quo, the unruffled functioning of administrative machinery, they shy away from an ethical assessment of professional differences.[11] The admission of differences between subordinates and superordinates often leads to withdrawal of mutual support followed by attacks on the integrity of each. It becomes advantageous, then, to resolve dilemmas of moral choice by referring to norms of institutional and group harmony even though inequalities of power and influence are thereby perpetuated without effective checks. Among these norms those of congeniality serve to keep subordinates in their place since it is apparently the less favored that stand to gain by raising problems, delineating conflicts and proposing new alignments of status and reward. Double think and double talk may become a cultivated art with such techniques of evasion as the apt witticism, seldom more than an oblique distraction from some unpleasant fact. Individual integrity may be kept impotent by devices calculated to prime conviviality. The anecdote, always contagious and sometimes devastating, about a subordinate's indiscretion spreads like hot rumor. The end in view is to maintain unwilling agreement or better, agreeableness in a *pseudo-gemeinschaft* community of like-minded men.[12]

Is Authority Reducible to Power?

A repertory of guiding images serves to maintain the power of those who hold authority. Presumably, academic boards are particularly qualified in respect to rational traits of leadership, and are, for this reason, impersonal managers of subordinates who tend to confuse private goals with organizational goals. Presumably, conflict of interest between superiors and subordinates can be rightly settled without reference to rules acceptable to subordinates. Presumably, since control and responsibility are vested in hierarchical authority, the latter can be held accountable for organizational failures. But, without apparent contradiction, many administrators claim that since social control is delegated, responsibility for organizational failure may be shifted to subordinates. In this context there is no admission that ability to make decisions has, through dependence upon specialized knowledge, been shared with subordinates.

Those who hold positions of authority often ignore the difference

between informally defined leadership and bureaucratically sponsored leadership, between leadership to meet personal or social needs
and leadership to meet organizational tasks. They often ignore questions concerning the possibility of reshaping institutional structures
to minimize the power of hierarchical positions and roles. They
assume that communications, demands, and manipulations down the
hierarchy are legitimate but generally disapprove of these processes
when directed up the hierarchy. Knowledge of what subordinates are
doing depends upon communication up the hierarchy. But when the
need for upward communication is admitted, dependence is admitted, and the legitimacy of commands and controls can be disputed.
How then, can authority be taken as legitimate and thus beyond
dispute when there are those who would dispute it? Moreover, the
assumption of legitimacy based on personal competence depends on
the (loyal?) cooperation of subordinates. But those subordinates
most "in the know" to maintain authoritative images are in the best
position to manipulate their superiors. The less the intimacy, the
greater the distance between superior and subordinate, the more
effective the authoritative image. With greater intimacy ("close supervision"), the judgment and morality of superiors can be more
readily challenged. To define the circumstances under which organizational maintenance requires compliances from subordinates, publicly recognized procedures for legitimating decisions are necessary.
When such procedures are absent, attempts to shift responsibility to
subordinates rest on a political fiction.

   To maintain hierarchical authority, personal goals realized through
specialization must be replaced by personal goals compatible with
the expected roles of those in command. A shift from specialized
competence to administrative ascendency, from emphasis on merit to
emphasis on loyalty to superiors, from "staff" interdependence to
"line" interdependence, is required. In place of universal standards of
judgment one must value partisan norms stemming from class culture, group status and college affiliation.[13] One must adhere to
organizational decisions directed by interest in public relations,
"managed consensus" and other instruments of political and economic support. In general, standards of operational efficiency must
be subordinated to standards compatible with the maintenance of
institutional controls.

Conclusion
   Certain unresolved dilemmas spring from legitimacy based on; (1)
hierarchical authority; (2) capacity to perform specialized skills; and,

(3) responsibility for organizational outcomes. If authority is legitimated by reference to specialized skills alone, the absence of specialized skills would make authority illegitimate, a condition which applies to many educational institutions. If authority is legitimated by reference to responsibility alone, the absence of responsibility would make authority illegitimate. The latter occurs when subordinates are held responsible for what is accountable to superordinates. On this analysis, claims in behalf of hierarchical authority have little foundation in educational requirements.

Other dilemmas arising from the assumption that hierarchical authority is essential in educational organizations may be briefly summarized as follows:

(1) Conflict occurs between the administrative requirement of disciplined compliance from automous experts and the latter's commitment to professional standards in the performance of duties.

(2) Conflict occurs between centralized directives based on restricted lines of communication, and the process of collective decision making based on the free exchange of ideas. The latter is essential to responsible problem-solving at all levels of organization.

(3) Conflict occurs between the competitive demand for rationality (advanced planning) and the administrative obstacles to acquiring adequate knowledge of future organizational outcomes.

(4) Conflict occurs between bureaucratized roles designed to maintain stable organizational goals and non-bureaucratized roles developing out of attempts to change or replace goals when organizational survival is threatened.

(5) Conflict occurs between the ascribed status of faculty in the community and their contractual status in school organizations. The former is based largely on tradition (kinship, economic and political class); the latter is based on criteria that represent technical and professional capacity to contribute to educational goals.

(6) Conflict occurs between "staff" expertness and "line" discipline insofar as staff personnel provide knowledge of line operations to administrative superiors. When critical knowledge leads to distrust of line personnel, coordination is difficult. To regain support of line subordinates, staff reports may be upgraded to the point of inaccuracy. When staff reports are known to be inaccurate, line superiors lose their effectiveness. The dilemma remains when the function of staff and line are reversed, as in a university.[14]

(7) Areas of decision-making not covered by bureaucratic rules and regulations are areas where administration and faculty judgments

conflict. Where faculty are defined as experts, administration is powerless to maintain its goals. Where administration is defined as experts, faculty are powerless to innovate.

(8) Administrative hierarchies create conditions which produce conflicting loyalties. The more loyal a superior is to his subordinates the less he will abide by the commands of those above him, and vice versa. Moreover, the more the superior compensates for disloyalty among his subordinates by enforcing organizational rules the more he alienates the latter. Thus hierarchical consensus is never complete.

Given the preceding dilemmas it is apparent that organizational coordination is more effective when founded on democratic choice and group deference (identification, loyalty, solidarity?). In the absence of equal opportunity to develop leadership experience and without some principle for defining a just distribution of rewards, the goals of education cannot be fully realized.

FOOTNOTES

1. This essay is part of a continuous dialogue between the writer, as department chairman, and members of the university faculty who would welcome (they claim) a more centralized administration. The reader should not conclude that the writer has little sympathy for those who occupy positions of authority. Instances in which behavior disruptive of scholarly pursuits cannot be dislodged against the principaled belief that "All academic endeavor is opportunistic," "Power politics is a necessity of life" and "Human communication is always a species of manipulation," invite authoritative decisions. But instances in which administrators must adopt intolerant stances to combat academic intolerance are so seldom that the case against authority appears to be more convincing than many professionals are willing to admit. Significant for education is the fact that the case against authority has yet to receive the kind of throughgoing analysis invested in the case for authority. This brief paper is no more than a preliminary statement on the subject.

2. Of the many essays on authority no two present the same detailed image. Cf. for instance, C. J. Friedrich (ed.), *Authority* (Cambridge: Harvard University Press, 1958).

3. A. E. Duncan-Jones, "Authority," *Aristotelian Society Supplement*, Vol. XXXII (1958) p. 256.

4. A basic question of modern organization concerns the conditions under which authority creates a division of labor which leads to social solidarity. Much of the work in modern factories is so simplified, microscopic, repetitive or automatic that the social needs of workers have few occasions for expression. To produce the kind of coordination that liberates potential solidarity the division of labor should be enlarged to include variable ("polyvalent") activities, allow scope for the worker's imagination and provide opportunities for intergroup planning. In some respects the worker should be able to control the character of the product and through it achieve some measure of personal worth and status.

Unless there is continuity of function between the worker's need to shape materials according to his own dispositions and rhythms and his need for response and interchange with coworkers, the division of labor cannot sustain any meaningful kind of social solidarity. Cf. G. Friedman, *The Anatomy of Work* (Toronto: Heineman, 1956) pp. 68-81.

5. The reader may be less convinced by documentation than by the following kind of sociological logic: (1) Authority rests in part upon status. (2) Status rests upon class, ethnic membership, inheritance, etc. (3) Therefore authority rests in part upon class, ethnic membership, inheritance, etc.

6. Impossible in the sense that no technically competent first rate mind can know as much about the effective instruments of organizational endeavor as a team of technically competent first rate minds, however subordinate the latter.

7. See V. A. Thompson, *Modern Organization,* (New York: Knopf, 1961) pp. 137-51.

8. That higher education has not always favored this arrangement has long been known. Referring to the democracy of the university in the authoritarian life of the Middle Ages, R. G. Bauer writes: "This democracy was expressed in an administrative arrangement whereby the faculty, as a body of equals, collectively made the important decisions concerning institutional standards, policies, organization, administration, control, and relations with the outside world . . . This method of institutional government and administration emphasized the equal status of all members of the faculty and allowed no opportunity for development of an administrative hierarchy or powerful administrators . . ." See *Cases in College Administration* (New York: Columbia, 1953) p. 17.

9. H. A. Simon, *et al* in *Public Administration* (New York: Knopf, 1950) write: "A pyramid of supervisions is needed because no single man can coordinate the activities of a large number of other persons—any individual's span of control is limited." (p. 131) . . . "If there were no acceptance of authority, each element of each decision would have to be examined each time it was communicated from one person to another; and the recipient of the communication would have to convince himself of the proposal. (p. 185). Is it beyond the potentials of any organization to have tiers of successively smaller groups with members composed of communicants chosen from the larger groups to which each belong? If this were done could not the span of *communication* accommodate organizations of any size?

10. It is sometimes claimed that board members are in better position than "partisan" educators to represent the public interest. Apart from the complex problem of what constitutes "representation" one may ask why citizens of average wealth or power are almost always excluded from such boards.

11. It should be said, however, that in universities and liberal arts colleges where academic freedom is prized, administrators often take heroic steps to understand the bases of professional differences, more often, sometimes, than do rank and file faculty.

12. Notwithstanding these remarks, respect for congeniality is essential to prevent the frustrations of research from seriously impeding faculty deliberations and, ultimately, scholarly productivity. Every department, it seems, has an active minority who cannot be satisfied with anything short of a Utopian satisfaction of their needs. Since dissatisfactions arise as rapidly as new needs are satisfied, this minority exemplified the principle that "needs grow with the opportunity to satisfy them." If, then, norms of congeniality are constructed as "species of manipulation" the administrator should make the most of it!

13. Cf. L. Gross, "A Theory of Power and Organizational Processes," *The School Review,* Vol. 70 (Summer, 1962) pp. 149-62.

14. Similar dilemmas are discussed in P. M. Blau and W. R. Scott, *Formal Organizations,* (San Francisco: Chandler Publishing Co., 1962) pp. 173, 225-49.

LISTEN TO WHAT YOU CAN'T HEAR

Norman B. Sigband

Today's executive spends roughly 40 per cent of his work day just listening. The higher he rises in the management hierarchy, the greater that percentage is apt to be, thanks to more meetings, as well as to interviewing, counselling, exchanging of information and decision making.

To the manager, it is vital to listen as the effective salesman must listen—to determine what the "prospect" will buy.

The manager must "sell" his ideas to his superiors; he must persuade his subordinates; he must inform his associates. But in every case he will not be aware of what to sell, how best to persuade, and in what areas to inform, if he first does not listen to those around him.

He must not only listen, he must try to hear what is not said.

Take the case of Supervisor Galvin. Joe has just approached him to report:

"Well, Mr. Galvin, I finally locked up the Bahr Co. order. Boy, was it a mess! But you said it was an emergency job, and I saw to it that it went out today—right on the button. You know, I've been here every night this week and almost all last weekend to tie that darned thing up. Bahr's specifications are ridiculous, but the order is on its way, even though my wife may throw me out. And let me tell you, if I never see another job as tough as that, I'll be plenty happy. It really required blood, sweat and tears."

If Mr. Galvin should answer, "Great, Joe. Now let's get to work on the Sunnyvale order," he hasn't really been listening.

From *Nation's Business*, June 1969, pp. 70-72. Reprinted by permission.

What was Joe really saying? We'll never be sure, but he was not simply saying the Bahr order was difficult. He probably was saying, "How about giving me a pat on the back, Mr. Galvin?" or "Why do you give me all the problem jobs?" or "I hate to work nights."

The sensitive, effective manager will hear what the other fellow often is inhibited from stating directly, due to ego, emotions, position held, or what have you.

Let's tune in on Supervisor Jackson's interview with extremely conscientious Jim Cantonelli, who has just been offered a promotion to section chief.

"I sure appreciate the offer, boss, but I don't think I can handle it. You know I only been in the States seven years, I murder the language, I don't write well. What am I goin' to do about the weekly reports? And I'm not too hot on the reading angle; wow, all those instructions that come down. And the guys laugh now when I try to talk; how can I hold meetings? And you know yourself that all I know about switching systems, I picked up aroung here."

If Supervisor Jackson continues to press, and points out the increased salary, new title, and other ego satisfying factors, Cantonelli may accept. This, however, may place a hard-working production man in a position over his head and result in failure for him, decreased morale in the department, and financial loss to the firm.

What should Jackson have perceived from Cantonelli's reaction to the offer? He probably should have heard him saying, "I'm not ready for the job, I'm afraid to take it on, I don't think the men will be with me."

Obviously a supervisor can't back away from every worker who appears reluctant to accept promotion. Many such promotions work out very well. But when a manager hears a Cantonelli say what he said, that is the time to perceive correctly.

You Have to Concentrate

One basic barrier to effective listening is simply inability to concentrate, which causes facts and ideas to be lost.

Lack of concentration may have several roots. Most of us speak at about 140 words per minute, but we can comprehend at a much faster rate. This permits us to take mental excursions into other areas as we listen.

For a few seconds, the listener thinks about that faulty car transmission; then he returns to the speaker's topic; then he is off again. This time he wonders about the football game: Will it be worth $5.50 per ticket? And again back to the speaker. But what about vacation? Two weeks in September should be O.K. And back to the speaker.

But now the speaker is too far ahead; the listener has missed something vital on one of his excursions. Besides, the topic seems very complex. Oh, well, not concentrating is easier than trying to concentrate. And another listener now is just hearing.

Opinions and prejudices can also cause poor concentration. When a statement the listener doesn't like is made, he may figuratively reach up into his brain and turn the communicator off. Or he may concentrate on a statement with which he disagrees, allowing other statements to go unheard.

The style of the speaker's clothes, the look on his face, his posture, his accent, the color of his skin, his mannerisms, or past experiences with him may also cause the listener to react emotionally and tune him out.

Try to put aside your preconceived ideas or prejudices. The man who is speaking may have a new concept that is worth putting into practice.

And if you want to concentrate, don't try to do something unrelated to the discussion while the man you wish to listen to is talking.

Also, by the way, make him realize you are concentrating. Look directly at him, and sit up straight, Don't protest that you listen best when you are relaxed, hands clasped behind your head and feet propped on the desk. This may be true, but the speaker may see lack of interest and perhaps discourtesy on your part. The result would be a barrier to clear communication.

Listening for Facts

The good listener makes a definite attempt to listen to every statement for facts and for feelings.

In listening for facts, you should first attempt to perceive the theme or the thesis of the presentation. In a speech, this may be stated in the first few minutes. It probably will be noted in different words several times during the talk, and may well serve as a concluding statement.

The basic ideas should then be recognized. What are the four key points in the entire talk? The alert listener will be able to perceive them, even if the speaker doesn't label each specifically. Facts to support the ideas should be assimilated. But once the ideas are firmly fixed in your mind, they will help you recall specific facts.

If you listen analytically, you can recognize major ideas and separate them from minor ones. Of course this requires your full effort. Effective listening is hard work.

Sometimes, you find yourself listening to someone who hasn't organized his ideas too well. He seems to be going in circles. He repeats himself. He barely mentions a key fact. It's up to you to organize his presentation in your mind, as he talks.

Taking notes during the talk will help you retain ideas and facts. But you should never become so absorbed in the task of taking notes that you lose the ideas being transmitted. And if the talk goes on for any length of time, the good listener occasionally will hastily review in his mind the ideas and facts which have already been cited.

All in all, to perceive the facts that are stated, you need to be attentive and analytical, and to develop an ability to be retentive.

Listening for Feelings

Listening for feelings is more difficult.

Here you must try to perceive what is really behind a seemingly obvious statement. You must give, insofar as you are able, the same connotations to words that the other fellow gives. You must also try to recognize his biases and his frame of reference. You must try to remember his salary level and his desires.

When a slow, easygoing man says, "We must get on this job right away," you interpret "right away" as "in a week or two." When an employee you know to be conscientious and slow to give praise calls another a "hard worker," your connotation probably will be very similar to his.

You must constantly "listen" to the other person's nonverbal communications. His inflections, his gestures, his finger tapping, the look in his eyes, and the changing lines in his brow.

If his words say, "Well, it really isn't very important to me anyway," but his posture is stiff, his knuckles white, his eyes hopeful and his forehead glistening with perspiration, you had better hear the nonverbal message. If you don't, communication will not be effective.

Here is a situation similar to one which may have occurred to you or one of your salesmen just yesterday. Mr. Big, President of the Acme Co., is very proud of the newly completed offices for his five immediate subordinates. They had been scattered in different sections of the plant; now they all will be on the same floor with him.

You are trying to sell him office furniture and you tell him you have an especially good buy for his company on five beautiful executive walnut desks. Mr. Big is unimpressed.

"They don't seem quite right," he says. "They're very modern and they look terribly short of drawer space. Of course they are beautiful, but they don't have file drawers. And holy smokes, why does our controller or purchasing head need so much surface area? Why, these desks must be twice as big as mine!"

Now, if you know Mr. Big at all, you should be able to tell what he is really saying.

There is no point in pressing him about how inexpensive, or beautiful or functional the five desks are. For what he is telling you is, "I don't want my subordinates to have bigger, more beautiful desks than mine. It hurts my ego."

Of course, he can't say that. Nevertheless, you must hear what he does say and respond tactfully to it. If you don't—no sale.

The Results

Effective listening on your part produces many salutary results.

First, there will be more effective listening on the other person's part. When he notes that you are sincerely and carefully listening, and not merely waiting for him to pause and inhale so you can jump in, he does not feel threatened. Thus, after he has had his complete say, he is ready to listen carefully to you.

Second, the speaker presents more information which may benefit you. Your careful listening usually will motivate him to cite as many facts as he can. Then you are in a better position to make correct decisions.

Third, your relationship with the speaker often is improved, and you understand him better. He has an opportunity to get facts, ideas and hostilities off his chest. And you may recognize that one man requires frequent praise, while another does not; that one responds favorably to counselling, while another resents it; that he is an extrovert, while she is an introvert.

Everyone wants understanding—with or without agreement—and there is no better way of giving it than through sensitive listening.

A fourth product of careful listening often will be unexpectedly easy solutions to problems. When the other person is permitted to speak in an unthreatening environment, and feels he has the listener's complete attention and respect, he may hear himself more clearly. As a result, solutions may come through to him or you more clearly.

All in all, effective listening, both to what is said and what isn't said, can bring major benefits to a businessman. Too often, the business manager says, "I don't have time to listen carefully." The only reply to that is, "You don't have time NOT to listen carefully."

PARTICIPATIVE MANAGEMENT: TIME FOR A SECOND LOOK

Robert C. Albrook

The management of change has become a central preoccupation of U. S. business. When the directors have approved the record capital budget and congratulated themselves on "progress," when the banquet speaker has used his last superlative to describe the "world of tomorrow," the talk turns, inevitably, to the question: "Who will make it all work?" Some people resist change. Some hold the keys to it. Some admit the need for new ways but don't know how to begin. The question becomes what kind of management can ease the inevitable pains, unlock the talent, energy, and knowledge where they're needed, help valuable men to contribute to and shape change rather than be flattened by it.

The recipe is elusive, and increasingly business has turned to the academic world for help, particularly to the behavioral scientists—the psychologists, sociologists, and anthropologists whose studies have now become the showpieces of the better business schools. A number of major corporations, such as General Electric, Texas Instruments, and Standard Oil (N. J.), have brought social scientists onto their staffs. Some companies collaborate closely with university-based scholars and are contributing importantly to advanced theoretical work, just as industry's physicists, chemists, and engineers have become significant contributors of new knowledge in their respective realms. Hundreds of companies, large and small, have tried one or

Albrook, Robert C., "Participative Management: Time for a Second Look," *Fortune*, May 1967, pp. 199-214. Reprinted from the May 1967 issue of Fortune Magazine by special permission; © 1967 Time Inc.

another formulation of basic behavioral theory, such as the many schemes for sharing cost savings with employees and actively soliciting their ideas for improved efficiency.

For forty years the quantity and quality of academic expertise in this field have been steadily improving, and there has lately been a new burst of ideas which suggest that the researchers in the business schools and other centers of learning are really getting down to cases. The newest concepts already represent a considerable spin-off from the appealingly simple notions on which the behavioral pioneers first concentrated. The essential message these outriders had for business was this: recognize the social needs of employees in their work, as well as their need for money; they will respond with a deeper commitment and better performance, help to shape the organization's changing goals and make them their own. For blue-collar workers this meant such steps as organizing work around tasks large enough to have meaning and inviting workers' ideas; for middle and upper management it meant more participation in decision making, wider sharing of authority and responsibility, more open and more candid communication, up, down, and sideways.

The new work suggests that neither the basic philosophy nor all of the early prescriptions of this management style were scientifically sound or universally workable. The word from the behavioral scientists is becoming more specific and "scientific," less simple and moralistic. At Harvard, M.I.T., the University of Michigan, Chicago, U.C.L.A., Stanford, and elsewhere, they are mounting bigger, longer, and more rigorous studies of the human factors in management than ever before undertaken.

One conclusion is that the "participative" or "group" approach doesn't seem to work with all people and in all situations. Research has shown that satisfied, happy workers are sometimes more productive—and sometimes merely happy. Some managers and workers are able to take only limited responsibility, however much the company tries to give them. Some people will recognize the need to delegate but "can't let go." In a profit squeeze the only way to get costs under control fast enough often seems to be with centralized, "get tough" management.

Few, if any, behaviorists espouse a general return to authoritarian management. Instead, they are seeking a more thorough, systematic way to apply participative principles on a sustained schedule that will give the theory a better chance to work. Others are insisting that management must be tailor-made, suited to the work or the people, rather than packaged in a standard mixture. Some people aren't and never will be suited for "democracy" on the job, according to one viewpoint, while others insist that new kinds of psychological training can fit most executives for the rugged give-and-take of successful group management.

As more variables are brought into their concepts, and as they look increasingly at the specifics of a management situation, the behaviorists are also being drawn toward collaboration with the systems designers and the theorists of data processing. Born in reaction to the cold scientism of the earlier "scientific management" experts with their stopwatches and measuring tapes, the "human relations" or behavioral school of today may be getting ready at last to bury that hatchet in a joint search for a broadly useful "general theory" of management.

Why Executives Don't Practice What They Preach

Before any general theory can be evolved, a great deal more has to be known about the difficulty of putting theory into practice—i.e., of transforming a simple managerial attitude into an effective managerial style. "There are plenty of executives," observes Stanley Seashore, a social psychologist at the University of Michigan's Institute for Social Research, "who'll decide one morning they're going to be more participative and by the afternoon have concluded it doesn't work."

What's often lacking is an understanding of how deeply and specifically management style affects corporate operations. The executive who seeks a more effective approach needs a map of the whole terrain of management activity. Rensis Likert, director of the Michigan institute, has developed a chart to assist managers in gaining a deeper understanding of the way they operate. A simplified version is on pp. 122-123. By answering the questions in the left-hand column of the chart (e.g., "Are subordinates' ideas sought and used?"), an executive sketches a profile of the way his company is run and whether it leans to the "authoritative" or the "participative." Hundreds of businessmen have used the chart, under Likert's direction, and many have discovered a good deal they didn't realize about the way they were handling people.

Likert leads his subjects in deliberate steps to a conclusion that most of them do not practice what they say they believe. First, the executive is asked to think of the most successful company (or division of a company) he knows intimately. He then checks off on the chart his answers as they apply to that company. When the executive has finished this exercise, he has nearly always traced the profile of a strongly "participative" management system, well to the right on Likert's chart. He is next asked to repeat the procedure for the least successful company (or division) he knows well. Again, the profiles are nearly always the same, but this time they portray a strongly "authoritative" system, far to the left on the chart.

Then comes the point of the exercise. The executive is asked to describe his own company or division. Almost always, the resulting profile is that of a company somewhere in the middle, a blend of the "benevolent authoritative" and the "consultative"—well to the left of what the executive had previously identified as the most success-ful style. To check out the reliability of this self-analysis, Likert sometimes asks employees in the same company or division to draw its profile, too. They tend to rate it as slightly more "authoritative" than the boss does.

Likert believes that the predominant management style in U. S. industry today falls about in the middle of his chart, even though most managers seem to know from personal observation of other organizations that a more participative approach works better. What accounts for their consistent failure to emulate what they consider successful? Reaching for a general explanation, Likert asks his sub-jects one final question: "In your experience, what happens when the senior officer becomes concerned about earnings and takes steps to cut costs, increase productivity, and improve profits?" Most reply that the company's management profile shifts left, toward the au-thoritarian style. General orders to economize—and promptly—often result in quick, across-the-board budget cuts. Some programs with high potential are sacrificed along with obvious losers. Carefully laid, logical plans go down the drain. Some people are laid off—usually the least essential ones. But the best people in the organization sooner or later rebel at arbitrary decisions, and many of them leave.

At the outset, the arbitrary cost cutting produces a fairly prompt improvement in earnings, of course. But there is an unrecognized trade-off in the subsequent loss of human capital, which shows up still later in loss of business. In due course, management has to "swing right" again, rebuilding its human assets at great expense in order to restore good performance. Yet the manager who puts his firm through this dreary cycle, Likert observes, is often rewarded with a bonus at the outset, when things still look good. Indeed, he may be sent off to work his magic in another division!

Likert acknowledges that there are emergencies when sharp and sudden belt-tightening is inescapable. The trouble, he says, is that it is frequently at the expense of human assets and relationships that have taken years to build. Often it would make more sense to sell off inventory or dispose of a plant. But such possibilities are overlooked because human assets do not show up in the traditional balance sheet the way physical assets do. A company can, of course, lose $100,000 worth of talent and look better on its statement than if it sells $10,000 worth of inventory at half price.

A dollars-and-cents way of listing the value of a good engineering staff, an experienced shop crew, or an executive group with effective, established working relations might indeed steady the hand of a hard-pressed president whose banker is on the phone. Likert believes he is now on the trail of a way to assign such values—values that should be at least as realistic as the often arbitrary and outdated figures given for real estate and plant. It will take some doing to get the notion accepted by bankers and accountants, however sophisticated his method turns out to be. But today's executives are hardly unaware that their long payrolls of expensive scientific and managerial talent represent an asset as well as an expense. Indeed, it is an asset that is often bankable. A merely more regular, explicit recognition of human assets in cost-cutting decisions would help to ensure that human assets get at least an even break with plant and inventory in time of trouble.

Likert and his institute colleagues are negotiating with several corporations to enlist them in a systematic five-year study, in effect a controlled experiment, that should put a firmer footing under tentative conclusions and hypotheses. This study will test Likert's belief that across-the-board participative management, carefully developed, sustained through thick and thin, and supported by a balance sheet that somehow reckons the human factor, will show better long-run results than the cyclical swing between authoritarian and participative styles reflected in the typical middle-ground profile on his chart.

Conversion in a Pajama Factory

Already there's enough evidence in industry experience to suggest that participative management gets in trouble when it is adopted too fast. In some cases, an authoritarian management has abruptly ordered junior executives or employees to start taking on more responsibility, not recognizing that the directive itself reasserted the fact of continuing centralized control. Sometimes, of course, a hard shove may be necessary, as in the recent experience of Harwood Manufacturing Corp. of Marion, Virginia, which has employed participative practices widely for many years. When it acquired a rival pajama maker, Weldon Manufacturing Co., the latter's long-held authoritarian traditions were hard to crack. With patient but firm prodding by outside consultants, who acknowledged an initial element of "coercion," the switch in style was finally accomplished.

Ideally, in the view of Likert and others, a move of this kind should begin with the patient education of top executives, followed by the development of the needed skills in internal communication, group leadership, and the other requisites of the new system. Given time, this will produce better employee attitudes and begin to harness personal motivation to corporate goals. Still later, there will be improved productivity, less waste, lower turnover and absence rates, fewer grievances and slowdowns, improved product quality, and, finally, better customer relations.

The transformation may take several years. A checkup too early in the game might prove that participative management, even when thoroughly understood and embraced at the top, doesn't produce better results. By the same token, a management that is retreating from the new style in a typical cost squeeze may still be nominally participative, yet may already have thrown away the fruits of the system. Some research findings do indicate that participation isn't producing the hoped-for results. In Likert's view, these were spot checks, made without regard to which way the company was tending and where it was in the cycle of change.

A growing number of behaviorists, however, have begun to question whether the participative style is an idea toward which all management should strive. If they once believed it was, more as a matter of faith in their long struggle against the "scientific" manager's machine-like view of man than as a finding from any new science of their own, they now are ready to take a second look at the proposition.

It seems plain enough that a research scientist generally benefits from a good deal of freedom and autonomy, and that top executives, confronted every day by new problems that no routine can anticipate, operate better with maximum consultation and uninhibited contributions from every member of the team. If the vice president for finance can't talk candidly with the vice president for production about financing the new plant, a lot of time can be wasted. In sales, group effort—instead of the usual competition—can be highly productive. But in the accounting department, things must go by the book. "Creative accounting" sounds more like a formula for jail than for the old behaviorists' dream of personal self-fulfillment on the job.

And so with quality control in the chemical plant. An inspired adjustment here and there isn't welcome, thank you; just follow the specifications.

In the production department, automation has washed out a lot of the old problem of man as a prisoner of the assembly line, the kind of problem that first brought the "human relations" experts into the factories in the 1920's and 1930's. If a shop is full of computer-controlled machine tools busily reproducing themselves, the boy with the broom who sweeps away the shavings may be the only one who can put a personal flourish into his work. The creativity is all upstairs in the engineering and programing departments. But then, so are most of the people.

"Look what's happened in the last twenty years," says Harold J. Leavitt, a social psychologist who recently moved to Stanford after some years at Carnegie Tech. "Originally the concern of the human-relations people was with the blue-collar worker. Then the focus began to shift to foremen and to middle management. Now it's concentrated in special areas like research and development and in top management. Why? Because the 'group' style works best where nobody knows exactly and all the time what they're supposed to be doing, where there's a continuous need to change and adapt."

Democracy Works Better in Plastics

One conclusion that has been drawn from this is that management style has to be custom-designed to fit the particular characteristics of each industry. The participative approach will work best in those industries that are in the vanguard of change. A Harvard Business School study has compared high-performance companies in three related, but subtly different, fields: plastics, packaged food, and standard containers. The plastics company faced the greatest uncertainties and change in research, new products, and market developments. The food company's business was somewhat more stable, while the container company encountered little or no requirement for innovation. The three achieved good results using markedly different management styles. The plastics firm provided for wide dispersal of responsibility for major decisions, the food company for moderate decentralization of authority, and the container company operated with fairly centralized control.

Less successful enterprises in each of the three industries were also examined, and their managements were compared with those of the high-performance companies. From this part of the study, Harvard researchers Paul Lawrence and Jay Lorsch drew another conclusion:

not only may each industry have its own appropriate management style, but so may the individual operations within the same company. The companies that do best are those which allow for variations among their departments and know how to take these variations into account in coordinating the whole corporate effort.

Both the sales and the research departments in a fast-moving plastics company, for example, may adopt a style that encourages employees to participate actively in departmental decision making. But in special ways the two operations still need to differ. The research worker, for example, thinks in long-range terms, focusing on results expected in two or three years. The sales executive has his sights set on results next week or next month. This different sense of time may make it hard for the two departments to understand each other. But if top management recognizes the reasons and the need for such differences, each department will do its own job better, and they can be better coordinated. On the other hand, if top management ignores the differences and insists, for example, on rigidly uniform budgeting and planning timetables, there will be a loss of effectiveness.

It seems an obvious point that sales must be allowed to operate like sales, accounting like accounting, and production like production. But as Lawrence comments, "The mark of a good idea in this field is that as soon as it is articulated, it does seem obvious. People forget that, five minutes before, it wasn't. One curse of the behavioral scientist is that anything he comes up with is going to seem that way, because anything that's good *is* obvious."

People, Too, Have Their Styles

Other behavioral scientists take the view that management style should be determined not so much by the nature of the particular business operation involved, but by the personality traits of the people themselves. There may be some tendency for certain kinds of jobs to attract certain kinds of people. But in nearly any shop or office a wide range of personality types may be observed. There is, for example, the outgoing, socially-oriented scientist as well as the supposedly more typical introverted recluse. There are mature, confident managers, and there are those who somehow fill the job despite nagging self-doubt and a consuming need for reassurance.

For a long time, personality tests seemed to offer a way to steer people into the psychologically right kind of work. Whether such testing for placement is worthwhile is now a matter of some dispute. In any case, the whole question of individual differences is often

reduced to little more than an office guessing game. Will Sue cooperate with Jane? Can Dorothy stand working for Jim? Will Harry
take suggestions?

The participative approach to management may be based upon a
greatly oversimplified notion about people, in the view of psychologist Clare Graves of Union College in Schenectady, New York. On
the basis of limited samplings, he tentatively concludes that as many
as half the people in the northeastern U. S., and a larger proportion
nationwide, are not and many never will be the eager-beaver workers
on whom the late Douglas McGregor of M.I.T. based his "Theory Y."
Only some variation of old-style authoritarian management will meet
their psychological needs, Graves contends.

Graves believes he has identified seven fairly distinct personality
types, although he acknowledges that many people are not "pure-
breds" who would fit his abstractions perfectly and that new and
higher personality forms may still be evolving. At the bottom of his
well-ordered hierarchy he places the childlike "autistic" personality,
which requires "close care and nurturing." Next up the scale are the
"animistic" type, which must be dealt with by sheer force or entice-
ment; the "ordered" personality that responds best to a moralistic
management; and the "materialistic" individual who calls for pragmatic, hard bargaining. None of these are suited for the participative
kind of management.

At the top of Graves's personality ladder are the "sociocentric,"
the "cognitive," and the "apprehending" types of people. They are
motivated, respectively, by a need for "belonging," for "information," and for an "understanding" of the total situation in which
they are involved. For each of these levels some form of participative
management will work. However, those at the very top, the unemo-
tional "apprehending" individuals, must be allowed pretty much to
set their own terms for work. Management can trust such people to
contribute usefully only according to their own cool perception of
what is needed. They will seldom take the trouble to fight authority
when they disagree with it, but merely withdraw, do a passable but
not excellent job, and wait for management to see things their way.
In that sense, these highest-level people are probably not ideal
participators.

Graves believes most adults are stuck at one level throughout their
lifetimes or move up a single notch, at best. He finds, incidentally,
that there can be bright or dull, mature or immature behavior at
nearly all levels. The stages simply represent psychological growth
toward a larger and larger awareness of the individual's relationship
to society.

If a company has a mixture of personality types, as most do, it must somehow sort them out. One way would be to place participative-type managers in charge of some groups, and authoritarian managers in charge of others. Employees would then be encouraged to transfer into sections where the management style best suits them. This would hardly simplify corporate life. But companies pushing the group approach might at least avoid substituting harmful new rigidities—"participate, or else!"—for the old ones.

The Anthropological View

Behaviorists who have been studying management problems from an anthropological viewpoint naturally stress cultural rather than individual differences. Manning Nash, of the University of Chicago's business school, for example, observes that the American emphasis on egalitarianism and performance has always tempered management style in the U. S. "No matter what your role is, if you don't perform, no one in this country will defer to you," he says. "Americans won't act unless they respect you. You couldn't have an American Charge of the Light Brigade." But try to export that attitude to a country with a more autocratic social tradition, and, in the words of Stanley Davis of Harvard, "it won't be bought and may not be workable."

Diagnose Your Management

The chart on the next two pages is adapted from a technique developed by Rensis Likert, director of the Institute of Social Research at the University of Michigan, to help businessmen analyze the management style used by their companies. Anyone—executive or employee—can use it to diagnose his own company or division. Check the appropriate answers, using the guide marks to shade your emphasis. After the first question, for example, if your answer is "almost none," put the check in the first or second notch of the "none" box. Regard each answer as a sort of rating on a continuous scale from the left to the right of the chart. When you have answered each question, draw a line from the top to the bottom of the chart through the check marks. The result will be a profile of your management. To determine which way management style has been shifting, repeat the process for the situation as it was three, five, or ten years ago. Finally, sketch the profile you think would help your company or division to improve its performance. Likert has tried the chart on a number of business executives. Most of them rated their own companies about in the middle—embracing features of System 2 and 3. But nearly all of them also believe that companies do best when they have profiles well to the right of the chart, and worse with profiles well to the left.

			System 1 Exploitive Authoritative	System 2 Benevolent Authoritative	System 3 Consultative	System 4 Participative Group
LEADERSHIP	1.	How much confidence is shown in subordinates?	None	Condescending	Substantial	Complete
	2.	How free do they feel to talk to superiors about job?	Not at all	Not very	Rather free	Fully free
	3.	Are subordinates' ideas sought and used, if worthy?	Seldom	Sometimes	Usually	Always
MOTIVATION	4.	Is predominant use made of 1 fear, 2 threats, 3 punishment, 4 rewards, 5 involvement?	1, 2, 3, occasionally 4	4, some 3	4, some 3 and 5	5, 4, based on group set goals
	5.	Where is responsibility felt for achieving organization's goals?	Mostly at top	Top and middle	Fairly general	At all levels
	6.	How much communication is aimed at achieving organization's objectives?	Very little	Little	Quite a bit	A great deal
COMMUNICATION	7.	What is the direction of information flow?	Downward	Mostly downward	Down and up	Down, up, and sideways
	8.	How is downward communication accepted?	With suspicion	Possibly with suspicion	With caution	With an open mind
	9.	How accurate is upward communication?	Often wrong	Censored for the boss	Limited accuracy	Accurate
	10.	How well do superiors know problems faced by subordinates?	Know little	Some knowledge	Quite well	Very well

DECISIONS	11. At what level are decisions formally made?	Mostly at top	Policy at top, some delegation	Broad policy at top, more delegation	Throughout but well integrated
	12. What is the origin of technical and professional knowledge used in decision making?	Top management	Upper and middle	To a certain extent, throughout	To a great extent, throughout
	13. Are subordinates involved in decisions related to their work?	Not at all	Occasionally consulted	Generally consulted	Fully involved
	14. What does decision-making process contribute to motivation?	Nothing, often weakens it	Relatively little	Some contribution	Substantial contribution
GOALS	15. How are organizational goals established?	Orders issued	Orders, some comment invited	After discussion, by orders	By group action (except in crisis)
	16. How much covert resistance to goals is present?	Strong resistance	Moderate resistance	Some resistance at times	Little or none
CONTROL	17. How concentrated are review and control functions?	Highly at top	Relatively highly at top	Moderate delegation to lower levels	Quite widely shared
	18. Is there an informal organization resisting the formal one?	Yes	Usually	Sometimes	No—same goals as formal
	19. What are cost, productivity, and other control data used for?	Policing, punishment	Reward and punishment	Reward, some self-guidance	Self-guidance, problem solving

Adapted with permission, from *The Human Organization: Its Management and Value*, by Rensis Likert, published in April, 1967, by McGraw-Hill.

Within the U. S. there are many cultural differences that might provide guides to managerial style if they could be successfully analyzed. Recent research by Lawrence and Arthur N. Turner at the Harvard Business School hints at important differences between blue-collar workers in cities and those in smaller towns, although religious and other factors fog the results. Town workers seem to seek "a relatively large amount of variety, autonomy, interaction, skill and responsibility" in their work, whereas city workers "find more simple tasks less stress-producing and more satisfying."

In managerial areas where democratic techniques *are* likely to work, the problem is how to give managers skill and practice in participation. The National Education Association's National Training Laboratories twenty years ago pioneered a way of doing this called "sensitivity training" (see "Two Weeks in a T Group," *Fortune*, August, 1961). Small groups of men, commonly drawn from the executive ranks, sit down with a professional trainer but without agenda or rule book and "see what happens." The "vacuum" draws out first one and then another participant, in a way that tends to expose in fairly short order how he comes across to others.

The technique has had many critics, few more vocal than William Gomberg of the University of Pennsylvania's Wharton School. Renewing his assault recently, he called the "training" groups "titillating therapy, management development's most fashionable fad." When people from the same company are in the group, he argues, the whole exercise is an invasion of privacy, an abuse of the therapeutic technique to help the company, not the individual. For top executives in such groups, Gomberg and others contend, the technique offers mainly a catharsis for their loneliness or insecurity.

"Psyching Out the Boss"
Undoubtedly the T group can be abused, intentionally or otherwise. But today's sensitivity trainers are trying to make sure the experience leads to useful results for both the individual and his firm. They realize that early groups, made up of total strangers gathered at some remote "cultural island," often gave the executive little notion of how to apply his new knowledge back on the job. To bring more realism to the exercise, the National Training Laboratories began ten years ago to make up groups of executives and managers from the same company, but not men who had working relationships with one another. These "cousin labs" have led, in turn, to some training of actual management "families," a boss and his subordinates. At the West Coast headquarters of the T Group movement, the business

school at U.C.L.A., some now call such training "task-group therapy."

Many businessmen insist T Groups have helped them. Forty-three presidents and chairmen and hundreds of lesser executives are National Training Laboratories alumni. U.C.L.A. is besieged by applicants, and many are turned away.

Sensitivity training is supposed to help most in business situations where there is a great deal of uncertainty, as there is in the training sessions themselves. In such situations in the corporate setting there is sometimes a tendency for executives to withdraw, to defer action, to play a kind of game with other people in the organization to see who will climb out on a limb first. A chief ploy is "psyching out the boss," which means trying to anticipate the way the winds of ultimate decision will blow and to set course accordingly.

The aim of sensitivity training is to stop all this, to get the executive's nerve up so that he faces facts, or, in the words of U.C.L.A.'s James V. Clark, to "lay bare the stress and strain faster and get a resolution of the problem." In that limited sense, such therapy could well serve any style of management. In Clark's view, this kind of training, early in the game, might save many a company a costly detour on the road to company-wide "democracy." He cites the experience of Non-Linear Systems, Inc. of Del Mar, California, a manufacturer of such electronic gear as digital voltmeters and data-logging equipment and an important supplier to aerospace contractors. The company is headed by Andrew Kay, leading champion of the participative style. At the lower levels, Kay's application of participative concepts worked well. He gave workers responsibility for "the whole black box," instead of for pieces of his complex finished products. Because it was still a box, with some definite boundaries, the workers siezed the new opportunity without fear or hesitation. The psychological magic of meaningful work, as opposed to the hopelessly specialized chore, took hold. Productivity rose.

Vice Presidents in Midair

But at the executive level, Kay moved too quickly, failing to prepare his executives for broad and undefined responsibilities—or failing to choose men better suited for the challenge. One vice president was put in charge of "innovation." Suspended in midair, without the support of departments or functional groups and lacking even so much as a job description, most of the V.P.'s became passive and incapable of making decisions. "They lost touch with reality—including the reality of the market," recalls Clark. When the industry suffered a general slump and new competition entered the field, Non-Linear wasn't ready. Sales dropped 16 percent, according to Kay. In time he realized he was surrounded with dependent men, untrained to participate in the fashion he had peremptorily commanded. He trimmed his executive group and expects to set a new sales record this year.

Sheldon Davis of TRW Systems in Redondo Beach, California, blames the behavioral scientists themselves for breakdowns like Non-Linear's. Too often, he argues, "their messages come out sounding soft and easy, as if what we are trying to do is build happy teams of employees who feel 'good' about things, rather than saying we're trying to build effective organizations with groups that function well and that can zero in quickly on their problems and deal with them rationally."

To Davis, participation should mean "tough, open exchange," focused on the problem, not the organizational chart. Old-style managers who simply dictate a solution are wrong, he argues, and so are those new-style managers who think the idea is simply to go along with a subordinate's proposals if they're earnestly offered. Neither approach taps the full potential of the executive group. When problems are faced squarely, Davis believes, the boss—who should remain boss—gets the best solution because all relevant factors are thoroughly considered. And because everyone has contributed to the solution and feels responsible for it, it is also the solution most likely to be carried out.

One of the most useful new developments in the behavioral study of management is a fresh emphasis on collaboration with technology. In the early days of the human-relations movement in industry, technology was often regarded as "the enemy," the source of the personal and social problems that the psychologists were trying to treat. But from the beginning, some social scientists wanted to move right in and help fashion machines and industrial processes so as to reduce or eliminate their supposedly anti-human effects. Today this concept is more than mere talk. The idea is to develop so-called "socio-technical" systems that permit man and technology *together* to produce the best performance.

Some early experimentation in the British coal mines, by London's Tavistock Institute, as well as scattered work in this country and in Scandinavia, have already demonstrated practical results from such a collaboration. Tavistock found that an attempt to apply specialized factory-style technology to coal mining had isolated the miners from one another. They missed the sense of group support and self-direction that had helped them cope with uncertainty and danger deep in the coal faces. Productivity suffered. In this case, Tavistock's solution was to redesign the new system so that men could still work in groups.

In the U. S. a manufacturer of small household appliances installed some highly sophisticated new technical processes that put the company well in the front of its field. But the engineers had broken down the jobs to such an extent that workers were getting no satisfaction out of their performance and productivity declined. Costs went up and, in the end, some of the new machinery had to be scrapped.

Some technologists seem more than ready to welcome a partnership with the human-relations expert. Louis Davis, a professor of engineering, has joined the U.C.L.A. business-school faculty to lead a six-man socio-technical research group that includes several behaviorists. Among them is Eric Trist, a highly respected psychologist from the Tavistock Institute. Davis hopes today's collaboration will lead in time to a new breed of experts knowledgeable in both the engineering and the social disciplines.

"It's Time We Stopped Building Rival Dictionaries"

The importance of time, the nature of the task, the differences within a large organization, the nature of the people, the cultural setting, the psychological preparation of management, the relationship to technology—all these and other variables are making the search for effective managerial style more and more complex. But the growing recognition of these complexities has drained the human-relations movement of much of its antagonism toward the "super-rationalism" of management science. Humanists must be more systematic and rational if they are to make some useful sense of the scattered and half-tested concepts they have thus far developed, and put their new theories to a real test.

A number of behaviorists believe it is well past time to bury the hatchet and collaborate in earnest with the mathematicians and economists. Some business schools and commercial consulting groups are already realigning their staffs to encourage such work. It won't be easy. Most "systems" thinkers are preoccupied with bringing all the relevant knowledge to bear on a management problem in a systematic way, seeking the theoretically "best" solution. Most behaviorists have tended to assume that the solution which is *most likely to be carried out* is the best one, hence their focus on involving lots of people in the decision making so that they will follow through.

Where the "experts" who shape decisions are also in charge of getting the job done, the two approaches sometimes blend, in practice. But in many organizations, it is a long, long road from a creative and imaginative decision to actual performance. A general theory of management must show how to build systematic expertise into a style that is also well suited to people.

The rapprochement among management theorists has a distinguished herald, Fritz J. Roethlisberger of Harvard Business School, one of the human-relations pioneers who first disclosed the potential of the "small group" in industrial experiments forty years ago. He laughs quickly at any suggestion that a unified approach will come easily. "But after all, we are all looking at the same thing," he says. "It's time we stopped building rival dictionaries and learned to make some sentences that really say something."

PERSONAL ADJUSTMENT AND CONFLICT
IN THE WORK ORGANIZATION

Arnold S. Tannenbaum

Man versus Organization

The conflict between man and organization has interested social philosophers for some time. One of the historical roots of this interest can be traced to Rousseau, who saw in institutionalization the destruction of man's true and better nature. Karl Marx and a number of other sociological theorists have written about the frustrations imposed on man by the nature of industrial organization. The conflict lies partly in the specialization and routinization of mass production and partly in the worker's lack of control over his work or over his destiny in the organization. According to Marx, the worker is "separated" from the means of production, which he does not own, and suffers "alienation"—a sense of powerlessness and a lack of positive identity with his work (106, 135).*

Contemporary social critics also have been concerned with the relationship of man to the organization in which he works. The term *organization man* has become common parlance since Whyte's "exposé" of the pressures for conformity among middle-level executives. These executives not only work for the organization, they *belong* to it. "They are the ones of our middle class who have left home, spiritually as well as physically, to take the vows of organization life, and it is they who are the mind and soul of our great

---

*See References printed at end of article.—Ed.

From *Social Psychology of the Work Organization* by Arnold S. Tannenbaum. © 1966 by Wadsworth Publishing Company, Inc., Belmont, California 94002. Reprinted by permission of the publisher, Brooks/Cole Publishing Company.

self-perpetuating institutions" (177, p. 3). The pressures toward conformity in organizations have been portrayed in the extreme through the fiction of Huxley and of Orwell. "Round pegs in square holes," as Huxley puts it, "tend to have dangerous thoughts about the social system and to infect others with their discontent" (73, p. xvi). Although the analogy lacks subtlety, one might say that the formal organization *does* imply square holes, and *some* people, at least, are round.

The issue of man versus organization was posed for psychologists a number of years ago by F. H. Allport, who stressed the importance of individual differences in the personal characteristics of organization members.

> There are many individuals having degrees of [a] trait which cannot be expressed if the individual is to act in obedience to the institutional requirement or in line with the general pattern of conformity. Social standardization thus means the thwarting of biological individual differences in function, and an acute problem for those who are trying to adjust their deviating personal characteristics to the system. Machine industry, which pushes the institutional mode up to the highest point in order to conform with a standardized pace of the machinery, is an extreme example. The worries and tensions which workers experience in their efforts to adjust their individual differences to this standard requirement play their part in the familiar occupational neuroses. In lesser degree, perhaps, the same problem arises throughout most of our business and professional life (3, p. 247).[1]

Not all observers of the industrial scene have agreed with the dire representations of industrial organization offered by social critics. Mary Parker Follett, the practical philosopher whose writings during the 1920s and 1930s had a significant impact on the thinking of many professors and some administrators, argued strenuously that organizations need not be frustrating or debasing to workers (109). In her view, the personal needs of members can be reconciled with the major purposes and requirements of organization, and all conflicts can be resolved "integratively"—in a way that is advantageous to everyone. But this hope requires attention to problems of "human relations" in a way that has been lacking in most approaches to administration. Many who share Follett's view see justification for her optimism in the results of the Hawthorne experiments. This research seemed to provide concrete evidence for the power of "human relations" in organizations and, more significantly, it offered some clues to how this power might be tapped.

Thus, the Hawthorne research has become one of the cornerstones of the "human-relations movement" in industry. A chief proponent of this movement was a Harvard Business School professor named Elton Mayo. Mayo stressed the overriding commonality of interest of all persons in the industrial organization. Conflict in organizations was for him a manifestation of "social disease"; cooperation was the more normal, "healthy" state of affairs. The Hawthorne test room epitomized for Mayo the kind of spontaneous cooperation that is latent in every industrial organization. Furthermore, it had the qualities of Follett's integrative solution: management's goal of efficiency advanced at the same time that the workers furthered their own "self-interest"; the girls earned higher wages, and what is more, they derived a considerable degree of satisfaction from their work.

This last point has not been lost on psychologists who have a natural penchant for studying satisfaction and other indices of personal adjustment. These variables in the organizational setting are distinctly psychological rather than administrative, sociological, or economic. Furthermore, these variables seemed to hold the key to productive efficiency—provided that the results of the Hawthorne experiments had any validity. For psychologists to have believed otherwise would have been less than natural.

Because some industrial managers also became interested in the possible relationship between job satisfaction and productivity, a growing number of studies since the 1930s have investigated (a) the attitudes of workers toward their work and (b) the relationship of these attitudes to productivity and to other factors on the job.

Morale and Worker Performance

Psychologists plunged into the study of morale and productivity with a mixture of faith and scientific zeal, setting out to document in business and industrial organizations generally what the Hawthorne research seemed to imply for the Western Electric test room: that the satisfied worker is a productive worker. Approximately thirty years and as many research studies later, however, psychologists must admit that the results of these studies are disappointingly tenuous. Some studies did show a positive association between the morale of workers and their level of productivity; but it is not always clear that positive attitudes *caused* the high productivity rather than vice versa. Moreover, the relationships found in many of these studies are weak, a number of the studies show no relationship at all, and a few even suggest a negative association.[2] In some cases, the results of these analyses were ironic. For example, Figure 1 shows the relationship between the productivity of a group of office workers and their participation in their company's recreational program. The figure

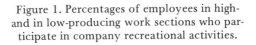

Figure 1. Percentages of employees in high-
and in low-producing work sections who participate in company recreational activities.

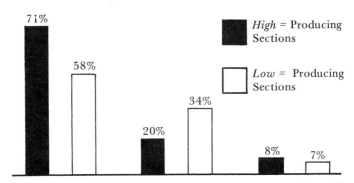

Never Participate   Occasionally Participate   Frequently Participate

(Adapted from Katz et al., 81, p. 58.)

shows that workers in high-producing sections participated less in the recreation program than did those in the low-producing sections. These recreational activities, which were designed at some expense to boost the morale of employees, obviously did not have the desired effect on the workers' productive efforts.

Psychologists do not agree fully about the meaning of these researches, but apparently the relationship between worker attitudes and productivity is not a direct and simple one. One weakness in the hypothesis that associates productivity with satisfaction is the failure to distinguish between satisfaction and motivation. Insofar as his needs are met, a person may be satisfied with his work. But his satisfaction indicates little about his motivation to work—particularly when his satisfaction does not depend on the amount of effort he puts into his work. Although job satisfaction may sometimes be associated with high productivity, as it evidently was in the Hawthorne test room, both of these variables are likely to be part of a more complex set of relationships.

Other indices of worker performance, however, may bear a more direct relationship to job satisfaction than does productivity. Measures of turnover and absenteeism, for example, correlate negatively with indices of worker morale (70, 169). Persons who dislike their jobs or their working conditions usually withdraw in one way or

Figure 2. Relationship between absenteeism
and satisfaction with wages.

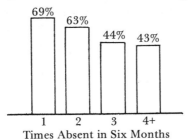

Per Cent Satisfied With Present Wages

Times Absent in Six Months

(From Mann and Baumgartel, 103, p. 19.)

another. For example, Ross and Zander found significant differences between two kinds of female skilled workers in a large company (127): those who quit were less satisfied with the recognition they obtained on their jobs, with their sense of achievement, and with their degree of autonomy than were those who continued their employment. Mann and Baumgartel (103) compared work groups that had high absence rates with groups that had low absence rates, and found that workers in the latter groups were relatively more satisfied than the others with their jobs, supervisors, work associates, wages, promotional opportunities, and the company in general. Figure 2, taken from the Mann-Baumgartel study, shows the relationship between absenteeism and satisfaction with wages for white-collar men.

Thus, although members' feelings of satisfaction are not directly related to productivity, these feelings do affect absenteeism and turnover. Furthermore, the satisfactions and dissatisfactions of members reflect important adjustments and conflicts in the organization. What are some of the factors that explain these adjustments and conflicts? We can begin our answer to this question by observing the effects of one of the most rudimentary elements of formal organization—the organizational hierarchy.

Hierarchy and Adjustment

The data of Figure 3 were collected during World War II by a group of psychologists, sociologists, and statisticians who produced the first major statistical study of attitudes in a large organization (150). This figure shows a relationship for the U. S. Army that is typical of the work organization; that is, persons at higher ranks are

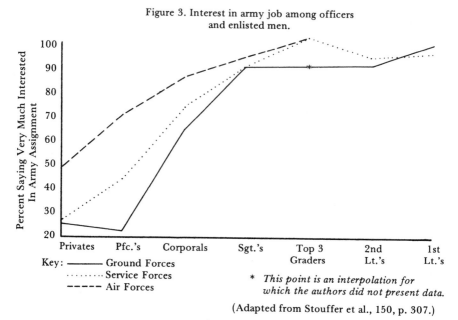

Figure 3. Interest in army job among officers
and enlisted men.

Key: ——— Ground Forces
········· Service Forces
––––– Air Forces

* *This point is an interpolation for
which the authors did not present data.*

(Adapted from Stouffer et al., 150, p. 307.)

Reprinted by permission of Princeton University Press.

generally more interested in or satisfied with their jobs than are
persons at lower levels. They are also more involved and personally
identified with their work, and their attitudes toward the organization itself are more favorable. These relationships are so general that
students of organization may react with surprise when exceptions to
them are found.

Organizational hierarchies are marked by several formal gradients,
which correlate with job satisfaction as shown in Figure 3. These
gradients are basic in explaining the relationship between rank and
adjustment. Although we shall discuss them under three separate
headings, the elements under each heading are interrelated.

Authority

Authority is generally distributed hierarchically in organizations.
Individuals at upper levels have more power and exercise more
control than those at successively lower levels. This distribution of
power has an important impact on job satisfaction. Studies of

organizations are reasonably consistent in showing a positive relationship between job satisfaction and the amount of control a person exercises in his work situation (26). Having some say in the affairs of the work situation contributes also to a member's sense of involvement in his work and in the organization, as well as his identification, personal commitment, and feeling of responsibility on the job.

The explanation for these relationships lies partly in the fact that organization members generally prefer exercising influence to being powerless—although there certainly are individual differences in this regard. Results from a number of studies show that workers and supervisors are more likely to feel that they have too little authority than too much. For example, several thousand workers in a large number of organizations were asked to describe how much control various groups in their workplace exercised and how much these groups *should* exercise. In 98 percent of these organizations, the "average" worker felt that the workers as a whole did not have as much control as they should (154).

Managers—all the way to the pinnacle of the organization—feel that they, too, have too little power. Figure 4 shows differences between the amount of authority associated with managerial positions and the amount that persons in these positions feel they should have. Porter obtained these data in a survey of nearly two thousand managers employed in a variety of companies (121). He questioned each manager about the following authority-related aspects of his position:

1. The authority connected with the position.
2. The opportunity in it for independent thought and action.
3. The opportunity for participation in the setting of goals.
4. The opportunity for participation in the determination of methods and procedures.

Porter asked two questions relative to each of these dimensions:

a. How much is there now?
   (min.) 1 2 3 4 5 6 7 (max.)

b. How much should there be?
   (min.) 1 2 3 4 5 6 7 (max.)

For each dimension and each respondent, Porter subtracted the answer to question *a* from the answer to *b*. He refers to this difference as the *perceived deficiency in need fulfillment.* Positive

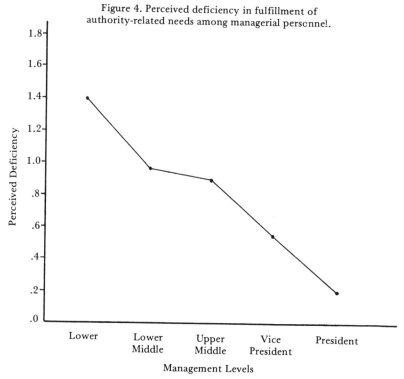

Figure 4. Perceived deficiency in fulfillment of
authority-related needs among managerial personnel.

(Adapted from Porter, 121. Professor Porter provided additional data upon
which this figure is based.)

scores imply that managers do not find as much authority in their
positions as they want, and negative scores mean that they find more
than they want. Since the perceived deficiencies in need fulfillment
for each of the four authority-related aspects of the job follow
essentially the same pattern, the results have been combined into the
single index shown in Figure 4.

There are two important points to note in this figure. First, the
average scores are *positive*; organization members generally perceive
themselves as having less authority than they should have or would
like to have. Second, the perceived discrepancies distinctly decrease
with hierarchical ascent; persons at upper levels are likely to

experience less dissatisfaction relative to their power or authority-related needs than are persons below them.

Status

Persons at higher levels are formally assigned greater status in the organization than persons at lower levels. Accordingly, persons at higher levels are considered more important and have greater responsibility, official respectability, and recognition. They also receive higher pay and enjoy greater privileges and perquisites: stock options, longer vacations, and paid sick leaves. The responsibility, respect, and recognition, along with the greater material rewards associated with status, contribute significantly to the satisfaction of important needs—*and to a sense of self-esteem.*

Porter asked his managerial respondents how much self-esteem they get from their positions and how much they *should* get, and he again found a positive relationship between need fulfillment and hierarchical rank (121). Persons at higher levels feel less deprived than do those below them in their sense of self-esteem.

There are indications that status and self-esteem (which accompanies status) affect not only the satisfactions of organization members, but also their mental and physical health. Here are a couple of quotations from interviews by Herzberg, Mausner, and Snyderman that illustrate how health problems may be associated with problems on the job (69, pp. 91-92):

I have angina [an inflammatory condition of the throat that may produce suffocative spasms]. Every time I have a run-in with my supervisor I get an attack.

When I came back and found that my chief had gone over my head in dealing with my section without telling me, I realized I was on the skids here. I started drinking and smoking too much. Never had an auto accident before but I banged up my fenders twice during that month. I must have lost twenty pounds.

Because research on this topic is extremely difficult to perform, it is not possible to draw unqualified conclusions. Nevertheless, some of the available research data are helpful. For example, in a study of two organizations Kasl and French made the assumption (based partly on earlier research) that the seeking of medical aid and the reporting of physical symptoms provides an index of mental ill health (77). These authors found that the number of visits of employees to the company dispensary, not including visits for injuries, correlates negatively with self-esteem (which in turn is positively related to status).

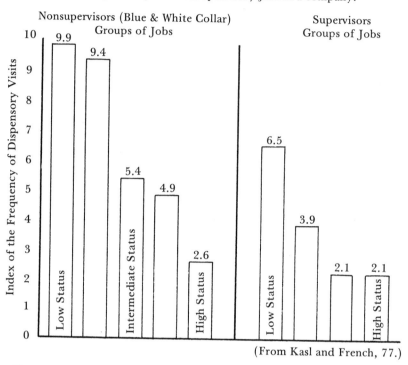

Figure 5. Frequency of dispensary visits on
supervisory and nonsupervisory jobs in a company.

(From Kasl and French, 77.)

Figure 5 illustrates the relationship Kasl and French found between job status and visits to the company dispensary for nonsupervisory and for supervisory employees. Within each of these groups, the higher the organization member's status (and self-esteem), the less likely he is to visit the company dispensary. The high rate of dispensary visits at the low-status supervisory level may be the result of an increase in responsibility at that point. This increase could be a source of worry or tension leading to health problems for some supervisors. Aside from this apparent exception, however, the data generally show a negative relationship between status and what Kasl and French call "illness behavior." Furthermore, these authors demonstrated that dispensary visits decreased among a group of men who moved into higher-status jobs, whereas visits increased for those who moved down in status.

Skill

As we move up the organization hierarchy, we find the jobs usually require more skill. At higher levels, jobs are also less repetitious, routinized, and fractionated; and they allow greater discretion and choice to organization members. Accordingly, jobs at upper levels permit greater individuality to members and a greater sense of self-fulfillment or "self-actualization." At lower levels, however, a worker may experience serious frustrations because his job fails to provide sufficient opportunity for him to use his abilities or to realize his potential.

Among the jobs most frustrating to workers are the low-skill jobs on assembly lines. Walker and Guest made detailed studies of the problems encountered by workers on assembly lines in automobile plants and concluded that mass-production technology eliminates "virtually everything that might be of real, personal value to the worker" (59, p. 502). The words of one worker interviewed by Walker and Guest convey the frustration and despair of many employees on the assembly line:

> You can't beat the machine. They have you clocked to a fraction of a second. My job is engineered, and the jigs and fixtures are all set out according to specifications. The foreman is an all right guy, but he gets pushed, so he pushes us. The guy on the line has no one to push. You can't fight that iron horse (171, p. 71).

Walker and Guest demonstrated how the low-skill requirements—along with the repetitiveness, routine, and lack of social interaction of mass-production jobs—adversely affect workers' attitudes toward their work as well as their rates of absenteeism and tardiness. Research by Morse in a large insurance company (112, Chap. 4) is consistent with the work of Walker and Guest. In clerical jobs, the greater the skill demanded, the greater the variety offered, and the more discretion and choice allowed to clerks in their work operations, the greater the job satisfaction the workers were likely to experience. Moreover, the increased satisfaction is not simply the result of the higher pay that often compensates skill. Morse demonstrated that the positive relationship between use of skill and job satisfaction exists regardless of pay level.

Some of the effects of low-skill jobs might be gleaned more readily from an analysis of workers who adjust well to such jobs than from those who have difficulty adjusting. Argyris considered this possibility by broaching a subject about which relatively little information is available because of its "touchiness"—the success of mentally retarded workers (11, pp. 66-67). Argyris quotes Brennan's description of two instances in which mentally retarded persons were successfully employed on unskilled jobs in a knitting mill and in a radio-manufacturing corporation. In both cases, the managers praised these employees for their excellence. In the knitting mill, the retarded girls "were more punctual, more regular in their habits, and did not indulge in as much 'gossip and levity.' " In the radio corporation,

> the girls proved to be exceptionally well-behaved, particularly obedient, and strictly honest and trustworthy. They carried out work required of them to such a degree of efficiency that *we were surprised they were classed as subnormals for their age.* Their attendance was good, and their behavior was, if anything, certainly better than that of any other employee of the same age (31, pp. 13-18, as quoted in 11; italics in original).

These dramatic illustrations do not mean that all low-skill jobs are designed for morons (although some jobs may be appropriate to this level of intelligence). Several studies suggest that within normal ranges, I.Q. alone does not affect workers' job satisfaction (70, 144, 169, pp. 135-138). *Education,* however, does sometimes lead to dissatisfaction (102, 112). An unpublished analysis by Mann shows that the negative correlation between education and job satisfaction is most striking for workers on unskilled jobs, is less strong for semiskilled workers, and is entirely absent for employees doing skilled work.

The education level of the work force has risen over the years, and it will continue to rise. With education, workers acquire abilities as well as aspirations which may not be easily realized. Thus, unskilled jobs at the lower levels of the hierarchy do not always match the capacities and aspirations of members. In mass-production operations particularly, jobs impose physical as well as mental constraints on workers. Such jobs cannot stimulate, challenge, or interest workers, and workers are therefore likely to perform them with less than a sense of complete involvement.

Hierarchy and Conflict

Hierarchy is a basic *organizational* characteristic, but it has the most profound *psychological* implications for the individual members. In the hierarchy, persons work together but are rewarded and motivated differently. Persons at higher levels are not only paid more; they are awarded greater *psychological* compensation. Organization, therefore is more or less compatible with the self-interests of members, depending partly on where they are in the organization hierarchy.

Organization, then, implies a kind of class society in the sense that, psychologically and economically, some members are more advantageously situated in it than others. Some members may also *give* more to the organization in the intensities of their involvements and efforts. It is not surprising therefore to find serious conflicts between persons in different positions. Symptoms of conflict, or of the potential for conflict, can be seen in three general differences between echelons in addition to the satisfaction gradients discussed above: (1) differences in perceptions and cognitions; (2) differences in ideals and norms; and (3) differences in loyalty.

Differences in Perceptions and Cognitions

Persons in different hierarchical positions may perceive or interpret important events in the organization quite differently. These differences are to be understood partly in terms of the principle . . . [that] perceptions and cognitions are affected by motivational states. Persons in different positions are motivated in different ways. They also have different sources of information and vantage points from which to view organizational events. Moreover, their immediate social and psychological environments are strikingly and systematically different. For example, the president interacts frequently with his vice-presidents and others at the executive level, whereas employees interact primarily with their co-workers and supervisors. These diverse groups live in worlds that are radically different. Furthermore, their worlds are composed in a number of respects, of *like-minded* individuals. Since persons at higher levels are more satisfied with and interested in their work than are those at lower levels, the president is in frequent touch with persons who share his relatively rosy picture of organizational life. These highly involved and interested persons feel relatively little dissatisfaction regarding authority, self-esteem, and self-actualization. It should not be surprising therefore to find them wondering occasionally why *everyone* in the organization does not have the same enthusiastic view they have. On the other hand, persons at the bottom of the hierarchy live in a psychologically depressed area, and each of them has considerable support from his fellow workers for his relatively jaundiced view of organizational life.

A number of research studies have documented some of the different perceptions and cognitions that are a function of hierarchical position. For example, Morse asked a group of clerical workers and their supervisors, "How does a person get ahead here in the company?" She found that supervisors were more likely than workers to explain advancement in terms of "merit," whereas workers were more likely to explain it more cynically (if not more

Figure 6. Comparative agreement between superior-subordinate
pairs on basic areas of the subordinate's job.

	Agreement on less than half the topics	Agreement on about half the topics	Agreement on more than half the topics
Job duties	15.0%	39.1%	45.9%
Obstacles in the way of subordinate's performance	68.2%	23.6%	8.1%

(Percentages based on study of 58 pairs. Adapted from 99, p. 10.)
Reprinted by permission of the publisher from *AMA Research Study #52.* ©
1961 by the American Management Association, Inc.

realistically), in terms of "knowing the right people, or luck" (112,
p. 100).

Striking perceptual differences also occur between persons at
managerial levels. Maier, Hoffman, Hooven, and Read asked high-
level managers and their immediate managerial subordinates to
describe aspects of the subordinates' jobs. Figure 6 shows the
amount of agreement and disagreement within these managerial
superior-subordinate pairs. Even though written job descriptions
were available, only about 46 percent of the pairs agreed on more
than half of the topics concerning the job duties of the subordinates.
A considerably greater discrepancy in perception can be noted with
regard to the obstacles which these persons see as preventing the
subordinate from performing well on the job. Needless to say,
potential (if not real) conflict exists when a supervisor and his
subordinate characteristically see different kinds of things interfering
with the subordinate's doing his job.

Part of the difficulty arises from authority and status differences,
which inhibit members from communicating freely with their superiors about important job matters. Thus, the different perceptions
between subordinates and supervisors are likely to remain differences. This problem of communication is illustrated in Figure 7,
based on a study by Mann in a large public utility. The table presents
results of several parallel questions asked of workers, their foremen,
and top staff. The first row indicates that between 85 and 90 percent
of the foremen and of top staff think that their subordinates feel
very free to discuss important job matters with them. However, only
about half of the men and two-thirds of the foremen say that they
feel very free to discuss important matters with their superiors. The

Figure 7. Extent to which superiors and subordinates agree
on aspects of communication between them.

	% Top staff say about fore-men	% Fore-men say about them-selves	% Fore-men say about the men	% Men say about them-selves
Feel very free to discuss important things about the job with superior	90	67	85	51
Always or nearly always tell sub-ordinates in advance about changes which will affect them or their work	100	63	92	47
Always or almost always get sub-ordinates' ideas	70	52	73	16

(From 102.)

second and third rows tell a similar story. Superiors are more likely than subordinates to think that communications between them are good.

Research has also revealed significant discrepancies in the perceptions by one hierarchical group of the motives or attitudes of another. Motives and attitudes are ambiguous referents, of course, and differences are to be expected. Yet the character of these differences is significant. For example, in their classic study of adjustment to army life, Stouffer and his colleagues found that officers overestimate enlisted men's (a) desire to be soldiers, (b) satisfaction with their jobs, (c) importance which they attach to the infantry, and (d) pride in their companies. To the question "How many of your officers are the kind who are willing to go through anything they ask their men to go through?" 92 percent of the officers, but only 37 percent of the enlisted men, answered "all" or "most." When asked to react to the statement "Most enlisted men do *not* respect their officers," only 25 percent of officers, compared to 54 percent of the enlisted men, agreed (150, p. 395). One reason for the officers' misjudging this basic fact of organizational life is that many men *act* as if they respect their officers when in fact they do not respect their officers.

Figure 8, based on a study by R. L. Kahn in a large appliance-manufacturing company (75), shows the results of two questions asked of members at different ranks. Workers were asked only the first question; supervisory and managerial persons were asked both:

1. Different people want different things out of a job. What are the things you yourself feel are *most important* in a job?

2. Different people want different things out of a job. What are the things you think most of the people you supervise feel are *most important* in a job?

All of the respondents were shown the list of variables in Figure 8. Kahn stresses several highlights of this table:

1. Foremen and general foremen misjudge the importance their subordinates attach to some, if not all, qualities of the subordinates' jobs.

2. Supervisors overestimate the desire of workers for economic rewards and for "not having to work too hard."

3. Supervisors underestimate the importance that subordinates attach to "social approval and self-expression—getting on well with one's supervisor and fellow workers, and having a chance to do work of high quality and interesting content" (75, p. 50).

4. These discrepancies in perception apply also to general foremen's ratings of foremen as well as to foremen's ratings of workers.

5. Supervisors apparently misperceive the job attitudes of their subordinates despite some basic similarities in what both groups want from their jobs. For example, 28 percent of the men and 28 percent of the foremen personally attach great importance to "getting along well with my supervisor"; yet only 14 percent of foremen and 15 percent of the general foremen ascribe this attitude to their subordinates—which indicates that the superior may be more like his subordinate than he thinks he is.

Differences in Ideals and Norms for the Organization

Persons express different ideals for their organization. In crucial respects, the kind of organization that workers want is a different kind from that preferred by their supervisors and managers. On the question of authority, for example, a compilation of results from a number of studies of work organizations reveals that workers, on the average, want to exercise more control over what goes on in the

Figure 8. What subordinates want in a job, compared with their superiors' estimates.

	AS MEN	AS FOREMEN		AS GENERAL FOREMEN	
	Rated the variables for themselves	Estimated men would rate the variables	Rated the variables for themselves	Estimated foremen would rate the variables	Rated the variables for themselves
Economic variables:					
Steady work and steady wages	61%	79%	62%	86%	52%
High wages	28	61	17	58	11
Pensions and other old-age-security benefits	13	17	12	29	15
Not having to work too hard	13	30	4	25	2
Human-satisfaction variables:					
Getting along well with the people I work with	36%	17%	39%	22%	43%
Getting along well with my supervisor	28	14	28	15	24
Good chance to turn out good-quality work	16	11	18	13	27
Good chance to do interesting work	22	12	38	14	43
Other variables:					
Good chance for promotion	25%	23%	42%	24%	47%
Good physical working conditions	21	19	18	4	11
Total	*	*	*	*	*
Number of cases	2,499	196	196	45	45

(From Kahn, 75. Reprinted by permission of author and publisher.)
*Percentages total over 100 because they include three rankings for each person.

workplace than they perceive themselves to exercise. However, in none of these organizations do *supervisors* want workers as a group to exercise more control than they are perceived to be exercising. Simply put, employees are likely to want a more democratic organization than supervisors want. By way of contrast, research in a *voluntary* organization, the League of Women Voters, showed that officers are as likely as members to prefer a democratic distribution of control (143).

The study of the American soldier to which we have referred provides further documentation for the important attitudinal and ideological differences that exist between ranks. Army discipline which implies emphasis on "spit and polish" and "military courtesy," was generally regarded as desirable by most officers but as undesirable by enlisted men (150). Figure 9 illustrates in more concrete detail how rank makes a difference in the preference which enlisted men, noncommissioned officers, and officers express regarding some of the standards of comportment for noncommissioned officers. Admittedly, most of these differences are not surprising; but they are nonetheless significant in reflecting the underlying bases of conflict within the organization. In small ways and in large, rank-and-file members tell us they want one kind of organization, and officers tell us they want another.

In the work organization, the preferences of officers correspond more closely than those of rank-and-file members to the official ideals of the organization. The operation of the organization, however, may conform more closely to what rank-and-file members want than to the wishes of officers. For example, a study of productivity and attitudes of workers and their foremen showed that (a) the level of productivity considered reasonable by workers is below that considered reasonable by their foremen, (b) the level considered reasonable by foremen is below that officially considered reasonable by the company, (c) most workers are producing at levels considerably below the official norm and below the level considered reasonable by their supervisors, and (d) the actual level of production corresponds more closely to what workers consider reasonable than to what their foremen or higher company officials consider reasonable (92, p. 48).

Differences in Loyalty and Support for the Organization
Superiors are more likely than their subordinates to identify with the organization and to support it psychologically; organizational policies and actions are more likely to seem to them morally correct,

Figure 9. Comparisons of privates, noncoms,
and officers on attitudes toward noncom behavior.

	PER CENT WHO AGREE WITH EACH STATEMENT		
	PRIVATES (384)	NONCOMS (195)	OFFICERS (31)
SOCIAL RELATIONS			
"A noncom will lose some of the respect of his men if he pals around with them off-duty"	13	16	39
"A noncom should not let the men in his squad forget that he is a noncom even when off-duty"	39	54	81
DISCIPLINE			
"A noncom has to be very strict with his men or else they will take advantage of him"	45	52	68
"A noncom should teach his men to obey all rules and regulations without questioning them"	63	81	90
WORK SUPERVISION			
"A noncom should always keep his men busy during duty hours, even if he has to make them do unnecessary work"	16	22	39
"The harder a noncom works his men the more respect they will have for him"	10	18	42
"On a fatigue detail, a noncom should see that the men under him get the work done, but should not help them do it"	36	37	68

(From 150, p. 408.)
Numbers in parentheses are the numbers of cases.

fair, and just. Superiors are more likely to take the view that what is good for the organization is good for *all* its members. The study of productivity that we have just reported, for example, showed that foremen are closer to accepting as reasonable the company policy regarding productivity than are the men. The foremen's immediate superiors in turn can be expected to agree more with the official productivity standard than do the foremen—and so on up the organizational hierarchy.

A member's attitudes of support for the organization and its policies are likely to change as his position in the hierarchy change. Workers who become foremen, for example, are likely to adopt attitudes similar to the attitudes of other foremen, and different from the attitudes of workers. This process of increasing loyalty and support that accompanies increasing rank has been investigated by Lieberman (90). This psychologist administered attitude questionnaires to more than two thousand workers in a large appliance-manufacturing concern. A year later, twenty-three workers who had been promoted to the rank of foreman and a group of workers who had not been promoted completed the questionnaire again. Workers in both groups were matched on a number of demographic characteristics, such as age and education, and on their responses to the initial questionnaire. Although both groups showed essentially the same attitudes toward the company and its policies on the first questionnaire, the data from the second questionnaire indicated that the foremen had changed to greater agreement with and support for the organization and its policies. The foremen felt that the company was concerned about the welfare of workers; they saw the union as an impediment to the organization; they changed markedly in their support for the controversial company incentive system; and they showed some shift in the direction of adopting the company's point of view rather than union's on the issue of seniority as the basis for promotion.

Some time after Lieberman had given the second questionnaire, the nation suffered an economic recession. As a result, the company returned eight of the foremen to worker status. Twelve others remained foremen and three left the company for unrelated reasons. Lieberman administered his questionnaire again and found that the demoted foremen had regained their original attitudes. Not only do persons change toward agreement with company policy as they move up the hierarchy, but they change away from agreement as they move down.

Lieberman also compared the attitudes of workers who were elected union stewards with the attitudes of workers who were promoted to foremen. Figure 10 indicates the changes these two groups underwent. It is based on the responses of twelve foremen and six union stewards who remained in their new roles about three years. The percentages in the figure represent the average proportions of the foremen and stewards who took a distinctly pro-management position on sixteen attitude measures.

Before their selection, these foremen and stewards did not differ in their attitudes toward the company and its policies. One year after assuming their new positions, however, the two groups diverged sharply, and after several years, they moved even further apart. On the basis of the data in this figure and other analyses, Lieberman concluded that differences in attitude between company foremen and union stewards do *not* result from the selection of pro-company workers as foremen nor the election of anti-company workers as stewards. Apparently, foremen and stewards acquire their attitudes as they move up their respective hierarchies.

Figure 10. Effects of foreman and steward roles:
Percent who express pro-management attitudes.

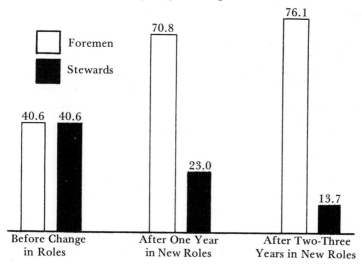

(Adapted from 90, p. 398.)

Adjustment, Conflict, and Organizational Performance

The problems of adjustment and conflict which we have discussed affect organizational performance in a number of ways: (a) they reduce the motivation of many members, (b) they impede effective control and coordination, and (c) they create opposition to the organization and its leaders.

Motivation

The success of the organization depends on the member's willingness to work assiduously and constructively in helping achieve the organization's goals. This willingness requires that

> each member of the organization . . . feel that the organization's objectives are of significance and that his own particular task contributes in an indispensable manner to the organization's achievement of its objectives. He should see his role as difficult, important, and meaningful. This is necessary if the individual is to achieve and maintain a sense of personal worth and importance (92, p. 103).

As we have seen through the data cited in this chapter, organizations do not fully meet this requirement—especially insofar as rank-and-file members are concerned.

Peter Blau, a sociological theorist, sees the motivational problem of organizational hierarchy this way:

> In a democracy . . . where status prerogatives are frowned upon, intense feelings of inequality among the lower echelons of a bureaucracy have several effects that are detrimental for operations. They inhibit identification with the organization and its objectives, lessen interest in performing tasks to the best of one's abilities, kill initiative, and reduce the chances that emergent operating problems will be readily met. Unless employees consider themselves partners in a common enterprise rather than tools in the hands of management, they are not prone willingly to assume responsibilities of their own (25, p. 80).

Control

Control and coordination are essential to any organized effort. A supervisor, however, can not exercise effective control over subordinates when his information about them is in serious error, and when he and they base their actions on seriously differing perceptions. At the very least, discrepancies in members' perceptions and cognitions make the job of control and coordination more difficult; at worst, they contribute—in the context of differences in rewards, satisfactions, interests, ideals, involvements, and loyalties—to resentment, distrust, hostility, and opposition.

Opposition

Opposition to the organization and its leaders, can manifest itself in various ways. It may express itself as a mild form of "passive resistance." Subordinates may simply withhold important information from their supervisors, keeping them in the dark about matters concerning which they should be informed. In some instances, subordinates may develop useful ideas for improving the product, or the work process, or the organization itself, but will not pass these on. Workers on jobs designed by time-study engineers, for example, may invent (often with considerable ingenuity) an "arsenal of secret weapons" such as jigs and fixtures that help them do their jobs more efficiently than is possible with the official method (176, p. 17). These workers do not always reveal their inventions to management, however, because they assume, sometimes realistically, that management will reset job rates. Such employees often hold these inventions in reserve to ease their jobs when the supervisor is not looking.

Certain forms of absenteeism, tardiness, "goldbricking," and slowdowns may also represent opposition that is relatively passive but nonetheless sometimes costly. Opposition may manifest itself in more aggressive forms too. Disputes, grievances, and strikes are the more aggressive forms of opposition, which workers employ through their unions. Employees may even resort to sabotage, although this is rare.

Forms of opposition of the type just described are symptoms of the "social disease," which Elton Mayo argues need not exist—except in organizations that do not conform to sophisticated principles of human relations. Organizations, in fact, differ in the degree to which they are subject to opposition, and one of our purposes is to understand why some organizations are relatively free of opposition while others verge on collapse because of it. The Hawthorne research offered a clue in answer to this question by revealing that opposition and cooperation frequently occur not as reactions of individual members but as collective reactions of members through groups.

FOOTNOTES

1. For a further, detailed analysis of the conflict between man and organization, see Argyris (9, 11) who argues that the work organization requires many members to act in immature rather than adult ways.

2. For comprehensive reviews and commentaries on such studies, see Brayfield and Crockett (30), Herzberg et al. (70), Katzell (83, pp. 243-244), and Likert (92, Chap, 2).

REFERENCES

1. Acton Society Trust. *Size and morale.* London: Acton Society Trust, 1953.
2. Adorno, T. W., Frenkel-Brunswik, Else, Levinson, D. J., and Sanford, R. N. *The authoritarian personality.* New York: Harper, 1950.
3. Allport, F. H. Individuals and their human environment. *Proc. Ass. Res. nerv. dis.,* 1933, 14, 234-252.
4. Allport, F. H. *Social psychology.* New York: Houghton Mifflin, 1924.
5. Allport, F. H. Teleonomic description in the study of personality. *Char. and pers.,* 1937, 5, no. 3, 202-214.
6. Allport, G. W. *Personality, a psychological interpretation.* New York: Holt, 1937.
7. American Psychological Association. Ethical standards of psychologists. *Amer. Psychologist,* 1963, 18, 56-60.
8. Arensberg, C., Barkin, S., Chalmers, W., Wilensky, H., Worthy, J., and Dennis, Barbara (Eds.). *Research in industrial human relations—A critical appraisal.* New York: Harper, 1957.
9. Argyris, C. *Integrating the individual and the organization.* New York: Wiley, 1964.
10. Argyris, C. *Interpersonal competence and organizational effectiveness.* Homewood, Ill.: Dorsey Press, 1962.
11. Argyris, C. *Personality and organization.* New York: Harper, 1957.
12. Asch, S. E. The effects of group pressure upon the modification and distortion of judgments. In (95) pp. 174-183.
13. Atkinson, J. W. (Ed.). *Motives in fantasy, action, and society.* Princeton, N. J.: Van Nostrand, 1958.
14. Atkinson, J. W., Heyns, R. W., and Veroff, J. The effect of experimental arousal of the affiliation motive on thematic apperception. In (13).
15. Bachman, J., Smith, C., and Slesinger, J. Control, performance and satisfaction: An analysis of structural and individual effects. *J. pers. soc. Psychol.,* 1966 (in press).
16. Back, K. The exertion of influence through social communication. *J. abnorm, soc. Psychol.,* 1951, 46, 9-23.
17. Bartiz, L. *The servants of power.* Middletown, Conn.: Wesleyan Univ. Press, 1960.
18. Barkin, S. Trade union attitudes and their effect upon productivity. In L. R. Tripp (Ed.). *Industrial productivity.* Madison, Wis.: Industrial Relations Research Association, 1951.
19. Bass, B. *Leadership, psychology and organizational behavior.* New York: Harper, 1960.
20. Bennis, W. G. Goals and meta-goals of laboratory training. In W. G. Bennis, E. H. Schein, D. E. Berlew, and F. I. Steele (Eds.), *Interpersonal dynamics, essays and readings on human interaction.* Homewood, Ill.: Dorsey Press, 1964, pp. 692-698.
21. Berlyne, D. E. *Conflict, arousal and curiosity.* New York: McGraw-Hill, 1960.
22. Birch, J. D., and Veroff, J. *Motivation.* Belmont, Calif., Wadsworth Publ. Co., 1966.
23. Blake, R. R., Mouton, J. S., Barnes, L. B., and Greiner, L. E. Breakthrough in organization development. *Harvard Bus. Rev.,* 1964, 42, no. 6, 133-135.

24. Blake, R. R., Mouton, J. S., and Bidwell, A. C. The managerial grid. *Advanced management office executive*, 1962, 36.
25. Blau, P. M. *Bureaucracy in modern society*. New York: Random House, 1956.
26. Blauner, R. Work satisfaction and industrial trends in modern society. In W. Galenson and S. Lipset (Eds.), *Labor and trade unionism*. New York: Wiley, 1960.
27. Bonini, C. P., Jaedicke, R., and Wagner, H. (Eds.), *Management controls: New directions in basic research*. New York: McGraw-Hill, 1964.
28. Bowers, D. Organizational control in an insurance company. *Sociometry*, 1964, 27, no. 2, 230-244.
29. Bradford, L. P., Gibb, J. R., and Benne, K. D. (Eds.). *T-group theory and laboratory method*. New York: Wiley, 1964.
30. Brayfield, H., and Crockett, W. H. Employee attitudes and employee performance. *Psychol. Bull.*, 1955, 52, no. 5, 396-424.
31. Brennan, N. *The making of a moron*. New York: Sheed & Ward, 1953.
32. Burns, T., and Stalker, G. M. *The management of innovation*. London: Tavistock Publications Ltd., 1961.
33. Canter, R. A human relations training program, *J. appl. Psychol.*, 1951, 35, 38-45.
34. Carp, F. M., Vitola, B. M., and McLanathan, F. L. Human relations knowledge and social distance set in supervisors. *J. appl. Psychol.*, 1963, 47, 78-80.
35. Cartwright, D. Influence, leadership, control. In J. G. March (Ed.) *Handbook of organizations*. Chicago: Rand McNally and Company, 1965, ch. 1.
36. Coch, L., and French, J. R. P., Jr. Overcoming resistance to change. *Hum. Rel.*, 1948, 4, no. 1, 512-533.
37. Copley, F. B. *Frederick W. Taylor*. New York: Harper, 1923.
38. Crozier, M. *The bureaucratic phenomenon*. Chicago: Univ. of Chicago Press, 1964.
39. Crutchfield, R. S. Conformity and character. *Amer. Psychologist*, 1955, 10, 191-198.
40. Dalton, M. *Men who manage*. New York: Wiley, 1959.
41. Day, R., and Hamblin, R. Some effects of close and punitive styles of supervision. *Amer. J. Sociol.*, 1964, 69, no. 5, 499-510.
42. Dent, J. K. Organizational correlates of the goals of business management. *Personnel Psychol.*, 1959, 12, 365-393.
43. Dunlop, J. T. *Industrial relations systems*. New York: Holt, 1959.
44. Emery, F. E., and Thorsrud, E. *Industrial democracy*. London: Tavistock Publications Ltd., 1965.
45. Emery, F. E., and Trist, E. L. Socio-technical systems. Paper presented at the 6th Annual International Meeting of the institute of Management Sciences. Paris: September 1959.
46. Ferguson, L. L. Social scientists in the plant. *Harvard Bus. Rev.*, 1964, 42, no. 3, 133-143.
47. Festinger, L., Schachter, S., and Back, K. *Social pressures in informal groups: A study of a housing project*. New York: Harper, 1950.
48. Festinger, L., and Thibaut, J. Interpersonal communication in small groups. *J. abnorm. soc. Psychol.*, 1951, 46, 92-99.
49. Fiedler, F. E. The influence of leader-laymen relations on combat crew

effectiveness. *J. abnorm. soc. Psychol.*, 1955, 51, 227-235.
50. Fleishman, E. Leadership climate, human relations training, and supervisory behavior. In (Ed.) *Studies in personnel and industrial psychology.* Homewood, Ill.: Dorsey Press, 1961, pp. 315-328.
51. French, J. R. P., Jr. The social environment of mental health. *J. soc. Iss.*, 1963, 19, no. 4, 39-56.
52. French, J. R. P., Jr., Israel, J., and As, D. An experiment in participation in a Norwegian factory. *Hum. Rel.*, 1960, 13, 3-19.
53. French, J. R. P., Jr., Kay, E., and Meyer, H. H. Participation and the appraisal system. *Human Relations*, 1966, 19 (1), 3-20.
54. Friedmann, G. *Industrial society.* Glencoe, Ill.: Free Press, 1955.
55. Gilbreth, F. B. *Motion study.* New York: Van Nostrand, 1911.
56. Golembiewski, R. T. *Behavior and the organization: O and M and the Small Group.* Chicago: Rand McNally, 1962.
57. Goodwin, H. G. Work simplification. *Factory Management and Maintenance*, 1958, 72-106.
58. Gouldner, A. W. *Patterns of industrial bureaucracy.* Glencoe, Ill.: Free Press, 1954.
59. Guest, R. H. Men and machines: An assembly-line worker looks at his job. *Personnel*, 1955, 31, 496-503.
60. Guetzkow, H. (Ed.). *Groups, leadership, and men.* Pittsburgh: Carnegie Institute of Technology, 1951.
61. Gurin, G., Veroff, J., and Feld, Sheila. *Americans view their mental health.* New York: Basic Books, 1960.
62. Haberstroh, C. Goals, programs and the training function. In (27).
63. Haire, M., Ghiselli, E., and Porter, L. W. An international study of management attitudes and democratic leadership. In *Proceedings CIOS XIII, International Management Congress.* New York: Council for International Progress in Management (USA), 1963, pp. 101-114.
64. Halpin, A., and Winer, B. A factorial study of the leader behavior descriptions. In (147) pp. 39-51.
65. Hariton, T. *Conditions influencing the effects of training foremen in new human relations principles.* Doctoral thesis, University of Michigan, 1951.
66. Harris, E., and Fleishman, E. Human relations training and the stability of leadership patterns. In Fleishman, E. (Ed.). *Studies in personnel and industrial psychology.* Homewood, Ill.: Dorsey Press, 1961, pp. 230-238.
67. Harrison, R. Impact of the laboratory on perception of others by the experimental group. In (10).
68. Hemphill, J., and Coons, A. Development of the leader behavior description questionnaire. In (147) pp. 6-38.
69. Herzberg, F., Mausner, B., and Snyderman, Barbara. *The motivation to work.* New York: Wiley, 1959.
70. Herzberg, F., Mausner, B., Peterson, R. O., and Capwell, Dora F. *Job attitudes: Review of research and opinion.* Pittsburgh, Pa.: Psychological Service of Pittsburgh, 1957.
71. Homans, G. C. *The human group.* New York: Harcourt, Brace, 1950.
72. Hugh-Jones, E. M. (Ed.). *Human relations and modern management.* Amsterdam: North-Holland Publ. Co., 1958.
73. Huxley, A. *Brave new world.* New York: Bantam, 1953.
74. James, W. *Principles of psychology.* New York: Holt, 1890.

75. Kahn, R. L. Human relations on the shop floor. In (72), Chapter 3.
76. Kahn, R. L., and Mann, F. C. Uses of survey research in policy determination. *Proc., Ninth Annual Meeting IRRA*, 1957, 256-274.
77. Kasl, S. V., and French, J. R. P., Jr. The effects of occupational status on physical and mental health. *J. soc. Issues*, 1962, 17, no. 3, 67-89.
78. Katona, G. Rational behavior and economic behavior. *Psychol. Rev.*, 1953, 60, no. 5, 307-318.
79. Katz, D., and Kahn, R. L. Leadership practices in relation to productivity and morale. In D. Cartwright and A. Zander (Eds.) *Group Dynamics*. Evanston, Ill.: Row, Peterson, 1953, pp. 554-570.
80. Katz, D., and Kahn, R. L. Some recent findings in human relations research in industry. In G. Swanson, T. Newcomb, and E. Hartley (Eds.), *Readings in social psychology*. (2nd ed.) New York: Holt, 1952, pp. 650-665.
81. Katz, D., Maccoby, E., and Morse, Nancy. *Productivity, supervision and morale in an office situation*. Ann Arbor: Institute for Social Research, Univ. of Michigan, 1950.
82. Katz, D., Maccoby, N., Gurin, G., and Floor, Lucretia. *Productivity supervision and morale among railroad workers*. Ann Arbor: Survey Research Center, Univ. of Michigan, 1951.
83. Katzell, R. A. Industrial psychology. In *Ann. Rev. of Psychol.* Palo Alto, Calif.: Annual Review Inc., 1957, pp. 243-244.
84. Kolaja, J. *Worker's Councils, the Yugoslov experience*. London: Tavistock Publications Ltd., 1965.
85. Krulee, G. K. The Scanlon plan: Cooperation through participation. *The Journal of Business of the University of Chicago*, 1955, 27, no. 2, 100-113.
86. Landsberger, H. A. *Hawthorne revisited*. Ithaca, N. Y.: Cornell Univ., 1958.
87. Leavitt, H., and Bass, B. Organization psychology. *Ann. Rev. Psychol.*, Palo Alto, Calif.: Annual Reviews Inc., 1964, pp. 371-398.
88. Lewin, K. Frontiers in group dynamics: Concept, method and reality in social science. *Hum. Rel.*, 1947, 1, 5-42.
89. Lewin, K. Group decision and social change. In (95) pp. 197-211.
90. Lieberman, S. The effects of changes in roles on the attitudes of role occupants. *Hum. Rel.*, 1956, 9, no. 4, 385-402.
91. Likert, R. Influence and national sovereignty. In J. G. Peatman and E. L. Hartley (Eds.), *Festschrift for Gardner Murphy*. New York: Harper, 1963.
92. Likert, R. *New patterns of management*. New York: McGraw-Hill, 1961.
93. Likert, R., and Seashore, S. E. Making cost control work. *Harvard Bus. Rev.*, 1963, 41, no. 6, 96-108.
94. Lysgaard, S. Some problems in connection with informal organization of workers. *Human Relations in Industry*. (Papers presented at Rome Conference) Paris: European Productivity Agency of the Organisation for European Economic Cooperation, 1956, pp. 44-48.
95. Maccoby, E. E., Newcomb, T. E., and Hartley, E. L. (Eds.) *Readings in social psychology*. New York: Holt, 1958.
96. McGehee, W. And Esau was an hairy man. *Amer. Psychologist*, 1964, 19, 799-804.
97. Maier, N. R. F. *The appraisal interview: Objectives, methods and skills*. New York: Wiley, 1958.
98. Maier, N. R. F. *Principles of human relations*. New York: Wiley, 1955.
99. Maier, N. R. F., Hoffman, L. R., Hooven, J. J., and Read, W. H.

Superior-subordinate communication in management. New York: American Management Association, 1961.

100. Maier, N. R. F., Solem, A. R., and Maier, Ayesha A. *Supervisory and executive development: A manual for role playing.* New York: Wiley, 1964.

101. Mann, F. G. Studying and creating change: A means to understanding social organization. In *Research in industrial Human Relations.* Madison, Wis.: Industrial Relations Research Association, 1957, 146-167.

102. Mann, F. G. *A study of work satisfactions as a function of the discrepancy between inferred aspirations and achievement.* Ann Arbor: unpublished doctoral dissertation, Univ. of Michigan, 1953.

103. Mann, F. G., and Baumgartel, H. G. *Absences and employee attitudes in an electric power company.* Ann Arbor: Survey Research Center, Univ. of Michigan, 1952.

104. March, J. G., and Simon, H. A. *Organizations.* New York: Wiley, 1958.

105. Marrow, A. J. *Behind the executive mask.* New York: American Management Association, 1964. .

106. Marx, K. *Selected writings in sociology and social philosophy.* T. B. Bottomore and M. Rubel (Eds.). New York: McGraw-Hill Book Co., 1964.

107. Maslow, A. H. A theory of human motivation. *Psychol. Rev.,* 1943, 50, 370-396.

108. Merton, R. K. Bureaucratic structure and personality. In Merton, Gray, Hockey, and Selvin, *Reader in bureaucracy.* Glencoe, Ill.: Free Press, 1952.

109. Metcalf, H. and Urwick, L., (Eds.) *Dynamic administration, the collected works of Mary Parker Follett.* New York: Harper, 1940.

110. Meyers, F. Workers' control of industry in Europe. *Southwestern soc. sci. Quart.,* 1958, 100-111.

111. Miller, D. R. The study of social relations: situation, identity, and social interaction. In S. Koch (Ed.). *Psychology: A study of a science,* Vol. 5. New York: McGraw-Hill, 1962, pp. 639-737.

112. Morse, Nancy. *Satisfactions in the white-collar job.* Ann Arbor: Survey Research Center, Univ. of Michigan, 1953.

113. Morse, Nancy, and Reimer, E. The experimental change of a major organizational variable. *J. abnorm. soc. Psychol.,* 1956, 52, 120-129.

114. Mulder, M., and Stemerding, A. Threat, attraction to group, and need for strong leadership; a laboratory experiment in a natural setting. *Hum. Rel.,* 1963, 16, 317-343.

115. Nussbaum, F. L. *A history of the economic institutions of modern Europe.* New York: Crofts and Co., 1933.

116. Odiorne, G. S. The trouble with sensitivity training. *Training Directors J.,* October 1963.

117. Patchen, M. Supervisory methods and group performance norms. *Admin. Sci. Quart.,* 1962, 7, no. 3, 275-294.

118. Patchen, M., Seashore, S., and Eckerman, W. Some dealership characteristics related to change in new car sales volume. Ann Arbor: Institute for Social Research, Univ. of Michigan, 1961. Unpublished report.

119. Pelz, D. Influence: A key to effective leadership in the first-line supervisor. *Personnel,* 1952, 29, 209-217.

120. Pfiffner, J. M., and Sherwood, F. P. *Administrative organization.* Englewood Cliffs, N. J.: Prentice-Hall, 1960.

121. Porter, L. W. Job attitudes in management: I. Perceived deficiencies in need fulfillment as a function of job level. *J. appl. Psychol.*, 1962, 46, no. 6, 375-384.
122. Revans, R. W. Human relations, management and size. In (72) pp. 177-220.
123. Rice, A. K. *Productivity and social organization.* London: Tavistock Publications Ltd., 1958.
124. Roethlisberger, F. J., and Dickson, W. J. *Management and the worker.* Cambridge, Mass.: Harvard Univ. Press, 1964.
125. Rose, A. M. The social psychology of desertion from combat. *Amer. soc. Rev.*, 1951, 16, 614-629.
126. Rosen, H. Desirable attributes of work: Four levels of management describe their job environments. *J. appl. Psychol.* 1961, 45, 155-160.
127. Ross, I. C., and Zander, A. F. Need satisfactions and employee turnover. *Personnel Psychol.*, 1957, 10, 327-338.
128. Sarnoff, I., and Zimbardo, P. Anxiety, fear, and social affiliation. *J. abnorm. soc. Psychol.*, 1961, 62, no. 2, 356-363.
129. Sayles, L. *Behavior of industrial work groups: Prediction and control.* New York: Wiley, 1958.
130. Schachter, S. Deviation, rejection and communication. *J. abnorm. soc. Psychol.*, 1951, 46, 190-207.
131. Schachter, S. *The psychology of affiliation, experimental studies of the sources of gregariousness.* Stanford, Calif.: Stanford Univ. Press, 1959.
132. Seashore, S. E. *Group cohesiveness in the industrial work group.* Ann Arbor: Survey Research Center, Univ. Of Michigan, 1954.
133. Seashore, S. E. The training of leaders for effective human relations. In R. Likert, and S. P. Hayes (Eds.), *Some applications of behavioral research.* Paris, Unesco, 1957, pp. 81-123.
134. Seashore, S. E., and Bowers, D. G. *Changing the structure and functioning of an organization.* Ann Arbor: Survey Research Center, Institute for Social Research, Monograph no. 33, 1963.
135. Seeman, M. On the meaning of alienation. *Amer. soc. Rev.*, 1959, 24, no. 6, 783-791.
136. Sells, S. Personnel management. In *Ann. Rev. Psychol.*, 1964, pp. 399-420.
137. Selvin, H. *The effects of leadership.* Glencoe, Ill.: Free Press, 1960.
138. Selznick, P. *TVA and the grass roots.* Berkeley: Univ. California Press, 1953.
139. Shepard, H., and Blake, R. R. Changing behavior through cognitive change. *Hum. Organization*, 1961, 21, 88-96.
140. Sherif, M. *The psychology of social norms.* New York: Harper, 1936.
141. Shipley, T. E., Jr., and Veroff, J. A projective measure of need for affiliation. In (13).
142. Simon, H. Authority. In (8), pp. 103-114.
143. Smith, C. G., and Tannenbaum, A. S. Organizational control-structure: A comparative analysis. *Hum. Rel.*, 1963, 16, no. 4, 299-316.
144. Smith, Patricia. The prediction of individual differences in susceptibility to industrial monotony. *J. appl. Psychol.* 1955, 39, no. 5, 322-329.
145. Starbuck, W. H. Organizational growth and development. In J. March (Ed.), *Handbook of organizations.* Chicago: Rand McNally, 1961, chapter 11.
146. Stock, Dorothy. A survey of research on T-groups. In (29) pp. 395-441.

147. Stogdill, R., and Coons, A. (Eds.). *Leader behavior: Its description and measurement.* Columbus, Ohio: Bureau of Business Research, Ohio State Univ. 1957.

148. Stotland, E. Peer groups and reactions to power figures. In D. Cartwright (Ed.), *Studies in social power.* Ann Arbor: Institute for Social Research, Univ. of Michigan, 1959, pp. 53-68.

149. Stouffer, S., Lumsdaine, A., Williams, R., Jr., Smith, M. B., Janis, I., Star, Shirley, and Cottrell, L., Jr. *Studies in social psychology in World War II* Vol. I. *The American soldier: Combat and its aftermath.* Princeton, N. J.: Princeton Univ. Press, 1949.

150. Stouffer, S., Suchman, E. A., DeVinney, L. C., Starr, Shirley A., and Williams, R. M., Jr. *Studies in social psychology in World War II* Vol. II, *The American soldier: Adjustment during army life.* Princeton, N. J.: Princeton Univ. Press, 1949.

151. Strauss, G. Some notes on power-equalization. In H. Leavitt (Ed.), *The social science of organizations: Four perspectives.* Englewood Cliffs, N. J.; Prentice-Hall, 1963, pp. 41-84.

152. Stuhr, A. W. Some outcomes of the New York employee survey. *Social science research report IV. Surveys and inventories.* Standard Oil Co. of New Jersey, 1962.

153. Sturmthal, A. *Workers councils.* Cambridge, Mass.: Harvard Univ. Press, 1964.

154. Tannenbaum, A. S. Control in organizations. New York: McGraw-Hill, 1968.

155. Tannenbaum, A. S. Control and effectiveness in a voluntary organization. *Amer. J. Sociol.,* 1961, LXVII, no. 1, 33-46.

156. Tannenbaum, A. S. Unions. In J. March (Ed.), *Handbook of organizations.* Chicago: Rand McNally, 1965. Chapter 17.

157. Tannenbaum, A. S., and Allport, F. H. Personality structure and group structure: An interpretative study of their relationship through an event-structure hypothesis. *J. abnorm. soc. Psychol.,* 1956, 53, no. 3, 272-280.

158. Tannenbaum, A. S., and Kahn, R. L. Organizational control structure: A general descriptive technique as applied to four local unions. *Hum. Rel.,* 1957, 10, no. 2, 127-140.

159. Tannenbaum, A. S., and Kahn, R. L. *Participation in union locals.* Evanston, Ill.: Row Peterson, 1958.

160. Tannenbaum, A. S., and Seashore, S. Some changing conceptions and approaches to the study of persons in organizations. Paper presented at XV International Congress of Applied Psychology, Ljubljana, Yugoslavia, 1964.

161. Tannenbaum, R., Weschler, I. R., and Massarik, F. *Leadership and organization: A behavioral science approach.* New York: McGraw-Hill, 1961.

162. Taylor, F. W. *Scientific management.* New York: Harper, 1911.

163. Trist, E., and Bamforth, K. Some social and psychological consequences of the Longwall method of coal-getting. *Hum. Rel.,* 1951, 4, no. 1, 3-38.

164. Trist, E., Higgin, G. W., Murray, H., and Pollock, A. B. *Organizational choice.* London: Tavistock Publications Ltd., 1963.

165. Turner, C. E. The test room studies in employee effectiveness. *Amer. J. pub. Health,* 1933, no. 23, 577-584.

166. Urwick, L. *The elements of administration.* New York: Harper, 1943.

167. Veroff, J. Development and validation of a projective measure of power motivation. *J. abnorm. soc. Psychcl.*, 1957, 54, 1-8.
168. Vroom, V. *Some personality determinants of the effects of participation.* Englewood Cliffs, N. J.: Prentice-Hall, 1960.
169. Vroom, V. *Work and motivation.* New York: Wiley, 1964.
170. Walker, C. R. *Modern technology and civilization.* New York: McGraw-Hill, 1962.
171. Walker, C. R., and Guest, R. H. The man on the assembly line. *Harvard Bus. Rev.*, 1952, 30, 71-83.
172. Weber, M. The essentials of bureaucratic organization: An ideal-type construction. In Merton, Gray, Hockey and Selvin (Eds.), *Reader in bureaucracy.* Glencoe, Ill.: Free Press, 1952.
173. Weber, M. *The theory of social and economic organization.* New York: Oxford Univ. Press, 1947 (trans. by A. M. Henderson and Talcott Parsons, Ed. Talcott Parsons).
174. Welker, W. I. Some determinants of play and exploration in chimpanzees. *J. comp. physiol. Psychol.*, 1956, 49, 84-89.
175. White, R., and Lippitt, R. *Autocracy and democracy: An experimental inquiry.* New York: Harper, 1960.
176. Whyte, W. F., Dalton, M., Roy, D., Sayles, L., Collins, O., Miller, F., Strauss, G., Fuerstenberg, F., and Bavelas, A. *Money and motivation: An analysis of incentives in industry.* New York: Harper, 1955.
177. Whyte, W. H., Jr. *Organization man.* New York: Simon and Schuster, 1956.
178. Wilensky, H. Human relations in the workplace: An appraisal of some recent research. In (8) pp. 25-50.
179. Worthy, J. C. Commentary on Mr. Wilensky's chapter. In (8) pp. 51-54.
180. Worthy, J. C. Factors influencing employee morale. *Harvard Bus. Rev.*, 1950, 28, no, 1, 61-73.

INDIVIDUAL ACTUALIZATION
IN COMPLEX ORGANIZATIONS

Chris Argyris

Recently the writer completed the first phase of a research project having two objectives. The first is to provide knowledge concerning mental health problems in industrial organizations; more specifically, with understanding the difficulties the individual faces and the opportunities he has for self-actualization in complex organizations. The second objective is to test parts of a theoretical framework about human problems of complex organizations and is reported in detail elsewhere (1).* The purpose of this paper is to present some recent results which may alter some commonly accepted notions of individual self-actualization in complex organizations.

Although the research to be discussed is being conducted in an industrial organization, the theory and the results are believed to apply to other kinds of complex organizations (for instance, hospitals, schools, banks, government agencies). Therefore, although the terms "management" and "employee" will be used, it is assumed that the results apply to any (genotypically) similar relationship between any administrator and employees.

Theoretical Framework

Since discussions of the theoretical framework and the many studies from which it is evolved are available in other publications (1, 2) only some of the main propositions are defined in order to give

*See References at end of article—Ed.

From *Mental Hygiene*, Vol. 44, No. 2, April 1960, pp. 226-237. Reprinted by permission of the publisher and the author.

the reader an acquaintance with the theoretical foundations of the research. The most relevant propositions follow:

• Personality is conceptualized as (a) being an organization of parts in which the parts maintain the whole and the whole maintains the parts; (b) seeking internal balance (usually called adjustment) and external balance (usually called adaptation); (c) being propelled by psychological as well as physical energy; (d) located in the need systems; and (e) expressed through the abilities. (f) The personality organization may be called "the self" which (g) acts to color all the individual's experiences, thereby causing him to live in "private worlds," and which (h) is capable of defending or maintaining itself against threats of all types.

• The development of the human personality can be hypothesized to follow the directions and dimensions outlined in the following model. It is assumed that human beings in our culture:

(a) Tend to develop from a state of passivity as infants to a state of increasing activity as adults. (This is what Erikson (3) has called self-initiative and Bronfenbrenner (4) has called self-determination.)

(b) Tend to develop from a state of dependence upon others as infants to a state of relative independence as adults. Relative independence is the ability to "stand on one's own two feet" and simultaneously to acknowledge healthy dependencies.[1] It is characterized by the liberation of the individual from his childhood determiners of behavior (for example, his family) and his development of his own set of behavioral determiners. The mature individual does not tend to react to others (for example, the boss) in terms of patterns learned during childhood.[2]

(c) Tend to develop from being capable of behaving only in a few ways as an infant to being capable of behaving in many different ways as an adult.[3]

(d) Tend to develop from having erratic, casual, shallow, quickly-dropped interests as an infant to having deeper interests as an adult. The mature state is characterized by an endless series of challenges; and the reward comes from doing something for its own sake. The tendency is to analyze and study phenomena in their full-blown wholeness, complexity and depth.[4]

(e) Tend to develop from having a short time perspective (that is, one in which the present largely determines behavior) as an infant, to a much longer time perspective as an adult (that is, one in which the behavior is more affected by the past and the future[5]). Bakke cogently describes the importance of time perspective in the lives of workers and their families and the variety of foresight practices by means of which they seek to secure the future (5).

(f) Tend to develop from being in a subordinate position in the family and society as an infant to aspiring to occupy an equal and/or superordinate position relative to their peers.

(g) Tend to develop from a lack of awareness of self as an infant to an awareness of and control over self as an adult. The adult who tends to experience adequate and successful control over his own behavior tends to develop a sense of integrity (Erikson) and feelings of self-worth.[6] Bakke (6, 7) shows that one of the most important needs of workers is to enlarge those areas of their lives in which their own decisions determine the outcome of their efforts.

• Most human problems in organizations arise because relatively healthy people in our culture are asked to participate in work situations which coerce them to be dependent, subordinate, submissive, to use few of their more than *skin-surface* abilities.

• There are three major sets of variables which cause the dependence and subordination. The formal organization structure is the first variable. (This includes the technology.) Directive leadership is the second, and managerial control (budget, incentive systems, quality control, motion and time studies) is the third.

• The degree of dependence and subordination that these three variables cause tends to increase as one goes down the chain of command, and the lower echelons of the organization take on the characteristics of mass-production.

• Healthy human beings (in our culture) tend to find dependence, subordination and submissiveness frustrating. They would prefer to be relatively independent, to be active, to use many of their deeper abilities; and they aspire to positions equal with or higher than their peers. Frustration leads to regression, aggression, and tension. These in turn lead to conflict. (The individual prefers to leave but fears doing so.) Moreover, it can be shown that under these conditions, the individual will tend to experience psychological failure and short time perspective.

• Individuals will adapt to the frustration, conflict, failure, and short time perspective by creating any one or a combination of the following *informal* activities.

(a) Leave the situation (absenteeism and turnover).

(b) Climb the organizational ladder.

(c) Become defensive (daydream, become aggressive, nurture grievances, regress, project, feel a low sense of self-worth).

(d) Become apathetic, disinterested, non-ego involved in the organization and its formal goals.

(e) Create informal groups to sanction the defense reactions in (c) and (d).

(f) Formalize the informal groups in the form of the trade unions.

(g) De-emphasize in their own minds the importance of self-growth and creativity, and emphasize the importance of money and other material rewards.

(h) Accept the above described ways of behaving as being proper for their lives outside the organization.

• Management will tend to increase the employees' dependence, subordination, submissiveness, which in turn will increase their frustration, and sense of failure, which in turn will increase the informal activities. Management will react to the increase in the informal activities by the formal structure, directive leadership and managerial controls. This closes the circuit and one has a circular process in seemingly perpetual motion.

The Focus of the Study and the Sample

The objective of the research, conducted in a multi-story manufacturing plant, is to study the mental health of highly skilled as compared to low-skilled employees. Our hypothesis is that since highly skilled employees tend to have a greater opportunity to express more mature behavior (be creative, use many abilities, be challenged in their work, and so on), they will tend to have a healthier work world. This in turn should lead to the highly skilled employees' behaving in more mature ways (as defined by our model above). For example, the high-skill employees (Department A) should express less indifference, apathy, dependence and submissiveness than the low-skill employees (Department B). Also the high-skill employees should express greater sense of self-worth, self-satisfaction, and develop more lasting friendships than the low-skill employees.

Thirty-four employees from Department A and 90 employees from Department B constitute the sample. The schedules of the questions used are semi-structured. They outline specific areas which ought to be covered but leave the interviewer free to decide upon the sequence of the questions.[7]

The interviews were held in the plant, on company time. Notes were taken during the interview and recorded immediately at the end of the day. Interviews were held on different days of the week for a period of seven months.[8]

Evidence that the Experimental Conditions Exist for the Employees

The design of the study calls for *a priori* predictions about employee behavior in Departments A and B. The differences, if any are found, are to be attributed to the differential characteristics assumed to exist in the technology of Departments A and B. (For example, A gives employees much more opportunity for varied, creative work than does B.) Before the hypotheses can be tested, however, we must show some evidence that the employees perceive the differences between A and B as we assume they do. The researcher's assumption of differences are based upon management's job-classification structure. It is one thing for management to classify the jobs in Department A as skilled and Department B as non-skilled and to pay the employees according to these classifications; it is quite another for the employees to perceive these differences.

Evidence that the employees experience the experimental conditions as the researchers assume can be obtained from a number of sources. Ninety-four percent of the employees in Department A (high-skilled) report that they have jobs in which they experience "plenty of variety," "as much variety as they can handle or more." Eighty-seven percent of the employees in Department B report that they have jobs which are "completely routine," "dull," "monotonous," "with little if any variety."

Further evidence is obtained by analyzing the data related to "perceived personal satisfaction" about their jobs. Eighty-five percent of Department B (low skill) report that they obtain "no satisfactions from their work excepting good wages." Eighty-three percent of the employees in Department A report that they gain "much personal satisfaction because they have challenging and creative work."

A few qualitative examples to illustrate the differential feelings are:

Department A: "I think the satisfaction I get is to know that I have done a job well. I like to do a perfect job; I like to feel something's done really good; it's really perfect. When I take a look at a piece that I can tell has been made well, I get a real sense of satisfaction."
Department B: 1. "If the work is all right, then I make money, and that's my biggest satisfaction. If I don't, I get pissed off. What else is there to be satisfied about? I learned long ago the only thing you can get out of a good job is good pay."

2. "The only reason I work is to make money. No other reason. Some guys (damn few) say they work for pleasure. They must be bats. How the hell am I supposed to get satisfaction from this job? I'd just as soon get out and dig holes, at least I'd be in the fresh air."

A second assumption made by the research design is that the degree of dependence and subordination required of the employees by the leadership and the managerial controls will not vary significantly between Departments A and B. These assumptions must also be verified as representing reality from the employees' point of view.

Seventy-five percent of the employees in B and 84% in A view the leadership as "excellent because they hardly ever bother us, because they continually try to help us earn good wages and have secure jobs." In discussing the contacts that they have with management, 63% in B and 68% in A view the management as being "friendly," "down-to-earth," "interested in the employees," and "continually striving to make the employees feel they are not simple machines."

Turning to controls, we find that almost no employees in either department describe the budgets as pressuring them. One explanation of this may be that the budget system is only a few months old and has not had an opportunity to be felt by the employees. Turning to the incentive system, 67% in Department B and 62% in Department A view the piece rates as "being fair," "some rates tough, some easy, but the overall average is fair," and "wish they were slightly higher, but this is not a complaint."

In response to a question on the freedom the employees feel, reflecting on the leadership and the controls together, 83% in Department B and 100% in Department A report they have "as much, or almost as much freedom as they desire." Finally, in an over-all indication of the degree of pressure the employees feel, 91% in Department B and 100% in Department A say that they "never, or hardly ever, experience pressure."

It seems reasonable to assume that the degree of dependence and subordination required of the employees in Departments A and B does not vary significantly between the departments. This says nothing about the amount of dependence and submissiveness *perceived* by the employees. We are simply saying that whatever the amount is, it is about equal in both departments.

Some Differences Between High Skill and Low Skill Employees

A method has been developed to infer the predispositions that individuals manifest *while at work*, plus their potency (in the Lewinian sense of the term).[9]

Table 1

High Skill	Statistical Significance [11]	Low Skill
1. Express a high sense of self-worth and self-regard related to their technological capabilities.	.001	1. Express a very low sense of self-worth and self-regard.
2. Express need to be active.	.001	2. Express need to be passive.
3. Express need to work with others.	.001	3. Express need to be alone.
4. Express need for variety and challenge in their work world.	.001	4. Express need for routine, nonchallenging work.
5. Express need to have some close friendships while at work.	.01	5. Express desire not to make close friendships while at work.
6. Express need to produce quality work.	.001	6. Express need to produce adequate (quantitative work to make a fair day's pay.
7. Express almost no need to overemphasize the importance of material rewards.	.01	7. Overemphasize the importance of material rewards.
8. Express need to learn more about other kinds of work within the same job family.	.001	8. Express almost no need to learn other kinds of work.
9. Participate in activities outside their workplace judged by the researcher to be creative.	.01	9. Participate in activities outside their workplace judged by the researcher to be noncreative.

A word about our use of the concept "predisposition." For the sake of consistency and simplicity the personality aspects upon which we focus are all categorized as "predisposition." A predisposition is defined as a tendency to act in a particular situation. The predispositions are inferred from the interview data. The analyst combs the interview for any themes from which he can infer the desires that the participant wishes to satisfy while at work.[10] An analysis of these data show that statistically the high-skill (HS) employees differ significantly from the low-skill (LS) employees as follows.

These data confirm the hypothesis that the technology has an impact upon the predispositions and activities of human beings. Further analysis, however, raises the question of how significant this impact is if one is focusing on mental health problems.

The Degree of Self-Actualization of HS and LS Employees

The answer to this question becomes evident when we note that the self-actualization scores of the LS and HS employees do *not* differ significantly. Both sets of employees have equally high scores. These scores purport to quantify (in a primitive manner) the degree to which an individual actualizes himself while in the organization.

In other words, even though the LS and HS employees differ significantly in terms of the characteristics listed above, their degree of self-actualization is the same. *Thus, in this case, the often-quoted generalization by mental health practitioners that low skill employees will tend to have a lower degree of self-actualization than high skill employees is not upheld.*

Similarities Between HS and LS Employees

If the HS and LS employees do not differ significantly in self-actualization, then it must be that in addition to the dissimilar predispositions, they must have similar ones which are of higher potency and which are being expressed. The data confirm this hypothesis. The four predispositions with the highest potency are similar for *both* groups of employees. They are:

	Frequency of Choice	
	(Percent)	
	HS	*LS*
1. To be left alone by management	97.0	89.0
2. To be non-involved, indifferent and apathetic about the formal goals and problems of the organization	96.0	86.0
3. To experience skin-surface interpersonal relationships	96.0	90.0
4. To earn fair wages and to have secure jobs	92.0	89.0

From the first two predispositions we may infer the employees desire to be left alone by the formal authorities and not to be required to become ego-involved in the objectives of the company. Apparently the employees have withdrawn psychologically from the organization. They may be said to be in a state of apathy.

Apathy also seems to characterize the employees' predispositions with regard to their interpersonal relationships with others. We note

Table 2. Frequency distribution of self-actualization scores in high skilled and low skilled employees

	HS(%)	LS(%)
0-49.5	..	..
50-54.5	2.9	1.1
55-59.5	2.9	1.1
60-64.5	..	3.3
65-69.5	5.9	8.9
70-74.5	5.9	16.7
75-79.5	8.8	11.1
80-84.5	23.6	16.7
85-89.5	20.6	21.1
90-94.5	14.7	10.0
95-100	8.8	10.0

that they desire few interactions and those to be mere skin-surface relationships. This apathy toward human relationships (as differentiated from apathy toward non-human relationships) may be defined as *alienation*. Employees who are alienated are therefore defined as those who do not tend to desire the rich interpersonal activity usually assumed by some personality theorists to be a basic characteristic of man.[12]   In short, alienated people are willing to separate themselves from human relationships.

From the employees' point of view (especially those on low-skill jobs) alienation may be a sensible way to adapt to their working world. Why, they reason, should they become ego-involved in a world that will not permit them to express mature aspirations and to gain satisfaction of their adult needs?

At this point, the data simply permit us to hypothesize that the primitive state of interpersonal relationship inferred to exist inside the plant also seems to exist in the activities the employees engage in during their non-working hours.[13]   Thus the employee may be hurting his "long-range self" without realizing it.

Here is an important area for research. What precisely are the mental health implications of prolonged experiences of apathy and alienation? Can prolonged apathy and alienation lead to mental illness? If so, by what processes and toward what types of illnesses?

Returning to the data, one may further hypothesize that the alienation (apathy towards others and towards one's self) will tend to lead the employees in *both* groups to express a low degree of competence in their relationships with people. At the same time, recalling the job differences between the LS and HS employees, we may hypothesize further that only the latter will tend to express a high degree of competence in their dealing with "things." These hypotheses are confirmed. LS and HS employees' sense of competence and regard for their competence in interpersonal relationships is low and about the same for both groups. On the other hand, we have seen (Table 2) that only the HS employees report a high degree of competence in their dealing with "things."

Some Comments on the "Human Climate" of the Organization

Let us now look briefly at the environmental culture of the organization in which these results are being obtained.

An analysis of the data shows that management believes, *and the employees agree*, that the organization is *not* pressure-oriented. (In fact, in the writer's experience, this is the least pressure-oriented plant he has ever studied.) The leadership consciously refrains from pressure tactics. As to managerial controls, they are just being established. One of the highest officials remarks that if controls upset people, the controls will go! The employees in both groups report they appreciate the lack of pressure. They are very loyal to the organization, produce an amount that is appreciated by all levels of management, have continually voted down a union, and have a long record of low absenteeism, low turnover, and low grievance rates.

Oversimplified Theories of Individual-Organizational Health

From the above, it is not difficult to see why both management and employees are quite content with each other and with the organization. Each group feels it is getting what it desires.

On the other hand, the employees report that they desire a world in which 1) they are not required to become ego-involved and made (partially) responsible for the organization's health, 2) they are permitted to be alienated and 3) they are paid well (from their point of view) and guaranteed a secure job. It must be stressed again that no adequate evidence exists to help the mental health practitioner decide how mentally unhealthy or healthy is this state of affairs. (As far as the writer is aware, not even a reliable and valid concept of mental health exists.) It may be that the situation herein described is not unhealthy for individuals and will not lead to mental health problems. On the other hand, there is enough evidence to hold with equal vigor the hypothesis that, as Fromm implies, alienation can lead us to become a sick society (8). I tend to believe Fromm has made an important point. However, much research is needed really to test the hypothesis.

The other side of the argument that must be kept in mind is that mental health of the individual is a product of his total life situation. It may be that an individual can endure a significant amount of deficiency in actualization within the plant and make up for it in activities outside the plant. What little evidence I have seen seems to suggest that there is a correlation between the in-plant actualization and outside activities. People with low actualization within the plant do not seem to make up for it as judged by the kind of community activities in which they participate.[14] Recent, and as yet unpublished, research by the writer reinforces the above conclusion. For example, most of the employees (low- and high-skill) do not participate in "outside" organizations in the community. However, systematic research is lacking and no definite conclusions may be drawn at this time.

On the other hand, we find that the managers' concept of organizational health is equally obscure if not invalid. Management is using a set of criteria about organizational health which leads the executives to diagnose the health of the organization as high. For example, they see that absenteeism, turnover, grievance rates are low and that the production and loyalty are high, and on the basis of their theory, judge that all is well. The problem is that their theory about organizational health is oversimplified and internally inconsistent. It is oversimplified because it does not include the health of the individuals working for the organization. It is inconsistent because it has two inconsistent and independent sets of criteria for organizational health rather than one unified set. For example, management assumes that an organization with low absenteeism, low turnover, low grievance, will also tend to have employees who are productive and who desire to be identified with the company, to participate in all decisions that directly influence them, to worry about making the company more effective, to feel some responsibility for the over-all health of the company, and to develop close relationships with management and each other so that such phrases as "one happy family," and "we're a close company," mirror reality.

Our data show that the above theory is not as integrated as management assumes. For example, the plant has a very low rate of absenteeism, turnover, and grievances. The employees are productive. Up to this point, management's theory holds. The same employees, however, also express little identification with the company, little desire to feel some responsibility for its over-all health, little desire to win promotions as foremen, little desire to have close friendships with management *or* with each other. Nor do they express strong needs to belong to cohesive groups.

This does *not* mean, however, that the plant isn't "one happy family." The employees, according to our measures, are very loyal to the organization because they need to be in situations where they are simply asked to produce and not required to become identified with, or deeply involved in, the company. As one employee puts it, "I love this company; it's a wonderful place. They pay excellent wages, give good benefits and they leave you alone. There's a relaxed friendly feeling here. You don't feel the constant pressure as you do in Company Y. No sir, I wouldn't leave this company even if someone wanted to pay me more." Thus, strong loyalty is not necessarily built upon an active, interested, healthy employee group. On the contrary, the opportunity to be apathetic, disinterested, non-involved, could generate strong loyalties within the employees as long as wages and job security remain high.

The most crucial needs HS and LS employees report are wages, job security, job control, non-involvement and togetherness, following that order. Does this mean that money is most important? Are we back to the economists' theory of rational man? The answer to the first question is, "Yes," and to the second, "No." If money is important, it is not because man is the inherently rational being pictured by some economists. The employee is still a complex organism with inner strivings to grow, to develop, to have a sense of inner worth. It is precisely because he is not permitted truly to actualize his potential that he makes a decision to "simplify" his personality, making money and other material factors most important. It is as if the employee says to himself, "I want to be a healthy creative human being; I cannot be, and still produce what I am required to produce. Therefore, I will say, 'To hell with my total personality,' and place the major emphasis on money."[15]

Such a decision is not a rational one. It is a *deep, emotional, human one.* Nevertheless, it makes money and job security very important to the employee. If this is valid, then administrators of complex organizations are faced with one of the most difficult human problems ever to challenge them. On the one hand, it becomes easy for both the administrator and the employees to deemphasize human values and to operate on a *quid pro quo* basis of money, job security, and benefits. As long as a minimum standard of human relationships is maintained, the "rational man relationship" could well flourish. But, as the data point out, such a theory will produce and reward apathy, indifference, alienation, and non-involvement.

Relating Individual Health to Organizational Effectiveness

If the above is valid, clearly individual and organizational "health" are so interrelated that it may be impossible to consider one without considering the other. Men like Lewin and Harry Stack Sullivan showed years ago that man cannot be separated from his environment. In studying the problems of industrial mental health, it may be that man may not be separated from the organization. The unit becomes the individual-organization.

In stating this position, are we making a value judgment that it is good for organizations to exist? The answer must be provided on two levels. First, as far as the researcher is concerned, organizational survival is not a matter of value. Organizations must exist for the researcher as do leaves for the botanist, human bodies for the biologist, and birds for the ornithologist. Without organizations, the researcher on organizations would have nothing to study.

Turning to the value problem from the mental health practitioner's point of view, the following may be said. Most students agree that, basically, organizations are created by man to fulfill needs that require the collective efforts of human beings. These needs are essential if man is to survive. Thus, stating that organizations must survive is simply affirming the most basic needs of mankind. *It is precisely because human survival and health are crucial that organization effectiveness is emphasized.* Without organizational effectiveness, man could lose his individual health.

This position is openly acknowledged by the employees. Interviews with the employees show quite clearly that they *feel* responsible for keeping the organization alive. The problem, from a mental health point of view, is that they too have internalized management's inadequate standards of organizational effectiveness. Consequently, they too, feel that low absenteeism, turnover, grievance rates and high production imply a healthy organization. They report a high degree of satisfaction with their mental health. In fact, our data lead us to predict that over 90% of the employees and 100% of the management in this plant would resist or even reject a mental health program that attempts to emphasize individual health "vs" or "over" the requirements of the organization. The employees report themselves to be "too realistic" to see such a program as in their interest.

Difficult as the situation may sound, there is at least one possible direction to consider. These feelings of responsibility for organizational effectiveness could become the foundations for the building of an effective *preventive* mental health program in industry. Is it not a sign of some health when an individual is willing to see himself in a realistic perspective in his relationship with his society? To be willing to give of one's self without feeling one is giving up one's self may be an important building block for a healthy society.

The argument is not being made that an overemphasis on organization could not lead to the ideal of an "organization man" who submits his uniqueness and his health to the demands of the organization. This possibility is admitted and must be avoided. It is the contention of the writer that, in the final analysis, the existence of organization-man is symptomatic of sick organizations. Organizations are tools which help man to survive. They are created by man. Man can change them to facilitate individual growth.

Changing organizations today, however, is a very difficult task and the major barrier is that there exists no theory or empirical knowledge that tells us in which direction changes ought to be made. As mentioned above, the traditional management theories are inadequate, but the new human relations theories may be equally inadequate. One must conclude from this study that the informal employee system, assumed by many social scientists to be one answer to the problem, does not offer a solution. *The informal employee system in this plant sanctions and protects employees apathy, indifference, and alienation.*

Herein lies the challenge of the future for preventive mental health. Much thinking needs to be done on developing dimensions of organizational effectiveness.[16] Much research needs to be conducted on how to maximize individual-organization health. In the organization studied only such a theory would appeal to both the employees and the management, who express a deep desire that the plant must survive, even, if necessary, at their psychological "expense."

FOOTNOTES

1. This is similar to Erikson's "sense of autonomy" and Bronfenbrenner's "state of creative interdependence."

2. White, Robert W., *Lives in Progress*. New York, Dryden Press, 1952.

3. Lewin and Kounin believe that as the individual develops needs and abilities the boundaries between them become more rigid. This explains why an adult is better able than a child to be frustrated in one activity and still behave constructively in another. See Lewin, Kurt, *A Dynamic Theory of Personality*, New York, McGraw-Hill Book Co., 1935, and Kounin, Jacob S., "Intellectual Development and Rigidity," *Child Behavior and Development*, edited by R. Barker, J. Kounin, and H. R. Wright. New York, McGraw-Hill Book Co., 1943, 179-198.

4. White, Robert W., *op. cit.*, pp. 347 ff.

5. Lewin also cites the billions of dollars that are invested in insurance policies. See Lewin, Kurt, "Time Perspective and Morale," *Resolving Social Conflicts*. New York, Harper & Brothers, 1958, p. 105.

6. Rogers, Carl R., *Client-Centered Therapy*. Boston, Houghton Mifflin Co., 1951.

7. For a more detailed discussion see Argyris, Chris, *Human Problems in a Large Hospital*. New Haven, Labor and Management Center, Yale University, 1956.

8. A monograph being written provides detailed discussion of the research methods and an analysis of the organization as a social system. This work is tentatively entitled *Theory and Method of Diagnosing Organizational Behavior*.

9. Lewin, Kurt, *op. cit.*

10. A predisposition is not assumed to be as basic as the "needs" or "need system" postulated by many psychologists. The psychologist's concept of "need" usually refers to those predispositions (to use our terms for the moment) that are more genotypic (that is, they are manifested in many different types of

situations). Our predispositions are limited to the organizational context being studied.

11. The probability of obtaining by chance a difference as large as that reported is computed by employing statistical procedures appropriate for use with independent proportions. See Quinn McNemar, *Psychological Statistics.* New York, John Wiley & Sons, 1955, p. 60.

12. See Lewin, Kurt, *A Dynamic Theory of Personality*, New York, McGraw-Hill Book Co., 1935; Fromm, Erich, *The Sane Society*, New York, Rinehart & Co., 1955; Sullivan, Harry Stack, *Conceptions of Modern Psychiatry*, William Alanson White Psychiatric Foundation, 1947; Rogers, Carl R., *op. cit.*

13. Argyris, Chris, *Personality and Organization.* New York, Harper & Brothers, 1957.

14. Argyris, Chris, *ibid.*

15. Two points worth noting are: It is not only industry which forces the employee to simplify his personality. The family, schools, churches, etc., may all have similar impacts. Second, the employee is willing to simplify his personality up to a point. This does not mean he will accept money to be treated in an inhuman manner.

16. For some preliminary dimensions of organizational health, see the author's "Organizational Leadership," ONR Conference, March, 1959, in a book to be edited by Luigi Petrullo.

REFERENCES

1. Argyris, Chris, "Individual-Organization Actualization," *Administrative Science Quarterly*, September 1959.
2. Argyris, Chris, *Personality and Organization.* New York, Harper & Brothers, 1957.
3. Erikson, E. H., *Childhood and Society.* New York, Norton, 1950. See also R. Kotinsky, *Personality in the Making.* New York, Harper & Brothers, 1952, pp. 8-25.
4. Bronfenbrenner, Urie, "Toward an Integrated Theory of Personality," *Perception*, (Blake, Robert R. and Glen B. Ramsey). New York, Ronald Press, 1951, pp. 206-257.
5. Bakke, E. W., *The Unemployed Worker.* New Haven, Yale University Press, 1940.
6. Bakke, E. W., *ibid*, p 247.
7. Bakke, E. W., *ibid*, p. 29.
8. Fromm, Erich, *The Sane Society.* New York, Rinehart, 1955, p. 275.

THE NATURE OF CONTROVERSY

Harold Full

Controversy, whether in education or in other areas of social life, has its basis in the contradictory yet interrelated needs, ideas, beliefs, and values of men. Controversy is the intellectual expression of the conflicts, anxieties, and hostilities in society and serves to ease these tensions by permitting the peaceful processes of discussion and debate to minimize the danger of open strife and rebellion. Though some form of conflict is a precondition for controversy, controversy itself can channel these continuing conflicts in desirable directions by creating an intellectual climate that, by moving beyond the immediate dispute, can permit opportunities to develop for reasoned evaluation or resolution. Such creative interaction can prepare the society for intelligent change and progress.[1]

Although conflict and controversy alone cannot account for all the myriad changes that take place in a society, they can, and do, set the stage for changes to occur. The United States as the most open, most mobile, most dynamic society in the world is also a society that is characterized by the greatest frequency of conflicts and controversies. The openness of a society is conducive to divergent ideas and beliefs. It creates an atmosphere for the acceptance of change. The society that resists change and controversy fails to realize the greater danger that confronts it, a danger arising from its inadaptability and static nature. In a society dominated by revolutionary changes that are taking place at an accelerating pace, characteristic of the United States today, it seems essential to develop an intelligent understanding of the nature of controversy and its role in a contemporary democratic society.

Controversy is embedded in the tradition of American democracy. The freedoms embodied in the Constitution were not given to Americans; they were the result of a long series of struggles and conflicts in which controversy played an important role. Controversy helped to resolve the enormous problems facing a growing nation. In the settling of forty million new immigrants, in the giant growth of industry, in the tremendous expansion Westward, in the zealous movements for social and political reform, and in the unique development of a system of free public schools open to all, the continuous give and take of conflicting points of view opened the way for development of levels of understanding that was more inclusive than the ideas or practices of the contending parties. Through this process new questions were raised and new alternatives were seen. Current pressing problems, some new, some reformulations of the old, are being tested in the fires of controversy, and, if intelligently directed, new concepts or new modes of behavior can emerge to provide the society with enough elasticity to meet the radical changes underway.

In examining past and present controversies, it seems that at least six basic phases can be identified. The term *phases of controversy (stages of controversy* would also be acceptable), rather than kinds or types of controversy, was deliberately selected to indicate the dynamic nature of controversy. *Phases* suggests the movement that takes place in any discussion that involves conflicting points of view. Even when a controversy becomes hardened into intransigent positions attracting few new participants or new ideas, it becomes static only temporarily and can flare up again in new dress to meet current fashion. Once this quality of controversy is recognized, it should be understood that the following identified phases are not intended to make distinctions so sharp that rigid boundaries between them are established. Nor do controversies proceed precisely in the manner outlined. They can, and do, begin at any one of the phases, or at several phases simultaneously. Being aware of these qualifications, the reader should find these classifications useful in stimulating him to closer examination of the conflicting points of view presented in the articles in this anthology and helpful in identifying the dominant phases in current disputes.

Phase One. This phase is represented by oversimplification. Very complicated problems are reduced to a single cause. Statements such as this are typical, "The way to prevent juvenile delinquency is to impose a curfew." Little effort is made to identify the issue under discussion or to evaluate it within the conditions that currently prevail. This leads to great fragmentation. What is seen are single units, individual parts, without any relationship to each other or to the whole.

Phase Two. This stage is identified by a polarization of thought. Arguments are put in the form of extremes; beliefs are formulated in an *either-or* context. The participants are so profoundly discontented that they are able to identify only the black and white contrasts between extreme opposites. Charges that cannot be substantiated are often made. This phase is further characterized by the introduction of irrelevant information, and frequently proponents of opposing views are derided and belittled by personal attacks. To bolster their views, the disputants will take refuge in the past, seeking to find "answers" for the contemporary problem or to discover authority figures whom they can romanticize and whose views can be made to conform to their opinions.

Phase Three. As controversy proceeds, the discussion is sometimes directed against a secondary object instead of the original cause of the conflict. The danger here is two-fold: it is possible to hurt or offend the secondary object, and it is possible, unless care is taken, to mistake the secondary object as the source of the problem. This practice makes repeated use of stereotype and exaggerated generalization as techniques for suppressing discussion of fundamental issues. For example, appeals were made by some politicians who were opposed to the recent Federal medical care program for the aged on the grounds that this was "socialized medicine," knowing that with many people this phrase would carry a negative connotation and knowing also that these people would be directed away from examining the basic need for medical care for the aged. These techniques used against objects, however, are harmless compared with their destructive quality when employed against individuals or groups. A moment's reflection can recall numerous instances in which group stereotype has done immeasurable harm to the group and to individuals within the group and that in turn has effectively prevented further examination of the real problem.

Phase Four. This phase concerns controversy among individuals within the same group. It can best be characterized by attempts among members of a group to gain conformity. This phase does not occur in all controversies.

Through discussions of controversial matters groups become established and are maintained. Controversy, in this instance, helps a group affirm its identity as a group. Conformity to the views of the group under these conditions has a positive value; it serves to maintain the unity of the group. If groups are engaged in continued controversy with those outside the group, however, they can in time become intolerant of individuals within the group who deviate from the common ideas, values, or beliefs shared by most of the other members. These conflicting positions are regarded as a threat both to the unity of the group and to its identity. The bitter controversy within the Republican Party during the 1964 presidential election campaign illustrates such intra-group conflicts and controversies.

Should the in-group hostility continue long enough, the group, believing, rightly or wrongly, that its identity is threatened, can restrict or limit its membership only to those who conform to the will of the majority. The group then tends to assume a sect-like character, and, in order to maintain cohesion, searches for disputes from an outside threat although none is actually present. Many extremist groups in the United States bear resemblance to this description.

Phase Five. This phase can be identified as a search for common ground. Participants in the controversy explore ways and means to resolve the conflict. They seek alternatives that may exist between the most extreme positions represented; they seek views or ideas that parallel and could displace other values or beliefs. Although their ultimate goals or beliefs remain widely separated, ground for compromise or for resolution of the controversy is sought on lesser values or interests which the participants may share. In fact, what is sought is some resolution of the controversy in terms that make possible the continuation of differences and even fundamental disagreements.

Charles Frankel puts it this way: "The failure to see that men can work well together without the same ultimate goals leads to a failure to take account of the most distinctive technique of a liberal society for maintaining voluntary cooperation—the technique of compromise. For compromise does not only take place when men are bound by a common creed. It takes place at least as often for a much simpler reason—that men have other values besides those that are in dispute. As a result, they do not choose to risk everything on a single issue."[2]

Phase Six. As controversy continues one can expect to discern a shifting of emphasis among participants. Positions change as new, more objective, ground is broken. New kinds of questions are asked;

new alternatives sought. Entirely different views of the world and new images of man may be introduced. From these varying views, new perspectives are gained from which to view old disputes in a new context and from which to discern new problems. The participants and those on the sidelines are educated to new ideas that without controversy may have taken longer to hear about or to understand.

It is evident from the description of this phase that it represents the most productive plane for a controversy to be waged on. Unfortunately, not all, perhaps only a few, controversies ever reach this stage. Often the participants are trapped, or trap themselves, at one of the beginning phases and fail to realize the potential of the issue under discussion or their own potential for intellectual growth. Yet the opposite is also true. Some controversies begin at this phase and descend to the level of oversimplification or polarization of thought where stereotypes are substituted for reason and logic. John Dewey's philosophy of education is a case in point. His theory of experience based on intellectual and moral standards for a scientific age offered a new vision of what education was all about, of what must be worthy of the name *education*. Soon, however, those who took up his banner, being either uninformed or misinformed, substituted catch phrases or slogans—"progressive" education versus "traditional" education—for the fundamental issue. They became more noted for what they opposed than what they stood for.

Implicit in the six phases just described is a hierarchy of stages through which controversy may move, proceeding from the least informed to the most informed. Also implicit in these descriptions are various levels at which controversy may be enjoined. *Levels*, in this sense, implies the ability to see the issue under discussion from its simplest formulation to its most complex proportions or to see its immediate and practical as well as its theoretical dimensions. The more levels one is able to identify, the greater is his understanding and the deeper his insight into the controversy.

An illustration of the levels of controversy is the great controversy surrounding the famous Scopes trial in Tennessee in 1925 concerning the teaching of Darwin's theory of evolution in the public schools. What began originally as a controversy between science and religion was later sharpened into a clash among the various shades of opinion held by the religious modernists and the religious fundamentalists. Still later the controversy was focused on the larger issues surrounding the relation of church and state in the control of education. Embedded within these central concerns was a range of opinion grouped around other conflicting themes—God versus atheism, rural versus urban, old versus new, conservative versus liberal, censorship versus freedom. Because much of the discussion represented extreme positions, attention was diverted from some of the major, overriding issues implicit in a thorough understanding of the controversy—What is science? What is religion? Should the will of a minority be forced upon the majority?

The negative and positive features of controversy are revealed from further examination of the six phases presented. At first glance the negative aspects do seem to loom large. Frequently in controversy thought is polarized, issues are oversimplified, objects and groups are stereotyped, and pressures are exerted to conform. In assessing the negative results of controversy, some see these factors as paramount, leading them to the conclusion that controversy should be avoided.

This view seems rather widespread in the field of education, where some teachers and administrators in the public schools and some of those engaged in teacher education in the colleges become overly sensitive, hence defensive, when conflicting opinions are aired concerning the important educational issues of our time. Part of this defensive posture might be accounted for by their lack of historical perspective. By being involved in the wealth of current educational controversy, some educators are led to believe that contemporary conflicts are the first, or at least the greatest, the schools have ever faced; they fail to realize that the disputes of the past were many and long and bitter.

Secondly, it is not uncommon that little distinction is made among the sources of controversy. Criticism of the schools comes from those who are dedicated in their support of public education, as well as from a minority who seek to subvert the goal of education for all American youth. Some educators' lack of discrimination in evaluating sources of criticism reflects unfortunately in their opposing arguments, which are often a strong defense of both the weaknesses and the strengths of public education. Quite naturally, this defensive stance gives the impression of weakness or implies that an apology is in order for the unsettled state of affairs in education today. Such reactions prevent professionals in education from rendering informed leadership to the public and limit their responsibility to develop with youth a mature, reasoned, and sophisticated approach to controversy.

The positive dimensions of controversy seems to outweigh those of the negative. Not all controversies are brought out into the open; some are suppressed by individuals or the group. The motivation for expressing a difference of opinion must be strong enough to overcome any doubts that a person or group may have about expressing the opinion. In this sense, then, conflicting points of view can have a counterbalancing effect on the pressures of conformity in society. The motivation for expressing differing views provides democracy with a vital spirit for self-renewal.

The act of entering into controversy serves to establish relations where none existed before and to provide the possibility that other relations are likely to follow. Once these new relationships are created the climate is ripe for additional interaction. Further, through the course of controversy, new situations develop that call for new rules, new norms, new ideas, new values to be created while old rules, norms, ideas, and values are being revised, reformulated, or replaced. Thus, the very nature of controversy safeguards the society from becoming static and helps the participants to derive inner satisfaction. And by reducing hostilities or by diminishing tensions controversy allows the participants to view their problems more objectively.

Controversy assists in maintaining a balance in society. The pluralistic structure of American society provides stability for its social system through the interdependence of conflicting groups whose crisscrossing controversies provide opportunities for individuals and groups to test their relative strength and to reassess their relative power. By intelligent discussion of controversial issues individuals and groups are allowed to shift and choose among various values and beliefs. This process brings about new forms of flexible social arrangements that create avenues for channeling positive and desirable social action. Thus, controversy is a vital form of social interaction. Through this form of social interaction the area is widened for man to act by free choice and not by coercion. The free give and take of conflicting ideas, values, and beliefs forces man to go beyond the parochial point of view, to expand his horizons. This process maintains the vitality of the democratic open society and provides the means by which the society can continue to be open.

Conformity, in its various guises, is the enemy of the very openness of society that controversy helps to sustain. By the throttling of discussion, conformity closes many avenues of social communication and reduces opportunities for individuals to think, to criticize, to evaluate for themselves. Further, in narrowing the choices available to the individual, or the opportunities for making choices, his personal and social responsibilities are severely restricted. Conformity encourages the receptive mind; controversy develops the inquiring mind. The unsettling pace of modern change breeds doubt and an uneasiness of the mind on which conformity, by providing a false sense of security, thrives. Thus, man is robbed of his vision of an endless future with unlimited possibilities, and his awareness of belonging to a larger community of mankind is dulled.

There are moments in the life of almost every man when he feels a yearning to escape into the past to a more simple age, when society and its problems were less complex, or to escape to some future utopia, where common agreement and consent will banish problems and conflicts and bring continual happiness, comfort, and security. There are other moments when man feels resentful that problems he did not create are imposed upon him. Yet in these resentful moments, as in the moments of escape, he knows that he cannot evade the exceptional moment in which he is living, with all its problems, crises, and controversies, nor can he ignore them. He knows that he must live in their full gravity under all conditions and with all consequences.

FOOTNOTES

1. Some ideas in this essay have been freely adapted from Lewis A. Coser, *The Functions of Social Conflict* (Glencoe, Ill.: The Free Press, 1956) and Georg Simmel, *Conflict and the Web of Group Associations* (Glencoe, Ill.: The Free Press, 1955).

2. Charles Frankel, *The Case For Modern Man* (New York: Harper and Brothers, 1956), p. 82.

REFERENCES

Bedyne, D. E. *Conflict, Arousal, and Curiosity*. New York: McGraw-Hill, 1960.

Coser, Lewis A. *Sociological Theory: A Book of Readings* (2nd ed.). New York: The Macmillan Company, 1964.

Coser, Lewis A. *The Functions of Social Conflict*. Glencoe, Ill.: The Free Press, 1956.

Falk, W. D. "Symposium: Reasons," *The Journal of Philosophy* (November 1963), pp. 702-718.

Henderson, Donald. "Minority Response and the Conflict Problem," *Phylon* (Spring 1964), pp. 18-26.

Horowitz, Irving L. "Concensus, Conflict, and Cooperation: A Sociological Inventory," *Social Forces* (December 1962), pp. 177-188.

Simmel, Georg. *Conflict and the Web of Group Associations*. Glencoe, Ill.: The Free Press, 1955.

SUPERORDINATE GOALS IN THE REDUCTION
OF INTERGROUP CONFLICT

Muzafer Sherif

ABSTRACT

This paper[1] summarizes an experimental study on intergroup relations, with emphasis on the reduction of conflict between groups. In the first phase, two groups were established independently by introducing specified conditions for interaction; in the second phase, the groups were brought into functional contact in conditions perceived by the members of the respective groups as competitive and frustrating. Members developed unfavorable attitudes and derogatory stereotypes of the other group; social distance developed to the point of mutual avoidance, even in pleasant activities. In the final phase of the experiment the measure that proved effective in reducing tension between groups was the introduction of goals which were compellingly shared by members of the groups and which required the collaborative efforts of all.

In the past, measures to combat the problems of intergroup conflicts, proposed by social scientists as well as by such people as administrators, policy-makers, municipal officials, and educators, have included the following: introduction of legal sanctions; creation of opportunities for social and other contacts among members of conflicting groups; dissemination of correct information to break down false prejudices and unfavorable stereotypes; appeals to the moral ideals of fair play and brotherhood; and even the introduction of rigorous physical activity to produce catharsis by releasing pent-up frustrations and aggressive complexes in the unconscious. Other measures proposed include the encouragement of co-operative habits

From *The American Journal of Sociology*, Vol. 63, No. 4, January 1958, pp. 349-356. Copyright © 1958 by the University of Chicago Press. Reprinted by permission.

in one's own community, and bringing together in the cozy atmosphere of a meeting room the leaders of antagonistic groups.

Many of these measures may have some value in the reduction of intergroup conflicts, but, to date, very few generalizations have been established concerning the circumstances and kinds of intergroup conflict in which these measures are effective. Today measures are applied in a somewhat trial-and-error fashion. Finding measures that have wide validity in practice can come only through clarification of the nature of intergroup conflict and analysis of the factors conducive to harmony and conflict between groups under given conditions.

The task of defining and analyzing the nature of the problem was undertaken in a previous publication.[2] One of our major statements was the effectiveness of superordinate goals for the reduction of intergroup conflict. "Superordinate goals" we defined as goals which are compelling and highly appealing to members of two or more groups in conflict but which cannot be attained by the resources and energies of the groups separately. In effect, they are goals attained only when groups pull together.

Intergroup Relations and The Behavior of Group Members

Not every friendly or unfriendly act toward another person is related to the group membership of the individuals involved. Accordingly, we must select those actions relevant to relations between groups.

Let us start by defining the main concepts involved. Obviously, we must begin with an adequate conception of the key term—"group." A group is a social unit (1) which consists of a number of individuals who, at a given time, stand in more or less definite interdependent status and role relationships with one another and (2) which explicitly or implicitly possesses a set of values or norms regulating the behavior of individual members, at least in matters of consequence to the group. Thus, shared attitudes, sentiments, aspirations, and goals are related to and implicit in the common values or norms of the group.

The term "intergroup relations" refers to the relations between two or more groups and their respective members. In the present context we are interested in the acts that occur when individuals belonging to one group interact, collectively or individually, with members of another in terms of their group identification. The appropriate frame of reference for studying such behavior includes the functional relations between the groups. Intergroup situations are not voids. Though not independent of relationships within the groups in question, *the characteristics of relations between groups cannot be deduced or extrapolated from the properties of in-group relations.*

Prevalent modes of behavior within a group, in the way of co-operativeness and solidarity or competitiveness and rivalry among members, need not be typical of actions involving members of an out-group. At times, hostility toward out-groups may be proportional to the degree of solidarity within the group. In this connection, results presented by the British statistician L. F. Richardson are instructive. His analysis of the number of wars conducted by the major nations of the world from 1850 to 1941 reveals that Great Britain heads the list with twenty wars—more than the Japanese (nine wars), the Germans (eight wars), or the United States (seven wars). We think that this significantly larger number of wars engaged in by a leading European democracy has more to do with the intergroup relations involved in perpetuating a far-flung empire than with dominant practices at home or with personal frustrations of individual Britishers who participated in these wars.[3]

In recent years relationships between groups have sometimes been explained through analysis of individuals who have endured unusual degrees of frustration or extensive authoritarian treatment in their life-histories. There is good reason to believe that some people growing up in unfortunate life-circumstances may become more intense in their prejudices and hostilities. But at best these cases explain the intensity of behavior in a given dimension.[4] In a conflict between two groups—a strike or a war—opinion within the groups is crystallized, slogans are formulated, and effective measures are organized by members recognized as the most responsible in their respective groups. The prejudice scale and the slogans are not usually imposed on the others by the deviate or neurotic members. Such individuals ordinarily exhibit their intense reactions within the reference scales of prejudice, hostility, or sacrifice established in their respective settings.

The behavior by members of any group toward another group is not primarily a problem of deviate behavior. If it were, intergroup behavior would not be the issue of vital consequence that it is today. The crux of the problem is the participation by group members in established practices and social-distance norms of their group and their response to new trends developing in relationships between their own group and other groups.

On the basis of his UNESCO studies in India, Gardner Murphy concludes that to be a good Hindu or a good Moslem implies belief in all the nasty qualities and practices attributed by one's own group—Hindu or Moslem—to the other. Good members remain deaf and dumb to favorable information concerning the adversary. Social contacts and avenues of communication serve, on the whole, as vehicles for further conflicts not merely for neurotic individuals but for the bulk of the membership.[5]

In the process of interaction among members, an in-group is endowed with positive qualities which tend to be praiseworthy, self-justifying, and even self-glorifying. Individual members tend to develop these qualities through internalizing group norms and through example by high-status members, verbal dicta, and a set of correctives standardized to deal with cases of deviation. Hence, possession of these qualities, which reflect their particular brand of ethnocentrism, is not essentially a problem of deviation or personal frustration. It is a question of participation in in-group values and trends by good members, who constitute the majority of membership as long as group solidarity and morale are maintained.

To out-groups and their respective members are attributed positive or negative qualities, depending on the nature of functional relations between the groups in question. The character of functional relations between groups may result from actual harmony and interdependence or from actual incompatibility between the aspirations and directions of the groups. A number of field studies and experiments indicate that, if the functional relations between groups are positive, favorable attitudes are formed toward the out-group. If the functional relations between groups are negative, they give rise to hostile attitudes and unfavorable stereotypes in relation to the out-group. Of course, in large group units the picture of the out-group and relations with it depend very heavily on communication, particularly from the mass media.

Examples of these processes are recurrent in studies of small groups. For example, when a gang "appropriates" certain blocks in a city, it is considered "indecent" and a violation of its "rights" for another group to carry on its feats in that area. Intrusion by another group is conducive to conflict, at times with grim consequences, as Thrasher showed over three decades ago.[6]

When a workers' group declares a strike, existing group lines are drawn more sharply. Those who are not actually for the strike are regarded as against it. There is no creature more lowly than the man who works while the strike is on.[7] The same type of behavior is found in management groups under similar circumstances.

In time, the adjectives attributed to out-groups take their places in the repertory of group norms. The lasting, derogatory stereotypes attributed to groups low on the social-distance scale are particular cases of group norms pertaining to out-groups.

As studies by Bogardus show, the social-distance scale of a group, once established, continues over generations, despite changes of constituent individuals, who can hardly be said to have prejudices because of the same severe personal frustrations or authoritarian treatment.[8]

Literature on the formation of prejudice by growing children shows that it is not even necessary for the individual to have actual unfavorable experiences with out-groups to form attitudes of prejudice toward them. In the very process of becoming an in-group member, the intergroup delineations and corresponding norms prevailing in the group are internalized by the individual.[9]

A Research Program

A program of research has been under way since 1948 to test experimentally some hypotheses derived from the literature of intergroup relations. The first large-scale intergroup experiment was carried out in 1949, the second in 1953, and the third in 1954.[10] The conclusions reported here briefly are based on the 1949 and 1954 experiments and on a series of laboratory studies carried out as co-ordinate parts of the program.[11]

The methodology, techniques, and criteria for subject selection in the experiments must be summarized here very briefly. The experiments were carried out in successive stages: (1) groups were formed experimentally; (2) tension and conflict were produced between these groups by introducing conditions conducive to competitive and reciprocally frustrating relations between them; and (3) the attempt was made toward reduction of the intergroup conflict. This stage of reducing tension through introduction of superordinate goals was attempted in the 1954 study on the basis of lessons learned in the two previous studies.

At every stage the subjects interacted in activities which appeared natural to them at a specially arranged camp site completely under our experimental control. They were not aware of the fact that their behavior was under observation. No observation or recording was made in the subjects' presence in a way likely to arouse the suspicion that they were being observed. There is empirical and experimental evidence contrary to the contention that individuals cease to be mindful when they know they are being observed and that their words are being recorded.[12]

In order to insure validity of conclusions, results obtained through observational methods were cross-checked with results obtained through sociometric technique, stereotype ratings of in-groups and out-groups, and through data obtained by techniques adapted from the laboratory. Unfortunately, these procedures cannot be elaborated here. The conclusions summarized briefly are based on results cross-checked by two or more techniques.

The production of groups, the production of conflict between them, and the reduction of conflict in successive stages were brought about through the introduction of problem situations that were real and could not be ignored by individuals in the situation. Special "lecture methods" or "discussion methods" were not used. For example, the problem of getting a meal through their own initiative and planning was introduced when participating individuals were hungry.

Facing a problem situation which is immediate and compelling and which embodies a goal that cannot be ignored, group members *do* initiate discussion and *do* plan and carry through these plans until the objective is achieved. In this process the discussion becomes *their* discussion, the plan *their* plan, the action *their* action. In this process discussion, planning, and action have their place, and, when occasion arises, lecture or information has its place, too. The sequence of these related activities need not be the same in all cases.

The subjects were selected by rigorous criteria. They were healthy, normal boys around the age of eleven and twelve, socially well adjusted in school and neighborhood, and academically successful. They came from a homogeneous sociocultural background and from settled, well-adjusted families of middle or lower-middle class and Protestant affiliations. No subject came from a broken home. The mean I.Q. was above average. The subjects were not personally acquainted with one another prior to the experiment. Thus, explanation of results on the basis of background differences, social maladjustment, undue childhood frustrations, or previous interpersonal relations was ruled out at the beginning by the criteria for selecting subjects.

The first stage of the experiments was designed to produce groups with distinct structure (organization) and a set of norms which could be confronted with intergroup problems. The method for producing groups from unacquainted individuals with similar background was to introduce problem situations in which the attainment of the goal depended on the co-ordinated activity of all individuals. After a series of such activities, definite group structures or organizations developed.

The results warrant the following conclusions for the stage of group formation: When individuals interact in a series of situations toward goals which appeal to all and which require that they co-ordinate their activities, group structures arise having hierarchical status arrangements and a set of norms regulating behavior in matters of consequence to the activities of the group.

Once we had groups that satisfied our definition of "group," relations between groups could be studied. Specified conditions conducive to friction or conflict between groups were introduced. This negative aspect was deliberately undertaken because the major problem in intergroup relations today is the reduction of existing intergroup frictions. (Increasingly, friendly relations between groups is not nearly so great an issue.) The factors conducive to intergroup conflict give us realistic leads for reducing conflict.

A series of situations was introduced in which one group could achieve its goal only at the expense of the other group—through a tournament of competitive events with desirable prizes for the winning group. The results of the stage of intergroup conflict supported our main hypotheses. During interaction between groups in experimentally introduced activities which were competitive and mutually frustrating, members of each group developed hostile attitudes and highly unfavorable stereotypes toward the other group and its members. In fact, attitudes of social distance between the groups became so definite that they wanted to have nothing further to do with each other. This we take as a case of experimentally produced "social distance" in miniature. Conflict was manifested in derogatory name-calling and invectives, flare-ups of physical conflict, and raids on each other's cabins and territory. Over a period of time, negative stereotypes and unfavorable attitudes developed.

At the same time there was an increase in in-group solidarity and co-operativeness. This finding indicates that co-operation and democracy within groups do not necessarily lead to democracy and co-operation with out-groups, if the directions and interests of the groups are conflicting.

Increased solidarity forged in hostile encounters, in rallies from defeat, and in victories over the out-group is one instance of a more general finding: Intergroup relations, both conflicting and harmonious, *affected the nature of relations within the groups involved.* Altered relations between groups produced significant changes in the status arrangements *within* groups, in some instances resulting in shifts at the upper status levels or even a change in leadership. Always, consequential intergroup relations were reflected in new group values or norms which signified changes in practice, word, and deed within the group. Counterparts of this finding are not difficult to see in actual and consequential human relations. Probably many of our major preoccupations, anxieties, and activities in the past decade are incomprehensible without reference to the problems created by the prevailing "cold war" on an international scale.

Reduction of Intergroup Friction

A number of the measures proposed today for reducing intergroup friction could have been tried in this third stage. A few will be mentioned here, with a brief explanation of why they were discarded or were included in our experimental design.

1. Disseminating favorable information in regard to the out-group was not included. Information that is not related to the goals currently in focus in the activities of groups is relatively ineffective, as many studies on attitude change have shown.[13]

2. In small groups it is possible to devise sufficiently attractive rewards to make individual achievement supreme. This may reduce tension between groups by splitting the membership on an "every-man-for-himself" basis. However, this measure has little relevance for actual intergroup tensions, which are in terms of group membership and group alignments.

3. The resolution of conflict through leaders alone was not utilized. Even when group leaders meet apart from their groups around a conference table, they cannot be considered independent of the dominant trends and prevailing attitudes of their membership. If a leader is too much out of step in his negotiations and agreements with out-groups, he will cease to be followed. It seemed more realistic, therefore, to study the influence of leadership within the framework of prevailing trends in the groups involved. Such results will give us leads concerning the conditions under which leadership can be effective in reducing intergroup tensions.

4. The "common-enemy" approach is effective in pulling two or more groups together against another group. This approach was utilized in the 1949 experiment as an expedient measure and yielded effective results. But bringing some groups together against others means larger and more devastating conflicts in the long run. For this reason, the measure was not used in the 1954 experiment.

5. Another measure, advanced both in theoretical and in practical work, centers around social contacts among members of antagonistic groups in activities which are pleasant in themselves. This measure was tried out in 1954 in the first phase of the integration stage.

6. As the second phase of the integration stage, we introduced a series of superordinate goals which necessitate co-operative inter-action between groups.

The social contact situations consisted of activities which were satisfying in themselves—eating together in the same dining room, watching a movie in the same hall, or engaging in an entertainment in close physical proximity. These activities, which were satisfying to each group, but which did not involve a state of interdependence and co-operation for the attainment of goals, were not effective in reducing intergroup tension. On the contrary, such occasions of contact were utilized as opportunities to engage in name-calling and in abuse of each other to the point of physical manifestations of hostility.

The ineffective, even deleterious, results of intergroup contact without superordinate goals have implications for certain contemporary learning theories and for practice in intergroup relations. Contiguity in pleasant activities with members of an out-group does not necessarily lead to a pleasurable image of the out-group if relations between the groups are unfriendly. Intergroup contact without superordinate goals is not likely to produce lasting reduction of intergroup hostility. John Gunther, for instance, in his survey of contemporary Africa, concluded that, when the intergroup relationship is exploitation of one group by a "superior" group, intergroup contact inevitably breeds hostility and conflict.[14]

Introduction of Superordinate Goals

After establishing the ineffectiveness, even the harm, in intergroup contacts which did not involve superordinate goals, we introduced a series of superordinate goals. Since the characteristics of the problem situations used as superordinate goals are implicit in the two main hypotheses for this stage, we shall present these hypotheses:

1. When groups in a state of conflict are brought into contact under conditions embodying superordinate goals, which are compelling but cannot be achieved by the efforts of one group alone, they will tend to co-operate toward the common goals.

2. Co-operation between groups, necessitated by a series of situations embodying superordinate goals, will have a cumulative effect in the direction of reducing existing conflict between groups.

The problem situations were varied in nature, but all had an essential feature in common—they involved goals that could not be attained by the efforts and energies of one group alone and thus created a state of interdependence between groups: combating a water shortage that affected all and could not help being "compelling"; securing a much-desired film, which could not be obtained by either group alone but required putting their resources together; putting into working shape, when everyone was hungry and the food was some distance away, the only means of transportation available to carry food.

The introduction of a series of such superordinate goals was indeed effective in reducing intergroup conflict: (1) when the groups in a state of friction interacted in conditions involving superordinate goals, they did co-operate in activities leading toward the common goal and (2) a series of joint activities leading toward superordinate goals had the cumulative effect of reducing the prevailing friction between groups and unfavorable stereotypes toward the out-group.

These major conclusions were reached on the basis of observational data and were confirmed by sociometric choices and stereotype ratings administered first during intergroup conflict and again after the introduction of a series of superordinate goals. Comparison of the sociometric choices during intergroup conflict and following the series of superordinate goals shows clearly the changed attitudes toward members of the out-group. Friendship preferences shifted from almost exclusive preference for in-group members toward increased inclusion of members from the "antagonists." Since the groups were still intact following co-operative efforts to gain superordinate goals, friends were found largely within one's group. However, choices of out-group members grew, in one group, from practically none during intergroup conflict to 23 percent. Using chi square, this difference is significant $(P < .05)$. In the other group, choices of the out-group increased to 36 percent, and the difference is significant $(P < .001)$. The findings confirm observations that the series of superordinate goals produced increasingly friendly associations and attitudes pertaining to out-group members.

Observations made after several superordinate goals were introduced showed a sharp decrease in the name-calling and derogation of the out-group common during intergroup friction and in the contact situations without superordinate goals. At the same time the blatant glorification and bragging about the in-group, observed during the period of conflict, diminished. These observations were confirmed by comparison of ratings of stereotypes (adjectives) the subjects had actually used in referring to their own group and the out-group during conflict with ratings made after the series of superordinate goals. Ratings of the out-group changed significantly from largely unfavorable ratings to largely favorable ratings. The proportions of

the most unfavorable ratings found appropriate for the out-group—
that is, the categorical verdicts that "all of them are stinkers" or ". . .
smart alecks" or ". . . sneaky"—fell, in one group, from 21 percent at
the end of the friction stage to 1.5 percent after interaction oriented
toward superordinate goals. The corresponding reduction in these
highly unfavorable verdicts by the other group was from 36.5 to 6
percent. The over-all differences between the frequencies of stereotype ratings made in relation to the out-group during intergroup
conflict and following the series of superordinate goals are significant
for both groups at the .001 level (using chi-square test).

Ratings of the in-group were not so exclusively favorable, in line
with observed decreases in self-glorification. But the differences in
ratings of the in-group were not statistically significant, as were the
differences in ratings of the out-group.

Our findings demonstrate the effectiveness of a series of superordinate goals in the reduction of intergroup conflict, hostility, and
their by-products. They also have implications for other measures
proposed for reducing intergroup tensions.

It is true that lines of communication between groups must be
opened before prevailing hostility can be reduced. But, if contact
between hostile groups takes place without superordinate goals, the
communication channels serve as media for further accusations and
recriminations. When contact situations involve superordinate goals,
communication is utilized in the direction of reducing conflict in
order to attain the common goals.

Favorable information about a disliked out-group tends to be
ignored, rejected, or reinterpreted to fit prevailing stereotypes. But,
when groups are pulling together toward superordinate goals, true
and even favorable information about the out-group is seen in a new
light. The probability of information being effective in eliminating
unfavorable stereotypes is enormously enhanced.

When groups co-operate in the attainment of superordinate goals,
leaders are in a position to take bolder steps toward bringing about
understanding and harmonious relations. When groups are directed
toward incompatible goals, genuine moves by a leader to reduce
intergroup tension may be seen by the membership as out of step
and ill advised. The leader may be subjected to severe criticism and
even loss of faith and status in his own group. When compelling
superordinate goals are introduced, the leader can make moves to
further co-operative efforts, and his decisions receive support from
other group members.

In short, various measures suggested for the reduction of intergroup conflict—disseminating information, increasing social contact, conferences of leaders—acquire new significance and effectiveness when they become part and parcel of interaction processes between groups oriented toward superordinate goals which have real and compelling value for all groups concerned.

FOOTNOTES

1. The main points in this paper were presented at the Third Inter-American Congress of Psychology, Austin, Texas, December 17, 1955.

2. Muzafer Sherif and Carolyn W. Sherif, *Groups in Harmony and Tension* (New York: Harper & Bros. 1953).

3. T. H. Pear, *Psychological Factors of Peace and War* (New York: Philosophical Library, 1950), p. 126.

4. William R. Hood and Muzafer Sherif, "Personality Oriented Approaches to Prejudice," *Sociology and Social Research*, XL (1955), 79-85.

5. Gardner Murphy, *In the Minds of Men* (New York: Basic Books, 1953).

6. F. M. Thrasher, *The Gang* (Chicago: University of Chicago Press, 1927).

7. E. T. Hiller, *The Strike* (Chicago: University of Chicago Press, 1928).

8. E. S. Bogardus, "Changes in Racial Distances," *International Journal of Opinion and Attitude Research*, I (1947), 55-62.

9. E. L. Horowitz, " 'Race Attitudes,' " in Otto Klineberg (ed.), *Characteristics of the American Negro*, Part IV (New York: Harper & Bros., 1944).

10. The experimental work in 1949 was jointly supported by the Yale Attitude Change Project and the American Jewish Committee. It is summarized in Sherif and Sherif, *op. cit.*, chaps. ix and x. Both the writing of that book and the experiments in 1953-54 were made possible by a grant from the Rockefeller Foundation. The 1953 research is summarized in Muzafer Sherif, B. Jack White, and O. J. Harvey, "Status in Experimentally Produced Groups," *American Journal of Sociology*, LX (1955), 370-79. The 1954 experiment was summarized in Muzafer Sherif, O. J. Harvey, B. Jack White, William R. Hood, and Carolyn W. Sherif, "Experimental Study of Positive and Negative Intergroup Attitudes between Experimentally Produced Groups: Robbers Cave Study" (Norman, Okla.: University of Oklahoma, 1954). (Multilithed.) For a summary of the three experiments see chaps, vi and ix in Muzafer Sherif and Carolyn W. Sherif, *An Outline of Social Psychology* (rev. ed.; New York: Harper & Bros., 1956).

11. For an overview of this program see Muzafer Sherif, "Integrating Field Work and Laboratory in Small Group Research," *American Sociological Review*, XIX (1954), 759-71.

12. E.g., see F. B. Miller, " 'Resistentialism' in Applied Social Research," *Human Organization*, XII (1954), 5-8; S. Wapner and T. G. Alper, "The Effect of an Audience on Behavior in a Choice Situation," *Journal of Abnormal and Social Psychology*, XLVII (1952), 222-29.

13. E.g., see R. M. Williams, *The Reduction of Intergroup Tensions* (Social Science Research Council Bull. 57 [New York, 1947]).

14. John Gunther, *Inside Africa* (New York: Harper & Bros., 1955).

BEYOND THEORY Y

John J. Morse
Jay W. Lorsch

During the past 30 years, managers have been bombarded with two competing approaches to the problems of human administration and organization. The first, usually called the classical school organization, emphasizes the need for well-established lines of authority, clearly defined jobs, and authority equal to responsibility. The second, often called the participative approach, focuses on the desirability of involving organization members in decision making so that they will be more highly motivated.

Douglas McGregor, through his well-known "Theory X and Theory Y," drew a distinction between the assumptions about human motivation which underlie these two approaches, to this effect:

Theory X assumes that people dislike work and must be coerced, controlled, and directed toward organizational goals. Furthermore, most people prefer to be treated this way, so they can avoid responsibility.

Theory Y—the integration of goals—emphasizes the average person's intrinsic interest in his work, his desire to be self-directing and to seek responsibility, and his capacity to be creative in solving business problems.

It is McGregor's conclusion, of course, that the latter approach to organization is the more desirable one for managers to follow.[1]

McGregor's position causes confusion for the managers who try to

From *Harvard Business Review*, May-June 1970, pp. 61-68. © 1970 by the President and Fellows of Harvard College; all rights reserved.

choose between these two conflicting approaches. The classical organizational approach that McGregor associated with Theory X does work well in some situations, although, as McGregor himself pointed out, there are also some situations where it does not work effectively. At the same time, the approach based on Theory Y, while it has produced good results in some situations, does not always do so. That is, each approach is effective in some cases but not in others. Why is this? How can managers resolve the confusion?

A New Approach

Recent work by a number of students of management and organization may help to answer such questions.[2] These studies indicate that there is not one best organizational approach; rather, the best approach depends on the nature of the work to be done. Enterprises with highly predictable tasks perform better with organizations characterized by the highly formalized procedures and management hierarchies of the classical approach. With highly uncertain tasks that require more extensive problem solving, on the other hand, organizations that are less formalized and emphasize self-control and member participation in decision making are more effective. In essence, according to these newer studies, managers must design and develop organizations so that the organizational characteristics *fit* the nature of the task to be done.

While the conclusions of this newer approach will make sense to most experienced managers and can alleviate much of the confusion about which approach to choose, there are still two important questions unanswered:

1. How does the more formalized and controlling organization affect the motivation of organization members? (McGregor's most telling criticism of the classical approach was that it did not unleash the potential in an enterprise's human resources.)

2. Equally important, does a less formalized organization always provide a high level of motivation for its members? (This is the implication many managers have drawn from McGregor's work.)

We have recently been involved in a study that provides surprising answers to these questions and, when taken together with other recent work, suggests a new set of basic assumptions which move beyond Theory Y into what we call "Contingency Theory: the fit between task, organization, and people." These theoretical assumptions emphasize that the appropriate pattern of organization is *contingent* on the nature of the work to be done and on the particular needs of the people involved. We should emphasize that we have labeled these assumptions as a step beyond Theory Y because of McGregor's own recognition that the Theory Y assumptions would probably be supplanted by new knowledge within a short time.[3]

The Study Design

Our study was conducted in four organizational units. Two of these performed the relatively certain task of manufacturing standardized containers on high-speed, automated production lines. The other two performed the relatively uncertain work of research and development in communications technology. Each pair of units performing the same kind of task were in the same large company, and each pair had previously been evaluated by that company's management as containing one highly effective unit and a less effective one. The study design is summarized in Figure 1.

The objective was to explore more fully how the fit between organization and task was related to successful performance. That is, does a good fit between organizational characteristics and task requirements increase the motivation of individuals and hence produce more effective individual and organizational performance?

An especially useful approach to answering this question is to recognize that an individual has a strong need to master the world around him, including the task that he faces as a member of a work organization.[4] The accumulated feelings of satisfaction that come from successfully mastering one's environment can be called a "sense of competence." We saw this sense of competence in performing a particular task as helpful in understanding how a fit between task and organizational characteristics could motivate people toward successful performance.

Organizational Dimensions

Because the four study sites had already been evaluated by the respective corporate managers as high and low performers of tasks,

Figure 1. Study design in "fit" of organizational characteristics

Characteristics	Company I (predictable manufacturing task)	Company II (unpredictable R & D task)
Effective performer	Akron containers plant	Stockton research lab
Less effective performer	Hartford containers plant	Carmel research lab

we expected that such differences in performance would be a preliminary clue to differences in the "fit" of the organizational characteristics to the job to be done. But, first, we had to define what kinds of organizational characteristics would determine how appropriate the organization was to the particular task.

We grouped these organizational characteristics into two sets of factors:

1. Formal characteristics, which could be used to judge the fit between the kind of task being worked on and the formal practices of the organization.

2. Climate characteristics, or the subjective perceptions and orientations that had developed among the individuals about their organizational setting. (These too must fit the task to be performed if the organization is to be effective.)

We measured these attributes through questionnaires and interviews with about 40 managers in each unit to determine the appropriateness of the organization to the kind of task being performed. We also measured the feelings of competence of the people in the organizations so that we could link the appropriateness of the organizational attributes with a sense of competence.

Major Findings

The principal findings of the survey are best highlighted by contrasting the highly successful Akron plant and the high-performing Stockton laboratory. Because each performed very different tasks (the former a relatively certain manufacturing task and the latter a relatively uncertain research task), we expected, as brought out earlier, that there would have to be major differences between them in organizational characteristics if they were to perform effectively. And this is what we did find. But we also found that each of these effective units had a better fit with its particular task than did its less effective counterpart.

While our major purpose in this article is to explore how the fit between task and organizational characteristics is related to motivation, we first want to explore more fully the organizational characteristics of these units, so the reader will better understand what we mean by a fit between task and organization and how it can lead to more effective behavior. To do this, we shall place the major emphasis on the contrast between the high-performing units (the Akron plant and Stockton laboratory), but we shall also compare each of these with its less effective mate (the Hartford plant and Carmel laboratory respectively).

Formal Characteristics

Beginning with differences in formal characteristics, we found that both the Akron and Stockton organizations fit their respective tasks much better than did their less successful counterparts. In the predictable manufacturing task environment, Akron had a pattern of formal relationships and duties that was highly structured and precisely defined. Stockton, with its unpredictable research task, had a low degree of structure and much less precision of definition (see Figure 2).

Akron's pattern of formal rules, procedures, and control systems was so specific and comprehensive that it prompted one manager to remark: "We've got rules here for everything from how much powder to use in cleaning the toilet bowls to how to cart a dead body out of the plant." In contrast, Stockton's formal rules were so minimal, loose, and flexible that one scientist, when asked whether he felt the rules ought to be tightened, said:

"If a man puts a nut on a screw all day long, you may need more rules and a job definition for him. But we're not novices here. We're professionals and not the kind who need close supervision. People around here *do* produce, and produce under relaxed conditions. Why tamper with success?"

Figure 2. Differences in formal characteristics
in high-performing organizations

Characteristics	Akron	Stockton
1. Pattern of formal relationships and duties as signified by organization charts and job manuals	Highly Structured, precisely defined	Low degree of structure, less well defined
2. Pattern of formal rules, procedures, control, and measurement systems	Pervasive, specific, uniform, compre-hensive	Minimal, loose, flexible
3. Time dimensions incorporated in formal practices	Short-term	Long-term
4. Goal dimensions incorporated in formal practices	Manufacturing	Scientific

These differences in formal organizational characteristics were well suited to the differences in tasks of the two organizations. Thus:

• Akron's highly structured formal practices fit its predictable task because behavior had to be rigidly defined and controlled around the automated, high-speed production line. There was really only one way to accomplish the plant's very routine and programmable job; managers defined it precisely and insisted (through the plant's formal practices) that each man do what was expected of him.

On the other hand, Stockton's highly unstructured formal practices made just as much sense because the required activities in the laboratory simply could not be rigidly defined in advance. With such an unpredictable, fast-changing task as communications technology research, there were numerous approaches to getting the job done well. As a consequence, Stockton managers used a less structured pattern of formal practices that left the scientists in the lab free to respond to the changing task situation.

• Akron's formal practices were very much geared to *short-term* and *manufacturing* concerns as its task demanded. For example, formal production reports and operating review sessions were daily occurrences, consistent with the fact that the through-put time for their products was typically only a few hours.

By contrast, Stockton's formal practices were geared to *long-term* and *scientific* concerns, as its task demanded. Formal reports and reviews were made only quarterly, reflecting the fact that research often does not come to fruition for three to five years.

At the two less effective sites (i.e., the Hartford plant and the Carmel laboratory), the formal organizational characteristics did not fit their respective tasks nearly as well. For example, Hartford's formal practices were much less structured and controlling than were Akron's, while Carmel's were more restraining and restricting than were Stockton's. A scientist in Carmel commented:

"There's something here that keeps you from being scientific. It's hard to put your finger on, but I guess I'd call it 'Mickey Mouse.' There are rules and things here that get in your way regarding doing your job as a researcher."

Climate Characteristics

As with formal practices, the climate in both high-performing Akron and Stockton suited the respective tasks much better than did the climates at the less successful Hartford and Carmel sites.

Perception of structure: The people in the Akron plant perceived a great deal of structure, with their behavior tightly controlled and defined. One manager in the plant said:

"We can't let the lines run unattended. We lose money whenever they do. So we make sure each man knows his job, knows when he can take a break, knows how to handle a change in shifts, etc. It's all spelled out clearly for him the day he comes to work here."

In contrast, the scientists in the Stockton laboratory perceived very little structure, with their behavior only minimally controlled. Such perceptions encouraged the individualistic and creative behavior that the uncertain, rapidly changing research task needed. Scientists in the less successful Carmel laboratory perceived much more structure in their organization and voiced the feeling that this was "getting in their way" and making it difficult to do effective research.

Distribution of influence. The Akron plant and the Stockton laboratory also differed substantially in how influence was distributed and on the character of superior-subordinate and colleague relations. Akron personnel felt that they had much less influence over decisions in their plant than Stockton's scientists did in their laboratory. The task at Akron had already been clearly defined and that definition had, in a sense, been incorporated into the automated production flow itself. Therefore, there was less need for individuals to have a say in decisions concerning the work process.

Moreover, in Akron, influence was perceived to be concentrated in the upper levels of the formal structure (a hierarchical or "top-heavy" distribution), while in Stockton influence was perceived to be more evenly spread out among more levels of the formal structure (an egalitarian distribution).

Akron's members perceived themselves to have a low degree of freedom vis-à-vis superiors both in choosing the jobs they work on and in handling these jobs on their own. They also described the type of supervision in the plant as being relatively directive. Stockton's scientists, on the other hand, felt that they had a great deal of freedom vis-à-vis their superiors both in choosing the tasks and projects, and in handling them in the way that they wanted to. They described supervision in the laboratory as being very participatory.

It is interesting to note that the less successful Carmel laboratory had more of its decisions made at the top. Because of this, there was a definite feeling by the scientists that their particular expertise was not being effectively used in choosing projects.

Relations with others. The people at Akron perceived a great deal of similarity among themselves in background, prior work experiences, and approaches for tackling job-related problems. They also perceived the degree of coordination of effort among colleagues to be very high. Because Akron's task was so precisely defined and the behavior of its members so rigidly controlled around the automated lines, it is easy to see that this pattern also made sense.

By contrast, Stockton's scientists perceived not only a great many differences among themselves, especially in education and background, but also that the coordination of effort among colleagues was relatively low. This was appropriate for a laboratory in which a great variety of disciplines and skills were present and individual projects were important to solve technological problems.

Time orientation. As we would expect, Akron's individuals were highly oriented toward a relatively short time span and manufacturing goals. They responded to quick feedback concerning the quality and service that the plant was providing. This was essential, given the nature of their task.

Stockton's researchers were highly oriented toward a longer time span and scientific goals. These orientations meant that they were willing to wait for long-term feedback from a research project that might take years to complete. A scientist in Stockton said:

> "We're not the kind of people here who need a pat on the back every day. We can wait for months if necessary before we get feedback from colleagues and the profession. I've been working on one project now for three months and I'm still not sure where it's going to take me. I can live with that, though."

This is precisely the kind of behavior and attitude that spells success on this kind of task.

Managerial style. Finally, the individuals in both Akron and Stockton perceived their chief executive to have a "managerial style" that expressed more of a concern for the task than for people or relationships, but this seemed to fit both tasks.

In Akron, the technology of the task was so dominant that top managerial behavior which was not focused primarily on the task might have reduced the effectiveness of performance. On the other hand, although Stockton's research task called for more individualistic problem-solving behavior, that sort of behavior could have become segmented and uncoordinated, unless the top executive in the lab focused the group's attention on the overall research task. Given the individualistic bent of the scientists, this was an important force in achieving unity of effort.

All these differences in climate characteristics in the two high performers are summarized in Figure 3.

As with formal attributes, the less effective Hartford and Carmel sites had organization climates that showed a perceptibly lower

Figure 3. Differences in "climate" characteristics
in high-performing organizations

Characteristics	Akron	Stockton
1. Structural orientation	Perceptions of tightly controlled behavior and a high degree of structure	Perceptions of a low degree of structure
2. Distribution of influence	Perceptions of low total influence, concentrated at upper levels in the organization	Perceptions of high total influence, more evenly spread out among all levels
3. Character of superior-subordinate relations	Low freedom vis-à-vis superiors to choose and handle jobs, directive type of supervision	High freedom vis-à-vis superiors to choose and handle projects, participatory type of supervision
4. Character of colleague relations	Perceptions of many similarities among colleagues, high degree of coordination of colleague effort	Perceptions of many differences among colleagues, relatively low degree of coordination of colleague effort
5. Time orientation	Short-term	Long-term
6. Goal orientation	Manufacturing	Scientific
7. Top executive's "managerial style"	More concerned with task than people	More concerned with task than people

degree of fit with their respective tasks. For example, the Hartford plant had an egalitarian distribution of influence, perceptions of a low degree of structure, and a more participatory type of supervision. The Carmel laboratory had a somewhat top-heavy distribution of influence, perceptions of high structure, and a more directive type of supervision.

Competence Motivation

Because of the difference in organizational characteristics at Akron and Stockton, the two sites were strikingly different places in which to work. But these organizations had two very important things in common. First, each organization fit very well the requirements of its task. Second, although the behavior in the two organizations was different, the result in both cases was effective task performance.

Since, as we indicated earlier, our primary concern in this study was to link the fit between organization and task with individual motivation to perform effectively, we devised a two-part test to measure the sense of competence motivation of the individuals at both sites. Thus:

The *first* part asked a participant to write creative and imaginative stories in response to six ambiguous pictures.

The *second* asked him to write a creative and imaginative story about what he would be doing, thinking, and feeling "tomorrow" on his job. This is called a "projective" test because it is assumed that the respondent projects into his stories his own attitudes, thoughts, feelings, needs, and wants, all of which can be measured from the stories.[5]

The results indicated that the individuals in Akron and Stockton showed significantly more feelings of competence than did their counterparts in the lower-fit Hartford and Carmel organizations.[6] We found that the organization-task fit is simultaneously linked to and interdependent with both individual motivation and effective unit performance. (This interdependency is illustrated in Figure 4.)

Figure 4. Basic contingent relationships

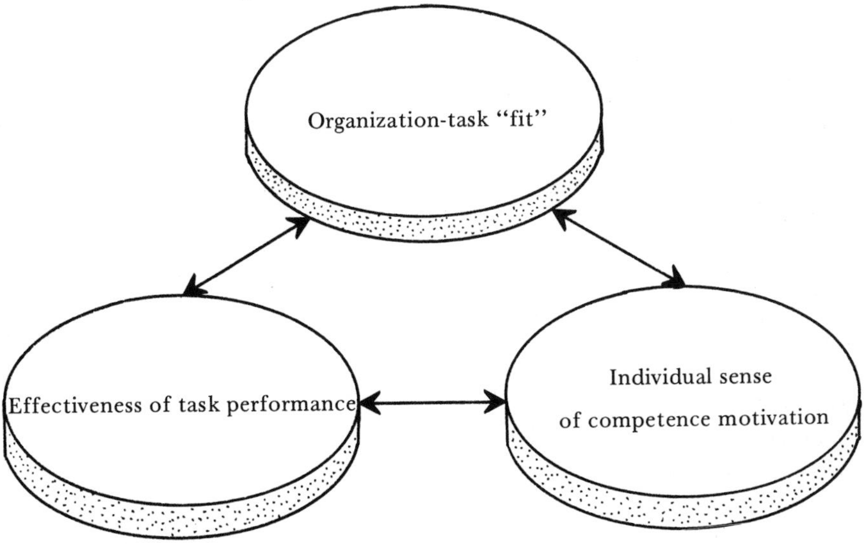

Putting the conclusions in this form raises the question of cause and effect. Does effective unit performance result from the task-organization fit or from higher motivation, or perhaps from both? Does higher sense of competence motivation result from effective unit performance or from fit?

Our answer to these questions is that we do not think there are any single cause-and-effect relationships, but that these factors are mutually interrelated. This had important implications for management theory and practice.

Contingency Theory

Returning to McGregor's Theory X and Theory Y assumptions, we can now question the validity of some of his conclusions. While Theory Y might help to explain the findings in the two laboratories, we clearly need something other than Theory X or Y assumptions to explain the findings in the plants.

For example, the managers at Akron worked in a formalized organization setting with relatively little participation in decision making, and yet they were highly motivated. According to Theory X, people would work hard in such a setting only because they were coerced to do so. According to Theory Y, they should have been involved in decision making and been self-directed to feel so motivated. Nothing in our data indicates that either set of assumptions was valid at Akron.

Conversely, the managers at Hartford, the low-performing plant, were in a less formalized organization with more participation in decision making, and yet they were not as highly motivated like the Akron managers. The Theory Y assumptions would suggest that they should have been more motivated.

A way out of such paradoxes is to state a new set of assumptions, the Contingency Theory, that seems to explain the findings at all four sites:

1. Human beings bring varying patterns of needs and motives into the work organization, but one central need is to achieve a sense of competence.

2. The sense of competence motive, while it exists in all human beings, may be fulfilled in different ways by different people depending on how this need interacts with the strengths of the individuals' other needs—such as those for power, independence, structure, achievement, and affiliation.

3. Competence motivation is most likely to be fulfilled when there is a fit between task and organization.

4. Sense of competence continues to motivate even when a competence goal is achieved; once one goal is reached, a new, higher one is set.

While the central thrust of these points is clear from the preceding discussion of the study, some elaboration can be made. First, the idea that different people have different needs is well understood by psychologists. However, all too often, managers assume that all people have similar needs. Lest we be accused of the same error, we are saying only that all people have a need to feel competent; in this *one* way they are similar. But in many other dimensions of personality, individuals differ, and these differences will determine how a particular person achieves a sense of competence.

Thus, for example, the people in the Akron plant seemed to be very different from those in the Stockton laboratory in their underlying attitudes toward uncertainty, authority, and relationships with their peers. And because they had different need patterns along these dimensions, both groups were highly motivated by achieving competence from quite different activities and settings.

While there is a need to further investigate how people who work in different settings differ in their psychological makeup, one important implication of the Contingency Theory is that we must not only seek a fit between organization and task, but also between task and people and between people and organization.

A further point which requires elaboration is that one's sense of competence never really comes to rest. Rather, the real satisfaction of this need is in the successful performance itself, with no diminishing of the motivation as one goal is reached. Since feelings of competence are thus reinforced by successful performance, they can be a more consistent and reliable motivator than salary and benefits.

Implications for Managers

The major managerial implication of the Contingency Theory seems to rest in the task-organization-people fit. Although this interrelationship is complex, the best possibility for managerial action probably is in tailoring the organization to fit the task and the people. If such a fit is achieved, both effective unit performance and a higher sense of competence motivation seem to result.

Managers can start this process by considering how certain the task is, how frequently feedback about task performance is available, and what goals are implicit in the task. The answers to these questions will guide their decisions about the design of the management hierarchy, the specificity of job assignments, and the utilization of rewards and control procedures. Selective use of training programs and a general emphasis on appropriate management styles will move them toward a task-organization fit.

The problem of achieving a fit among task, organization, and people is something we know less about. As we have already suggested, we need further investigation of what personality characteristics fit various tasks and organizations. Even with our limited knowledge, however, there are indications that people will gradually gravitate into organizations that fit their particular personalities. Managers can help this process by becoming more aware of what psychological needs seem to best fit the tasks available and the organizational settings, and by trying to shape personnel selection criteria to take account of these needs.

In arguing for an approach which emphasizes the fit among task, organization, and people, we are putting to rest the question of which organizational approach—the classical or the participative—is best. In its place we are raising a new question: What organizational approach is most appropriate given the task and the people involved?

For many enterprises, given the new needs of younger employees for more autonomy, and the rapid rates of social and technological change, it may well be that the more participative approach is the most appropriate. But there will still be many situations in which the more controlled and formalized organization is desirable. Such an organization need not be coercive or punitive. If it makes sense to the individuals involved, given their needs and their jobs, they will find it rewarding and motivating.

Concluding Note

The reader will recognize that the complexity we have described is not of our own making. The basic deficiency with earlier approaches is that they did not recognize the variability in tasks and people which produces this complexity. The strength of the contingency approach we have outlined is that it begins to provide a way of thinking about this complexity, rather than ignoring it. While our knowledge in this area is still growing, we are certain that any adequate theory of motivation and organization will have to take account of the contingent relationship between task, organization, and people.

FOOTNOTES

1. Douglas McGregor, *The Human Side of Enterprise* (New York, McGraw-Hill Book Company, Inc., 1960), pp. 34-35 and pp. 47-48.
2. See for example Paul R. Lawrence and Jay W. Lorsch, *Organization and*

Environment (Boston, Harvard Business School, Division of Research, 1967); Joan Woodward, *Industrial Organization: Theory & Practice* (New York, Oxford University Press, Inc., 1965); Tom Burns and G. M. Stalker, *The Management of Innovation* (London, Tavistock Publications, 1961); Harold J. Leavitt, "Unhuman Organizations," HBR July-August 1962, p. 90.

3. McGregor, op. cit., p. 245.

4. See Robert W. White, "Ego and Reality in Psychoanalytic Theory," *Psychological Issues*, Vol. III, No. 3 (New York, International Universities Press, 1963).

5. For a more detailed description of this survey, see John J. Morse, *Internal Organizational Patterning and Sense of Competence Motivation* (Boston, Harvard Business School, unpublished doctoral dissertation, 1969).

6. Differences between the two container plants are significant at .001 and between the research laboratories at .01 (one-tailed probability).

3

Organizational Development
and
Human Resources

The emerging concern with organizational development and human resources is based on a recognition that change and change processes are irrevocably tied to the environment within which the change takes place. The articles in this part were selected to provide a greater familiarity with this problem and some methods of facilitating needed change.

An overview is provided in Bogue's article, "The Context of Organizational Behavior." Flacks explores the question of whether to change within an established framework or to change the framework.

Organizational change is related to a need for efficient and effective organizational structures. The adequacy of a structure is based on the functional characteristics of that structure. Miles discusses criteria for assessing the health of an organization. Articles by Golembiewski and Dyer, Maddocks, Moffitt, and Underwood suggest change models helpful to practitioners embarking on this difficult path. Stutz and Jesser and Dickenson, Foster, Walker, and Yeager provide examples of major change efforts initiated in the field of education and educational administration.

Trusty and Sergiovanni conclude this part with a suggestion for restructuring teacher roles based on identified human needs of teachers and administrators.

THE CONTEXT OF ORGANIZATIONAL BEHAVIOR:
A CONCEPTUAL SYNTHESIS FOR THE
EDUCATIONAL ADMINISTRATOR

E. G. Bogue

Since the German sociologist Max Weber first outlined the characteristics of a bureaucracy, the literature on organizational theory has been growing with exponential rapidity. The recent books by Bass,[1] Thompson,[2] Scott,[3] and March[4] manifest the interest commanded by this relatively new field of inquiry. And the diversity of organizational inquiry is revealed by the variety of disciplines participating in both separate and interdisciplinary ventures. Economists, sociologists, psychologists, management specialists, educators, and mathematicians have initiated studies into one or more phases of organizational theory.

For the educational administrator, the array of research and reporting in organizational theory presents a dilemma not unlike that faced by the teacher confronting the literature of educational psychology. From the research and writing of the behavioral, stimulus-response, cognitive, neuro-physiological, and developmental psychologists, the teacher searches for those conceptual threads which he may weave into the fabric of his classroom teaching. Constructing a conceptual framework which can serve as a guide to more enlightened practice proves to be a formidable task.

A similar challenge faces the educational administrator as he surveys the literature of organizational theory, which is as diverse as that of educational psychology. The orchestration of personnel, material resources, and ideas which leads to the harmonious integra-

From the *Educational Administration Quarterly*, Vol. 5, No. 2, Spring 1969, pp. 58-75. Reprinted by permission.

tion of man and organization is a complex task. It is natural, therefore, that the practicing administrator would also search for those concepts and principles which would assist him in developing a more commanding professional competency.

Certainly there are considerable risks in any attempt to distill the numerous points of inquiry found in organizational theory. Entire books have dealt with the topics of job satisfaction, motivation, communication, supervisory behavior, organizational conflict, and decision-making processes. A paper of this length could hardly capture the full impact of these topics. Yet our conviction is that we may profitably consider a portion of organizational inquiry of immediate utility to the practitioner—whether he be an elementary school principal, school superintendent, or university president.

Principal focus of the paper will be on the determinants of organizational behavior. We will suggest a simple model composed of four elements and then proceed to examine the relationship of each element to individual behavior. The reader will readily discern considerable interaction among the elements, but for purposes of exposition we have chosen to treat them separately. Our objective is to provide a concise conceptual framework of value to the educational administrator.

A Simplified Model of Behavior Determinants

In the literature of organizational theory, one can find research and theorizing related to a number of organizational concepts. Since this paper is an attempt to capsule some of these concepts into a more concise scheme, we present a highly simplified model involving four elements.

As Figure 1 indicates, we are suggesting that individual behavior in organizations can be viewed in terms of four-perspectives: manage-

Figure 1. Simplified Model of Behavior Determinants

Individual Behavior Within Organizations			
Management Philosophy	Organizational Structure	Group Membership	Individual Personality

ment philosophy, organizational structure, group membership, and individual personality. Each of these elements has important implications for practice as the educational administrator develops structures and relationships designed to free the creative energies of those with whom he works.

The Influence of Management Philosophy

Our thesis in this discussion is that management philosophy is a keystone variable in influencing individual behavior within the organization. In treating management philosophy, we mean to consider those value dispositions and assumptions which managers hold about the nature of man and his work. We will suggest that management philosophy has changed significantly over the past half century, primarily as a result of intense research into the nature of leadership and organizations.

Three rather distinct periods of thought may be discerned in the literature of administration and management. The first of these is often called "scientific management." Scientific management was born in the late 19th century and flourished in the early 20th century, principally as a result of the research and writing of Frederick Taylor.[5] Based predominantly on the philosophy of Adam Smith, the focus of scientific management was on the economic nature of man. In essence, scientific management embraced the study of work specialization and wage analysis. Jobs were dissected in order to find the most efficient way of doing a particular task and for the purpose of setting a fair wage. Some of the assumptions about the nature of the average worker were not very noble, and the central theme was that money was the principal motivator.

Although scientific management produced a number of more effective management practices, its influence began to wane in the 1920's as industrial psychologists began to reveal that the problem of motivation-satisfaction was not as simple as the economic model assumed by scientific management. At the Western Electric Company, the now familiar Hawthorne studies by Elton Mayo and his colleagues committed mayhem on many hallowed assumptions held about the attitudes of workers toward their jobs. These and other studies also punched large holes in the concept of an organization as a blue print in action, as a series of line and staff relationships with fixed job responsibilities and closely specified interrelationships as initially proposed by Weber.

Organizations were revealed as social systems composed of both formal and informal elements, of grapevines and cliques, of overt and covert power structures, of both logical and non-logical behaviors. The economic assumption of the scientific management era was not adequate to account for the diverse need patterns uncovered, among which were the psychological needs for recognition, for security, for accomplishment and for involvement.

Out of the research of the industrial psychologists in the 1920's and 1930's emerged the "human relations" movement. This movement stressed the notion that if managers became more sensitive to the diversity of human needs, they could deal more effectively with the problems of motivation and conflict within organizations.

A host of training and development programs for executives and supervisors were developed in human relations. Reaching its zenith in the 1950's, the movement began to lose some of its momentum, however. Human relations was the first movement to introduce in a systematic way the findings of behavioral science into management practice, and this represents no small contribution. Perhaps its demise in recent years may be attributed to a lack of hard research validating the effectiveness of human relations training and the inhospitable environment to which many managers trained in human relations returned.

"Industrial humanism" is the rubic which describes the current trend in management philosophy.[6] The writing of scholars such as Chris Argyris, Douglas McGregor, and Rensis Likert provide much of the empirical and theoretical bases for this movement. Relying heavily upon the hierarchial need structure proposed by the psychologist Maslow, these theorists have suggested a number of concepts which merit serious reflection.

A brief digression to consider the motivation theory of Maslow may prove of value for our continued discussion. Maslow proposed a hierarchy of human needs beginning with the basic physiological needs and culminating in the higher social and ego needs, such as need for self-actualization.[7] The need for self-actualization can be described as a desire to feel that one's abilities are being fully utilized in some worthwhile and creative manner. We shall see in a moment how this theory makes a contribution to contemporary management philosophy.

Returning now to our discussion of industrial humanism, we should recall that one of the traditional assumptions about man and his work was that man is generally opposed to work. Notions of control and authority have therefore occupied prominent positions in traditional management philosophy. Scholars of the industrial humanist movement suggest that restrictive managerial control, coupled with inadequate opportunities for self-actualization, inhibits the development of trust among managers and between managers and employees. This paucity of trust and honesty in human relationships leads to serious dysfunctional consequences.

An experienced administrator has observed such dysfunctional consequences many times. Consider the following example of how trust and communication may be related. If there exists no feeling of trust between the administrator and the employee, then communication is filtered as information moves both up and down in the organizational hierarchy. The results are as follows. Failure to communicate downward means that employees are prevented from relating their individual and group objectives to the overall organizational objectives. Failure of employees to communicate upward prevents the administrator from obtaining accurate information about the true status of organizational operations. Eventually, of course, organizational productivity is affected.

We can begin to see how the motivation psychology of Maslow has had an impact on management philosophy, for Maslow has suggested that once the physiological needs are satisfied, the higher level needs become operative. Opportunity for self-actualization—for using his full array of talents in a creative venture—may transform work into an activity from which the individual may derive real pleasure and satisfaction.

In developing his Theory X and Theory Y notions of management in *The Human Side of Enterprise* McGregor leans heavily on Maslow's theory.[8] There are traces of the theory to be found also in Likert's *New Patterns of Management* emphasizing the participative approach to management.[9] And the influence of Maslow is to be seen in the theoretical presentation of Argyris' *Integrating the Individual and the Organization.*[10] The essential theme of these scholars is that relationships encouraging dependence, submissiveness, conformity, and imposed evaluation must give way to relationships which hold opportunity for development of trust, for independence of action, for risk taking, and for self-evaluation. The thrust of the industrial humanist movement thus encourages development of greater interpersonal competency on the part of managers. In addition, therefore, to learning more about the rational approaches to management—decision theory, operations research, simulation, etc.—managers must learn to work at the "gut level" of feelings and emotions.

As we close our discussion of management philosophy, we do not wish to leave the reader with the notion that contemporary management thought abandons the ideas of authority and control in organizational relationships. As we have pointed out in this discussion, it seems apparent that the trend in management thought is toward the development of more positive approaches to the motivation of man in organizational situations, with emphasis on trust and participation as vehicles for developing opportunity for self-actualization.

Yet the literature is equally clear on another point. It is that rigid and stereotyped notions of management styles belong, to borrow a phrase from Galbraith, in the museum of irrelevant ideas. There is no personality syndrome characteristic of all effective leaders nor a management style appropriate for all organizational situations. Flexibility is the key word. There is a time for independence and a time for control, a time for participation and a time for authority. Contrary to what some may think, flexibility in management style demands a greater competency than does a single approach. Flexibility requires the development of a broad knowledge base, the exercise of balanced judgment in matching style with situation, and careful consideration of values so that flexibility does not degenerate into opportunism.

We append a brief postscript to this discussion of motivation and management philosophy to mention another approach to the study of motivation in modern organizations, one which the reader may find particularly provocative. Whereas our analysis of the changing mood of human motivation and management philosophy has proceeded from a psychological base, in *The New Industrial State* Galbraith suggests that the motivation of men in organizations has changed; but the basis of his argument is economic rather than psychological. Briefly, he says that:

Power in economic life has over time passed from its ancient association with land to association with capital and then on, in recent time, to the composite of knowledge and skills which comprises the technostructure. Reflecting the symmetry that so conveniently characterizes reality, there have been associated shifts in the motivations to which men respond. Compulsion has an ancient association with land. Pecuniary motivation had a similar association with capital. Identification and adaptation are associated with the technostructure.[11]

Here the word "technostructure" is a term coined by Galbraith to describe the organized intelligence found in the various groups of highly trained specialists providing the motive power in modern organizations. Though his analysis proceeds from a basis of economic change rather than from a consideration of psychological needs, the results are strikingly parallel. Compulsion is the motivation of authority. Pecuniary motivation is that of money. Identification and adaptation are the motivations associated with the merging of individual goals and aspirations with the organization's goals.

From whatever framework one may view contemporary management philosophy—whether from an economic, psychological, or sociological perspective—it is apparent that the concepts of trust, participation, and self-actualization are key elements in all frames of reference. Having thus briefly explored management philosophy as one of the determinants of individual behavior, we turn now to the second element of our simplified model, organizational structure.

The Effect of Structure

In contemporary society, a term frequently tossed about is "bureaucracy." Most often the context of its use will be an unfavorable one. Yet the various forms of bureaucracy found today are perhaps the most efficient means that man has found for accomplishing complex tasks.

Indeed, we might even observe that bureaucracy represents a kind of innovation in human relationships. It is apparent, however, that the formal and static kind of structure described by Weber has significant limitations when measured against the demands of contemporary society. In this discussion, we will mention four such limitations which illustrate how organizational structure has an impact on individual behavior.

Reduces Opportunity for Individual Psychological Success

One of the most critical indictments of contemporary organizational patterns is that they reduce the opportunity for individuals to achieve psychological success. This point of view is especially prominent in the research and writings of Chris Argyris.[12] The concept is essentially this. Modern hierarchial structures are based on the principles and philosophy of scientific management—which includes the familiar ideas of chain of command, span of control, task specialization, etc. And, as we have pointed out in the previous section, the prevalent managerial philosophy is that man is opposed to work. Thus, a combination of restrictive managerial controls and jobs fragmented by technology and specialization act to reduce opportunities for individual challenge and psychological success— especially at the lower levels in the hierarchy.

Thus, at some levels in our organizational structures we have so fragmented job responsibilities that employees are using only a narrow range of their talents. Faced with the frustration which comes from lack of challenge, employees may react in a variety of ways by expending much of their energy in non-productive activities. Expenditure of energy in these adaptive activities reduces the productive output of the organization. And the cycle is made complete, because these types of employee behaviors convince administrators that more controls are needed.

Here then is a vivid example of interaction between management philosophy and organizational structure. The results of rigid management, lack of opportunity for participation, and narrowly conceived responsibilities are becoming painfully apparent to many educational administrators today. Teachers and students are becoming more forceful in making known their objections to such approaches.

Contributes to Organizational Inertia

Another serious criticism of contemporary organizational structures is that they contribute to inertia by reducing opportunity for change. John Gardner has pointed out the need for continued "self-renewal" at both the individual and organizational level and has clearly explained that a readiness to grow and change is critical in contemporary society.[13] Yet those familiar with the workings of large organizations know that the rigidity which comes with formalization of activities is difficult to surmount. One of the mechanisms of the impedance is explained by Thompson:

Hierarchical relations overemphasize the veto and underemphasize approval of innovation. Since there is no appeal from the superior's decision, a veto usually ends the matter. However, an approval will often have to go to the next higher level where it is again subject to veto. A hierarchial system always favors the status quo.[14]

Thus, communication if often inhibited in the hierarchical structure. Of course, there are other more complex concepts involved in this problem of resistance to change. We refer especially to the problem of individual status and role expectations associated with hierarchial structures. The basic idea is, however, that organizational inertia is encouraged by the "chain of command" concept inherent in contemporary patterns.

Inhibits Effective Decision Making

Today's society is one of specialization and increased interdependence, but we find it difficult to integrate specialists into hierarchial organizational patterns. In times gone past, the "boss" usually had come up through the ranks so that he knew every job under his supervision better than anyone working for him. This, of course, is no longer true. The diversity of organizational activities makes it impossible for one man to know it all. What school principal, school superintendent, or college president can possess an effective command of the variety of activities that take place in modern educational organizations?

Galbraith emphasizes the contribution of specialization as he points out that:

The real accomplishment of modern science and technology consists of taking ordinary men, informing them narrowly and deeply and then through appropriate organization, arranging to have their knowledge combined with that of other specialized but equally ordinary men.[15]

He goes on to emphasize the need for coordination:

Finally, following the need for this variety of specialized talent, is the need for its coordination. Talent must be brought to bear on the common purpose. More specifically, on large and small matters, information must be extracted from the various specialists, tested for its reliability and relevance, and made to yield a decision.[16]

The tasks of designing an "appropriate organization" and achieving "coordination" are the ones which are made more difficult by contemporary organizational patterns.

Thompson maintains that:

Modern bureaucracy is an adaptation of older organizational forms altered to meet the need of specialization. Modern specialization is grafted into it, but old traces of the past remain. Along with technological specialization, we find survivals of Genghis Khan and the aboriginal war chiefs. We find the latest in science and technology associated with the autocratic, monistic, hierarchial organization of a simpler time.[17]

His thesis is that in modern organizations there is a growing imbalance between ability and authority—between the right to make decisions, which is authority, and the power to do so, which is specialized ability. Through the creation of staff agencies, cabinet methods of governance, and various council and committee structures some of the limitations outlined by Thompson have been overcome, but a number of problems remain unresolved.

Encourages Mechanistic View of Organization

Finally, we mention the fact that contemporary organizational patterns encourage a mechanistic view of organizational functions. With a mechanistic perspective, little relationship is discerned among the various parts of the organization. This restricted perspective has little correspondence with the reality of organizational functions, which is that the vitality of an organization depends upon the vitality of each component.

The dysfunctional consequences of an administrator's failure to take an organic view of an organization are readily apparent. For example, the school principal who evaluates his teaching faculty without regard to the capabilities of students or availability of teaching resources is taking a mechanistic view of his organization. The school superintendent who evaluates the effectiveness of his records division without any thought to the status of his computer and data processing division is taking a mechanistic view of his school system. The college president who feels that he can develop a strong department of psychology while neglecting to build strength in departments with which psychology may relate is taking a mechanistic view of the university. Indeed, any administrator who makes decisions without careful reflection of the impact throughout the organization has a bad case of "tunnel vision" with regard to the true nature of organizations today.

What implications do these concepts of structure have for the educational administrator? What points of focus and emphasis are suggested for practice? Clearly, the administrator must address himself to the challenges of (1) defining job responsibilities so that a greater array of human talents are called into play, (2) creating a sensitive balance between organizational control and independence of action so that change and innovation are facilitated rather than inhibited, (3) designing organizational relationships so that maximum contribution of specialists can be realized, and (4) developing an organic perspective of organizations so that he remains vigilant to the interdependency of organizational components.

In closing this discussion, let us admit readily that it is easier to recommend than it is to transform recommendation into action. At the same time, however, a more professional approach to administration begins with awareness. The writer shares with other practicing administrators the obligation of translating awareness into action.

The Impact of Group Membership

Occasionally administrators fall into the habit of thinking that the most important variables related to individual behavior within organizations are those associated with the vertical relationships formally expressed in line and staff charts. However, these formal relationships are only the above-surface part of the "iceberg" of organizational structure. In the words of Iannaccone:

> For centuries, some students of organization have thought that the formal organization is only what appears on the surface of organizational life and is given lip service. They have felt that beneath the formal organization, and obscured in part by it, there lies a "real" world consisting of the way things actually get done and how people truly behave in organizations.[18]

If research into organizational life has produced any finding of significance to the practicing administrator it is that peer relationships—both formal and informal—are critical variables in organizational productivity.

The study of group dynamics has produced a number of fruitful concepts concerning human behavior. It is not our purpose in this discussion to attempt a synopsis of the fields included in the study of group dynamics. To capsule areas such as the study of communication networks, leadership styles, attitude shaping, group counseling would be impossible; but perhaps with one or two examples we may illustrate the importance of group membership on individual behavior.

One of the things known from the study of group dynamics is that every individual in an organization is a member of both formal and informal groups and that these groups can have particular impact upon his attitudes and behavior. The literature abounds with laboratory and action research studies which reveal how group pressures can affect both the quality and speed with which tasks are accomplished and how groups can influence judgement. Administrators are in no way free from such influence, for research reveals that higher levels of education provide no immunity from pressures to conform. Thus, in understanding behavior within the organization, the alert administrator must remain sensitive to horizontal and diagonal relationships, the lines of which may extend outside the framework of the organization.

In the study of community and school relationships, administrators learn to define both the overt and covert power structures in the community of which the school is a part. A sensitivity to these structures is a valuable asset in a number of ways. Perhaps, an equally attentive study of both the above-surface and the "subterranean" structures within the organization may also prove fruitful.

Since our emphasis in this discussion is predominantly on the group membership effect on individual attitudes and behavior, perhaps it would be appropriate to take a short digression for the purpose of outlining an interesting motivation psychology which has emerged from the study of group behavior. We refer to the "cognitive dissonance" theory proposed by Festinger.[19] The core ideas of this theory are rather straight forward. Individuals are often confronted with conflicting notions or "cognitions" which do not fit well together. For example, a teacher may feel that a strike is an appropriate professional action but at the same time may feel that such action is unfair to the student. It is easy to see how different group memberships can bring pressure to bear on this point of individual conflict or dissonance.

Or consider the dissonance generated for an administrator who finds that the organizational chart dictates that he relate directly to another administrator for whom he has an intense personal dislike, a dislike derived from an extra-organizational association. According to Festinger, these conflicts or dissonances have motivation features because the dissonance will lead to behavior designed to reduce the dissonance. The teacher may decide that a temporary sacrifice of student welfare may be necessary for the long range welfare of other students, thus weighing in favor of the strike action. The administrator may decide that his personal feelings are less important than the welfare of his division, or he may find ways to circumvent the formal line of relationships. Cognitive dissonance theory has proved to be of considerable utility in predicting a wide range of behavior, and a basic familiarity with the concepts involved could prove to be of value in understanding, and predicting, behavior.

A number of other variables have been researched with regard to their effect on group performance and individual behavior. Research has included probes into (1) task variables, such as the effect of time required and task complexity; (2) structural variables, such as size of group, opportunity for interaction, and homogeneity of group talent; (3) leadership style, such as task orientation and group maintenance functions; and (4) communications, such as the study of network composition of speed of task completion and member satisfaction. This brief discussion is highly inadequate. Yet our purpose was limited. It was to stimulate the administrator to remain sensitive to the importance of both informal and formal relationships.

The Influence of Individual Personality

A careful review of the three previous sections of this paper will reveal that the determinants of individual behavior thus far considered have been external rather than internal. In effecting a more harmonious integration of individual and organization, our emphasis has been on adjusting the external factors of management philosophy, organizational structures, and group membership.

However, there is another perspective—and associated psychology —which is in contrast to the three points of view previously considered. This perspective is most clearly captured in the writings of Zaleznik, who suggests that:

> The energy and vitality that make organizations move depend upon individual initiative. Leaders with brilliant ideas and the capacity to inspire thought and action in others are the main generators of energy. The effects of their personality induce a contagion to perform that is considerably stronger in directing organizations than depersonalized systems such as interlocking committee structures or participative management. The release of individual energy and the contagion to perform occur within organizational structures. But the impulse and inspiration derive from individual personality.[20]

Zaleznik goes on to analyze man-organization interaction from a framework of Freudian psychology. His theme is that many of the problems encountered in man-organization conflict may be better understood from an internal view rather than from an external one. From the standpoint of Freudian psychology, the determinants of present behavior are to be found in the past experience of the individual. Zaleznik's thesis is that much dysfunctional behavior in organizations may be explained as a failure of the individual to achieve psychological maturity.

His exposition of leadership dilemmas, subordinancy relationships, status conflict, and other organizational problems in terms of individual personality development is conceptually rich. Perhaps we could explore one or two concepts which illustrate the importance of this idea for the educational administrator.

Let us take as our first example, the problem of communication in administrative behavior. We may recall that there has been significant emphasis given to the development of the ability to listen creatively and to empathize. Such an emphasis has a client-centered counseling orientation as proposed by Carl Rogers.[21] Certainly, the administrator will admit to frequent situations when listening is the appropriate administrative behavior. But, as Zaleznik points out, there are also situations which call for a posture more directive in character:

It is important for both superior and subordinate to know where one stands on issues of work or personal conflict. We usually hear that it is important to listen to the other person and understand his point of view. This is good advice as far as it goes. What gets left out to the misfortune of all concerned is the fact that competent behavior depends on the ability of the individual to know where he stands and what he would like to see happen. In particular, the authority figure may find himself tyrannized by his own vacillations. If the subordinate is confused and torn by mixed feelings, it will do him little good to find his boss is equally confused. In this sense, knowing where one stands and being prepared to take a position has a salutary effect on human relationships.[22]

Our purpose here is not to emphasize one point of view at the expense of the other. It is to reinforce the idea of flexibility which earlier we proposed in our discussion of management philosophy.

Another concept of special interest to the administrator concerns the relationship of "personality orientation and executive functions." One of the really significant findings of behavioral research is that there is no personality syndrome characteristic of all effective leaders. Another way of saying this is to point out that research has suggested that effective leadership is often as much determined by situational variables as by personality variables. In his book *Management by Objectives*, Odiorne makes the point clear by analogy.[23] He suggests that effective management is similar to effective acting. The successful actor, knowledgeable of his strengths and limitations, pays attention to the selection of the play so that it will be compatible with his strengths and limitations. Likewise the administrator should learn to assess his abilities so that he can achieve a harmonious and productive match of personality with function. Zaleznik neatly illustrates the interaction between administrator personality and administrative functions by the following diagram:

The interaction model of Figure 2 may be interpreted as follows. There are three types of organizational requisites or functions— homeostatic, mediative, and proactive. Homeostatic functions are passive in character and are associated with maintaining the internal stability of the organization. On the opposite end of the continuum are the proactive functions, which are those more active functions necessary for adapting the organization to its environment. These are change-oriented functions required for modifying organizational goals or the means by which the goals are achieved. Occupying an intermediate position on the continuum are the mediative functions.

Corresponding to these three types of organizational functions are three types of personality orientation. For example, the individual who is person-oriented will most probably give his major attention to

Figure 2. The Interaction of Executive Functions and Personality Orientations.[24]

Executive Functions—Organizational Requisites

		Homeostatic	Mediative	Proactive
	Persons	1	2	3
	Persons & Tasks	2	1	3
Personality Orientation	Ideas & Tasks	3	2	1

Investments In

1—Major Performance
2—Secondary Performance
3—Avoided Performance

the homeostatic organizational activities. In contrast, the idea and task oriented personality will find his major challenge and satisfaction in the proactive functions of the organization. There is a rough analogy here with some of the findings from group dynamics which suggest that two types of leaders may emerge within a group, a task oriented leader and a group maintenance leader. The task leader keeps the group focused on goals, whereas the maintenance leader insures the coherence and stability within the group.

The important implication of this model is that a match of personality with organizational function may be critical for both organizational productivity and individual personality development. Thus, a person-oriented individual thrust into an organizational position requiring a focus on tasks and goals may experience stress arising from the incompatibility of his personality and the organizational function. The same would be true of a task-oriented person finding himself in a position calling for a primary focus on interpersonal relations. These comments are not meant to suggest that individuals may be neatly and finally categorized in disregard of growth and change in personality. They do suggest, however, that it is inappropriate to ignore personality orientation in the integration of individual and organizational function.

This particular concept also relates to a suggestion which Zaleznik makes earlier in his book. It is that the administrator must develop a strong sense of identity:

The exercise of leadership requires a strong sense of identity—knowing who one is and who one is not. The myth of the value of being an "all-around guy" is damaging to the striving of an individual to locate himself from within and then to place himself in relation to others. This active location and placement of oneself prevents the individual from being defined by others in uncongenial terms. It prevents him also from being buffeted around the sea of opinion he must live within. A sense of autonomy, separateness, or identity permits a freedom of action and thinking so necessary for leadership.

Not the least significant part of achieving a sense of identity is the creative integration of one's past. There is no tailor who can convert a hayseed into a big-city boy—anymore than a dude can become a cowboy for all the hours he spends on the range. Coming to terms with being a hayseed or a dude permits the development of a unique person who goes beyond the stereotypes offered to him as models.[25]

The message is clear. Before he can hope to direct effectively the action of others, the administrator must first acquire a mastery of himself.

We have hardly circumscribed the full range of concepts which are embodied in this emphasis on individual personality. But hopefully, the illustrations presented were sufficiently pertinent to reveal the importance of individual personality in the influence of individual behavior at all levels of the organizational hierarchy.

Summary

In closing this paper it is appropriate that we ask what points of emphasis are suggested for the educational administrator aspiring to develop a more commanding professional competence. Among the many concepts which may be extracted from our discussion, we deem these to be most important.

Perhaps it is a trivial point, but it bears repeating that the causes of individual behavior in organizations are multivariate. The administrator needs to remember, therefore, that the determinants of behavior emerge from a matrix composed of management philosophy, organizational structure, group memberships, and individual personality.

As we consider the elements of this matrix, we find that contemporary research and theorizing in management philosophy indicate that the most productive relationships are those in which dependence, submissiveness, conformity, and external evaluation give way to relationships which hold opportunity for the development of trust, for independence of action, for risk taking, and for self-evaluation. The latter elements are essentials in providing organizational opportunity for the individual to achieve self-actualization.

This is not to suggest that the notions of authority and control are absent in current thought. It does mean that rigid and stereotyped ideas of administrative style must be replaced by a more flexible perspective which encourages matching style with situation. Such administrative flexibility requires the development of a strong interpersonal competency, and this competency derives from a broad knowledge base and a willingness to work at the "gut level" of feelings and emotions where there are few rational guides for action. Finally, a flexible administrative style demands also the development of a carefully considered value framework which prevents flexibility from degenerating into opportunism.

We have also seen that contemporary hierarchical organizational patterns often tend to impede (1) the achievement of individual self-actualization, (2) the occurrence of change and innovation, (3) the effective use of specialists in decision making, and (4) the development of an organic view of the organization. While it is easier to verbalize about these limitations than it is to suggest remedies, the administrator must confront the challenge of designing organizational patterns and relationships so that a greater array of human abilities are called into play, of creating a sensitive balance between control and independence so that change and innovation are facilitated, of overcoming rigid notions of relationships so that efficient use of specialists in decision making is achieved, and of developing an organic perspective of organizations so that the interdependence of organizational components is seen.

From a consideration of group membership on individual behavior, the administrator learns to acquire a sensitivity to the importance of diagonal and horizontal relationships within the organization. Individuals in the organization are members of groups, both informal and formal, whose lines of influence may extend well beyond the formal boundaries of the organization. An awareness, then, of both the overt and covert power relationships—of the above-surface and subterranean aspects of the organization—is indispensable for the administrator interested in understanding and predicting individual behavior.

Although what we have said thus far emphasizes the importance of external forces on individual behavior, a point not to be forgotten is that powerful internal forces for action are present in the personalities of individuals. The energy which moves organizations comes from individuals *acting on* their environment. It is not particularly proper, therefore, to see members of an organization simply as passive elements, moving to and fro at the whim of external forces. A harmonious integration of individual and organization is more likely to emerge when careful attention is given to the interaction between individual personal orientation and the various organizational tasks.

FOOTNOTES

1. Bernard M. Bass, *Organizational Psychology* (Boston: Allyn and Bacon, 1965).

2. Victor Thompson, *Modern Organizations* (New York: Alfred Knopf, 1961).

3. William G. Scott, *Organization Theory: A Behavioral Analysis for Management* (Homewood: Richard Irwin, Inc., 1967).

4. J. G. March (ed.), *Handbook of Organizations* (Chicago: Rand McNally, 1965).

5. Frederick Winslow Taylor, *Scientific Management* (New York: Harper and Row, 1947).

6. Scott, *op. cit.*, p. 43.

7. Abraham H. Maslow, *Motivation and Personality* (New York: Harper and Brothers, 1954).

8. Douglas McGregor, *The Human Side of Enterprise* (New York: McGraw-Hill, 1960).

9. Rensis Likert, *New Patterns of Management* (New York: McGraw-Hill, 1961).

10. Chris Argyris, *Integrating the Individual and the Organization* (New York: John Wiley and Sons, 1964).

11. John Kenneth Galbraith, *The New Industrial State* (Boston: Houghton Mifflin, 1967), p. 143.

12. Argyris, *op. cit.*

13. John Gardner, *Self-Renewal* (New York: Harper and Row, 1964).

14. Thompson, *op. cit.*, p. 61.

15. Galbraith, *op. cit.*, p. 62.

16. *Ibid.*, p. 63.

17. Thompson, *op. cit.*, p. 5.

18. Laurence Iannaccone, "An Approach to the Informal Organization of the School," *Behavioral Science and Educational Administration: The Sixty-third Yearbook of the National Society for the Study of Education, Part II*, Daniel E. Griffiths, editor (Chicago: University of Chicago Press, 1964), p. 223.

19. Leon Festinger, *Theory of Cognitive Dissonance* (Evanston, Illinois: Peterson and Company, 1957).

20. Abraham Zaleznik, *Human Dilemmas of Leadership* (New York: Harper and Row, 1966), pp. 3-4.

21. Carl Rogers, *Client Centered Therapy* (New York: Houghton Mifflin, 1951).

22. Zaleznik, *op. cit.*, p. 68.

23. George S. Odiorne, *Management by Objectives* (New York: Pitman Publishing Corporation, 1965).

24. Zaleznik, *op. cit.*, p. 191.

25. *Ibid.*, pp. 41-42.

PROTEST OR CONFORM:
SOME SOCIAL PSYCHOLOGICAL PERSPECTIVES
ON LEGITIMACY

Richard Flacks

When John Kennedy received his discharge from the armed forces after World War II, he wrote in his notebooks, "War will exist until that distant day when the conscientious objector enjoys the same reputation and prestige that the warrior does today."

In a certain sense, the "distant day" apparently hoped for by the young John Kennedy has arrived. On the American campus, the draft resister assuredly has more prestige than the willing conscript. Drs. Howard Levy and Benjamin Spock likely are more widely honored among many medical students than those in the medical profession who have dutifully served in Vietnam. National magazines have provided us with more sympathetic details concerning the exploits of Pvt. Andrew Stapp, the Fort Hood Three, the Reverend William Sloane Coffin, and David Harris than of Medal of Honor winners, ace bomber pilots, and even Green Berets. I have no doubt that a poll of attendees at this conference would show more respect for the actions of Captain Dale Noyd, a psychologist court-martialed for refusal to use his skills in support of the Vietnam war effort, than for those psychologists who continue to aid military training, psychological warfare, and counterinsurgency. In the ghetto high schools of the country, it seems likely that the great hero of this war is Muhammed Ali. At my own university, 49 percent of the graduate students and

Reproduced by special permission from *The Journal of Applied Behavioral Science,* "Protest or Conform: Some Social Psychological Perspectives on Legitimacy," Richard Flacks, pp. 127-150, copyright 1969 by the NTL Institute for Applied Behavioral Science.

graduating seniors responding to a student government poll declare that they would not serve in the armed forces if drafted; Louis Harris finds that 20-30 percent of male students nationally say they will refuse to serve. If John Kennedy's "distant day" still seems far off, it is nevertheless already here on certain campuses and in certain neighborhoods of the country (9).*

Current discussion of legitimacy focuses on this situation and is concerned particularly with speculation that instances of defiance, resistance, and disruption by young people, directed against established authority, represent a trend leading to the erosion and destruction of the legitimacy of military and other authority. This concern is too recent to have produced very much in the way of systematic research; instead, one is struck by the fact that whatever empirical social psychological research we have which bears directly on the problem of authority tends to dramatize the extent to which people do what they are told to do by those with authority.

There is, for example, a small tradition of rather striking experimental studies which demonstrate that persons tend to do what they perceive to be clearly expected of them by others whom they regard as having the right to have such expectations. Among the earliest of such studies[1] were those by Jerome Frank (5) in which subjects were asked to perform impossible or disagreeable tasks, such as balancing a marble on a steel ball or eating dry soda crackers. In Frank's studies, subjects would continue to carry out the experimenter's instructions without overt resistance, unless explicitly informed of their right to refuse.

There are even more dramatic demonstrations of willing obedience in the recent experimental literature. Pepitone and Wallace (6) encountered little resistance from subjects who were asked by experimenters to sort garbage. Martin Orne and his associates (12; 13) attempted to design tasks which would be refused by normal subjects so that the effects of hypnosis on subjects' willingness to accept commands could be demonstrated. In general, he found that it was extremely difficult to design a task so boring or meaningless that an unhypnotized subject would refuse an experimenter's request to continue with it. In later experiments, Orne and his associates were able to get subjects to do extremely disagreeable and harmful things by asking them to pretend that they were hypnotized. Subjects who simulated hypnosis were as fully willing as hypnotized subjects to pick up a poisonous snake, put their hands in nitric acid, and throw

---

*See References at end of article.—Ed.

acid in an assistant's face. Even subjects who were told they were "normal controls" tended to show compliance with these requests. It should be added, of course, that steps were taken by the experimenters to prevent actual injury to the participants in the experiments.

There are, finally, the well-known experiments by Stanley Milgram (11) which have demonstrated the capacity of the experimental situation to create what Milgram calls "destructive obedience." Subjects asked to deliver what they believed to be extremely dangerous electric shocks to another person, in a situation in which the administration of shocks was defined as necessary to the success of an experiment, tended to deliver the maximum voltage even when they heard or saw the victim in pain and pleading for mercy. Even though they gave a variety of indications of stress and dislike for the situation, the majority of subjects in Milgram's basic situation continued to perceive an obligation to the experimenter to follow his orders.

Milgram's studies suggest some limits on the tendency of subjects to do what they are told to do. For instance, when commands conflict with one's personal inclinations, the latter are more likely to prevail if there is a way to evade the command without being detected or if one observes others defying the command openly. There is also the suggestion in his work that individuals who accept orders they regard as legitimate tend to believe that the primary responsibility for the consequences of such orders rests with the experimenter rather than themselves.

This small literature of experimentation on obedience is not entirely easy to interpret. Most obviously, these studies show that, at least in our culture, persons tend to be highly trusting of scientists and tend, consequently, to accept the authority of a scientist once they have committed themselves to helping him in an experiment. Although one might not wish to go very far in generalizing responses to scientific authority to other power relationships, it does seem that these experiments do constitute rather pure demonstrations of the effects of legitimacy, with other sources of motivation largely removed. These studies suggest that under conditions where authority is defined by subjects as legitimate, they appear highly ready to do what is expected of them, highly likely to delegate processes of judgment to the authority figure—even when coercion and reward are virtually absent and the consequences of obedience are likely to be negative. One concludes from these studies that it would be perilous to treat forms of compliance with national authority—such as readiness to enter military service or to pay taxes or to otherwise support war—as merely instrumental acts designed to avoid the severe negative sanctions associated with noncompliance or evasion. By the same token, obedience to national authority cannot be explained solely as positively instrumental nor as positively expressive of sentiments like patriotism or ideological commitment to the regime. What makes the experiments we have cited so striking is that they illustrate behavior undertaken *in spite of personal motive and without positive emotional commitment.* It is for this reason that they appear to be valid microscopic replications of such mass instances of obedience as submission to conscription or participation in bureaucratically organized genocide.

It is clear that Milgram's subjects and draft resisters stand for opposing aspects of the same culture and social system. Milgram's subjects seem to typify what C. Wright Mills called the "cheerful robot"; the prevalence of compliance in his experiments seems to support critics of modern society who fear the rise of "mass conformity." Yet the emergence of youthful opponents of militarism and of forms of protest based on civil disobedience and confrontation suggests the possibility of an opposing trend. Indeed, one of the more pressing tasks for social analysis is to attempt to understand which figure—Milgram's subject or the conscientious resister—best symbolizes the central trends in individual-authority relations in American society.

Some Structural Determinants of Legitimacy

Although no coherent framework is yet available which can provide us with such systematic understanding, two lines of investigation in social psychology may be relevant for constructing such a framework. The first derives from the experiments we have cited and focuses on the way in which perceived characteristics of the authority structure influence the likelihood of obedience. Milgram's findings provide a basis for extrapolating at least three general propositions concerning those features of the authority structure which are central to the maintenance of its legitimacy.

1. Individuals tend to attribute legitimacy to authority when the exercise of that authority is perceived as beneficial to groups, institutions, or values to which the individual is committed. We have argued that explanations of compliant behavior cannot rest on notions of reward and punishment; indeed, the very definition of legitimacy involves the assumption that individuals comply with authority in spite of their personal motives. In other words, we can measure the legitimacy of a particular authority structure by the degree in which it can obtain conformity without the use of positive or negative sanctions. Nevertheless, claims to legitimacy by authorities in modern society usually must include an argument that the exercise of this authority is instrumental to the achievement of benefits or values collectively desired by subordinates. Thus, subjects in the experiments we have cited tended to assume that the orders given them were designed to advance science; they acted against their personal inclinations, not because they were coerced or rewarded but because they perceived their actions as instrumental to the achievement of a collective goal and they perceived the experimenter as a valid representative of that goal.

All modern nation-states are "pluralist" in the sense that they govern societies consisting of diverse classes, ethnic groups, institutions, and subcultures. The legitimacy of national authority in such societies depends in part on the maintenance of the perception that common interests and values are shared by these diverse groups, transcending that which divides them, that the national authority is the authentic guarantor of those common interests, and that continued support for national authority is relatively beneficial for each such group. In such a society, legitimacy is in danger of erosion if, for example, there is a persistent pattern of inequity experienced by members of a particular class or stratum, if adherents of particular value systems or subcultures feel threatened, unrepresented, or disillusioned by the going system, if the established common values of the national culture are weakened by rapid social change and the national authorities are seen as incompetent to generate or support new values, or if members of particular institutions experience significant discontinuities between their collective goals and those of the authorities. The erosion of established authority under these conditions is probably hastened if alternative structures are perceived or envisioned by those who are disaffected.

2. Attribution of legitimacy is a function of trust; that is, the perception that those in authority are not biased against one or that the working of the system does not result in special costs for oneself or one's group. The importance of trust in the experiments we have cited is rather clear; in both the Orne and Milgram experiments, it seems likely that subjects were willing to obey commands to commit destructive acts in the belief that the experimenter knew what he was doing and was able to eliminate or control any real danger in the situation. For Orne's subjects, this perception was probably reinforced when they observed that they were prevented from actually picking up the poisonous snake by the sudden appearance of a glass screen between themselves and the snake.

At the level of national authority, trust depends on such matters as the objectivity of the authorities in mediating conflicts, the degree in which the police and the courts implement the principle of equality before the law, the openness of the political system and the media of opinion to emergent groups and dissenting views, the trustworthiness of statements made by national leaders, the degree in which officially espoused policies are actually implemented and actually have the results claimed for them, and so on.

It should be clear that trust, as we have defined it, constitutes a somewhat different basis for legitimacy than perceived benefit. Certainly, the perception that a regime or political system is biased in one's favor constitutes an important source of legitimacy; nevertheless, as Gamson (6, p. 57) has suggested, such perceptions by some members are likely to be less stable supports for a system than a general perception of nonbias—for if one group feels particularly advantaged by the system, others are likely to feel disadvantaged and will tend to withdraw their support. Gamson argues that the optimal level of trust for maintaining legitimacy in situations of high conflict is one in which conflicting parties see the authorities as unbiased.

3. Individuals tend to attribute legitimacy to authority if they perceive a generalized consensus supporting legitimacy. This consensus may be manifested through expressions of popular opinion; it may also be manifested by the ease with which the authority in question can call upon the backing of other centers of power in the society. The Milgram experiments, in addition to suggesting the importance of trust and perceived benefit as supports for legitimacy, indicated that compliance was substantially reduced when subjects perceived others disobeying. This finding is, of course, congruent with those of other experiments in conformity to group pressure which have repeatedly shown that subjects tend not to conform if they have social support for nonconformity.

No principle in social psychology is better established than the idea that individual attitudes depend on the perceived attitudes of significant others. In the case of legitimacy, the usual psychological mechanisms which bind people to accept consensual attitudes are importantly supplemented by the principle of consent of the governed. In a political democracy, the existence of general consensus about the legitimacy of a regime or a policy is a very powerful support because majority support is defined as the ultimate basis for legitimacy in the system. Thus those who are inclined to challenge legitimacy confront moral as well as psychological difficulties when they do so. These difficulties can be reduced, it appears, by the example of individuals who refuse to comply. Acts of noncompliance can have the effect of undermining the "pluralistic ignorance" which often underlies popular consensus. Many with private doubts conform because they believe others lack doubts; examples of open disobedience serve to make private doubts public. Furthermore, they can provide models of effective resistance: often, as Milgram has argued, persons tend to obey because they believe they have no alternative or because they lack the skills necessary for resistance; the overt resistant may make alternatives visible and skills available. In situations where compliance to authority entails major individual sacrifice and where obedience is demanded primarily because the commands are legitimate, public acts of individual noncompliance can be precursors of large-scale popular disaffection. This was surely the faith of Thoreau and those who have followed him.

Arthur Stinchcombe has recently argued that "power based *only* on the shifting sands of public opinion and willing obedience is inherently unstable" (16, p. 161). In his view, it is not popular consent or the willing obedience of subordinates which is decisive for legitimating a power; rather "a power is legitimate to the degree that, by virtue of the doctrines and norms by which it is justified, the power-holder can call upon sufficient other centers of power, as reserves in case of need, to make his power effective" (16, p. 162). From a psychological point of view, we may interpret this statement to predict that individuals will tend to perceive the action of an authority as legitimate if that action has or is likely to have the support of other centers of power. We can also draw from it the prediction that popular disaffection and weakening consensus about legitimacy are less clear-cut signs of eroding legitimacy than is the failure by role-players in key institutions adequately to support the power of national authority. Finally, although Stinchcombe in his brief exercise in conceptual analysis does not deal with this point, we can expect a reciprocal relationship between popular opinion and the responsiveness of institutional leaders to the needs of national authority. In situations of growing popular disaffection, institutional authority may be decisive as a conservative force in backing up the legitimacy of the national authority; but if cracks should appear in the institutional structure, then popular disaffection may be accelerated. At any rate, Stinchcombe's strictures against overemphasizing the importance of popular consent as a basis for legitimacy are quite suggestive; they lead us to consider measuring the stability of a political system by looking at the intactness of the institutional framework rather than simply at public opinion and the distribution of attitudes.

Individual Character and the Capacity To Resist

Drawing on the Milgram and other experiments concerning obedience, we have been able to suggest some variables which seem centrally useful in describing the conditions under which persons tend to attribute legitimacy to political regimes and national authority. These variables have to do with perceived characteristics of the authority structure and with perceptions about the social context in which the authorities operate.

Another social psychological perspective on legitimacy is possible. This involves emphasis on the characteristics of the situation. In the Milgram studies, individual differences in the degree of compliance, in reaction time, and in eagerness to administer shock were observed. It is important to note that Milgram found that these differences were correlated with such "personality" measures as the F scale. The existence of such individual differences and such correlations leads us quite directly to that long tradition of research on "character" which has been a distinctive contribution of psychology to political analysis.

Familial Influences

Starting at least with Freud, there has been the hypothesis that the family constitutes a miniature political system and that attitudes toward parental authority are generalized or projected onto other political figures. Freud's view of the matter was notoriously pessimistic: the family was inherently authoritarian; in it men learned habits of submission, learned to repress or deflect their anti-authoritarian impulses, and, if well-socialized, came to idealize forms of paternal domination. But the psychoanalytic perspective does not require a view of socialization which emphasizes the repressive outcome of early childhood experience; Wilhelm Reich was among the earliest to suggest that children raised in democratic, egalitarian, and nonrepressive social settings could become adults with the capacity to resist irrational or tyrannical authority.

Speculation and investigation about the political effects of early socialization reached an important culmination with the research on the Authoritarian Personality (1). Whatever its methodological flaws, this research made quite credible the idea that attitudes of submission may be based on enduring personality dispositions, and that such dis-

positions have their origins in families characterized by highly dominant fathers, strongly hierarchical structures, rigorously differentiated
fathers, strongly hierarchical structures, rigorously differentiated
sexual and generational roles, and low tolerance for free expression
of impulses. Subsequent experimental studies, including Milgram's as
we have noted, show positive relationships between F scores and
submissive or conforming behavior.

Democratic or anti-authoritarian "personalities" have been far less
well studied. Research with which I am most familiar concerns
characteristics of student protesters; our own studies (4), those of
Brewster Smith and his associates (2, in press), and of Kenneth Keniston (7) all provide evidence that student activists tend to come from
families which are more egalitarian and democratic and less repressive
than the families of students who are uninvolved in protest movements.
Finally, one might call attention to case studies by Wolfenstein (17) of
"revolutionary personalities." They suggest a pattern in which
paternal authority has been weak or absent at crucial stages in the
development of these future revolutionaries; there is the suggestion
in Wolfenstein's work that an important experience for creating the
capacity for revolutionary leadership is that of having replaced one's
father in the family in early adolescence. The psychoanalytic perspective contains grave and notorious dangers of psychological
reductionism; still, I am convinced that the central hypotheses—that
the family is a political system; that one learns within it habits of
response to authority and attitudes toward appropriate behavior by
authorities which can carry over to the larger political system—
remain viable and fruitful ones for those who want to understand the
capacities of individuals for conformity and resistance and the
tendencies within cultures to facilitate or inhibit such capacities.
Since political radicals and dissenters have often borne the brunt of
psychoanalytic scrutiny used for *ad hominem* attack on their
position, there is legitimate concern that the psychoanalytic tradition
is conservative when applied to political theory. (A provocative
treatment of the general problem of psychoanalysis and politics
appears in Sampson, 14.) But ever since Reich, it has been clear
that psychoanalytic hypotheses on the formative role of parental
authority could have radical critical functions. At any rate, we may
relate our discussion of authoritarianism to the problem of legitimacy by asking such questions as: Does the persistence of authoritarian institutions and practices depend in part on the ability of these
institutions to recruit appropriate character types? Is the legitimacy

of, say, military authority likely to be materially affected by the emergence in the society of significant numbers of youths who are characterologically indisposed to submit to it?

The psychoanalytic tradition emphasizes the relationship between character development and political behavior, and tends to ignore explicit learning about government and politics. There is, however, a growing body of research on the latter. Briefly stated, the mass of such studies can, I believe, be summarized by saying that children tend to adopt the political beliefs and preferences of their parents, and moreover, that white children tend to be highly supportive of the American political system. In the words of Easton and Dennis (3), summarizing their findings on children's images of government, "The small child sees a vision of holiness when he chances to glance in the direction of government—a sanctity and rightness of the demigoddess who dispenses the milk of human kindness. The government protects us, helps us, is good, and cares for us when we are in need, answers the child." The authors believe that this early set of emotions and perceptions forms the basis for later adult attitudes toward the state. This pattern of socialization is undoubtedly crucial in maintaining the legitimacy of authority in American society.

Although no one has studied blacks or student protesters in quite the same way, we may suspect that among both groups a high proportion had somewhat different images of government in early childhood. Black respondents are far more suspicious of government authorities than whites; this undoubtedly reflects not only their actual experience but also the received experience of their parents (10). Student activists' political attitudes are in large measure continuous with those of their parents; it is probable that from a very early age they were reared to be skeptical about the sanctity and benevolence of established authority (4). If the white majority tends to socialize their children to support the legitimacy of the national government, it seems also to be the case that significant minority subcultures tend to rear their children rather explicitly to have doubts about that authority. If the majority of white children talk as if they were raised in the nurseries of *Brave New World,* this would seem to ensure the stability of national authority as we now know it—and this appears to be the assumption underlying much of the work on political socialization. But the existence of at least two counter-cultures, socializing their children quite differently, suggests a more dynamic, less predictable political scene.

Competence

In recent years, psychologists have displayed increasing interest in the ways in which individual conceptions of self influence the capacity for initiative, autonomy, and rationality. In a recent review Brewster Smith (1968) suggests that "competence" is a useful summary term for a variety of traits and attitudes which have been defined and measured in recent studies. The competent person, as Smith defines him, perceives the self as "causally important, as effective in the world . . . as likely to be able to bring about desired effects, and as accepting responsibility when effects do not correspond to desire. In near equivalent, the person has self-respect." Although competence is likely to be associated with favorable levels of general self-evaluation or esteem, general esteem is less important then the sense of efficacy or potency (15, pp. 281-282).

Although competence bears some relationship to authoritarianism, since both concepts address the capacity of individuals for independence and self-determination, it clearly is a different sort of concept. In particular, references to competence have to do with aspects of self-awareness rather than with unconscious determinants. Whereas authoritarianism as a concept asks us to focus on early socialization and enduring traits as influences on the capacity for self-determination, a focus on competence leads us to emphasize the continuing role of experience and social interaction in shaping this capacity.

If there is a generalized capacity for independence, a generalized tendency to perceive oneself as causally important and potent, then this has clear implications for political behavior and relations to authority. Indeed, there exist a considerable number of studies relating efficacy to aspects of political behavior such as voting, activism, and alienation.

With reference to legitimacy, we may hypothesize that competence is related to the individual's readiness to delegate processes of judgment and evaluation to superordinate authority, or to participate smoothly in situations where decisions which affect him are beyond his control. For persons with high competence, the legitimacy of authority depends on the degree to which they have access to the decision-making process or believe that their judgments are taken seriously by superiors, or, perhaps most importantly, have the freedom to shape their own situation without reference to higher authority. Persons with low sense of competence, on the other hand, tend to view authority as untrustworthy, but also lack trust in their own ability to affect those in authority. They are, consequently, likely to be politically apathetic, fatalistically enduring what is imposed upon them (while sometimes trying to evade the most severe consequences), unless some route to efficacy becomes manifest (as is sometimes the case).

In modern society, formal education is the socializing experience which is supposed to be most directly relevant to enhancing competence. In practice, of course, it very often has the opposite effect, particularly on children of impoverished or working class background (8). Nevertheless, it seems clear that achieving high levels of education does increase the sense of competence of many individuals, particularly in the political sphere.

Alongside the rise of mass higher education in modern society has been the increasing dominance of bureaucratic forms of authority. Bureaucratic organization rewards competence, but at the same time bureaucratic hierarchy rests on the assumption that there are major differences among men in their capacity to exercise authority, and that competence in this regard ought to give a few men great legitimate power to coordinate the lives of many others who ought not to expect much voice in decisions which control them.

There is, then, a contradiction between two of the great shaping institutions of the contemporary period—mass higher education and bureaucratic authority—a contradiction which has to do with opposed definitions of competence embodied in each of these institutions. This contradiction was noted by Max Weber in his classic essay on bureaucracy. Weber felt that the tension between liberal education and bureaucracy would probably be resolved by the erosion of liberal education and its replacement by technical training. It is clear that his expectations were to a very great extent accurate. Narrow specialization, emphasis on technique, and value neutrality in higher education are widely seen as the central trend; critics continue to see these as reducing the likelihood that the highly educated person will feel himself to be competent to take part in general citizenly activity.

Still, liberal education has not been totally erased, and more and more young people are getting exposed to it. These same young people, unlike their predecessors in the educated middle class, are very likely to spend much of their lives, both in the educational system and beyond it, under bureaucratic authority if they follow conventional career lines.

The heightened sense of competence produced by mass higher education and by comfortable status constitutes, I believe, one of the more important sources of instability for the legitimacy of established authority, particularly those authority structures which assume little competence and provide little autonomy for those subordinate to it.

Risk Taking

There is one final personal characteristic which seems to deserve mention as relevant to understanding the stability of authority in American society. This is the capacity to take risks in order to defy authoritative orders. There are undoubtedly numerous determinants of this capacity, and one doubts whether there is, in fact, a generalized trait—call it courage—which predicts willingness to take risks in all spheres of life. I particularly want to emphasize the possibility that one's socioeconomic status is an important determinant of one's capacity to take risks involving disobedience. In particular, it seems likely that high status and material security, particularly if one is born into them, tend to weaken the impact of those incentives and sanctions which are usually utilized by authority to maintain conformity. Obviously, most people at the top do a great many things to stay there; still, it seems to be empirically true that they also have more objective and subjective freedom of action. This is, in part, because the status and income incentives of the society are less attractive; in part, because one has been raised to exercise rather than defer to authority; in part, because one may have a certain degree of guilt about being affluent in an egalitarian society; in part, because one discovers the limitations and psychological costs of a life-style organized around material consumption and preservation of social status. At any rate, on this analysis, one should not find it surprising that among those most willing to be defiant of the draft; among those most prepared to face prison with some degree of equanimity; among those ready to take risks with respect to their future careers, a disproportionate number of children of affluence will be represented. Furthermore, on this analysis, one predicts that rising levels of affluence will greatly increase the number of young who are prepared to take the risks of challenging established authority.

Speculations on the Future of American National Authority

I have formulated the foregoing propositions and hypotheses in what appears to be a deductive style; actually, however, this discussion should be read as *post hoc* argument. On the one hand, much of the previous discussion was designed to try to identify some general principles which would explain some of the data which we and others have obtained concerning the characteristics of student protesters. Second, this discussion was in large part an attempt to provide some rational grounds for the feeling, which I am sure I share with others, that present student protest movements against university administrations, against the war and the draft, are not isolated or ephemeral outbursts, but that they have major historical implications, particularly for the legitimacy of national authority in advanced industrial societies like our own.

The burden of social research which has relevance to anticipating the future of legitimacy in this society strongly suggests that the prudent observer will place his bets on continued stability. That is the implication of Milgram's studies and other experiments demonstrating the willing obedience of subjects undergoing scientific manipulation. It is the burden of research on the effects of political socialization. It is the clear implication of studies of political behavior, of voting habits and patterns, and public opinion. The main body of theory and research from diverse fields seems to say that the legitimacy of national authority in the United States rests on a broad consensus among Americans about political rules, about common values, about the trustworthiness of the system in general and the current regime in particular; and that this consensus is powerfully supported by the process of socializing the young on the one hand and by the prosperous and progressive consequences of the system on the other.

This kind of reasoning did not help social scientists to predict either the black revolt or the mass disaffection and rebelliousness of educated youth. Given the emergence of these movements, conventional social analysis leads us to expect that their effects will be neither symptomatic of, nor productive of, fundamental changes in the nature of authority and its legitimation in American society.

Such reasoning seems increasingly less credible with each passing day. And we need not rely solely on our emotional reactions to immediate turmoil to provide grounds for thinking that the legitimacy of established authority in the United States is reaching an historical turning point.

The Black Revolt

The black revolt is, of course, a primary reason for expecting a transformation of authority. The shift in its terms, from a movement for integration to a movement for colonial liberation, means that, by definition, a major portion of the black community has already decided that established authority on national and local levels is illegitimate. Current proposals for dealing with the racial crisis fall roughly into three categories: they are either proposals for the institutionalization of new forms of authority or proposals to restore the legitimacy of the political system by efforts to rapidly meet the economic needs of the black population, or they are frank appeals to recognize the collapse of legitimacy by proposing to maintain power through force.

Some of our previous discussion is helpful in understanding why legitimacy of authority has so rapidly eroded for black people. Without attempting a detailed analysis, the following points are worth mentioning:

1. Negroes have of course never felt particularly rewarded by the system nor have they been given any opportunity to see it as trustworthy. As we have previously suggested, this disaffection and mistrust is a product of direct and graphic experience; it is also a feature of the political socialization of Negro children and youth in the family.

2. The past decade has been one of increased disillusionment. Although the postwar period was expected to be one of rapid progress for Negroes, matters did not turn out this way. The gap between black and white economic position has tended to widen. Laws and government enactments which promised change were not effectively implemented. The promise of migration to the city has turned to despair. Of particular importance in intensifying distrust of and disaffection with the political system is the situation of black youth. The rising generation experiences enormous rates of unemployment and the knowledge that future opportunity will be meager; it contributes disproportionately to the casualties in Vietnam, suffers almost universal harassment at the hands of the local police—and all this in the context of an endless stream of promises and seductions. To vast numbers of black youth, it is clear that the system is strongly biased against them and that nothing is to be gained from further adherence to it.

3. The integration movement was crucial in the development of new stances toward authority. Its failure, of course, intensified disaffection. But its success in creating organization had the effect of increasing the competence and risk-taking capacity of many black people. It also transformed the consensus of the black community from one organized around accommodation and acceptance of established authority to one favoring assertiveness and independent power.

Of course, no elaborate framework of theorizing is needed to account for the emergence of deepening revolutionary sentiment in the black community. On the other hand, one need not assume that the existence of such a sentiment is particularly threatening to the long-term legitimacy of the American political system. Partial incorporation of Negro demands, it may be argued, can offset the most threatening implications of the movement; anyway, it may be said, the blacks are a special case of disaffection, with little resonance among whites.

The General Erosion of Legitimacy

I believe, however, that the inability of the American polity to deal effectively with Negro grievances is not the only source of erosion of its legitimacy. Indeed, the so-called youth revolt indicates that more general problems are, in fact, emerging. these, I would argue, have to do with major shifts in aspects of American culture to which I have already briefly referred. Among these changes I would emphasize the following:

1. *There has been a general decline of commitment to traditional "middle class values" throughout the society.* Many observers have commented on the erosion of the "Protestant Ethic"—a process which probably began with the turn of the century and which has been due largely to the impact of bureaucratization and increasing economic surplus. These processes have virtually destroyed the traditional capitalist economy; the cultural and characterological patterns associated with it have likewise lost their vitality. On the other hand, it is important to emphasize that the existing political and institutional élites continue to represent themselves in traditional ways and that large sectors of the populace still adhere to some version of the classic virtues of entrepreneurial success, self-discipline, and individualism which derive from the Protestant Ethic.

2. *The rapid growth of a sector of the middle class whose status depends on high education rather than property.* This group tends to be most critical of traditional values and of traditional capitalism generally, in part because of the exposure of these people to humanist values, in part because their vocations are often not tied directly to the business sector of the economy. In addition, as we have suggested, high education is likely to increase the interest of individuals in having autonomy and a voice in decision making.

3. *Associated with these trends has been the transformation of the American family, especially the family of the educated middle class.* This transformation involves increased equality between husband and wife, declining distinctiveness of sex roles in the family, increased opportunity for self-expression on the part of children, fewer parental demands for self-discipline, and more parental support for

autonomous behavior on the part of children. Evidence from studies of student protesters suggests the existence of an increasingly distinct "humanist" subculture in the middle class, consisting primarily of highly educated and urbanized families, based in professional occupations, who encourage humanist orientations in their offspring as well as questioning attitudes to traditional middle class values, to arbitrary authority, and conventional politics (4). Although this humanist subculture represents a small minority of the population, many of its attributes are more widely distributed; and the great increase in the number of college graduates suggests that the ranks of this subculture will rapidly grow.

4. *These cultural changes inevitably generate discontent with established authority.* As we have already suggested, persons raised in these "new" ways are likely to be resistant to authority which is hierarchical, bureaucratic, or symbolic of traditional capitalist and nationalist goals. On the other hand, one might imagine that authority on the national and institutional levels in America could be flexible enough to offset serious disaffection on the part of this emergent group. Change in the direction of providing greater personal autonomy and participation, élites who speak the language of modernity and change, and the adoption of public programs that fulfill the vocational and personal needs of the educated humanists might be sufficient to keep their unrest within the framework of legitimacy.

There is, however, an awesome barrier to the achievement of this kind of incorporation, namely, the commitment of American political and corporate élites to the maintenance of an international empire. This commitment has numerous internal consequences. The most central for our purposes is that it necessitates the militarization of the youth—the imposition of conscription on the one hand and the "channeling" of youth into "necessary" occupations on the other. It is this situation, more than anything else, which converts the restiveness of educated youth into direct opposition, which leads them to challenge the legitimacy of established authority, and which, incidentally, connects them to militant black youth. For both black and white humanist youth, the persistence and growth of militarism and empire building constitute a fundamental violation of central values and a severe threat to individual and collective fulfillment of central aspirations.

Militant black and humanist white youth are most directly affronted by conscription and other consequences of American imperialism, and the result is that they come into direct and continuing conflict with authority as they try to resist its imposition. But imperialism has other consequences for political stability. For instance, continued commitment to massive military expenditures forces the postponement of domestic reform, thereby alienating, rather than incorporating, deprived minority groups and the educated middle class. Imperialist foreign policy seems to require a steady deterioration in the perceived trustworthiness of national authority: for instance, it requires the elaboration of covert, paramilitary institutions, management of information, and other practices which signify a loss of democratic control over foreign policy and an increase in direct efforts by the state to manipulate the domestic political process. The massive defense budget greatly enhances the power of the military and defense corporations, who exert powerful influence over policy without responsibility to the electorate. Those who oppose the military or who want to change foreign policy become increasingly convinced that national authority is biased against them, and legitimacy is further eroded.

One could go on in elaborating the many ways in which dissent and opposition to the Johnson Administration and its policies, or more general grievances on the part of the disadvantaged, have systematically been converted into more fundamental challenges to the legitimacy of national authority, in large part as a consequence of its imperialist character.

One might accept the above analysis and still seriously doubt whether the increasingly revolutionary mood of some sectors of the population represents an unmanageable challenge to the legitimacy of the present authority structure. The challenge is serious; the widespread use of armed force to occupy cities and protect various public installations and functions is a demonstration of this, as is the steadily rising number of jailed draft resisters, and ultimately, Lyndon Johnson's decision not to seek re-election. But its unmanageability depends on whether and in what manner the present mood spreads to other parts of the population.

If there is a potential for growing delegitimization of national authority beyond the strata who are presently disaffected, it ought to become manifest in the ranks of the armed forces. For, as we have suggested, if widespread potential discontent with legitimate authority exists, it can be catalyzed by the example of a small number of active disobedients. That small number has now begun to appear—in the form of public deserters, men who refuse orders, servicemen who participate in peace marches and love-ins. Now, a miniscule but growing movement for a union of servicemen has emerged, as well as a number of underground newspapers which are passed around army bases. Do these events represent the early stages of general disaffection among conscripts? This seems far less unlikely today than it did even a few months ago.

Catalysts and Cracks

We have also suggested that legitimacy depends on the readiness of other centers of power to provide backing for the challenged authority. There have, it seems to me, already developed some minor, if interesting, cracks in the institutional support for American national authority. One illustration of this is the willingness of some university authorities to accede to student demands to withhold class rank information from Selective Service boards and to readmit students convicted of violating the draft laws.[2] These are rather trivial gestures; still they are symbolic of the fact that some institutional authorities—particularly university administrators and church officials—find it increasingly difficult to support the establishment in general. At the opposite pole, one observes the increasingly open hostility of the police to efforts by local authorities to moderate civil disorder, resulting in increasing tension within the authority structure at least at the municipal level. Whether these actions suggest a more fundamental series of splits in the institutional framework again remains to be seen.

In short, I have been trying to say that there appears to be a fundamental incompatibility between the commitment of American national authority to the maintenance of a world empire and the continued legitimacy of that authority. The commitment to empire prevents the authorities from adequately meeting the demands of the disadvantaged. It necessitates forms of domination and social control which are antidemocratic and which reduce the trustworthiness of the authorities. It perpetuates forms of organization which prevent the political system from reflecting the vast cultural changes which are sweeping the society. It requires the deployment of youth for military and related purposes while cultural changes have made many youths characterologically unsuitable for such purposes.

These are some of the reasons for feeling that the draft resister and the Black Panther rather than the cheerful robot or the black bourgeois are the authentic vanguard of an emerging social and political order, and that the example of the resistant few is likely to continue to be catalytic for the ambivalent and passive many. The danger of a repressive response by beleaguered authority is quite real, as is the mobilization of popular support for the imposition of order at the expense of freedom. Yet the emergent characterological and cultural trends, and the revolutionary movements they have spawned, promise a new social system, in which militarism, racism, narrow nationalism, and imperialism have become illegitimate and where individual dignity, individual conscience, and collective participation become the primary bases for legitimate authority. This promise makes the risks worthwhile for many of us.

FOOTNOTES

1. This discussion of the literature on conforming is indebted to Gamson (1968, pp. 127-135).
2. Another illustration would be the decision of Yale University officials to strip the ROTC there of its academic status. As reported in *The News American* (Baltimore, Md.) Editorial. Feb. 3, 1969. Similar actions were taken by other universities in recent months.

REFERENCES

1. Adorno, T. W., Frenkel-Brunswik, E., Levinson, D., & Sanford, N. *The authoritarian personality*. New York: Harper & Row, 1950.
2. Block, J., Haan, N., & Smith, M. B. Activism and apathy in contemporary adolescents. In J. F. Adams (Ed.), *Contributions to the understanding of adolescence*. New York: Allyn & Bacon, in press.
3. Easton, D., & Dennis, J. The child's image of government. *The Annals*, September 1965, 361, 40-57.
4. Flacks, R. The liberated generation. *J. soc. Issues*, 1967, 23, 52-75.
5. Frank, J. Experimental studies of personal pressure and resistance. *J. gen. Psychol.*, 1944, 30, 23-64.
6. Gamson, W. *Power and discontent*. Homewood, Ill.: Dorsey Press, 1968.
7. Keniston, K. *Young radicals*. New York: Houghton-Mifflin, 1968.
8. Kozol, J. *Death at an early age*. Boston: Houghton-Mifflin, 1967.
9. Lauter, P., & Howe, Florence. The draft and its opposition. *The New York Rev. of Books*, June 20, 1968, X (12), 25-31.
10. Marvick, D. The political socialization of the American Negro. *The Annals*, September 1965, 361, 112-127.
11. Milgram, S. Some conditions of obedience and disobedience to authority. In I. D. Steiner & M. Fishbein (Eds.), *Current studies in social psychology*. New York: Holt, Rinehart & Winston, 1965. Pp. 243-262.
12. Orne, M. T. On the social psychology of the psychological experiment. *Amer. Psychologist*, 1962, 17, 776-783.
13. Orne, M. T., & Evans, F. J. Social control in the psychological experiment. *J. Pers. soc. Psychol.*, 1965, 1, 189-200.
14. Sampson, R. V. *The psychology of power*. New York: Vintage, 1968.
15. Smith, M. B. Competence and socialization. In J. Clausen (ed.), *Socialization and society*. Boston: Little, Brown, 1968. Pp. 270-320.
16. Stinchcombe, A. *Constructing social theories*. New York: Harcourt, Brace & World, 1968.
17. Wolfenstein, F. V. *The revolutionary personality*. Princeton, N. J.: Princeton Univer. Press, 1967.

PLANNED CHANGE AND ORGANIZATIONAL HEALTH: FIGURE AND GROUND

Matthew B. Miles

Any observer of the applied behavioral sciences today would have to note a remarkable interest in the entire problem of planned change. Scientists and practitioners alike are concerned with the stages of planned change in groups, organizations, and communities; with the question of how change processes can be managed in a meaningful sense of that word; and with the characteristics of the "change agent," that miraculous middleman between What Science Has Proved and What We Are Up Against. The very existence of this seminar is a case in point.

There is a growing literature, in journals as diverse as *Applied Anthropology* and *Petroleum Refiner*; there have already been thoughtful attempts to collect this literature, and to conceptualize the problems involved. (19*; 7). All this is gratifying to beleaguered school administrators—and to everyone who, following Kurt Lewin's most frequently-quoted dictum, believes that "there is nothing so practical as a good theory."

Yet it seems to me that there is an important, but often-overlooked aspect of what is being said and done about planned change: the notion that any particular planned change effort is deeply conditioned by the state of the system in which it takes place. For example, properties of the organization such as communication

---

*See References at end of article.—Ed.

From *Change Processes in the Public Schools,* Carlson *et. al.,* editors, Center for the Advanced Study of Educational Administration, University of Oregon, 1965, pp. 11-34.

adequacy, and the distribution of influence have a powerful effect on the speed and durability of adoption of any particular innovation, from *English 2600* to data processing of teacher marks. To use an image from Gestalt psychology, specific planned change attempts have most typically been "in figure," occupying the focus of attention, while the organization itself has remained the "ground."

I believe this emphasis is both practically and theoretically unfortunate. It is time for us to recognize that successful efforts at planned change must take as a primary target the improvement of *organization health*—the school system's ability not only to function effectively, but to develop and grow into a more fully-functioning system.

Perhaps I can illustrate my assertion that organization properties have often been treated peripherally, or left to sit as background phenomena. If you have examined the literature on the diffusion of innovations, perhaps with the aid of Everett Rogers' excellent compendium (27) you will notice that a good deal of attention is paid to the individual innovator, to when he adopts the innovation, and why. But the literature remains nearly silent on the organizational setting in which innovation takes place. I suspect this has several antecedents.

For one thing, the typical adopter in most rural sociological studies is an individual farmer rather than a collectivity such as an organization. The farmer's role in the community setting turns out to be important, but aside from studies on "traditional" versus "modern" community norms, the influence of the larger social setting tends to be underplayed.

Paul Mort did, on the other hand, make extensive studies of innovation by organizations—school districts (see 28). But Mort, far from being even an amateur sociologist, appeared almost aggressively ignorant of available knowledge about the functioning of organizations and communities. His "common sense" categories and demographic indices gave us no inkling of what was really going on in the districts who supplied his with data.

Even Dick Carlson's (11) study of the adoption of modern math by school superintendents suffers a bit, I think, from a kind of "great man" tendency; the internal dynamics of the school system are seen as less important than characteristics of the local superintendent, such as his position in the reference group of administrators in the region. His data are compelling, but I suspect they would have been even more powerful had he gone into more depth on the dynamics of the local setting.

From the anthropological side, I think it fair to say that there has been an over-emphasis on the properties of a particular innovation itself, its diffusion across systems, and its integration within systems —without a corresponding degree of interest in the dynamics and functioning of the receiving organization as such. Art Gallaher (15) has thoughtfully discussed power structure in innovation-receiving systems, the actual prestige of advocates of the innovation, and other matters influencing how (or if) an innovation will be integrated into the local organization. But even here, I think the analysis is over-focused on the "thinginess" of the particular innovation, taking the local system itself as a kind of unmodifiable ground against which the innovation shows up in stark figure.

One more example. The currently wide-spread emphasis on the importance of "dissemination of research findings," and even the recent effort of the U.S. Office to provide development and demonstration centers, likewise avoid the problem. They share the popular view that the *content* or demonstrated efficacy of a particular educational innovation, as such, is the crucial thing in determining whether or not it will be adopted and used effectively. As you can gather, I am taking a decidedly processual view here: organization dynamics are the focus of attention.

I hope I have not misrepresented the views of my colleagues. It would please me to be corrected, in fact. What I do want to counter in this paper is a set of assumptions (by scientists or practioners) that organization properties—from decision-making methods to interpersonal climate—are simply "there," that they are relatively invariant, and cannot (or should not) themselves be made the subject of planned change efforts.

More generally, the position being taken is this. It seems likely that the state of health of an educational organization can tell us more than anything else about the probable success of any particular change effort. Economy of effort would suggest that we should look at the state of an organization's health as such, and try to improve it—in preference to struggling with a series of more or less inspired shortrun change efforts as ends in themselves.

To analogize with persons for a minute: the neurotic who struggles through one unavailing search for "something new" after another will never be genuinely productive until he faces and works through fundamental problems of his own functioning. Genuine productiveness—in organizations as in persons—rests on a clear sense of identity, on adequate connection with reality, on a lively problem-solving stance, and on many other things, to which I would like to turn in a moment. Here I only wish to leave you with the root notion that attention to organization health ought to be priority one for any administrator seriously concerned with innovativeness in today's educational environment.

In the remainder of this paper, I should like, first, to deal with some problems in the very concept of health, both generally and as applied to organizations. The next section reviews the conception of "organization" employed in the rest of the paper, and outlines some dimensions of organization health as I see them. All this is rather general, and I should then like to turn to some discussion of the special properties of *educational* organizations, as such, and what their particular ways of departing from optimum organization health seem to be. Lastly, as an applied behavioral scientist, I would be remiss if I did not discuss some representative technologies for inducing organization health, and suggest some principles underlying them.

Most of this paper is frankly speculative, though it is informed by a good deal of current work in the applied behavioral sciences—and even, now and then, by some contact with phenomena such as superintendents, principals, teachers and children. All of the notions in the paper need vigorous discussion and testing.

Some Problems in the Concept of "Health"

The historical, common-sense notion of health is that it represents absence of illness, disease, suffering, wrongness in an organism. If not arrested, a serious "sickness" may lead to irreversible changes, such as organ impairment, atrophy or death. But beginning (to my knowledge) with the interesting British work in preventive medicine dubbed the "Peckham Experiment," there has been more and more medical concern with the notion of positive well-being or optimal functioning. That is, disease-freeness, in and of itself, does not guarantee that an organism will in fact be coping with life's adventures with a sense of *élan,* and growing while it does so.

This conception of positive health—in many ways a sneaky, vague notion—has also been receiving more and more attention in the mental health literature (see 17). And there is increasing interest in the fields of psychotherapy and human relations training with the notion of "self-actualization." Both "positive health" and "self-actualization" imply a considerable gap between sheer disease-freeness, and something that might be called the fully functioning human being. This is an attractive idea; it is consistent with much of our common sense experience, and it caters to the American notion of the (nearly) infinitely-improvable man.

But even if something like "positive health" or "self-actualization" can be said to exist—and Maslow's (22) case studies are instructive and plausible in this respect—there are some traps and difficulties in applying such concepts to organization functioning. One, of course, is the tendency to go "over-organismic," reifying the organization into some kind of gigantic person, or least organism. This, of course, leads into the hoary disputation about whether systems larger than that of the individual person are "real" (see, for example, Warriner, 31), a totally unprofitably byway which I do not propose to enter at the moment.

Another danger is that the notion of health implies "sickness"; school administrators are having enough difficulty as it is without being accused of being at the helm of pathological vessels on the stormy seas of innovation. The very image of "sickness" itself diverts attention away from the notion of positive growth and development, implying that only correction of some negative or painful state is required.

Finally, there are the risks involved in any discussion involving "ideal types"—distortion of reality, or blindness to large portions of it, and a prevalence of normative, preachment-type statement-making about any particular organization (or, more usually, *all* organizations).

All these objections have some validity; I do not propose to eradicate them here, only to bring them to awareness, so they do not hamper the subsequent discussion unduly. In brief, the intellectual risks of an "organization health" approach seem to me far outweighed by the advantages. A reasonably clear conception of organization health would seem to be an important prerequisite to a wide range of activities involving organizations: research of any meaningful sort; attempts to improve the organization as a place to live, work, and learn; and—not least—the day-to-day operations of any particular organization, such as your own school system.[1]

Organizations: Their Nature

Formal definitions show that the author of the paper has paid his debt to "the literature"; they may sometimes even help in de-limiting the sphere of discussion. "Organization" is here treated as a special case of the more general concept "system," more particularly "open system." The latter is defined as:

A bounded collection of interdependent parts, devoted to the accomplishment of some goal or goals, with the parts maintained in a steady state in relation to each other and the environment by means of (1) standard modes of operation, and (2) feedback from the environment about the consequences of system actions. (23, p. 13).

Argyris (1, p. 120) poses a broadly similar definition: "(1) a plurality of parts, [which] (2) maintaining themselves through their interrelatedness and, (3) achieving specific objective(s), (4) while accomplishing (2) and (3) adapt to the external environment thereby (5) maintaining their interrelated state of parts."

Either of these definitions would apply to a system such as a candle flame, an air-conditioning unit, or a school district. For our purposes, it is perhaps sufficient to say that the above definitions, in the special case of the "organization," are expected to apply to social systems larger than a face-to-face group, and with a reasonable degree of goal specification (this latter to exclude larger systems, such as communities and nations).

Somewhat more specifically, reference to Figure 1 will indicate the notion "educational organization" used as a backdrop for this paper. Notice that the usual hierarchical arrangement is absent, since the "parts" are not seen as persons or work groups, but as social-psychological components of the system which cross-cut persons and groups. The figure indicates that the organization exists in an environment from which it receives inputs (money, personnel, and children) and to which it releases outputs in terms of goal achievement, and morale and learning motivation of the clients in the organization (children).

Between the input and output, to paraphrase T. S. Eliot, falls the shadow of a number of other components. The inhabitants of an educational organization must have reasonably clear perceptions of the goal or goals to which the system is devoted; these in turn affect role specifications and performance for the inhabitants. Systems of reward and penalty regulate role performance, as do the norms governing the style of interpersonal transactions in the system. The arrows in the diagram are intended to indicate directions of influence between parts of the system, as well as to suggest that a variety of feedback loops exist which serve to maintain the system in a reasonably steady state.

If all goes well, desired system outputs are achieved. But this is not all: above and beyond the network of parts and their functioning, we can conceive of a set of system "health" characteristics, which have to do with the continued adequacy and viability of the organization's coping. More of this below. Here it is perhaps sufficient to sketch out

Figure 1. Schematic Model of Organization Functioning and Change Environment

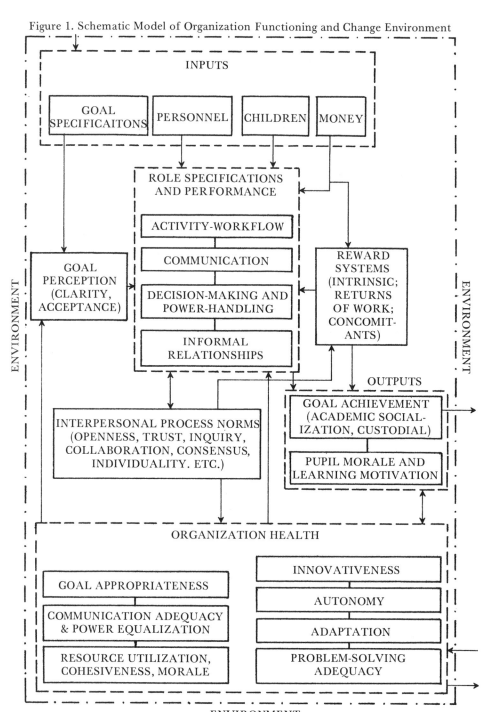

the schematic model, and point out that it assumes nothing about the specific kinds of structures—planful or emergent—appearing in any particular system. The model will presumably fit a classical pyramidal scheme, as well as a number of more or less radical variants from this (e.g., those suggested by Argyris, 1).

Organization Health

Our present thinking about organization health is that it can be seen as a set of fairly durable *second-order* system properties, which tend to transcend short-run effectiveness. A healthy organization in this sense not only survives in its environment, but continues to cope adequately over the long haul, and continuously develops and extends its surviving and coping abilities. Short-run operations on any particular day may be effective or ineffective, but continued survival, adequate coping, and growth are taking place.

A *steadily* ineffective organization would presumably not be healthy; on balance, "health" implies a summation of effective short-run coping. But notice that an organization *may* cope effectively in the short run (as for example by a speed-up or a harsh cost-cutting drive), but at the cost of longer-run variables, such as those noted below. The classic example, of course, is an efficiency drive which cuts short-run costs and results in long-run labor dissatisfaction and high turnover.

To illustrate in more detail what is meant by "second-order property," here is a list of ten dimensions of organization health that seem plausible to me. Many of them are drawn by heuristic analogy from the behavior of persons or small groups; this does *not* mean, of course, that organizations necessarily are precisely homologous to persons or groups—only that thinking in this way may get us somewhere on what, it must be admitted, is a very complex problem indeed. Here then are ten dimensions. They are not, of course mutually exclusive, and interact with each other vigorously within any particular organization. Both Jahoda (17) and Argyris (1) have commented on the importance of a multiple-criterion approach to the assessment of health, given the present state of our knowledge and the fact, that as a college roommate of mine once remarked with blinding insight, "You know, everything is really connected to everything else."

The first three dimensions are relatively "tasky," in that they deal with organizational goals, the transmission of messages, and the way in which decisions are made.

1. *Goal focus.* In a healthy organization, the goal (or more usually goals) of the system would be reasonably clear to the system members, and reasonably well accepted by them.[2] This clarity and acceptance, however, should be seen as a necessary but insufficient condition for organization health. The goals must also be *achievable* with existing or available resources, and be *appropriate*—more or less congruent with the demands of the environment. The last feature may be most critical. Switching back to the person level for a moment, consider the obsessive patient who sets the clear, accepted, achievable goal for himself of washing his hands 250 times a day. The question remains: is this an appropriate goal in light of what else there is to do in life?

2. *Communication adequacy.* Since organizations are not simultaneous face-to-face systems like small groups, the movement of information within them becomes crucial. This dimension of organization health implies that there is relatively distortion-free communication "vertically," "horizontally," and across the boundary of the system to and from the surrounding environment. That is, information travels reasonably well—just as the healthy person "knows himself" with a minimum level of repression, distortion, etc. In the healthy organization, there is good and prompt sensing of internal strains; there are enough data about problems of the system to insure that a good diagnosis of system difficulties can be made. People have the information they need, and have gotten it without exerting undue efforts, such as those involved in moseying up to the superintendent's secretary, reading the local newspaper, or calling excessive numbers of special meetings.

3. *Optimal power equalization.* In a healthy organization the distribution of influence is relatively equitable. Subordinates (if there is a formal authority chart) can influence upward, and even more important—as Likert (18) has demonstrated—they perceive that their boss can do likewise with *his* boss. In such an organization, inter-group struggles for power would not be bitter, though inter-group conflict, (as in every human system known to man) would undoubtedly be present. The basic stance of persons in such an organization, as they look up, sideways and down, is that of collaboration rather than explicit or implicit coercion. The units of the organization (persons in roles, work groups, etc.) would stand in an interdependent relationship to each other, with rather less emphasis on the ability of a "master" part to control the entire operation. The exertion of influence in a healthy organization would presumably rest on the competence of the influencer *vis-à-vis* the

issue at hand, his stake in the outcome, and the amount of knowledge or data he has—rather than on his organizational position, personal charisma, or other factors with little direct relevance to the problem at hand.

These then are three "task-centered" dimensions of organization health. A second group of three dimensions deals essentially with the internal state of the system, and its inhabitants' "maintenance" needs. These are resource utilization, cohesiveness, and morale.

4. *Resource utilization.* We say of a healthy person, such as a second-grader, that he is "working up to his potential." To put this another way, the classroom system is evoking a contribution from him at an appropriate and goal-directed level of tension. At the organization level, "health" would imply that the system's inputs, particularly the personnel, are used effectively. The overall coordination is such that people are neither overloaded nor idling. There is a minimal sense of strain, generally speaking (in the sense that trying to do something with a weak or inappropriate structure puts strain on that structure). In the healthy organization, people may be working very hard indeed, but they feel that they are not working against themselves, or against the organization. The fit between people's own dispositions and the role demands of the system is good. Beyond this, people feel reasonably "self-actualized"; they not only "feel good" in their jobs, but they have a genuine sense of learning, growing, and developing as persons in the process of making their organizational contribution.

5. *Cohesiveness.* We think of a healthy person as one who has a clear sense of identity; he knows who he is, underneath all the specific goals he sets for himself. Beyond this, he *likes himself*; his stance toward life does not require self-derogation, even when there are aspects of his behavior which are unlovely or ineffective. By analogy at the organization level, system health would imply that the organization knows "who it is." Its members feel attracted to membership in the organization. They want to stay with it, be influenced by it, and exert their own influence in the collaborative style suggested above.

6. *Morale.* The history of this concept in the social-psychological literature is so appalling that I hesitate to introduce it at all. The implied notion is one of well-being or satisfaction. Satisfaction is not enough for health, of course; a person may report feelings of well-being and satisfaction in his life, while successfully denying

deeplying hostilities, anxieties, and conflicts. Yet it still seems useful to evoke, at the organization level, the idea of morale: a summated set of individual sentiments, centering around feelings of well-being, satisfaction, and pleasure, as opposed to feelings of discomfort, unwished-for strain and dissatisfaction. In an *un*healthy system, life might be perceived rosily as "good," or as unabashedly bad; in a healthy organization it is hard to entertain the idea that the dominant personal response of organization members would be anything else than one of well-being.

Finally there are four more dimensions of organization health, which deal with growth and changefulness: the notions of innovativeness, autonomy, adaptation *vis-à-vis* the environment, and problem-solving adequacy.

7. *Innovativeness.* A healthy system would tend to invent new procedures, move toward new goals, produce new kinds of products, diversify itself, and become more rather than less differentiated over time. In a sense, such a system could be said to grow, develop, and change, rather than remaining routinized, and standard. The analogue here is to the self-renewing properties of a Picasso; or to Schachtel's (29) "activity" orientation (curious, exploring) as contrasted with "embeddedness" orientation (tension-reducing, protective) in persons.[3]

8. *Autonomy.* The healthy person acts "from his own center outward." Seen in a training or therapy group, for example, such a person appears nearly free of the need to submit dependently to authority figures, *and* from the need to rebel and destroy symbolic fathers of any kind. A healthy organization, similarly, would not respond passively to demands from the outside, feeling itself the tool of the environment, and it would not respond destructively or rebelliously to perceived demands either. It would tend to have a kind of independence from the environment, in the same sense that the healthy person, while he has transactions with others, does not treat their responses as *determinative* of his own behavior.

9. *Adaptation.* The notions of autonomy and innovativeness are both connected with the idea that a healthy person, group, or organization is in realistic, effective contact with the surroundings. When environmental demands and organization resources do not match, a problem-solving, re-structuring approach evolves in which *both* the environment and the organization become different in some respect. More adequate, continued coping of the organization, as a result of changes in the local system, the relevant portions of the

environment, or more usually both, occurs. And such a system has sufficient stability and stress tolerance to manage the difficulties which occur during the adaptation process. Perhaps inherent in this notion is that the system's ability to bring about corrective change in itself is faster than the change cycle in the surrounding environment. Explanations for the disappearance of dinosaurs vary, but it is quite clear that in some way this criterion was not met.

10. *Problem-solving adequacy.* Finally, any healthy organism— even one as theoretically impervious to fallibility as a computer— *always* has problems, strains, difficulties, and instances of ineffective coping. The issue is not the presence or absence of problems, therefore, but the *manner* in which the person, group, or organization copes with problems. Argyris (1) has suggested that in an effective system, problems are solved with minimal energy; they stay solved; and the problem-solving mechanisms used are not weakened, but maintained or strengthened. An adequate organization, then, has well-developed structures and procedures for sensing the existence of problems, for inventing possible solutions, for deciding on the solutions, for implementing them, and for evaluating their effectiveness. Such an organization would conceive of its own operations (whether directed outward to goal achievement, inward to maintenance, or inward-outward to problems of adaptation) as being *controllable*. We would see active coping with problems, rather than passive withdrawing, compulsive responses, scapegoating, or denial.

Here then are ten dimensions of a healthy organization,[4] stated abstractly, even vaguely in many instances. They must, of course, be operationalized into meaningful indicators of organization functioning; the staff of our project is currently into this with more than a little trepidation, but with keen interest to see whether these ways of viewing the health of a system prove to have a reasonable amount of empirical steam behind them.

The Special Case of Educational Organizations

These dimensions can presumably be applied to any type of organization. Much of the theory and empirical data on which they are based was generated in industrial organizations in which "organization improvement" programs have become more and more widespread in the last few years. (See, for example, Bennis, 5; 6.) We need, however, to determine the special properties of *educational* systems (if any) which pre-dispose them to particular types of ill health. It is also necessary to examine whether the technologies of organization improvement which have proved successful industrially need adaption in certain directions before they are likely to be efficacious in schools. If this is not done, we might well expect a recrudescence of the unfortunate enthusiasm of schoolmen for Taylorism and "scientific management" which occurred in the first decades of this century. (See the excellent treatment of this appalling subject in Callahan & Button, 10.)

In our own time, it has taken a good deal of agitation by people like Dan Griffiths to get school administrators and professors of education to accept the possibility that the school is in fact an organization, and as such shares certain properties with all other organizations, and that administrative theory, if well developed in any field of human endeavor, could apply to the school business. This is quite correct. However, emphasis on the commonality of all types of organizations has tended to obscure the fact that educational systems have special properties which condition the propositions of organization theory in reasonably predictable ways. What, then, are some of these properties?

1. *Goal ambiguity.* For many different reasons, it has seemed difficult to specify the output of educational organizations very precisely. Some of this is realistic: change in human beings is going on, with presumably cumulative effects over a long period of time. But part of this output measurement difficulty also seems to be a form of organization defense or protection against criticism from the surrounding environment (see below).

Whatever the reasons, supposed "unmeasurability" of organizational output (hence, of the effectiveness of particular role occupants) seems a fairly durable feature of educational organizations as we know them today.

In addition, certain goals of the school (such as "academic learning") are often given primacy in public pronouncements while others (for example, the socialization of achievement motivation and appropriate *Gesellschaftlich* behavior for the incoming denizens of an industrial society) are treated as background phenomena. Still others (such as keeping the kids off the streets and out of Mother's way—call it custodial care) are usually taboo as legitimate goal statements.[5]

It is possible, of course, that school system goals are not all that unmeasurable and ambiguous. In some exploratory interviewing we have been doing in two suburban school systems, teachers and principals, almost without exception, denied that "it is difficult to know when you are doing a good job"[6] and denied that "disagree-ment over the goals of the school" was present. We intend to pursue this further, because our hunch is that such protestations of agree-ment reflect defensive solutions to the actual problems of goal ambiguity and goal disagreement, which do in fact exist.

I believe that this ambiguity and pseudo-consensus around school output measurement encourages the institutionalization and ossifica-tion of teaching procedures. If it cannot really be determined whether one course of action leads to more output than another, then why stop lecturing? There is a further consequence (stemming particularly from the unacknowledged but powerful custodial func-tion of the school): highly rigid time and personnel allocations in most American schools. Hall passes, the forty-seven-minute period, and the difficulty some teachers have in finding time to go to the toilet are all examples. It is interesting that the increasing use of computers for class scheduling has not, to my knowledge, exploited the enormous potential of information-processing machines for making a *more* rather than less flexible learning environment. In any event, I wish only to make the point that goal ambiguity and procedural rigidity may very well turn out to be closely connected.

2. *Input variability.* Another, possibly unique, property of educa-tional organizations is a very wide variation in input from the environment, particularly in relation to children and personnel. Since the school is defined in America as publicly responsible, it must accept children of a very wide range of ability and motivation to carry out its activities (this holds true, of course, for custodial and socialization goals as well as academic learning goals). The current stress on programs for the "culturally deprived" only serves to divert attention from the fact that the American schools seem never to have been able to cope effectively with children from lower socioeco-nomic levels.[7]

This is no place to review in any detail the problem of variability in teacher performance, but here again it is important to note that the range of intellectual ability, interpersonal skill and knowledge of subject matter among teachers is probably at least as great as that among pupils. This variability causes considerable stress in educa-tional organizations, and develops the need to provide teaching personnel with methods and procedures which are (in effect) teacher -proof. Wayland (1964) has reviewed this problem as a function of the enormous historical expansion of the scope of American educa-tion; he suggests that the teacher's role is now essentially that of a bureaucratic functionary, all protestations of "professionalism" to the contrary.

3. *Role performance invisibility.* Classrooms are in effect the production departments of the educational enterprise; in them teachers teach. Yet, this role performance is relatively invisible to status equals or superiors. Children can observe, usually very acutely, the quality of a teacher's execution of her role, but they are not allowed to comment on this, and have few (if any) sanctions to bring to bear. Thus, rewards in the teaching profession seem relatively detached from others' estimates of one's performance; the average teacher, as Lortie (20) has pointed out, gains most satisfaction from intrinsic properties of the role behavior involved. Teaching thus becomes a craft-like occupation, rather than a profession, and substitute criteria for teaching effectiveness, such as "how interested the kids are" begin to appear and are used vigorously. Perhaps this is what our teachers meant when they said it was not difficult to know when they were doing a good job.

4. *Low interdependence.* A further characteristic of educational organizations, when compared with thing-producing systems, seems to be a relatively low interdependence of parts. Teacher A's failure to teach anything to her minions affects the job-relevant behavior of teacher B very little—except in a rather diffuse, blaming sense, as when junior high-school teachers devoutly declare their belief that basic skills are not present in newly-arrived seventh graders.

This low interdependence has several consequences. First, it tends to reinforce the pyramidal "man-to-man" style of supervision which Likert (18) and others have shown to be inimical to organization effectiveness. In the case of teachers of young children, it tends to promote a kind of infantilism and boredom; in many teachers, as suggested by a recent study (26) the peak of productive contribution tends to be in the twenties, with distancing from students and potential routinization starting in the mid-thirties. The reported stresses and strains in most accounts of team teaching—an attempt to increase interdependence in educational organizations—are mute testimony to the strength with which "separatist" norms have become institutionalized in the American public school.[8]

High interdependence is not without its difficulties, of course. As Golembiewski (16) has pointed out, the classical division of industrial organizations into specialized departments tends to promote hostility, competitiveness, and disjunction between the authority system and other aspects of the organization such as communication patterns, friendship relationships, and work flow. He suggests an alternative organization model involving the existence of "product divisions," each of which contains in it all the specialties necessary to undertake an operation such as buying materials for, producing and marketing a washing machine. Schools are organized in a product division manner, in effect. But Golembiewski's analysis—this is crucial—depends on the existence of simple, rapidly-available output measures, so that the performance of a product division can be monitored. As we have seen, the absence of such measures—and more fundamentally, the belief that they can never be produced—is a serious barrier to the effectiveness of educational organizations.

5. *Vulnerability.* The American public school, even more than other public organizations, is subject to control, criticism, and a wide variety of "legitimate" demands from the surrounding environment: everyone is a stockholder. Any public organization tends to generate this type of relationship with systems and persons outside its boundary. But a people-processing organization such as the school is dealing with extremely valuable property—children—who return to their parents each night with more or less accurate news of how they have been treated. Thus, in the special kind of organization termed a school, almost any role occupant—board member, superintendent, principal, staff specialist, or teacher can be criticized by parents or citizens at large. To the system inhabitants, the organization skin seems extremely thin. Many kinds of ingenious defenses are adopted to solve this problem—policies about visiting the classroom, brain-washing of new board members by the superintendent and the old members (cf. Sieber, 30, in press), buffer devices such as the PTA, and so on. Yet, the fact remains that a consumer who doesn't like the octane rating of his gasoline cannot go to the refinery and criticize the operation of a cat-cracker—but a parent who feels conflicted about her child's reading ability can be pretty violent with the first grade teacher. (I might comment that this vulnerability seems most sharp when viewed from the inside. Many parents apparently feel that the school is impregnable, and that they must not raise complaints, rock the boat, etc.)

In any event, this state of affairs represents, I believe, a serious failure of adaptation skills of schools as organizations, and tends to reduce school system autonomy sharply. In recent years, I have met only one school superintendent who told me he was going ahead actively (and successfully) with curriculum and organization changes to which a majority of his community were opposed. As it turned out, he was an old private school man.

6. *Lay-professional control problems.* Public schools are governed by laymen, most of whom have not been inside a school for twenty years prior to their succession to the board. As a result, they often

agree tacitly or explicitly on a division of labor with the superintendent and his staff (the policy—procedure distinction developed by
Brickell and Davies is one such example). But even where the board
is "well trained" and leaves the execution of policy to the superintendent, notice that the question of *educational policy* determination still remains a moot one.

And there are internal lay-professional problems as well. In many
respects, the principal of an elementary or high school, in terms of
expert knowledge, may find himself far behind the capabilities of
particular teachers on his staff—and is in this sense a layman as well.
The problems of organizations with high proportions of professionals
have been studied vigorously (ex: hospitals, and research organizations); I only wish to indicate here that the fruits of such study so far
have found little application in schools.[9]

7. *Low technological investment.* Lastly, it seems very clear that
the amount of technology per worker in schools is relatively low.
From 60% to 75% of a local school system's budget ordinarily goes
to salary, with a fraction for equipment and materials. Even if we
count buildings as "technological investment," the picture is rather
different from that in most industries. This has consequences: social
transactions, rather than socio-technical transactions, come to be the
major mode of organization production. Because of this, it is possible
that education, as James Finn has suggested, has never made it out of
the folk culture stage. And we are back once again to goal ambiguity
and its problems.

These, then, strike me as special strains, ways in which educational
organizations as such and the public school in particular depart from
the generalized model of organization health outlined earlier. In sum,
I would suggest that, in terms of the dimensions above, the major
difficulties to be expected in most public schools would center
around goal focus, (as a consequence of goal ambiguity), difficulties
in communication adequacy and power equalization stemming from
low interdependence; and perhaps most centrally, failures in innovativeness, autonomy, adaptation, and problem-solving adequacy, because of vulnerability and lay-professional conflict.

Interestingly enough, I do not see any clear reason for believing
that internal "maintenance problems" (such as those involved in
effective resource utilization, cohesiveness, and morale) are sharp
points of strain in most school systems; it may very well be that low
interdependence, plus orientation to a professional reference group,
carry with them a willingness to "settle for less" than the optimum in
these areas.

The Induction of Organization Health

The particular degree of health of any local school system, given a multiple-criterion approach such as that suggested here, undoubtedly varies from time to time. A question of considerable interest is: what can be done to induce a greater degree of organization health in any particular system? By now a fair amount of experience exists, drawn from the interesting blend of consultation and research in which an increasing number of behavioral scientists now find themselves involved, primarily with industrial organizations. These methods can perhaps most usefully be considered as *interventions* in the on-going life of a system; this term implies an action which interferes with or reorients processes—either pathological or normal—ordinarily occurring in the system. A teacher's intervention in a child's problem-solving serves to reorient his thinking; perhaps more importantly, it can aid the child to mobilize his own energies more effectively. Thus the usual aim of an intervention is to start internal change processes going in the system at hand, rather than only causing an immediate change.

Below are described six interventions aimed at improving organization health.[10] In some cases, plausible statements can be made about which dimensions of health are most typically influenced by a particular intervention. For the most part, however, we do not really know; it is exactly the function of our research project to discover how these are likely to work in educational organizations. In conclusion, some common principles underlying the six interventions are discussed.

1. *Team training.* In this approach, the members of an intact work group (for example, the superintendent and his central office personnel) meet for a period of several days away from their offices, with consultant help. They examine their own effectiveness as a problem solving team, the role of each member in the group and how it affects the group and the person himself, and the operations of the group in relation to its organizational environment. This problem-solving may be based on fairly careful prior data collection from individuals as to their views on the current problems of the system; these data are summarized and form the beginning of the group's agenda. Occasionally, exercises and theoretical material on group and organization functioning may be supplied by the outside consultant.

Under these circumstances, the members of the group usually improve in their abilities to express feelings directly, and to listen to—and understand—each other. Communication adequacy is thus considerably increased. The members also deal with internal conflicts in the team, and learn to solve problems more effectively as a unit, thus presumably increasing their ability to meet the demands placed upon them by other parts of the system. Over a period of time, beginning with the top decision-making group of the system, this intervention may be repeated with other groups as well. Industrial programs of this sort have been described by Argyris (2) and Blake and Mouton (8).

2. *Survey feedback.* In this approach, data bearing on attitudes, opinions, and beliefs of members of a system are collected via questionnaire. An external researcher summarizes the data for the organization as a whole, and for each of a number of relevant work groups. Each work group, under the guidance of its own superior, and perhaps with consultant help, examines its own summarized data, in comparison with those for the organization as a whole. The group makes plans for change stemming from these discussions and carries them out. The focus of this intervention is on many or all of the work groups within a total setting. The aim is to free up communication leading to goal clarification and problem-solving work. The relative objectification involved in looking at data helps to reduce feelings of being misunderstood and isolated, and makes problems more susceptible to solution, rather than retaining them as a focus for blaming, scapegoating, griping and so on. For an account of survey feedback procedure, see Mann (21); Gage (13) has tried a similar approach effectively with student-to-teacher feedback, and is now studying teacher-to-principle feedback.

3. *Role Workshop.* Sometimes called the "horizontal slice" meeting, this intervention involves all the people in a particular role (for example, elementary principal). They fill out research instruments dealing with role expectations which various others hold for them, the fit between their own wishes and these expectations, their actual role performance, etc. These data are summarized, and form the vehicle for a series of activities (discussion, role practice, decision-making exercises, problem-solving and so on) at a workship attended by all the people in the role. The main focus here is on role clarity, effectiveness, and improved fit between the person and the role. By sharing common role problems, people occupying the role may develop alternative solutions which result in better performance of that role and more "self-actualized" operation in general.

4. *"Target setting" and supporting activities.* In this approach, periodic meetings are held between a superior and each of his subordinates, separately. In a school system, this might involve the

superintendent and his staff members, or a principal and his teachers. The work of each subordinate is reviewed in relation to organizational and personal goals, and the superior and subordinate agree collaboratively on new targets for the subordinate's work and personal development. These "targets" are in turn reviewed after some work time (usually six months or so) has elapsed. During that period, other activities such as role meetings, consultation, self-operated data collection, academic courses, and workshops, may be engaged in by the subordinate to develop needed skills and understandings as he works toward the collaboratively-set goals. The focus of attention here is the working relationship between superior and subordinate, and the degree to which they are together able to help the subordinate grow and develop on the job. Improved trust, feelings of support, better and more satisfying role performance, and more open communication usually result. Zander (33) has reviewed thoroughly the problems and values of performance appraisal, including commentary on the target-setting approach.

5. *Organizational diagnosis and problem-solving.* This intervention involves a residential meeting of members of an intact work group, usually at the top of the organization (or in small organizations, up to size 40-50, the entire work force). They meet for several days to identify problems facing the system, and the reasons for the existence of these; to invent possible solutions; to decide on needed system changes; and to plan implementation of these through regular channels and newly-constructed ones. It differs from team training as described above in that relatively less attention is given to team relationships and interpersonal effectiveness as such, and more to system problems in the large. The main focus of attention is on the organization and its current functioning. The improvement of problem-solving activity and communication adequacy are typical results. For an account of two such meetings conducted with an industrial organization, see Zand, Miles, and Lytle (32, forthcoming).

6. *Organizational experiment.* In this approach, a major organizational variable of interest is changed *directly*,[11] by agreement of the responsible administrators, and needed implementation efforts. One such approach is described vividly by Morse and Reimer (25): in several divisions of a large organization, the level of decision-making was moved radically downward, thus giving more autonomy to subordinates; in several other divisions the level of decision-making was moved up; and in several divisions no change was made. Such an approach requires the careful collection of pre-post data, and the use of control groups in order to test the consequences of the change.

The halo of "experiment" is an aid to acceptance, since the arrangement is seen as not only temporary, but scientific, and responsibly managed. Such an approach ordinarily includes a feedback stage, in which the results are examined carefully and implications for the continuing functioning of the organization drawn.

These, then, are six possible approaches to the induction of organization health. Certain common threads appear to flow through all of them.

1. *Self-study.* These approaches reject the "technocratic" change model involving the recommendations of a detached expert, and actively involve the system itself in what might be called organizational introspection. The same holds true for approaches involving group self-study for various teams in the organization, and personal introspection and re-examination by role occupants.

In common with the action research movement in education, these approaches also carry the assumption that an operant stance on the part of the organization is both theoretically and practically preferable to the problems involved in dependence on outsiders for system change.

2. *Relational emphasis.* These approaches do not conceive of the organization as a collection of jobs with isolated persons in them, but as a network of groups and role relationships; it is the functioning of these groups and relationships, as such, which requires examination and self-operated, experimental alteration. The aim is not to ferret out and change the "attitude" of old-fogey Principal A, but to focus on the relationships and group settings in which Principal A's attitudes are evoked.

3. *Increased data flow.* These approaches all involve the heightening or intensification of communication, especially vertically, but also diagonally and horizontally. New feedback loops are often built in to the existing system. The use of status-equalizing devices such as intensive residential meetings also encourages fuller and freer flow of information through channels which may have been blocked or have always carried distorted messages.

4. *Norms as a change target.* By focusing on groups and relationships, and increasing data flow, these approaches have the effect of altering existing norms which regulate interpersonal transactions in the organization. If, for example, a work group where the norms are "play it close to the vest, and don't disagree with the boss" engages in a team training session, it is quite likely—since all group members

have participated in the experience—that norms such as "be open about your feelings whether or not they tally with the boss' wishes" will develop. These approaches thus have a strong culture-changing component, based on intensive, data-based interaction with others.[12]

5. *Temporary-system approach.* But norm-changing is by definition very difficult under the usual pressures of day-to-day operation in the organization. "Business as usual" has to prevail. Most of the interventions described involve the use of residential meetings, which constitute a detached, "cultural island" approach to organizational introspection and self-correction. They are in effect temporary systems,[13] where new norms can develop, and where, given the suspension of the usual pressures, meaningful changes can be made in the structure and functioning of the permanent system.

6. *Expert facilitation.* All of these interventions also include the presence of a semi-detached consultant figure, whose main functions are to facilitate, provoke, and support the efforts of the system to understand itself, free up communication and engage in more adequate problem-solving behavior. The outsider role, however, is seen as impermanent; it is only associated with the system during the actual period of the intervention itself. If the intervention is successful, the organization itself continues the self-corrective processes which have been begun by the intervention.

Whether or not these interventions, drawn from work with thing-producing organizations, can be used plausibly with people-processing organizations such as schools is an interesting question, to which my colleagues and I are beginning to gather some answers. One impulse at the moment is to believe that the answer will be affirmative. With the assistance of two or three school systems, we expect to have some empirical data on intervention results in about two years, an eventuality to which we look forward with a good deal of pleasure.

In Conclusion

It might be useful to point out in conclusion that the position taken in this paper is *not* that an organization must necessarily be brought to a state of perfect health before it can engage in any meaningful short-run innovative projects at all. Rather, we feel it is quite likely that the very act of carrying out small scale projects in planned change can undoubtedly strengthen the health of an educational organization—but only if *direct attention is paid concurrently to the state of the organization.* The basic innovative project, we believe, must be one of organization development itself.

FOOTNOTES

1. For additional comments on the importance of the concept of organization health, see Bennis (4).

2. Note that the question of actual goal achievement as such is here conceived of as separate, analytically speaking, from the question of organization health. Argyris has suggested that organization effectiveness, a concept resembling the health notion, resides in the organization's ability to (1) achieve goals, (2) maintain itself internally, (3) engage in adaptation processes with the environment—and to accomplish these three "core activities" at a constant or increasing level of effectiveness, given the same or decreasing increments in energy input (1, p. 123). This three-way scheme is also used in the present discussion.

3. Clark (12) has suggested that organization health resides primarily in the continuous possibility of *both* kinds of orientation: toward change and development, and for stability and maintenance. This dual possibility should be realized, he suggests, at the personal, group, inter-group, and total organizational levels.

4. Little has been said here about the actual form of the organization which is most likely to meet these criteria of organizational health at some optimal level. Some applied work in organization change (1; 4) suggests that strongly pyramidal organizations designed around strict division of labor, accountability, limited span of control, etc., are uniquely *ill*-fitted to the demands of survival in today's world. Argyris (1) has suggested a number of alternatives to the pyramidal model, (such as the use of temporary "product teams" with power base on functional contribution rather than position) which he feels are not only more likely to lead in the direction of organization health but respect the "essential properties" of organizations as open systems. Empirical data on this question are not numerous; however, work with communication nets in small simulated organizations has suggested that relatively loose, power-equalized, full-communication models of organization are much more effective than traditional models when the environment is shifting and changing. This finding also appeared in a study of Scottish electronic firms by Burns and Stalker (9). See also Likert (18).

5. If you doubt for a minute that custodial care is an important goal of the American public school, try this "Gedanken-experiment." Which would be the most effective form of teacher strike: (a) for teachers to stay home; (b) for teachers to come to school, but teach the children nothing?

6. This is a remarkable assertion, in light of the encyclopedic (and to me gloomily inconclusive) research findings on teacher effectiveness (see 14).

7. See, for example, the really staggering data on reading retardation and advancement as a function of social class in Barton and Wilder (3).

8. Lortie's (20) comments on a three-part norm system are relevant here: He comments on the teacher as subscribing to the following beliefs: a) the teacher should be free of interference in his teaching; b) other teachers should be considered and treated as equals (in spite of the fact that they obviously differ in interests and skill); c) teachers should act in a friendly manner toward one another in informal contacts. Note that these norms reinforce each other in such a way as to inhibit effective, interdependent work.

9. It is interesting to note that the greatest inroads of applied behavioral science seem to have been in research-based organizations, in areas such as aerospace, electronics, and petroleum refining. Why this has not happened in

schools (and universities!) is an interesting question. It may very well be that a knowledge-*spreading* organization (such as a school) operates rather differently from a knowledge-*making* one (such as a research group).

10. See Bennis (5; 6) for a thorough review of alternative approaches being used.

11. I am reminded of Hollis Caswell's classic remark when asked in 1943 how the newly-formed Horace Mann-Lincoln Institute would proceed in its program of school experimentation: "We'll change the curriculum by changing it."

12. In retrospect, the crucial role of norms in the maintenance of organizational health has probably been underplayed in this paper. In our research, we are planning to collect data on norms such as those regulating interpersonal authenticity and awareness, trust, objectivity, collaboration, altruistic concern, consensual decision-making, innovativeness, and creativity. Most of these are directly co-ordinated to the dimensions of organizational health reviewed above.

13. See Miles (24) for an analysis of the special properties of temporary systems for change-inducing purposes.

REFERENCES

1. Argyris, C. *Integrating the Individual and the Organization.* New York: Wiley, 1964.

2. ————. *Interpersonal Competence and Organizational Effectiveness.* Homewood, Ill.: Dorsey Press, 1962.

3. Barton, A. H. and Wilder, D. E. "Research and Practice in the Teaching of Reading: A Progress Report." In M. B. Miles (Ed.), *Innovation in Education.* New York: Bureau of Publications, Teachers College, Columbia University, 1964. Pp. 361-398.

4. Bennis, W. G. "Towards a 'Truly' Scientific Management: The Concept of Organization Health." In A. Rapaport (Ed.), *General Systems.* (Yearbook of the Society for the Advancement of General Systems Theory). Ann Arbor, Michigan: 1962.

5. ————. "A New Role for the Behavioral Sciences: Effecting Organizational Change." *Administrative Science Quarterly,* 1963, 8 (2), 125-165.

6. ————. "Theory and Method in Applying Behavioral Science to Planned Organizational Change." Cambridge: Alfred P. Sloan School of Management, M.I.T., 1964. Mimeographed.

7. ————., Benne, K. D., and Chin, R. *The Planning of Change: Readings in the Applied Behavioral Sciences.* New York: Holt, Rinehart and Winston, 1961.

8. Blake, R. R., Blansfield, M. G., and Mouton, J. S. "How Executive Team Training Can Help You." *Journal American Society of Training Directors,* 1962, 16 (1), 3-11.

9. Burns, T. and Stalker, G. M. *The Management of Innovation.* London: Tavistock Publications. 1961.

10. Callahan, R. E. and Button, H. W. "Historical Change of the Role of the Man in the Organization, 1865-1950." In D. E. Griffiths (Ed.), *Behavioral Science and Educational Administration.* Sixty-third Yearbook (Part II), National Society for the Study of Education. Chicago: University of Chicago Press, 1964.

11. Carlson, R. O. "School Superintendents and the Adoption of Modern Math: A Social Structure Profile." In M. B. Miles (Ed.), *Innovation in Education.*

New York: Bureau of Publications, Teachers College, Columbia University. Pp. 329-342.

12. Clark, J. V. "A Healthy Organization." Los Angeles, California: Institute of Industrial Relations, University of California, 1962.

13. Gage, N. L. "A Method For 'Improving' Teacher Behavior." *Journal of Teacher Education,* 1963, 14 (3), 261-266. (a)

14. ———. (Ed.) *Handbook of Research on Teaching.* Chicago: Rand McNally, 1963. (b)

15. Gallaher, A. "The Role of the Advocate and Directed Change." Paper presented at the Symposium on Identifying Techniques and Principles for Gaining Acceptance of Research Results of Use of Mass Media in Education. Lincoln, Nebraska: November 24-27, 1963.

16. Golembiewski, R. "Authority as a Problem in Overlays." *Administrative Science Quarterly,* 1964, 9 (1), 23-49.

17. Jahoda, M. *Current Concepts of Positive Mental Health.* New York: Basic Books, 1958.

18. Likert, R. *New Patterns of Management.* New York: McGraw-Hill, 1961.

19. Lippitt, R., Watson, J. and Westley, B. *The Dynamics of Planned Change.* New York: Harcourt, Brace, 1958.

20. Lortie, D. C. "Craftsmen and Colleagueship, A Frame for the Investigation of Work Values Among Public School Teachers." Paper read at American Sociological Association meetings, 1961.

21. Mann, F. C. "Studying and Creating Change." In W. G. Bennis, K. D. Benne, and R. Chin, *The Planning of Change: Readings in the Applied Behavioral Sciences.* New York: Holt, Rinehart and Winston, 1961. Pp. 605-615.

22. Maslow, A. "Self-actualizing People: A Study of Psychological Health." In W. Wolff (Ed.), *Personality Symposium.* New York: Grune and Stratton, 1950. Pp. 11-34.

23. Miles, M. B. *Innovation in Education.* New York: Bureau of Publications, Teachers College, Columbia University, 1964. (a)

24. ———. "On Temporary Systems." In M. B. Miles (Ed.) *Innovation in Education.* New York: Bureau of Publications, Teachers College, Columbia University, 1964. (b) Pp. 437-492.

25. Morse, N. and Reimer, E. "The Experimental Change of a Major Organizational Variable," *Journal of Abnormal and Social Psychology,* 1956,120-129.

26. Peterson, W. A. "Age, Teacher's Role, and the Institutional Setting." In B. J. Biddle and W. J. Ellena (Eds.), *Contemporary Research on Teacher Effectiveness.* New York: Holt, Rinehart and Winston, 1964. Pp. 264-315.

27. Rogers, E. M. *Diffusion of Innovations.* New York: Free Press, 1962.

28. Ross, D. H. (Ed.) *Administration for Adaptability.* New York: Metropolitan School Study Council, 1958.

29. Schachtel, E. G. *Metamorphosis.* New York: Basic Books, 1959.

30. Sieber, S. D. "The School Board as an Agency of Legitimation." *Sociology of Education,* in press. Bureau of Applied Social Research Reprint No. A-404, Columbia University.

31. Warriner, C. J. "Groups are Real: A Reaffirmation. *American Sociological Review,* 1956, 21, 549-554.

32. Zand, D., Miles, M. B., and Lytle, W. O. Jr. "Organizational Improvement Through Use of a Temporary Problem-Solving System." In D. E. Zand and P.

C. Buhanan, (Eds.), *Organization Development: Theory and Practice.* Forthcoming.

33. Zander, A. (Ed.) *Performance Appraisals: Effects on Employees and Their Performance.* Ann Arbor, Michigan: Foundation for Research on Human Behavior, 1963.

PLANNED ORGANIZATIONAL CHANGE:
A MAJOR EMPHASIS IN A BEHAVIORAL
APPROACH TO ADMINISTRATION

Robert T. Golembiewski

This paper seeks to look at "planned organizational change." To paraphrase Bennis, Benne, and Chin, that is, the focus is on "the application of systematic and appropriate knowledge to human affairs for the purpose of creating intelligent action and change." To the same point, the emphasis is on "conscious, deliberate, and collaborative effort to improve the operations of an [organizational] system . . . through the utilization of scientific knowledge."[1] Perhaps *the* distinguishing adjective is "collaborative," as compared to such approaches as Scientific Management. Defined in these terms, planned organizational change potently requires attention to the two basic questions of scientific effort: What is related to what?; and How can we get what we want based on a knowledge of what is related to what?

Despite the complex detail necessary to provide some glimpses of planned organization change as a major emphasis in a behavioral approach to administration, the analytical target and intent are uncomplicated. The focus of this paper provides three perspectives on planned change in organizations, all based on the "laboratory approach," and the motivation for the review is direct. William Gore provides our basic text. He noted: ". . . quantum jumps in capability have begun to allow the possibility of our striking out for a quantitatively different kind of adaptation to environment; one based upon

Reproduced by permission of the publisher, F. E. Peacock, Publishers, Inc., Itasca, Illinois. From Robert T. Golembeiwski and F. E. Blumberg (eds.), *Sensitivity Training and the Laboratory Approach,* 1970, pp. 361-390.

the potentiality of our manipulating [the] environment." The point of the manipulation is profoundly human, the goal being no less than to increase the gratification of man's needs in the large organizations that are so much with us.

The Laboratory Approach as a Feedback Model: Necessary Skills and Values[2]

Basically, the laboratory approach seeks to provide learning designs that maximize the chances of effective feedback. Using the cybernetic analogy, "feedback" may be defined as information concerning the efficacy of some data processor's adaptations to his environment. Thus a home furnace is linked with a temperature sensor so that the heating unit can approximate some desirable temperature setting. If that feedback linkage does not function, the furnace will reflect maladaptive behaviors as temperatures vary. Individuals and organizations can similarly expect maladaptive responses if their feedback processes are inadequate.

A viable feedback linkage depends upon the nature of both the "input" and the "throughput," in the popular vernacular of systems theory. As for feedback viewed as input, human beings and large organizations are alike in that they are no better in adapting than their feedback is timely, is presented in useful form, and validly reflects what exists. Figure 2 suggests the point in a generalized but useful way. That figure schematizes a typical degenerative feedback cycle, with attention to both interpersonal as well as to organizational relations.

In addition, note only the self-heightening features of such degenerating sequences. Thus an *existential* reason to distrust A often will generate an *anticipatory reaction* that A is not to be trusted. Hence B is likely to be less open, and low trust in A is thereby reinforced. Further organizational elaborations of such feedback cycles could easily be made, and particularly in the case of line-staff relations.[3] But let Figure 2 stand as a stark and uncomplicated reminder of the profound importance of feedback viewed as input.

The crucial role of feedback is clearest in the T-Group, or a small unstructured group which is the basic learning vehicle in "sensitivity training."[4] "How did I come across to you when I did that?," may be group member A's signal that he wants feedback. And other group members may respond by providing that evidence on which they have a monopoly, their own reactions, feelings, and attitudes. The essential products are profoundly simple. Participants see how difficult but rewarding it is to risk sharing their ideas or feelings; they

Figure 1. A Typical Self-Heightening, Degenerative Feedback Cycle

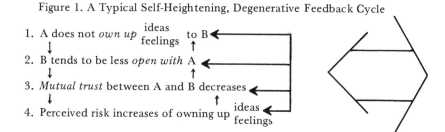

1. A does not *own up* $\frac{\text{ideas}}{\text{feelings}}$ to B
2. B tends to be less *open with* A
3. *Mutual trust* between A and B decreases
4. Perceived risk increases of owning up $\frac{\text{ideas}}{\text{feelings}}$

experience how much they limit themselves and others by not being
open; they demonstrate for themselves the prime importance to
others of their ideas and feelings and reactions; and they gain skill and
insight in giving and receiving feedback, as well as in reversing
degenerating feedback cycles.

Human beings and organizations will be *no better* in adapting than

Figure 2. A Typical Degenerative Feedback Cycle and Some of Its
Typical Interpersonal and Organizational Outcomes.

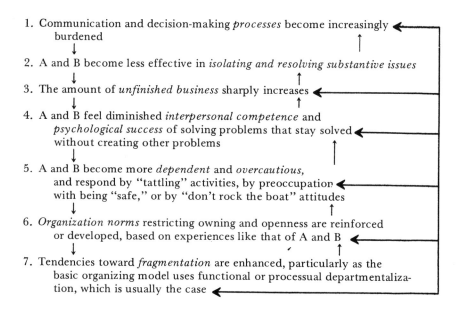

1. Communication and decision-making *processes* become increasingly
   burdened
2. A and B become less effective in *isolating and resolving substantive issues*
3. The amount of *unfinished business* sharply increases
4. A and B feel diminished *interpersonal competence* and
   psychological success of solving problems that stay solved
   without creating other problems
5. A and B become more *dependent* and *overcautious,*
   and respond by "tattling" activities, by preoccupation
   with being "safe," or by "don't rock the boat" attitudes
6. *Organization norms* restricting owning and openness are reinforced
   or developed, based on experiences like that of A and B
7. Tendencies toward *fragmentation* are enhanced, particularly as the
   basic organizing model uses functional or processual departmentaliza-
   tion, which is usually the case

their feedback is timely, usefully presented, and valid, then; but they can be *worse*. Like all servomechanisms, that is, man-in-organizations must be appropriately programmed to provide and to process feedback. As with the furnace, that is, the ideal is not providing it with just any feedback that is to be processed in just any way. How the feedback is given and how it is responded to—the style of the throughput—is patently of great significance. For our purposes, we consider only two throughputs: *skills* of giving and processing feedback, and *values* underlying these skills.

Figure 3 attempts to do the complex job of sketching both the skills and the values appropriate to the laboratory approach. Column C, particularly, implies the skills required for the sensitive inducing and processing of feedback. "You are a stereophonic SOB, Charlie, and I'll bet it's because your father rejected you," illustratively, is not a skillful piece of feedback in a group situation. That is, the statement contrasts sharply with the ground rules for effective feedback in column 2 of Figure 3. In quick summary, the example of feedback is

—Evaluative and judgmental, and leaves open only the options of accepting or rejecting the conclusion;
—It rushes to "there-and-then" interpretations beyond the competence of perhaps anyone but the analyst of the target of the feedback;
—It refers to the total person rather than to some act;
—The outburst does not encourage trust between the two individuals or between the initiator and other group members;
—The proffered feedback does not contribute to a sense of the organic solidarity of the group, as could be done by an open invitation to group members by the speaker to cross-validate his reactions; and
—Paramountly, it does not indicate even remotely how the SOB can gain non-SOB status.

Skillful feedback might be phrased this way: "When you did x, Charlie, I got furious. I doubted your motives, and I believe I know one of the reasons why. I hope others can help, but at least I hear you sneering when you say 'Yes sir.' I wonder if others in this group also feel that you were sneering at me? Do you want to make me furious? If so, keeping saying 'Yes, sir,' just the way you did."

The other three columns of Figure 3 apply more broadly to the value environment within which the conditions are optimum for

Figure 3. Four Value-Loaded Dimensions Relevant in Laboratory Approaches to Organization Change and Development

A Meta-Values of Lab-Training*	B Proximate Goals of Lab Training	C Desirable Means for Lab Training	D Organization Values Consistent with Lab Training†
1. An attitude of inquiry reflecting (among others): a. A "hypothetical spirit"; and b. Experimentalism 2. "Expanded consciousness and sense of choice" 3. The value system of democracy, having as two-core elements: a. A spirit of collaboration; and b. Open resolution of conflict via a problem-solving orientation 4. An emphasis on mutual "helping relationships" as the best way to express man's interdependency with man	1. Increased insight, self-knowledge 2. Sharpened diagnostic skills at (ideally) all levels, that is, on the levels of the a. Individual; b. Group; c. Organization; and d. Society 3. Awareness of, and skill-practice in creating, conditions of effective functioning at (ideally) all levels 4. Testing self-concepts and skills in interpersonal situations 5. Increased capacity to be open, to accept feelings of self and others. To risk interpersonally in rewarding ways	1. Emphasis on "here and now" occurrences 2. Emphasis on the individual act rather than on the "total person," acting 3. Emphasis on feedback that is nonevaluative in that it reports the impact on the self of other's behavior, rather than feedback that is judgmental or interpretive 4. Emphasis on "unfreezing" behaviors the trainee feels are undesirable, on practice of replacement behaviors, and on "refreezing" new behaviors 5. Emphasis on "trust in leveling," on psychological safety of the trainee 6. Emphasis on creating and maintaining an "organic community"	1. Full and free communication 2. Reliance on open consensus in managing conflict, as opposed to using coercion or compromise 3. Influence based on competence rather than on personal whim or formal power 4. Expression of emotional as well as task-oriented behavior 5. Acceptance of conflict between the individual and his organization, to be coped with willingly, openly, and rationally

*Adapted from Edgar H. Schein and Warren G. Bennis, *Personal and Organizational Change through Group Methods* (New York: Wiley, 1965), pp. 30–35; and Leland P. Bradford, Jack R. Gibb, and Kenneth D. Benne, *T-Group Theory and Laboratory Method* (New York: Wiley, 1964), pp. 10, 12.

†Philip E. Slater and Warren G. Bennis, "Democracy Is Inevitable," *Harvard Business Review*, Vol. 42 (1964), pp. 51 ff.

encouraging others to give feedback, as well as optimum for increasing the probability that the feedback will be responded to effectively and efficiently. Such an environment is difficult to induce, but its main properties should be generally clear in Figure 3. Hence the lack of further attention here.

The T-Group also clearly illustrates the significance of feedback viewed as throughput. Thus the T-Group ideal may be described as the development of a supportive environment within which group members feel it possible to share ideas and feelings, to test out their own perceptions against the perceptions of fellow group members, to judge the appropriateness of behaviors for attaining personal goals, and to experiment with new behaviors. The goal is to do all this, and to do it openly, with increasing honesty, and in a spirit that is increasingly helpful.

The Laboratory Approach: Three Basic Limitations

The laboratory approach is no stranger to messianic claims of its always-and-everywhere applicability; some of my best friends make such claims, indeed. But the reader is advised to keep three points in mind. First, not every organization is a potential host for the laboratory approach. The cultural preparedness of the host organization is an issue of moment in any decision to begin a change program via the lab approach, in other words. Warren Bennis has spelled out the factors involved in testing for such cultural preparedness,[5] and his work is required reading for those who want to avoid being licked before they start.

Second, the laboratory approach is only one of a family of possible approaches to organization change. I believe the laboratory approach is a particularly useful one. But the histories and traditions of some organizations are not congenial to the approach; and not all organizational problems can be ameliorated by the laboratory approach. Indeed, the laboratory approach can aggravate some problems. Greiner's typology isolates seven such alternative approaches to organization change.[6] They are:

1. *The Decree Approach.* A person with high formal authority originates a "one-way" order to those of lesser authority.

2. *The Replacement Approach.* One or more officials leave or are replaced and the new personnel trigger organizational changes.

3. *The Structural Approach.* Organizational relations are changed, presumably with effects on behavior.

4. *The Group Decision Approach.* Group agreement is sought

concerning the implementation of alternatives specified by others, as opposed to involving groups in isolating or solving problems.

5. *The Data Discussion Approach.* Data are presented to a host organization by an internal or outside consultant, and organization members are encouraged to develop their own analyses of the data.

6. *The Group Problem-Solving Approach.* Problems are identified and solved in group discussions.

7. *The T-Group or Laboratory Approach.* The emphasis is on sensitivity to individual and group behavior, with improvements in inter-personal relations and in openness serving as a foundation for changes in organization structure and policies.

As in medicine, in short, therapy and prognosis depend on the diagnosis of the organizational illness. Moreover, there is no single "magic bullet" organizational therapy. Thus a highly authoritarian organization which has recruited members with appropriate and extreme personality constellations may usually find alternative 1 more useful and comfortable than 6 or 7.

Third, a change agent may intervene in an organization in a number of major ways, not all of which are always appropriate for a specific organizational problem and not all of which require or even use the laboratory approach. Blake and Mouton, for example, identify nine kinds of interventions. There are interventions that stress:[7]

1. *Discrepancy*, by calling attention to contradictions in or between policy, attitudes, and behavior;

2. *Theory*, by presenting research findings or concepts that enlarge the client's perspective;

3. *Procedure*, by critiquing existing methods;

4. *Relationships*, as by focusing attention on tensions between individual and groups;

5. *Experimentation*, by encouraging comparisons of several alternative approaches before a decision is made;

6. *Dilemmas*, by pointing up significant choice-points or dilemmas in problem-solving, with attention to testing action-assumptions and seeking alternatives;

7. *Perspective*, by providing situational or historical understanding;

8. *Organization Structure*, by identifying problems as inhering in structure or the organization of work; and

9. *Culture*, by focusing on traditions or norms.

The laboratory approach might be variously useful as a tool in each of the nine kinds of interventions, and particularly in types 4, 6, 8, and 9. But the laboratory approach is nowhere indispensable nor even necessarily useful.

Three Applications of the Lab Approach: Diverse Designs for Personal/Organizational Learning

Diverse learning designs have been developed consistent with the brief characterization above of the laboratory approach as a feedback model. We can only sample that diversity of designs here, but even sampling suffices to demonstrate the usefulness of the laboratory approach. Three types of applications will comprise our sample. In turn, they emphasize the use of laboratory designs to:

1. Modify the problem-solving perspectives of individuals on work-related issues;
2. Modify organizational styles by inducing changes in interpersonal and group behavior; and
3. Modify the attitudes of individuals in organizations so as to develop attitudes favorable to more effective performance.

A Sensitivity Training Design: Modifying Problem-Solving Perspectives of Individuals

The first learning design is the most simple and the most limited, in organizational terms. Basically, it focuses on before/after changes in the ways individuals define work-related problems. We can only extract a few details from the technical report.[8] An orthodox, week-long experience in T-Groups intervened between two administrations of a questionnaire designed to determine participants' perspectives on work-related problems. Each participant chose his own reference problem. Briefly, before their training began, participants were asked to choose and describe a problem they were having at work. Five criteria were to guide the selection of the organizational problem:

1. The respondent was *directly* involved;
2. The problem was *unresolved*;
3. The respondent was *dissatisfied* with the lack of resolution and wished to initiate some change;

Figure 4. An Overview of Sensitivity Training

Basic Approach of Laboratory Training	Kinds of Target Data	Kinds of Learning	Levels of Learning	Basic Goals for Outcomes
"Sensitivity training attempts to accomplish the end of behavioral change through a philosophy and technique of training which is best described as a concern with "how"—how a trainee appraises himself, how a group behaves, how another would react in a given situation. In short sensitivity training has as its purpose the development of an executive's awareness of himself, of others, and of group processes, and of group culture."* The basic learning vehicle in any laboratory program is the T-Group. The T-Group is intended to help people:† 1. Explore the impact of their behaviors and values on others; 2. Determine whether they want to change their behaviors and values; 3. Test new behaviors and values, if individuals consider them desirable; and 4. Develop awareness of how groups can both stimulate and inhibit personal growth and decision making.	The focus is on the public, "here-and-now" data available only to T-Group members. These here-and-now data include: 1. The specific structures developed, such as the leadership rank-order; 2. The processes of group life, with especial attention to getting a group started, keeping it going, and then experiencing its inevitable "death"; 3. The specific emotional reactions of members to one another's behavior and to their experiences; and 4. The varying and diverse styles or modes of individual and group behavior, as in "fighting" the trainer or in "fleeing" some issue that has overwhelmed group members.	Interaction in T-Groups generates three basic kinds of learning by participants, to varying degrees in individual cases: 1. Learning that is largely cognitive and oriented toward effective committee functioning; 2. Learning that highlights deep emotional needs of which the participant was variously aware, and that shows how such needs can be satisfied; and 3. Learning that demonstrates the significance of "unfinished business," and that illustrates how and with what effects the press against the consciousness of such matters may be relieved.	Laboratory programs typically try to touch on three loci at which learning can be applied; but the first level receives most attention: 1. Personal learning, when the person learns about himself in-interaction in the T-Group; 2. Transfer learning, when personal learning is extended to "external" contexts (e.g., a worksite) to increase understanding or to improve functioning; and 3. Environmental learning, when the concern is to restructure some external context (e.g., an organization) so as to make it more personally satisfying and rewarding while also enhancing the effectiveness of those involved.	Laboratory programs enhance authenticity in human relations by seeking to increase: 1. Individual awareness about self and others; 2. Acceptance of others; and 3. Acceptance of self. Laboratory programs seek to free individuals to be more effective while they are more themselves, both as persons and as members of organizations, by seeking to enhance the development of: 1. Sensitivity to self and others; 2. Ability to diagnose complex social situations and to conceptualize experience in behavioral science terms; and 3. Action skills and attitudes required to capitalize on increased sensitivity and enhanced diagnostic skills.

From Robert T. Golembiewski, "Theory in Public Administration: Defining One 'Vital Center' for the Field." Florida State University Lecture Series, November 17, 1967.
*From William G. Scott, Organization Theory (Homewood, Ill.: Richard D. Irwin, Inc., 1967), p. 332.
†Based on Chris Argyris, Interpersonal Competence and Organizational Effectiveness (Homewood, Ill.: Dorsey Press, 1962), p. 156.

4. The problem was *interpersonal*, that is, it involved the respondent's relation to some person or persons; and

5. The problem was *important* to the respondent.

The problem chosen became the reference problem for each participant on before/after administrations of questionnaire items designed by Oshry and Harrison.[9]

Although the problems described by participants were not referred to before or during the week-long experience in T-Groups, our expectations were that a successful laboratory experience would influence the ways in which a participant would view his reference problem in the "after" administration of the questionnaire. Our expectations had two basic sources. First, many interpersonal problems at work stem from a violation of such norms for the processes of problem solving as those sketched in Figure 3. A successful laboratory experience would encourage participants to internalize the values in Figure 3, and consequently it should modify in predictable ways the participants' definitions of their problem situations.

Second, the typical T-Group covers an incredible range of learning opportunities. Figure 4 attempts to provide some sense of this range of target data, of kinds and levels of learning, and of basic outcome goals. Individual T-Groups will vary widely in focus and extent of attention. Since the laboratory experience is a replica of life in these various senses, however, consultants felt it very probable that participants would experience analogs of their reference problems. Moreover, a T-Group presents sharp differences with life in what is discussed and how problems are solved. Consequently, again, we expected that a successful laboratory experience would probably provide participants with success experiences in working with a framework of feedback values/skills which could be generalized to the reference problems of individuals in back-home situations.

More specifically, Oshry and Harrison have developed nine scales that permit testing before/after changes in the problem-solving perspectives of individuals. Figure 5 names and illustrates these nine scales. Three types of outcomes were predicted for changes in participant responses to the scales after a successful laboratory experience. First, increases in scores were expected on Scales 1, 2, 7, and 8. That is, a successful laboratory experience should suggest to participants how both they and others had exacerbated their reference problem by avoiding the expression of opinions or feelings (Scales 1 and 7), and by not being open (Scales 2 and 8). Second, significantly lower scores were expected on Scales 3 and 4 in the "after" administration

Figure 5. The Problem Analysis Questionnaire of Oshry and Harrison,
with Data from Tests of Two Populations
(Each N = 20)

Description of Scales and Possible Ranges of Scores	Test I			Test II		
	Initial Scores, Means	Predicted Outcomes	Actual Outcomes, Means	Initial Scores, Means	Predicted Outcomes	Actual Outcomes, Means
1. *Self: Rational-Technical* (8-40) Example: I have not let others know just where I stand on this problem.	20.23	Sig. Higher	27.4†	17.33	Sig. Higher	27.4†
2. *Self: Closed* (8-40) Example: I have been relatively difficult to approach.	16.76	Sig. Higher	21.4*	12.72	Sig. Higher	18.88†
3. *Organizational: Rational-Technical* (8-30) Example: The organization lets things go too far before taking action.	15.35	Sig. Lower	11.35†	13.94	Sig. Lower	13.77
4. *Organization: Closed* (8-40) Example: The organization has become inflexible.	16.00	Sig. Lower	13.52*	16.47	Sig. Lower	18.00
5. *Others: Rational-Technical* (8-40) Example: The other person has not planned adequately.	17.35	Insig. Change	17.35	16.94	Insig. Change	18.44
6. *Others: Closed* (8-40) Example: Others are resentful of outside suggestions or help.	19.00	Insig. Change	20.05	21.64	Insig. Change	24.61
7. *Self and Others: Rational-Technical* (8-40) Example: The other person and I have not tried hard enough to work this problem out.	22.15	Sig. Higher	27.47†	15.06	Sig. Higher	23.83†
8. *Self and Others: Closed* (7-35) Example: The other person and I really don't trust each other.	15.58	Sig. Higher	19.94†	14.57	Sig. Higher	20.61†
9. *Situational* (5-25) Example: Both the other persons' and my jobs are such that we must work toward opposing goals.	10.00	Insig. Change	10.41	8.53	Insig. Change	8.38

*Designates a statistically significant difference at the .05 level
†Designates a statistically significant difference at the .01 level
Based upon Arthur Blumberg and Robert T. Golembiewski, "The PAQ and Laboratory Goal Attainment." Mimeographed, 1968.

Figure 6. One Scale from Likert's "Profile of Organizational and Performance Characteristics"

Illustrative Dimension *Character of Motivational Forces*	System 1 "Exploitative, Coercive, Authoritative"	System 2 "Benevolent Authoritative"	System 3 "Consultative"	System 4 "Participative Group-Based"
b. Manner in which motives used	Fear, threats, punishment, and occasional rewards	Rewards and some actual or potential punishment	Rewards, occasional punishment and some involvement	Economic rewards based on compensation system developed through participation; group participation and involvement in setting goals, improving methods, appraising progress toward goals, etc.

From Rensis Likert, *The Human Organization: Its Management and Value* (New York: McGraw-Hill Book Co., 1967), pp. 190-99.

of the questionnaire, as participants were less likely to scapegoat "the organization" as a contributor to their reference problem. Third, insignificant before/after changes were expected on the other three scales, Scales 5, 6, and 9. On Scales 5 and 6, our rationale was that a participant in a successful laboratory experience would be less likely to place blame for his reference problem on others, but the same participant also probably would be more sensitive to the manifold ways in which others can preoccupy themselves with the rational-technical and can be closed to feedback. On Scale 9, similar cross-pressures were felt to be at work.

As Figure 5 shows, most predicted outcomes were realized. Thus 17 of the 18 paried scores changed in the predicted directions. Only Scale 4 on Test II is a deviant case. In addition, of the 12 cases in which significant differences were expected, 10 reached usually accepted levels of statistical significance. The pattern of results reported in Figure 5, in short, strongly supports the efficacy of the laboratory approach in modifying the perspectives from which organization members view problems. Although consultants could not arrange for a control group, there seems no reason to doubt that the observed effects were due to sensitivity training.[10] This implies the potency of the learning design, which potency is also established by a wide range of other research.[11]

Additional data urge that the changes in problem diagnosis were more than attitudinal phantoms. Although it is too early to state the conclusion flatly, the changes seem to have remained stable over the interval of a year. Replications of the research design, most convincingly, have yielded similar patterns of results.[12] Hence it does not seem that respondents were simply giving us the answers we sought, even though their insights on their reference problems were not deepened or sharpened or augmented by sensitivity training. We lack specific evidence that behavioral change has occurred, however.

The strength of the research design above is also its major weakness to put the conclusion above in terms of the training design. The narrowness of the training intervention implies real shortcomings. Specifically, our goal was not change per se, but attitudinal change that would lead to behavioral change and to increased effectiveness in the back-home situation. But the training design touched only one part of the necessary organizational change process, which Mann notes "needs to be concerned with altering both forces within an *individual* and the forces in the *organizational situation* surrounding the individual."[13] Our focus on the individual thus may have worked at cross-purposes with our ultimate purpose of inducing change in the back-home situation. That is, research concerned with back-home impact of laboratories training has yielded mixed results. Success stories exist, of course. But Bennis talks about the fadeout of attitudinal/behavioral changes when participants in sensitivity training return to organizations whose values were presumably different than the values of sensitivity training.[14] Similarly, Fleishman and his associates demonstrated the potency of the organizational situation.[15] Training did result in immediate changes but changes were variously washed out if the trainee's back-home superior used a leadership style that was incompatible with the training.[16]

Reactions to the mixed results concerning back-home changes often have been phrased in sharp terms. Thus Bennis, Benne, and Chin observe of programs and technologies of planned change that:

Isolating the individual from his organizational context, his normative structure which rewards him and represents a significant reference group, makes no sense. In fact, if it sets up countervailing norms and expectations, it may be deleterious to both the organization and the individual.

In sum, an individual programmed for feedback consistent with Figure 3 may find his behaviors are maladaptive in an organization which implies different rules-of-the-game.

Consultants in the design above were aware of such back-home issues, and did what we considered the next best thing to explicitly extending our design to the broader organization. Participants were told, to use the terminology of Figure 4, that personal learning would be emphasized. We hoped they saw some opportunities for transfer learning, and also noted that—since they were a "cousin" laboratory group—future cooperative environmental learning also was possible. "Cousin" groups are composed of people from the same organization and from similar levels, but do not usually work together. Primarily, we stressed the vast difference between personal learning and environmental learning. The accepted symbolism was to that point. Consultants noted that they hoped participants would become organizational crusaders for sensitivity training, if they saw value in it. As matters then stood, however, we felt it was appropriate to emphasize this lesson from the experience of the crusaders of old: more went than came back. Thus the watchwords were: experience, evaluate, and test for useful extensions. The organization's chief executive provided useful counterpoint to the theme, by stressing the developmental nature of the experience and by encouraging tests of extensions of the approach into the back-home situation. These structuring cues seem to have been accepted at face-value.

A Sensitivity Training Design: Modifying Organizational Styles
The basic design for sensitivity training sketched in Figure 4 also has been used to induce broad systemic changes in what may be called "organizational styles." Two examples establish the efficacy of laboratory training for these broader purposes. One example derives from the work of a University of Michigan team on a change program at the Weldon Manufacturing Company;[17] and the other example comes from Friedlander's carefully controlled study at one of the armed services' largest research and development stations.[18]

The two examples were chosen to complement as well as to supplement each other. Thus the macroscopic focus in Weldon was the style of the total firm. This focus makes the Weldon effort an important one. For one of the fundamental criticisms of the laboratory approach to organization change is that it attempts the impossible or highly improbable job of inducing in large organizations processes and dynamics analogous to those that are rooted specifically in small-group behavior.[19] In contrast, Friedlander's concern is with the style of a number of small, decision-making groups in a large organization. Both examples are complementary, in addition, in that they essentially attempt to test this basic premise:[20]

Training which does not take the trainee's regular social environment into account will probably have little chance of modifying behavior. It may very well be that human relations training—as a procedure for initiating social change—is most successful when it is designed to remodel the whole system of role relationships. . . .

The Weldon experience dealt with a massive effort to reorient a newly acquired company, in which change agent specialties from industrial engineering to sensitivity training were used.[21] At the global level, then, it is difficult to isolate *the* significant interventions. Basically, however, the combined effects of these diverse inputs were such as to improve performance by technically and behaviorally changing the ways in which the firm went about its business, that is, by fundamentally changing the firm's style.

Likert's useful distinction between four "management systems" helps illustrate these changes in style at Weldon. The style changes in Weldon were documented in part by Likert's 43-factor "Profile of Organizational and Performance Characteristics," which includes seven basic dimensions, variations in which can be described as composing different management systems. For example, "Manner in which motives are used" is one of the component scales of Likert's dimension "Character of Motivational Forces." Members of an organization can describe its systemic style by checking an appropriate descriptive point on a scale of 20 intervals, as illustrated in Figure 6. Likert's Profile has considerable value in organizational analysis. For example, respondents on the Profile can indicate where they perceive their organization to be and also where they would ideally prefer it to be. Reducing the gap between the real/ideal thus could be the goal of an organizational change program.

That the change program at Weldon succeeded in modifying the organization's style in profound ways can be illustrated via Likert's Profile of management systems. To provide some necessary detail, managers completed the Profile three times in 1964, their instructions asking them in turn to describe the management system at Weldon from three perspectives: before its acquisition, the contemporary (1964) system, and the management system they felt was ideal.

Figure 7 shows the patent movement over time in Weldon's style, as rated anonymously by the firm's top management. The gap between the pre-acquisition scores and the ideal was diminished sharply. In other terms, Weldon in 1964 was seen by its top managers as a System 3 organization, moving toward its System 4 ideal. Before the acquisition, it was seen as System 1 by its top managers. Nor was top management alone in perceiving such change in their organization's style. Ratings by other levels of management reflect a similar movement.

The movement in Figure 7 cannot all be attributed to sensitivity training, but its value seems undeniable in "building relationships of cooperation and trust in the Weldon organization" required to move toward a System 4 management system. Within the context sketched in Figure 4, Gilbert David thus describes the learning strategy applied at Weldon:[22]

A "family group" format would be used. That is, the training groups would be formed of people who were related in their normal work and who would bring their regular roles and relationships into the training sessions. This is probably the most difficult kind of group to engage in such training as the participants may well be reluctant to speak frankly with their superiors, and with colleagues with whom they must have future relations. It was felt, however, that this risk had to be taken as no other format would be likely to affect, in the short run, an internal organizational situation as critical as the one we had to deal with.

That this learning strategy employing sensitivity training proved successful is clear in Figure 8. That figure graphically portrays the movement of some Weldon managers along continua that should be

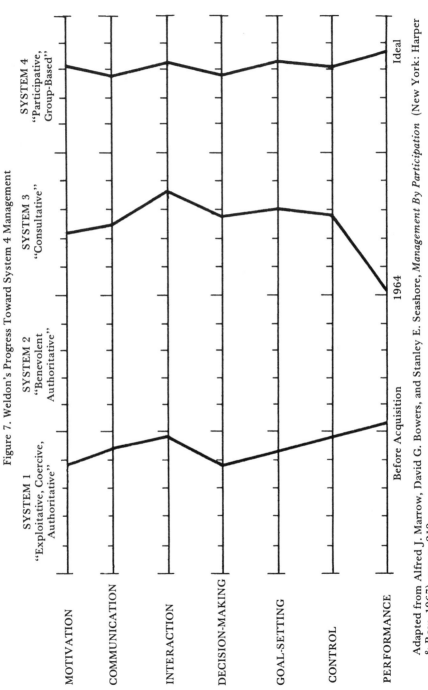

Figure 7. Weldon's Progress Toward System 4 Management

Adapted from Alfred J. Marrow, David G. Bowers, and Stanley E. Seashore, *Management By Participation* (New York: Harper & Row, 1967), esp. p. 219.

Figure 8. Retrospective Self-Ratings of Managers in Weldon, Immediately Before Training Seminars, Immediately After, and Approximately Two Years Later.

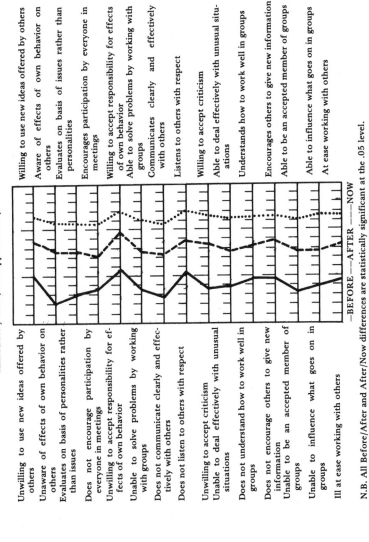

—BEFORE ——AFTER ——NOW

N.B. All Before/After and After/Now differences are statistically significant at the .05 level.

Based Upon Alfred J. Marrow, David G. Bowers, and Stanley E. Seashore, *Management By Participation* (New York: Harper & Row, 1967), p. 210.

positively affected by a successful laboratory experience. For example, a laboratory experience should generally make participants more aware of the effects of their own behavior on others. Figure 8 shows that such an effect actually did occur after a sensitivity training experience. Figure 8 also shows that a variety of other expected changes in perceptions of behavior occurred in response to the sensitivity training.

Several additional factors augment the present claim of the laboratory approach's potency in helping to modify the organizational style of a large firm with its own longish history of a contrary way of doing business. Although the data in Figure 8 are retrospective self-ratings, they receive powerful support from the ratings of superiors and peers.[23] The data providing that latter support are not presented here. Essentially, those data establish that the perceptions of changes in behavior reported by individuals were validated by their peers and superiors. If the retrospective self-ratings of how a person saw himself changing are fantasies, in short, those fantasies are corroborated by both superiors and peers. Various tests of logical internal consistency also support the value of laboratory training in modifying the style at Weldon. Thus the data in Figure 8 are consistent with the movement toward a System 4 managerial style depicted in Figure 7. For example, the greater willingness to accept criticism reported in Figure 8 is consistent with the movement toward a System 4 style.

This conclusion seems appropriate, then. Sensitivity training patently aided various interventions designed to alter the organizational style at Weldon. Which intervention contributed how much defies an answer, but the data in Figure 8 demonstrate that the laboratory approach at least contributed its share toward inducing appropriate modifications in Weldon's behavioral system.

Friedlander similarly found that a sensitivity training design could induce desired changes in the style of small decision-making groups in a public agency. Members of these groups had expressed disapproval with their meetings, and Friedlander[24] used factor analytic techniques to isolate six dimensions that accounted for most of the variance in member attitudes toward the groups. The six dimensions are:

1. *Group Effectiveness:* This dimension describes group effectiveness in solving problems and in formulating policy through a creative, realistic team effort.

2. *Approach to vs. Withdrawal from Leader:* At the positive pole

of this dimension are groups in which members can establish an unconstrained and comfortable relationship with their leader—the leader is approachable.

3. *Mutual Influence:* This dimension describes groups in which members see themselves and others as having influence with other group members and the leader.

4. *Personal Involvement and Participation:* Individuals who want, expect, and achieve active participation in group meetings are described by this dimension.

5. *Intragroup Trust vs. Intragroup Competitiveness:* At the positive pole, this dimension depicts a group in which the members hold trust and confidence in each other.

6. *General Evaluation of Meetings:* This dimension is a measure of a generalized feeling about the meetings of one's group as good, valuable, strong, pleasant, or as bad, worthless, weak, unpleasant.

The success of a laboratory program of organization change was estimated in terms of movement along these six dimensions. That is, Friedlander developed a Group Behavior Inventory (GBI) based on these six dimensions. The GBI was administered to 12 decision-making groups, to establish a baseline for descriptions of group styles. Four "Trainee Groups" participated in laboratory training sessions; and 8 "Comparison Groups" did not. In order to determine any before/after changes in the ways members viewed their groups, the Trainee Groups took the GBI a second time six months after their training; and the Comparison Groups did so six months after the first administration.

Friedlander's results support the success of the laboratory training, on balance. That is, in essence, his subgoals for change were increased ratings on each of the six dimensions of the GBI. For example, increased intragroup trust was one of these subgoals. Complex data indicate that the Trainee Groups, to spell out some of the supporting data, markedly improved on the six dimensions of the GBI. Figure 9 presents the relevant data. In sum, improvements were recorded on 5 of the 6 dimensions of the GBI. In addition, three of these five positive changes reached the .05 level of statistical significance. The one deviant result—a small decrease in Leader Approachability—did not reach statistical significance.

Given the obvious difficulty of inducing change in any social system, the trend in Figure 9 by itself constitutes solid proof of the impact of sensitivity training on organization style. But the environment was also changing significantly. The data in the Trainee Groups are all the more remarkable, that is, given what was happening in the

Figure 9. Some Summary Data of Before/After Changes in Style Properties of Small, Decision-Making Groups

GBI Dimensions	Before/After Changes in GBI Ratings by Members Trainee Groups			Comparison Groups		
	Before	After	Change	Before	After	Change
I. Group effectiveness	2.08	2.31	.23*	2.35	2.28	−.07
II. Leader approachability	2.46	2.37	−.09	2.78	2.62	−.16†
III. Mutual influence	2.44	2.61	.17*	2.40	2.37	−.03
IV. Personal involvement	2.53	2.63	.15*	2.57	2.51	−.06
V. Intragroup trust	2.13	2.25	.12	2.58	2.45	−.13
VI. Evaluation of meetings	2.04	2.08	.04	2.13	2.02	−.11

Taken from Frank Friedlander, "The Impact of Organizational Training upon the Effectiveness and Interaction of Ongoing Work Groups," *Personnel Psychology*, Vol. 20 (Autumn, 1967), esp. p. 302.
*Designates a statistically significant difference at the .05 level
†Designates a statistically significant difference at the .01 level

Comparison Groups. As Figure 9 also shows, in short, the relations in those groups had deteriorated between the two administrations of the GBI. Negative changes occurred in the Comparison Groups on all six of the GBI dimensions, in sharp contrast to the marked positive drift of changes in the Trainee Groups. Apparently, the parent organization was undergoing some trauma that encouraged and/or reinforced the deterioration of relations among its members. The Trainee Groups, as it were, successfully swam against this tide of worsening relations.

The Confrontation Design: Modifying Attitudes of Individuals in Groups

Given the undoubted value of sensitivity training for organization change and development, a co-worker and I have been concerned with developing "spin-offs" of the technique.[25] These spin-offs dually attempt to take some advantage of T-Group dynamics while avoiding some of the fears that, for example, an individual in a "family group" could reveal information about himself that might jeopardize his career. I know of one case, for example, in which an individual decided to set a standard for openness in a family group by revealing a medical problem that had escaped official notice. Although the medical condition did not affect his performance, it did disqualify him for his present job as well as for a highly desired promotion. Did he get caught up in the spirit of the moment, and live to regret it? Or did he really want to unburden himself of the secret? It was the latter in this case, but the potential for the former still inheres in the laboratory approach. Of less ethical concern, on a similar point, sensitivity training requires considerable time and expense. Thus it is difficult to extend very far down an organization's hierarchy. There are multiple values, then, in seeking spin-offs of sensitivity training.

The "confrontation design" is one spin-off of the laboratory approach that seems to have considerable usefulness in organizations.[26] The central[27] properties of the design may be listed in a summary way:

1. Confrontation designs involve as participants individuals who are hierarchically and/or functionally involved in some common flow or work. The results at issue here concern four levels of the same marketing organization, and some nine of its component activities.

2. Confrontations involve two or more organizational entities whose members have real and unresolved issues with one another, e.g., labor and management. In this case, the focus was on the

relations between various headquarters' activities and supervisors of a field sales force.

3. Confrontation designs involve the mutual development of images as a basis for attempting to highlight unresolved issues. "3-Dimensional Images" are developed to answer these questions:

1. How do we see ourselves in relation to the Relevant Other?
2. How does the Relevant Other see us?
3. How do we see the Relevant Other?

4. Confrontation designs provide for sharing 3-D Images between the involved parties.

5. Confrontation designs assume that significant organizational problems often are caused by blockages in communication.

6. Confrontations are short-cycle affairs. The one in question here took approximately 12 hours.

7. Confrontations designs typically are seen as springboards for organizational action. In this case, "Core Groups" were set up to work on specific organization problems. The general theory is that confrontations can improve degenerating feedback sequences, which improvement leaves individuals with a sudden surplus of energy no longer needed to repress data. That energy can be applied to task.

Basically, the confrontation design attempts to encourage participants to join in a mutual escalation of truthfulness, so as to reverse such degenerative feedback sequences as that described in Figure 5. A few details of the design imply how this is done. "Learning groups" are set up and asked to choose and describe their relations with "Relevant Others," that is, those in their organization with whom better relations are necessary in order for both to do a more effective job.[28] Each learning group then develops 3-Dimensional Images for each of the Relevant Others they chose, with results like those illustrated in Figure 10. Willing Relevant Others then share their 3-D Images, with the focus certainly being on understanding and illustrating individual items on the images and, perhaps, on beginning to work toward more desirable adaptations.

The confrontation design has a compelling internal logic. In terms of Figure 5, the design encourages owning and openness concerning organizational issues, with the goals of increasing mutual trust and decreasing the perceived risk of owning and being open. Owning and openness could be too radical, of course. But considerable reality testing and disciplining seems to take place in the confrontation design. At one extreme, very hurtful feedback is made improbable because of the processes of consensual validation going on in each

Figure 10. A Sample 3-D Image by One Regional Aggregate with
Promotion as the Relevant Other

A. *How Members of Regional Aggregate I See Themselves in Relation to Promotion Department*
    1. Circumvented
    2. Manipulated
    3. Receiving benefits of their efforts
    4. Nonparticipating (relatively)
    5. Defensive
    6. Used
    7. Productive
    8. Instrument of their success
    9. Have never taken us in to their confidence in admitting that a promotion "bombed"
    10. The field would like to help but must be a two-way street

B. *How Members of Regional Aggregate I Feel Promotion Department Sees Them*
    1. Insensitive to corporate needs
    1. Insensitive to corporate needs
    2. Noncommunicative upwards, as holding back ideas and suggestions
    3. Productive in field saleswork
    4. Naïve about the promotion side of business
    5. Unappreciative of promotion efforts
    6. As lacking understanding about their sales objectives
    7. Belligerent
    8. Overly independent operators
    9. Not qualified to evaluate the promotions sent to us
    10. Honest to opinions

C. *How Members of Regional Aggregate I Characterize Promotion Department*
    1. Autocratic
    2. Productive
    3. Unappreciative of field efforts
    4. Competent with "things" but not "people"
    5. Industrious
    6. Inflexible
    7. Unrealistic
    8. Naïve
    9. Progressive in promotion philosophy and programs
    10. Overly competitive within own department
    11. Plagiarists who take field ideas but do not always give credit

learning group. For the learning groups know they are going to have to live with whatever they communicate on their 3-D Image, and this obvious stake is an important disciplining feature in what gets communicated. At the other extreme, the confrontation design marshals significant dynamics that discourage safe blandness. The 3-Dimensional Images are formulated in isolation, and the design permits such complicated cross-checking of images that a learning group cannot safely take refuge in safe but spurious niceties. For while Group A is considering telling only the highly varnished truth, they know that Group B may be deciding to be more direct. And any obvious differences would be later targets for gleeful derision as the products of Group A's "fudge factory." Such processes induce an escalation of truthfulness, as the participants see reality.

The available data suggest that the confrontation design does indeed induce dynamics analogous to those in a T-Group. The attitudinal changes from one application of the design support this conclusion with margin to spare. Pre- and postconfrontation administrations of a questionnaire solicited data about changes in a wide range of attitudes toward a number of units and positions in the parent organization. Three types of attitudinal questions may be distinguished:

A. *Volitional Criteria Questions* which tapped attitudes the consultants viewed as relatively easy to change in a positive[29] direction via the confrontation (e.g., How much do you want to collaborate with Unit A?);

B. *Objective Criteria Questions*, which tapped attitudes that might

Figure 11.

		Types of Units		
		I *Involved*	*II* *Underrepresented*	*III* *New Business*
Types of Criteria- Questions	A. Volitional	Most significant favorable shifts in attitudes	Intermediate	Least favorable shifts in attitudes
	B. All	Favorable shifts in attitudes	Intermediate	Least favorable shifts in attitudes
	C. Objective	Least unfavorable shifts in attitudes	Intermediate	Most unfavorable shifts in attitudes

drift toward negative changes as people felt more free to be open about self and others, but which could not be changed in a positive direction by a confrontation (e.g., What is the level of productivity of Unit A?);

C. *All Criteria Questions*, composed of 11 Objective and 10 Volitional Criteria Questions, which consultants assume would show an overall favorable drift in attitudinal changes.

These attitudinal data were gathered for nine organizational units of which three types were distinguished before the data were processed "blind." These three types are:

I. Units that were deeply involved in the design, towards whom the most positive shifts in attitudes were expected;

II. Units that had token or no representation in the design, towards whom (at best) only modest shifts toward more favorable attitudes were expected; and

III. Units which essentially reneged on full participation in the confrontation, towards whom the least favorable shifts in attitudes were expected.

Roughly, then, consultants' expectations could be expressed in terms of a 3 x 3 matrix, as below:

The pattern of attitudinal changes above was not only expected, it was the intended outcome of the learning design. This may seem paradoxical or even perverse. As was noted elsewhere, however, developing a design that induced "negative" or "unfavorable" shifts in attitudes on the Objective Criteria Questions was intended:[30]

Basically, the learning design was a dilemma-invention model that characterizes much of the essence of the dynamics of T-Groups. Let us simplify grievously. Consultants concluded that members of the host organization had entered into a mutual-defense pact expressed, for example, in terms of unrealistically-high but mutual public estimates of performance. The lack of openness, in short, obscured basic organizational dilemmas. The confrontation design attempts to induce the public recognition of such dilemmas by greater openness and risk-taking, by explicitly dealing with the "real reality" of the actual state of affairs perceived by organization members. Hence negative changes in attitudes on the Objective Criteria-Questions do not signal a dangerous deterioration of "morale." Rather, such changes establish that dilemmas requiring attention have been acknowledged. During a confrontation, that is, organization members are encouraged to activate the "dilemma" part of the dilemma-invention learning model, as by seeing themselves and others as less productive than they were willing to admit previously. At the same time, however, the confrontation design encourages organization members to work harder on the "invention" aspects of the learning model. That is, the confrontation design is intended to favorably change the attitudes of organization members on the Volitional Criteria-Questions, e.g., toward greater desire to cooperate in coping with organizational dilemmas.

The matter may be summarized briefly. In its basic intent, then, the confrontation design proposes to raise to public attention unacknowledged dilemmas in an organization that must be dealt with. The confrontation design also intends to induce greater commitment and effort toward developing inventions capable of minimizing or eliminating the dilemmas, as in the Core Groups built into the confrontation design or in the back-home situation. These two intents are realized, in turn, as participants accept norms for giving and receiving feedback consistent with the laboratory approach [such as those sketched in Figure 3 above].

The pattern of a priori expectation proved to mirror the actual trends in the pre/postattitudinal changes, as Figure 12 shows. That table reports various ratios of positive/negative changes in attitudes, as well as ratios of statistically significant positive changes vs. statistically significant negative changes. The trends are quite clear.

Figure 12. Ratios of Positive/Negative Changes in Attitudes toward Various Organization Units Following a Confrontation Design, Based on Pre- and Postconfrontation Administrations of Questionnaire Items

				Types of Units	
			I	*II* Under-	*III* New
			Involved	*represented*	*Business*
Ratios by Types of Criteria-Questions	A. Volitional	+ / − ss+ / ss−	14.00 INFINITY	2.33 4.45	1.86 1.67
	B. Objective	+ / − ss+ / ss−	.65 .25	.42 0	.38 .18
	C. All	+ / − ss+ / ss−	1.86 .25	.95 .82	.83 .58

Based upon Robert T. Golembiewski and Arthur Blumberg, "Confrontation as a Training Design in Complex Organizations," *Journal of Applied Behavioral Science*, Vol. 3 (December, 1967), esp. pp. 538-39. Reproduced by special permission from NTL Institute for Applied Behavioral Science.

That is, Involved Units had 14 times as many positive changes in attitudes toward them on the Volitional Items, comparing the results of the second administration of the questionnaire with the results of the first administration. In contrast, the New Business Units had less than two times more positive than negative changes. All statistically significant changes in attitudes toward the Involved Units were positive, in addition. The New Business units did only slightly better than to break even on such changes.

Other data not reported above also suggest the real, if necessarily limited, value of the confrontation design in programs of organization change and development. Although the focus above is on attitudes, for example, we are quite certain that the confrontation design released new energies into work on task. Moreover, a third administration of the questionnaire shows that the attitudinal changes remained roughly stable over a six-month interval. Impressively, this stability existed in the face of massive and unfavorable changes in the organization's external environment.

Conclusion

The illustrations above have been necessarily sparse and hurried. They do support the premise that a behavioral approach must be included in organizations change programs. Such change, of course, helps establish how effective are existing behavioral theories. But the linkages are not clearly unidirectional, even on balance. *Applied* efforts at planned organization change, in short, not only profit from *pure* organization research but they vitally contribute to it. Indeed, the terms "pure" and "applied"—whatever their usefulness in other areas—profoundly misrepresent the complex linkages of concept and technique that alone can enrich our analysis of organizations.

FOOTNOTES

1. Warren G. Bennis, Kenneth D. Benne, and Robert Chin (Eds.), *The Planning of Change* (New York: Holt, Rinehart, & Winston, Inc., 1962), p. 3.

2. This section was part of an address, "Individual Freedom in Organizations," delivered at Northern Illinois University, October 28, 1967.

3. Robert T. Golembiewski, *Organizing Men and Power: Patterns of Behavior and Line—Staff Models* (Chicago: Rand McNally & Co., 1967).

4. For detail on the laboratory approach, consult Robert T. Golembiewski, "The 'Laboratory Approach' to Organization Change: The Schema of a Method," *Public Administration Review*, Vol. 27 (September, 1967), pp. 211-30, and especially the Bibliographical Note, pp. 229-30.

5. Warren G. Bennis, *Changing Organizations* (New York: McGraw-Hill Book Co., 1966), esp. pp. 131-52.

6. Larry E. Greiner, "Organization Change and Development" Unpublished Ph.D. Dissertation, Harvard University, 1965. See also Louis B. Barnes, "Organizational Change and Field Experiment Methods," in Victor H. Vroom (Ed.), *Methods of Organizational Research* (Pittsburgh, Pa.: University of Pittsburgh Press, 1967), esp. pp. 58-77.

7. Robert B. Blake and Jane S. Mouton, "A 9, 9 Approach to Organization Development," in Dale Zand (Ed.), *Organization Development: Theory and Practice* (in process).

8. Arthur Blumberg and Robert T. Golembiewski, "The PAQ and Laboratory Goal Attainment." Mimeographed, 1968.

9. Barry I. Oshry and Roger Harrison, "Transfer from Here-and-Now to There-and-Then: Changes in Organizational Problem Diagnosis Stemming from T-Group Training," *Journal of Applied Behavioral Science*, Vol. 2 (June, 1966), pp. 185-98.

10. If anything, conditions in the host organization were such as to encourage contrary learning. The two training periods coincided with a massive and long-overdue shakeup of personnel and programs in the organization. Our best estimate is that the laboratory program had to weather the strong and hostile winds generated by these changes.

11. Generally, see Dorothy Stock, "A Survey of Research in T-Groups," in Leland P. Bradford, Jack R. Gibb, and Kenneth D. Benne (Eds.), *T-Group Theory and Laboratory Method* (New York: John Wiley & Sons, Inc., 1964), pp. 305-441; and *A Bibliography of Research* (Washington, D.C.: NTL Institute for Applied Behavioral Science, 1967), *1947-1960* by Lewis E. Durham and Jack R. Gibb and *Since 1960* by Eric S. Knowles.

12. Oshry and Harrison, *op. cit.*, present generally parallel results although their research design is different.

13. F. C. Mann, "Studying and Creating Change," in Warren G. Bennis, Kenneth D. Benne, and Robert Chin (Eds.), *The Planning of Change* (New York: Holt, Rinehart & Winston, Inc., 1962), p. 612.

14. Warren G. Bennis, "A New Role for the Behavioral Sciences: Effecting Organizational Change," *Administrative Science Quarterly*, Vol. 8 (September, 196⌐), pp. 125-65.

15. Edwin A. Fleishman, E. F. Harris, and H. E. Burtt, *Leadership and Supervision in Industry* (Columbus, Ohio: Bureau of Educational Research, Ohio State University, 1955).

16. Bennis, Benne, and Chin, *op. cit.*, p. 620.

17. Alfred J. Marrow, David G. Bowers, and Stanley E. Seashore (Eds.), *Management by Participation* (New York: Harper & Row, 1967).

18. Frank Friedlander, "The Impact of Organizational Training Laboratories upon the Effectiveness and Interaction of Ongoing Work Groups," *Personnel Psychology*, Vol. 20 (Autumn, 1967), pp. 289-307.

19. The theoretical nexus of laboratory dynamics is considered from the structural point of view in Robert T. Golembiewski, *The Small Group* (Chicago: University of Chicago Press, 1962). Herbert Thelen, *The Dynamics of Groups at Work* (Chicago: University of Chicago Press, 1954) emphasizes emotional dynamics.

20. Mann, *op. cit.*, p. 608.

21. Marrow, Bowers, and Seashore, *op. cit.*, esp. pp. 63-139.

22. Gilbert David, "Building Cooperation and Trust," in Alfred J. Marrow, David G. Bowers, and Stanley E. Seashore (Eds.), *Management by Participation* (New York: Harper & Row, 1967), p. 98.

23. Marrow, Bowers, and Seashore, *op. cit.*, esp. pp. 211-12.

24. Frank Friedlander, "Performance and Interaction Dimensions of Organizational Work Groups," *Journal of Applied Psychology*, Vol. 50 (1966), pp. 257-65.

25. Robert T. Golembiewski and Arthur Blumberg, "Confrontation as a Training Design in Complex Organizations: Attitudinal Changes in a Diversified Population of Managers," *Journal of Applied Behavioral Psychology*, Vol. 3 (December, 1967), pp. 525-47.

26. For some reservations about the confrontation design, see Stokes Carrigan, "A Plug for Non-T-Group Confrontation" and especially Donald Klein, "A Complex Process of Social Surgery—or 'Technocrat, Don't Forget the Sutures,' " *Journal of Applied Behavioral Science*, Vol. 3 (December, 1967), pp. 548-55.

27. The following was part of an address, "Individual Freedom in Organizations," delivered at Northern Illinois University, October 28, 1967.

28. A confrontation design is most simple when it can be built around pre-existing groups with a developed collective sense and with immediate shared interests. Thus "labor" and "management" in a collective bargaining situation could be both the "learning groups" and the "Relevant Others." The situation underlying the present research was far more complex. For details of this complexity, consult Golembiewski and Blumberg, "Confrontation as a Training Design in Complex Organizations," *op. cit.*, esp. pp. 526-32.

29. "Positive" and "favorable" are shorthand for higher scores on such scales as "desire greater collaboration with." "Negative" and "unfavorable," similarly, are lower before/after ratings. The "direction" of scales for items on the questionnaire were varied so as to preclude the development of a "response set." But the data were coded in such ways as to keep consistent the direction of all attitudinal changes.

30. Robert T. Golembiewski and Arthur Blumberg, "The Laboratory Approach to Organization Change: The 'Confrontation Design'," *Journal of the Academy of Management* 11, 2, June, 1968, 199-210.

A LABORATORY-CONSULTATION MODEL
FOR ORGANIZATION CHANGE

William G. Dyer
Robert F. Maddocks
J. Weldon Moffitt
William J. Underwood

Behavioral change agents engaged in management and organization development efforts recognize as crucial, solutions to the recurring problems of entry and transfer. The major feature of the project reported here and still under way is the attempt to optimize both entry methods and transfer activities by a single developmental approach which includes the unique feature of using laboratory training to build a consulting relationship between internal consultants and their operating managers in an industrial organization.

The essential elements of the total design included: (a) laboratory training as an initiating vehicle, (b) the use of internal Trainer-Consultants, (c) the use of data collection and feedback, and (d) a single management and organizational conceptual framework. A single framework was used to overlay prelaboratory, laboratory, and postlaboratory activity. Data about each of the 25 participating managers were collected from peers and subordinates prior to the laboratory. The laboratory allowed each manager to receive data from other participants, to receive data from backhome work peers and subordinates, to establish a working consulting relationship with

---

Reproduced by special permission from *The Journal of Applied Behavioral Science*, "A Laboratory-Consultation Model for Organization Change," William G. Dyer, Robert F. Moddocks, J. Weldon Moffitt, and William J. Underwood, pp. 211-227, copyright, 1970 by the NTL Institute for Applied Behavioral Science.

internal consultants, and, with them, to begin to formulate a plan of action for back-home application.

Initial results from back-home application within the organization indicate that these design features have reduced the entry and transfer problems experienced in utilizing laboratory learnings in organization development. However, certain problems still exist in transfer of learning, namely: uneven skill on the part of the managers to implement laboratory learnings, some lack of skill on the part of the Trainer-Consultants to intervene effectively, and the existence of certain organization conditions that do not support change.

With the increasing number of organizations turning to management and organization development as avenues for increased effectiveness, two difficult problems have arisen as a real challenge to those engaged in such endeavors.

The first problem is mainly the result of organizations which place management and organization development in staff functions and hence confront the staff manager with the task of entry into the line organization. This problem of appropriate entry and responsibility is a recurring one for behavioral change agents.

The second and broader problem is that of the transfer of laboratory learnings to organizational improvement. Most of the attempts to do so can be subsumed under three models.

1. *The training model.* Managers can be sent to training programs geared to develop a motivation and conception for organizational improvement. Popular examples are Grid Seminars, NTL Institute laboratories, and company-sponsored programs.

2. *The survey-feedback model.* Data can be collected about the organization and fed back to management as a basis for initiating problem solving. Examples are Beckhard's (1966) or Blake's (Blake, Mouton, & Sloma, 1965) confrontation designs and much of the survey action-research work of The University of Michigan (Mann, 1957).

3. *The process-consultation model.* A consultant can engage directly with a management group and use their ongoing business activities as a vehicle. Much of the development work at Esso R & E and Union Carbide Corporation serves as examples.

The Organizational Setting Prior to the Change Program

Recently, a method of combining desirable features from all three models into a single approach for initiating an organizational improvement project was completed by the Radio Corporation of America (RCA) training group in conjunction with two external consultants. The enthusiastic response of management and the training group suggests its usefulness to those working in the organization field as well as to those more specifically concerned with the issue of transfer of training.

RCA is a large international organization of some 120,000 employees engaged in manufacturing a variety of products and providing services primarily in the field of electronics. The organization has a highly successful business image in terms of growth and financial return.

In the company there are two organization development persons at the corporate staff level, and out in the divisions are six experienced staff persons and five others who are less experienced. This makes a total staff of 13 persons available for OD work in the company, but only eight staff members considered experienced in OD.

There was no sense of urgency in the company on the part of management or the OD staff for beginning immediately an organization change program. Certain conditions were identified as pushing for change, but the desire was to build an OD model carefully with thoughts toward long-range results rather than some immediate transformations.

Previous Work of the OD Staff

Prior to the beginning of the organization change program, most of the internal OD staff were thought of as trainers (i.e., persons who diagnose management and organization needs, design a training program for certain personnel, and then conduct the program). The strategy for change was the hope that such training programs would lead to a change in management performance and perhaps in some organization change. It was felt by the staff that the training programs they were conducting were not producing adequate transfer into the organization, and that a different model of change was necessary—including a different way for the OD staff to work with managers. Although the staff felt competent in training and felt comfortable with their knowledge of new methods of OD, they lacked experience in carrying out new OD programs, e.g., consulting, team building, intergroup building. The image that the managers saw in the OD staff was a trainer image—these were people who conducted training programs but did not work regularly and consistently in the organization with the manager. It was felt necessary to change this image.

Features of The Change Program

For this project, laboratory training was chosen as an initiating vehicle. However, the problems of entry for the internal training group and connecting the laboratory learnings with the organization were critical design issues. Recognizing the continuing problem of transfer of training, the authors knew that some organizations provide internal consultants to serve as an application resource to their managers who attend residential laboratories, while others use the "family" concept of composing the training group of managers who have ongoing working relationships.

It was within these experiences that the authors designed the RCA project and attempted to optimize both entry and transfer by a single approach. The essential elements of the design included: (a) the use of internal Trainer-Consultants, (b) the use of a single management and organization conceptual framework, and (c) the use of data collection and feedback.

Internal Trainer-Consultants

The key factor in the total design was the utilization of a corps of full-time internal Trainer-Consultants (presenting the trainer image mentioned above). The individuals used were RCA division training staff who carried the training responsibility for managers in their organizations. This group was to be the major link between the training laboratory and back-home organizational application. The Trainer-Consultants (hereafter called T-Cs) had been attempting to establish a working consulting role with management as a supplement to their normal training activities; however, at the time this project was conceived, the consultant-manager relationship had not been fully developed. It was decided that this project would be used to build such a relationship and that this relationship would be the instrument for back-home application. The T-Cs would be expected to follow their managers back into their organizational units and to continue to find ways of transferring laboratory learnings into the organizational setting.

It was decided, therefore, that the laboratory would be restricted to only those managers who would be willing to come to the program with their respective internal T-C and who would commit themselves to working with him prior to, during, and following the laboratory experience. A description of the proposed development project was discussed with a select group of managers who, in the past, had indicated a desire to initiate development activity within their organizational units. All 25 managers who were invited agreed to participate in the project.

It was necessary to build a set of conditions within the laboratory which would enable the consultant-manager relationship to be established. One requirement, therefore, was to bring the T-Cs and managers into contact during the laboratory in such a way as to establish an open and trustful relationship similar to the one which often develops between laboratory trainers and participants.

The design must also allow the T-Cs and managers to share the learnings of the laboratory, thereby cementing the consultant-manager relationship and avoiding the blocks that often appear when two people have to work together on issues which have not been shared in a common experience. This is particularly important since an effective consultant-manager relationship can be blocked by forces in the organization.

Since establishing a working relationship would also require that the T-Cs be seen by their managers from the beginning as being an integral part of the laboratory, the design of the project called for the internal T-Cs to do the following:

1. Collect data prior to the laboratory about each of their managers from his subordinates and peers.

2. Consult with their managers during the laboratory regarding the experiences the latter were having in the laboratory itself and on the back-home data which were given to the managers at a precise time during the laboratory.

3. Develop the kind of relationship with their managers which would carry over to the organization.

4. Continue to work with their managers within their organizational units after the laboratory to design and implement a plan of action to move the laboratory learnings toward organization application.

Unifying Conceptual Framework

A second major design feature was the decision to provide a single unifying framework to the total project which would provide a cognitive map for the learning taking place in the laboratory and for relating laboratory learnings to the organizations of each of the participating managers.

The idea of a cognitive framework is not new. "We should always be sure in designing learning experiences that they have both confrontation and a support for current orientations built into them. Cognitive models have particular value in the analysis of problems of transfer of learning" (Harrison, 1965).

The idea of using a single framework to overlay prelaboratory, laboratory, and postlaboratory activity *is* new. We wanted to avoid the fairly typical response to laboratory learning, "I think I learned a lot, but I really can't say what it is or how it applies"; or the condition stated as, "Laboratory values are so different from the values of most organizations that if the individuals learned well while at the laboratory, they would probably tend to conclude that they should *not* use their new learning back home except where they have power and influence" (Argyris, 1966). The choice of a single framework for simplicity and understanding but which was broad enough to avoid oversimplification was seen as critical. Likert's (1961) system of organizational characteristics, which arranges several behavioral categories into a matrix with four general styles, was chosen as an appropriate vehicle.

Data Collection and Feedback

Another important project element was the use of three separate data-collecting instruments. While each was geared to a different purpose, all three were designed under the Likert conceptual framework. The instruments measured behavior along the following dimensions: leadership, motivation, communication, interaction-influence, decision making, goals, and control. Measurements of each dimension were differentiated across four broad management styles ranging from autocratic to participative.

One instrument was built to focus on the individual behavior of the manager in his organizational role. Each manager had subordinates and peers fill our this intstrument just prior to the laboratory. Data were received, profiled by T-Cs, and held to be fed back to the manager at a certain point in the laboratory.

Another instrument was constructed for the dual purpose of assessing the processes of a T Group and for assessing individual T-Group member behavior. The latter purpose provided the manager with systematized feedback on his behavior from his fellow T-Group members in the same conceptual framework used for the data gathered from his organizational subordinates and peers.

The third instrument designed for the project was cast at the organization level and built specifically to assess the processes of an organizational simulation exercise used in the laboratory.

The use of this instrumentation was expected to meet several objectives, the most important of which was to aid learning transfer. The instruments appeared to be an effective method of illustrating the operational value of the management and organizational conceptual framework. Data collected under a common framework were expected to be useful in helping the manager relate his laboratory behavior to his organizational behavior. In addition to their transfer value, the instruments were expected to aid the laboratory learning process and to illustrate for the managers the feasibility and value of collecting quantitative data about human behavior and relationship processes.

These three key elements—internal consulting resources, a single conceptual framework, and data collection—were viewed as bringing together for this project successful approaches from prior experience in the fields of training and organizational improvement.

Preparing Internal Consultants

Prior to the beginning of the laboratory, the seven internal T-Cs were brought together to prepare them for the laboratory experience and for their follow-up work with their managers in the back-home organizational application. During the two and one-half days thus spent, part of the time was used for giving the T-Cs an opportunity to contribute to the general design elements of the laboratory since its preliminary design had been done by the outside consultants and two internal trainers. The design work completed to this point called for the internal T-Cs to have a major decision role in locating and prescribing the timing and nature of consultations which would take place between them and their managers.

The major role of T-Cs during the laboratory experience was to act as ongoing consultants to their managers. They were to observe their managers in all aspects of the laboratory—T Groups, exercises, and theory sessions. They were to interact with their managers in a consulting capacity which would help them to function more effectively during the total laboratory experience. The week was to be used to practice their consultation skills and to build the type of consultant-manager relationship which would be functional when they went back to their organizations.

The T-Cs were also briefed on the use of data. They were responsible for feeding instrumented data back to their managers. Time was spent in helping the T-Cs interpret data and in examining ways data could be fed back in usable form so that the managers could identify those characteristics in the Likert system relating to their managerial performance which required planning for improvement.

Time was also spent in talking about and role-playing the building of the consultant role. A model of the consulting process was presented which examined the various dimensions of control. The

T-Cs looked at the types of requests which could be made of them by the managers during the laboratory and the ways in which varying response to these requests would result in the T-Cs' either exercising control over the managers or allowing the managers more autonomy. The T-C saw that his function with his manager was to help the manager increase his awareness of the processes going on around him, recognize the feedback given in the T Group, and to begin to plan more effective behaviors for himself without relying on the T-C for direction.

The Laboratory Phases

By way of overview, the major phases of the laboratory design were as follows:

Overview

Phase I—2 days. Concentrated T Grouping focused on general personal and interpersonal issues. A day-long marathon was used on the first full day.

Phase II—2 days. T Grouping was combined with organizational exercises and theory sessions. The learning focus was shifted to group and organizational issues.

Phase III—1 day. The collection, feedback, and analysis of data. Managers were supplied with data from both their organizational colleagues and their laboratory colleagues. The learning focus was the manager's impact on others along managerial and organizational dimensions.

Phase IV—1 day. Participants were assigned to use this period in whatever way they considered to be important. They chose concentrated T Grouping both to process their instrumented data with others and to resolve remaining issues developed in the T Group.

Because these phases were intersected by the key elements previously described, the laboratory will now be described to illustrate the use of each feature.

Phase I

During the concentrated T Grouping in Phase I, the T-Cs took three roles. First, they acted as observers watching the behaviors of their managers as they interacted with others. Second, they met with their managers in three private consultations interspersed throughout this period. The initial consultation was used to clarify the purpose of the several consultation periods scheduled in the laboratory agenda. Generally, this was described as helping the manager obtain

maximum value from the laboratory events. The remaining consultation periods in this phase were used to help the manager focus more
deeply on his experiences in the T Group. The third role taken by
the T-C was to collect, tabulate, and feed back data. During the
marathon on the first day, managers completed a group questionnaire designed around the Likert format. The results, in profile form,
revealed to the managers that nearly all perceived their T Groups to
be operating somewhat autocratically but that each perceived himself
to be operating more participatively. This brought into the design the
features of the conceptual framework and data collection as well as
opening up data for analysis in the T Group.

Phase II

During the focused exercises on group decision making and organizational processes in Phase II, three more private consultations were
scheduled. Each of these was located immediately following either an
exercise or a theory session and in turn was immediately followed by
a T-Group session. This scheduling gave the T-C an opportunity to
help the manager assess his behavior in structured task work and to
relate it to his behavior in the T Group. These consultations tended
to open for the manager new dimensions of concern which he could
then test out in the T Group.

Also during the second phase, a Likert-type questionnaire assessing
organizational processes was used during the organizational exercise.
For the second time the managers were exposed to the use of
quantitative data by a replication of the conceptual framework, but
applied to a different context.

Phase III

Phase III was entirely to collect, feed back, and analyze data.
First, each manager completed a questionnaire on every other manager in his T Group. The questionnaire was designed within the
Likert framework but geared to assess individual behavior in a T
Group. After each manager had received the results from his T-Group
peers, he met with the T-C for help in analyzing the data. A T-Group
session following this analysis was used for processing concerns raised
by the data.

The final event in this phase was particularly significant to the
entire design. It consisted of the T-C's making available to the
manager the profiled results of data collected prior to the laboratory
from the manager's organizational subordinates and peers.

Thus, at this point the manager had available comprehensive data which included: (a) systematized perceptions of his management behavior in his organization; (b) feed-back he had obtained from the T Group and exercise sessions of the laboratory, and the analysis of this in previous consultations; (c) systematized perceptions of his T-Group behavior; and (d) the resources of a T-C.

The hazard of data overload was reduced by the single conceptual organization of most of the data and by allowing a considerable amount of time for processing in private consultation. The substantial impact of this event derived from the direct relatability of laboratory data to organizational data by the single framework. Plainly, the manager had considerable data about himself in relevant roles—and in what to him was management language. The T-C helped the manager relate the various pieces of data and make his own personal assessments.

Phase IV

In Phase IV the managers were requested to decide for themselves what activities would be most useful. They chose continuous T Grouping. There were, therefore, no further consultations or data collections.

Application to the Organization

The first laboratory took place in May 1968. Since that time two more laboratory programs have been conducted which utilized the same design. Approximately 90 managers have gone through the change programs. After the first group, the next groups included the subordinates of those managers who had attended the first session, with the plan in mind of building a pool of persons with a common experience with whom the consultant could continue to work in the organization.

Initially, the T-Cs had no specific design for working with the participants back in the plant, except for a general notion of continuing the consulting started at the laboratory. However, it was discovered that practically all the managers felt a strong desire to reveal to their subordinates something about their laboratory experiences, including data and analysis of the questionnaire ratings which the subordinates had given them. It became the role of the T-C to help the managers plan and carry out such a communication process. Sometimes the T-C agreed to present the Likert framework in order to give the subordinates background and introduction to the data analysis.

Results of these meetings with subordinates have varied widely.

Some managers presented the data, had a limited discussion, but did little follow-through for reasons to be discussed. Others used this as a base for continuing a set of problem-solving meetings to work on the issues raised by the data. As might be predicted, the meetings of a manager with his staff were characterized by the following processes:

1. *Initial Threat.* This was a unique experience for almost all of the persons involved. By and large the culture of the company did not have norms that supported such openness of discussion. People were often embarrassed and uncertain about what to say and do.
2. *Reluctance To Respond and Flight.* After the manager and/or T-C had reported the laboratory experience and data, subordinates were asked to respond. This invitation was met by reluctance and often by elements of flight behavior.
3. *Provisional Resolution.* If the units were able to deal with the first two conditions, an attempt to work out resolutions to problems raised followed. The units which decided to continue generally set up procedures and times to work on the issues raised in the early meetings. It was noted that the units that did not continue could not make decisions to work on their own staff problems. The continuing groups have gone in different directions: Some have initiated direct family T Groups; some have used data collection-feedback sessions; others have stayed with the discussion of the original laboratory-generated data.

Continued OD Efforts

Results of the program have been determined by reports coming directly from the T-Cs working with the managers; systematic research designs have not been used. The direct reporting and anecdotal data indicate that about 25 percent of the managers who have participated in the three laboratories over a one-and-one-half-year period have *not* continued in any detectable OD efforts beyond the first meetings. Another 50 percent are continuing to make an effort toward OD, but the results are not considered totally effective by the T-Cs who are working with them. The remaining 25 percent have accomplished and are continuing to work on organizational change efforts that are considered significant improvements.

One manager who has been seen as particularly effective was perceived in the prelaboratory data as being very stiff and formal with his men; and since he was younger in age than most of his subordinates, some real barriers were created in working effectively with them. His organization, a staff service to a production operation, was, up to that time, widely judged to be mediocre in effectiveness. As a result of the laboratory experience, the manager and his T-C began a series of team-building meetings which reduced the level of formality, rigid role differentiation, intellectualization, and one-way influence. As this manager's staff team changed, the effect spread to the other parts of the organization because of the renewed energy exhibited by his staff. Organization improvement in terms of hard data began to emerge. As the case continues, recently this manager was given an unusually substantial promotion. He was placed in charge of a sizable plant whose business is critical and which has experienced considerable difficulty. His superior acknowledged that a year before this manager would not have been considered for the new position, but the fact that he was able to change and was able to bring about an improvement in his organization gave them some confidence that perhaps he had learned how to bring about change in another problem situation.

Characteristics of Abortive OD Efforts

Where managers have not continued to develop an improvement program, it has been felt that one or a combination of negative factors has been present in the following organizational components:

1. *The Manager.* Some managers have not seemed to benefit from the laboratory experience either for certain personal reasons or because their own anxiety about engaging in an open, leveling process with subordinates has been so high as to make further action difficult.

2. *The Organization.* It has become painfully evident that certain parts of the organization culture do not support continuing OD efforts. Sometimes the manager who went through the laboratory was faced with a boss who would not support new behaviors. Others found that work pressures requiring frequent travel, heavy overtime, and urgent time deadlines prevented the manager from moving ahead with the development meetings he would have liked holding.

3. *The T-C.* It must be admitted that this is no "game" for a novice. Inappropriate interviewing or mistimed or inadequately handled interventions by the T-C have undoubtedly had negative effects. This issue is so sensitive that a single fault by a T-C has in some instances permanently blocked further OD efforts for some units.

Four models are now being used to engage the participating managers in development activity. These are: (a) private consulting with the participating manager, (b) process interventions in regular business meetings, (c) direct and instrumented examination of staff teamwork in meetings established especially for this purpose both on and off plant premises, and (d) data collection and feedback from subordinates and other organizational members using a Likert conceptual framework to assess interpersonal data and as a data source for staff group action. (No T-C is engaged in private consulting with his participating manager as an exclusive process. Private consulting when used is being done in combination with one or more of the other processes.)

Critique

In reviewing the approach thus far, several weak and strong points can be identified. Two problems emerged during the laboratory, and another became visible during the application period.

Weaknesses

One problem concerns the number of managers worked with by the T-Cs. One T-C brought nine managers to the laboratory while another brought only one. The remaining ratios fell between these. Therefore, while in the 1-to-1 ratio team the T-C could spend a given time period in individual consultation, team ratios of more than one manager required the T-C either to reduce the individual time or work in subgroups. Although the design was timed to provide as much balance as possible, the consensus among the training staff was that more consulting time was available than the low-ratio teams could productively use and not enough time was available for the high-ratio teams. The optimum ratio for this design seemed to be about three managers per T-C.

Another problem concerned the use of one of the questionnaires. It was anticipated that collecting and feeding back group process information via the Likert framework during the first-day marathon would aid group development as well as introduce the framework and the use of quantitative methods. In fact, the managers displayed very little interest in these data, and it was not observable that the method had any effect, positive or negative. It is probable that such quantitative data were too "cold" to fit the context of the personal involvement of a marathon in a T Group.

Another problem has become visible during organizational application attempts. A few of the managers, while highly motivated to apply, have defined change goals more in terms of others than of themselves.

Strengths

The entire project to date has yielded several results which are considered highly valuable. It is clear that a successful relationship has been built between the T-C and his managers. From all observations of the T-Cs, their managers see them as useful resources, understand the nature of their role, and are desirous of utilizing them as adjuncts in the manager's back-home application efforts.

As indicated, a majority of the managers have either initiated application activity or have voiced intentions of doing so. This is interpreted as a clear indication that the project has produced an intention to apply laboratory learnings. At this point, there is every reason to believe that training will be transferred to the job in significant ways.

With respect to the laboratory features which can be judged as helpful, the following appear salient:

First-day marathon. This "up-front" period of continuous and intensive T Grouping was judged by the staff as moving the groups to a point approximating the third day of a standard laboratory design.

Single conceptual framework. The staff considered the use of a single overall framework to be quite useful. During the laboratory it provided a consistent set of dimensions which were inclusive enough to refer and relate most of the laboratory phenomena as well as organizational phenomena. This framework has continued to be highly useful as an organizing system for considering application goals and approaches.

Relating laboratory and organizational data. It was apparent to all the staff that having an opportunity to compare laboratory-produced data with data from their organizational realities was highly valuable for the managers. It provided a means of cross-validation and of relating similar concepts. It seemed a sufficient method for combating the typical tendency to compartmentalize laboratory experiences.

Cross-feed between consultations and other laboratory activities. The T Group and focused exercises provided the data source for consultations; on the other hand, the consultations had a visible effect on managerial behavior in the T Groups and focused exercises. Many a T-C observed his manager's explicit attempts in the T Groups to explore dimensions which the consultations had previously exposed and dealt with. It is difficult to assess, but the staff impression was that private consultations produced a beneficial effect on the more traditional laboratory experiences.

Application Problems

In terms of organization application it seems that the Likert framework has given an expectation for and a focus on changing an entire organization. The managers have worked at the level of their own staff—a small-group orientation. They are impatient with the length of time which is seemingly required to change a total organization. We feel it important that the laboratory give the small-group element a greater emphasis and that it help managers to see that the place to begin to influence the total organization is to improve group process within their own staff.

More attention needs to be given to careful selection of participants for the program. It seems that there are some types of managers located in certain kinds of situations for whom the laboratory experience can result only in minimal change efforts. If these can be identified, perhaps managers can be selected in whom greater possibilities for change are present.

It is our belief also that the laboratory should focus more attention on change strategies in addition to self-insight, interpersonal, and group and organization learning. Managers who plan to engage in change efforts need to learn more skills, e.g., how to conduct confrontation meetings, data collection and feedback sessions, process analysis of meetings, team-building meetings, and so on.

Conclusion

The field of behavioral science interventions has developed a number of approaches to planned organizational change. The one reported here has been a systematic attempt to utilize workable features from a variety of methods. It has been shown to be possible to build a laboratory design which incorporates internal T-Cs, quantitative data collection and feedback, and a single general conceptual framework into the more traditional laboratory experiences of T Group, exercises, and theory input. The total approach, which has been evaluated as successfully facilitating entry into the organization and transfer of laboratory learnings into the back-home setting, hinges tightly on the continued use of an internal resource person.

REFERENCES

Argyris, C. Explorations and issues in laboratory education. *Explorations in human relations Training and Research*, 1966, 3, 15.
Beckhard, R. An organizational improvement program in a decentralized organization. *J. appl. Behav. Sci.*, 1966, 2 (1), 3-25.
Blake, R. R., Mouton, Jane S., & Sloma R. L. The union-management intergroup laboratory. *J. appl. Behav. Sci.*, 1965, 1 (1), 25-57.

Harrison, R. Cognitive models for interpersonal and group behavior: A theoretical framework for research. *Explorations in human relations Training and Research*, 1965, 2, 109-110.

Likert, R. *New patterns of management*. New York: McGraw-Hill, 1961.

Mann, F. C. Studying and creating change: A means to understanding social organizations. In C. M. Arensberg, S. Barkin, W. E. Chalmers, H. L. Wilensky, J. C. Worthy, & Barbara D. Dennis (Eds.), *Research in industrial human relations*. New York: Harper & Row, 1957.

FOCUS ON PEOPLE: IMPROVING LEARNING
ENVIRONMENTS, OPPORTUNITIES AND PROCEDURES

Rowan C. Stutz
David L. Jesser

Considerable attention has already been given to the problems of education, of state and local organization, and of the necessary interrelations in a society that is experiencing change at an ever-increasing rate. The need for changes in the roles, functions and relations of the organizations and institutions that have fundamental responsibilities for education has also been emphasized. But if "schools are for kids," as Gibson[1] has suggested, what changes would appear to be necessary? What changes should be made in the roles, functions and relations of state and local education agencies in order that the primary *focus will be on people*—and especially on students?

Before examining possible changes in the roles, functions and relations of state and local education agencies, however, a brief summary of some apparent inadequacies in education as they relate to the individual learner seems to be appropriate. Such a review should provide these agencies with directions or mandates for needed changes. Any realistic review would probably reaffirm such inadequacies in educational programs as the following:

• Most of these programs do not seem to be designed to provide for individual needs, but instead appear to be geared to some vague and nebulous "norms."

From *Emerging State Responsibilities for Education,* pp. 83-101. Copyright 1970 by Improving State Leadership in Education, Denver, Colo. Reprinted by permission.

- The present programs seem to be primarily oriented to "motivation through punishment" rather than "motivation through reward."
- These programs do not seem to facilitate the attainment of clearly stated and meaningful goals.
- Most programs do not seem to have a high degree of relevance to emerging and changing societal needs and demands.
- These programs appear to be subject-centered, with each subject-matter program having little, if any, relationship to the other aspects of the program provided.

The degree to which educational agencies at the state and local levels are attempting to correct inadequacies that exist varies considerably from state to state and from one school system to another. Commendable efforts, with some successes, are noticeable; at the same time indefensible inactivity in situations in which the "status quo" is maintained can also be observed. *However, the serious consequences of the inadequacies in educational opportunities provided are clearly evident in virtually every state and local school district.* Throughout the nation, nearly one out of four students will drop out of school prior to graduation. (There are schools in which the drop-out rate is nearly double that for the nation.) Students, in increasing numbers, are protesting against various aspects and elements of the educational program, and are pleading for an educational system that is more responsive, more relevant, more personalized, and more productive. Parents and other taxpayers are demonstrating disaffection with the system through negative votes in elections relating to educational matters. Parents and students alike are expressing discontent in some areas through a relatively new phenomenon in education—the school boycott.

The problems and developments noted above are not intended to be used as evidence that "everything is wrong and nothing is right" in education. They should be construed as evidence—or symptoms—that there are some aspects of education in which serious problems exist, and that concerted efforts must be made to resolve these problems.

Educational leaders, as they recognize such inadequacies and their consequences, seem to have two fundamental alternatives: they could perceive the inadequacies to be of a scope and magnitude that would prohibit the development of any feasible method of coping with them; or they could determine that "because something *must* be done, something *will* be done." The first alternative (or perspective) could result only in a sense of frustration; the second, however, suggests a sense of urgency that must be developed and nurtured if these inadequacies are to be corrected.

Educational institutions and agencies at all levels need to direct their attention in a more forthright manner than ever before to the "feedback" that students, parents, taxpayers, teachers and legislators are furnishing. If they do not do so—if they fail to receive, evaluate and correctly interpret these signals—they are not likely, as Johns has observed, "to survive very long in this rapidly changing world."[2]

To "receive and evaluate" feedback, however, is only the first phase of the task. The second phase, which must be considered of paramount importance, consists of *planning for* and *implementing* the changes that the feedback signals indicate are needed.

As has been pointed out, some educational agencies have already responded to the need for change. Many state education agencies, for example, have attempted to redefine their roles, and have redirected their efforts in ways such as:

- Placing less emphasis on regulatory activities and more on leadership and service activities.
- Giving less attention to short-range "expedient" planning and much more to comprehensive long-range planning.
- Placing less emphasis on traditional organizational structures and more on developing functional organizational patterns.
- Placing less emphasis on issuing "pronouncements" and more on helping local districts to plan and develop appropriate policies and programs.

Many local education agencies—local schools and school systems—have also attempted to respond positively to the feedback signals that emanate from virtually every segment of society. Educational programs in which meaningful efforts are made to "compensate" for social and economic deprivations have been developed and implemented. Individualized learning programs, in which the individual student is of prime concern, have been initiated. Pre-school programs and other types of readiness activities have been effected. Educational enrichment activities, summer programs, and a wide variety of programs designed to meet special needs have been instituted.

Unfortunately, most efforts of the kind mentioned above have been made on a somewhat sporadic and limited basis. They apparently have been dependent upon factors such as: (1) the amount of external (federal, state, private foundation, etc.) dollars available; (2) the administrative philosophy and attitude in the school or school system; and (3) the existence of conditions that are obviously indefensible. Far too little attention seems to have been given to the "why" of education—to long-range planning, coordination of effort, and to re-evaluating, restructuring and reorganizing the overall educational program.

Many local education agencies are in need of significant assistance in these and similar areas that relate to planning and implementing improvements in the educational program. It is in such areas that meaningful help must be provided by state education agencies. In an ever-increasing manner, these agencies need to identify, develop and implement procedures that, in response to the all too evident feedback, *will assist local schools and school systems to plan for improvements in learning environments, in learning opportunities, and in learning procedures.*

Improving Environments for Learning

Where does learning take place? In what kinds of environment should education and learning be expected to occur? Under what kinds of conditions is learning best achieved? Obviously, questions such as these cannot be answered in simple terms. It cannot be said at present, for example, that learning takes place in one situation and not in another, that education and learning can take place only in *this* setting and not in *that* setting, or that learning can best be achieved only under *these* conditions and not under *those* conditions.

Some learning can—and may—take place anywhere, in almost any kind of setting, and within an almost limitless range of conditions. There are, however, certain kinds of locations, settings and conditions in which factors may be found that are more conducive to learning than in others. These will have to be more clearly identified, and strategies will need to be developed in order for educators to utilize them to the fullest advantage as efforts to facilitate learning are made.

If educational leaders at both the state and local levels are sincere in their statements relating to the need to improve or strengthen education, it is imperative that they consider the environments in which the less desirable or handicapping factors might at least be minimized if not eliminated entirely. At the same time, educators must devise strategies that will enable them to retain and strengthen those factors within the various environments that are conducive to—or which facilitate—learning. Educators need to be cognizant of the many kinds of environments that play an important part in the educational process, including the *physical* environment, the *socio-economic* environment, the *intellectual-emotional* environment and various combinations of these such as those found in the homes and neighborhoods in which students live.

The Physical Environment

Most state education agencies have demonstrated some concern about the physical environment of students. Standards have been established and statutory provisions and codes relating to sites and housing have been enforced in every state. In addition, many state education agencies have demonstrated · considerable leadership in providing assistance to local school systems as they plan for the construction or improvement of facilities.

Most state education agencies, for example, include staff members who are competent in the area of facilities planning, and have worked effectively in helping local school systems to plan for, design, and construct educational facilities that are conducive to learning. At least partly as a result of efforts by these consultants, many local school systems are constructing educational facilities—physical environments—that are quite different from those that were used by an earlier generation. Many schools have changed from massive and foreboding institutions to informal and friendly structures in which the learner, rather than the "establishment," is the central concern in the physical environment.

But the physical environment in which learning may take place is not limited to school buildings or educational facilities. It includes all physical conditions that exist in the home and community—even the food, noise, smog and many other often ignored factors. Every facet of the total physical environment may affect learning in either a positive or negative way.

Facilities consultants have moved far beyond the concept that the school building constitutes the only aspect of the physical environment that should be of concern. They have developed a much broader perspective regarding the physical environment that exists in relation to learning, and have experimented boldly with attractive structures and sites, "parkway schools," "educational parks," and other similar developments.

Because of their concerns, facility planning consultants have attempted to assist in developing strategies that would encourage educators and other citizens to cooperate in efforts to modify all aspects of the physical environment in which deficiencies are found. Unfortunately, concerns of this nature have not been demonstrated to any great degree for the socio-economic environment within which learning must also take place.

The Socio-Economic Environment

All too often educators and lay citizens have indicated—by actions if not words—that social conditions and economic factors are of no special concern for education. Such educators, perhaps in their ignorance, seem to expect learning to take place *in spite of* social and economic factors. Yet the work of Maslow and others makes it abundantly clear that there is an essential and vital relationship between this type of environment and education. Little if any bona fide learning can be effected or encouraged when basic needs—such as hunger and friendship—have not been met. Little, if any, effective learning occurs when the potential learners are undernourished, poorly clothed, are handicapped by poor health, or believe that they are discriminated against by their fellow students or the school staff.

Educators who assume that such students will progress satisfactorily in the formal education program will be disappointed. Instead of learning—and thus improving themselves and society—students who are alienated in this manner are likely to drop out of school at an early opportunity and be considered failures in education and probably also as contributing members of society.

Educational leaders need to become more aware—and help others become aware—of the relationships between socio-economic conditions and education. Only when these relationships are clearly recognized can constructive efforts be made to modify the social and economic factors that handicap progress in learning.

The Intellectual-Emotional Environment

The educative process—the total effort that is made to guide and facilitate learning—cannot be conducted effectively in a school that is isolated from the community in which it exists, or without appropriate consideration of all relevant factors in the internal and external environments. Two such environments have already been discussed. Still another aspect of the environment that exerts considerable influence and much pressure upon both the system and process of education is the intellectual-emotional environment in the school, the home, the community, and even in the state and nation.

This aspect of the environment is one of the most intangible and, sometimes, one of the most rapidly changing of all the environments in which education exists. Attitudes and values held by people can be quickly altered as a result of some unexpected or unforeseen occurrence. As a consequence of an environmental change of this nature, some of the goals and priorities that have been established and accepted for education may need to be reconsidered. For example, as a consequence of a campus disturbance, a news release relating to "underachievers," or the publication of a book that is critical of some aspect of education, the attitudes toward some of the accepted goals, priorities, or procedures may change rather significantly.

Some educators may well feel frustrated as they attempt to identify ways of coping with this aspect of the educational environment. They may adopt a somewhat fatalistic attitude about it—a "*que sera sera*" (what will be will be) attitude—and make no attempt to deal with it. Such educators, however, also are often frustrated by the lack of effectiveness that may be demonstrated by existing educational provisions.

As personnel of state education agencies attempt to provide the leadership and services needed to devise procedures to assist local schools and school systems to solve their own problems, special attention must be devoted to the environment in which these problems exist. In all too many instances efforts to bring about some desired and necessary change have failed, and a major cause for these failures can be attributed to a lack of concern about—or a total ignorance of—the environmental setting.

Educational leaders, at all levels, should recognize that the various environments may serve as effective deterrents to needed change, and that in some instances, changes in education may not be effected until there has been some modification in the environment. *Where environmental modification is needed in order to facilitate learning, educational leaders must be aware of this need, and be willing to attempt to meet it.*

Improving Opportunities for Learning

While needed improvements in education encompass every dimension of the educational system—including facilities, finance patterns, personnel practices, administrative arrangements and curricular organization—the major areas in which reforms are most urgent are those relating to (1) the environments in which learning must take place; (2) the opportunities for learning that are provided; and (3) the procedures that are developed and instituted for the purpose of facilitating learning. The first of these broad areas has been discussed earlier; the latter two are discussed in this and subsequent sections of this chapter.

Each of these broad areas, however, is or should be concerned primarily with people—students, parents, teachers, administrators, and lay citizens. As the state education agency addresses itself to the task of helping local schools and school systems to effect improvements, whether in aspects of the environment, learning opportunities or instructional practices and procedures, the concern for and about people must always be at the forefront—*the focus must be on people.*

The major conceptual structure of education in America was established at a time when the culture was relatively simple. Since its inception, however, the context in which education functions has changed considerably. It is no longer possible for citizens to play a responsible role in the culture and society without having benefited from the contributions that the system of education should make. Unfortunately, in many instances, this system has not developed in a manner that makes possible the contributions that are needed in light of present and future conditions. Many of the learning opportunities that are provided are outmoded and obsolete and consequently are irrelevant. The inadequate opportunities in the areas of subject matter, curriculum, application of objectives to instructional programs, materials and methods of instruction, and the deployment of both students and teachers continue to lend credence to the observation that "many teachers in the 20th Century are using 19th Century methods to educate children who will live most of their lives in the 21st Century." As a direct consequence of outmoded, obsolete and irrelevant learning opportunities, education (both as a process and a system) is not affecting the critical behavior of people as much as it should. The following characteristics of existing educational programs provide background for this statement:

- Instructional objectives are often stated in broad general terms that are somewhat related to the educational goals of the system. They identify desired *qualities* of behavior and desired *end products* of behavior, but not the actual behaviors to be produced through education.
- Many of the current practices are based on assumptions, often implicit, that are not defensible in terms of the developing reservoir of knowledge relating to learning. These assumptions include: verbal learning will change behavior; learning consists of receiving, memorizing and reciting verbal information; only about one-third of all students can learn adequately what is taught, another third will learn much of what is taught, and about a third of all students will inevitably fail or just get by; all learners in a

given group will have been provided with the preparation that will enable them to take the next proposed learning step; and those who fail or become excessively bored can drop out of school and be tolerated by society without any great concern.
- Little if any consideration is given to determining what kinds of learning are of most importance.
- Motivation for learning is achieved through punishment or threats of punishment.

Efforts to improve the equality and quality of the educational opportunities available to children, youth and adults must take existing inadequacies into consideration, and obviously must be concerned with ways of eliminating them.

If learning opportunities for all students, regardless of their location, are to be significantly improved, strategies and programs must be developed that will provide for effective implementation of numerous kinds of changes including: facilitating the development of appropriate educational goals and measurable objectives; improvements or modifications in the learning environments; and bringing together the salient features of what is known about the processes of teaching and learning. Implementation of these strategies and procedures will require many—and perhaps drastic—changes in the component aspects of education, including curricular provisions, teacher preparation programs, organizational structures, and the like. A careful examination of each of these needed changes with the leadership of state education agency personnel will not only enable the agency to describe more accurately existing patterns, but also will enable it to help local education agencies examine and select some of the more viable options for improving learning environments, developing viable curricular patterns, and effecting instructional improvements.

Developing Educational Goals and Objectives

The task of developing meaningful educational goals that are acceptable to a majority of those concerned is a challenging one that requires skillful leadership and broad involvement. Unless goals are clearly spelled out, agreed upon, and generally accepted, school improvement efforts are likely to be directionless, ineffective, and frequently merely labels without substance.

Every education agency, therefore, should continuously be involved in the development and revision of statements of educational goals, because there can be effective planning only when goals are clearly enunciated. Moreover, evaluation and accountability are feasible only when goals are stated and most are defined in behavioral terms.

But how are meaningful and mutually acceptable goals arrived at? Many times educational "goals" are spelled out, in unilateral fashion, by some agency, institution or organization. When established in this manner, "goals" do not in fact exist. What does exist, in this kind of situation, is in reality a set of mandates that presumably must be implemented. In the past, a primary function of many state education agencies has been that of preparing such "mandates" for local schools and school systems. In recent years, however, it has become increasingly apparent that goals when established *for* subordinate groups or organizations are empty and relatively meaningless. Just as planning cannot be effectively accomplished when it is done *for* one agency *by* another, goals likewise cannot be effectively established *for* one group *by* another.

Everyone concerned with the development of goals for education probably would agree that: (1) many of these goals are appropriate for every school system in a state and, therefore, should be recognized as state-wide goals; and (2) most local school systems and schools have some problems and needs that are not common to all districts and will need to develop supplementary goals. Most people will also agree that the procedures for achieving these goals will differ in some respects from one school and district to another, and that they should not be expected to be uniform.

State education agencies, therefore, have three major responsibilities relating to educational goals, each of which will necessitate high quality leadership and services and, in most cases, the involvement of other competent people. These are: (1) developing, revising as necessary, and obtaining agreement on appropriate statements of state-wide goals; (2) devising and utilizing pertinent procedures for measuring and reporting on progress and problems in achieving these goals; and (3) assisting local school systems and schools to develop appropriate statements of their own supplementary goals, and to devise pertinent procedures for measuring and reporting on problems and progress in achieving both state-wide and supplementary local goals.

Any strategy that is developed or designed to assist in the definition of goals for education should have built into it the concept of involvement if the goals are to be acceptable to a majority of those affected or concerned. Some local schools and school systems possess a considerable degree of the expertise necessary to work with representative advisory committees and other groups to define and establish goals. Most local school systems, however, do not—probably largely because they have relied on "others" to define and establish goals. Providing such school systems with practical guidelines concerning utilization of the concept of involvement would seem to be an important role of the evolving state education agency.

As state education agencies prepare to provide leadership in the formulation of state goals for education and to assist local school systems in the formulation of their own goals, the considerations suggested in Figure 1 should be kept in mind. There must be a focus on people—a concern for others—as goals are formulated; at the same time, there must be a thoughtful and rational approach. All too often, as has already been pointed out, new goals for education are established primarily on an emotional or impulsive basis. When goals are so established, they are, in effect, "straws in the wind," and will be just about as stable.

Obviously, information concerning quality, scope, and other aspects of the learning opportunities must be available in usable form before valid goals for education can be established. There are many ways in which these kinds of information can be assembled and made

Figure 1. Important Considerations Relating to the Formulation of Goals

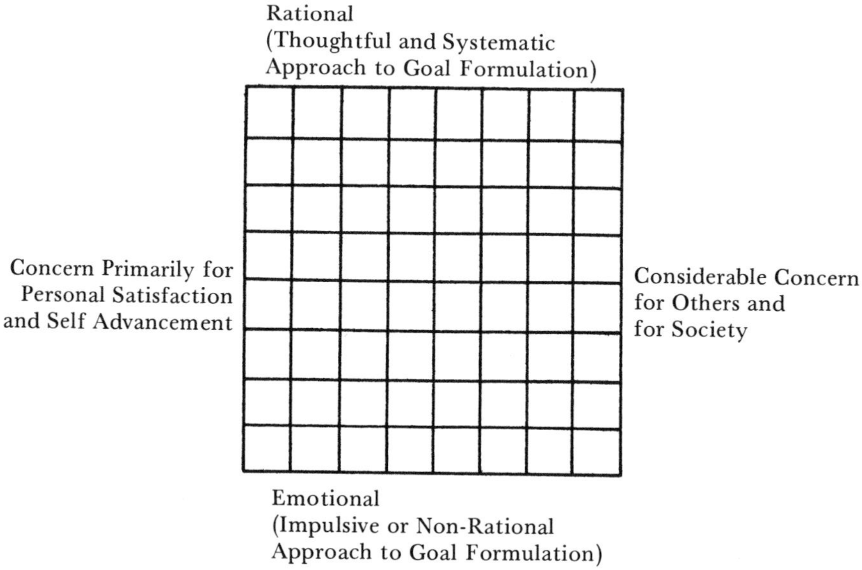

Rational
(Thoughtful and Systematic
Approach to Goal Formulation)

Concern Primarily for Personal Satisfaction and Self Advancement

Considerable Concern for Others and for Society

Emotional
(Impulsive or Non-Rational
Approach to Goal Formulation)

available. State education agency personnel should help to determine which could be used most effectively in specific circumstances. The information that is made available should relate, however, in rather direct fashion to the learner. All too often information concerning some aspect of education is collected and disseminated with little or no attention devoted to the probable implications for the learner.

After goals of and for education are identified and stated, viable and significant relationships must be developed between what is desired for learners and ways of advancing them toward these goals. In defining these, it is crucial that specific educational objectives for each goal be developed, and that school processes and services which are designed to advance students toward those objectives and goals include provisions for the measurement and evaluation of all steps in the sequence. If state education agency personnel can provide the kind of assistance that is needed by local schools and school systems in defining goals and objectives, learning opportunities are likely to be improved. But assistance is needed in many other areas as well.

Developing Relevant Curriculum Content

As has been suggested, needed improvements in learning opportunities must be directly related to the *goals* for education that are established and agreed upon. Some answer to the question, "What kind of persons do we want to produce?" must be provided. But goals, if they are to be achieved, must relate to specific courses of action. One such course of action, mandated by existing inadequacies, must be concerned with *what is taught*—with *what is to be learned.*

Curriculum development, over the years, has been the responsibility of a variety of agencies and institutions. Textbook publishers have been the major producers of curriculum materials and guides. State agency curriculum and textbook committees and commissions have provided teachers with guides, syllabi and suggested lists of materials. The major responsibility for the ultimate decision about what was to be learned, however, has been left largely to individual teachers. So long as the decision was related to what the total group should be learning, the individual teacher was relatively comfortable. But the increasing emphasis in recent years upon the individualization of instruction has made necessary an entirely different set of curricular decisions. A wide variety of instructional tasks—learning opportunities—that will enable the student to be relatively independent and flexible in pursuing a block of learning activities that relate to his own needs is essential. State education agency personnel, curriculum supervisors, classroom teachers, and publishers will need to identify and implement procedures that will enable the individual teacher to make the necessary and appropriate choices.

Just how best to get at needed changes in the curriculum is receiving considerable attention but as yet has not been resolved. Even so, state education agencies have the central responsibility to lead in effecting curriculum reforms. However, the curriculum reforms that are essential to meet crucial needs cannot be of a piecemeal or "bandaid" nature. Major revisions, rather than minor modifications, are called for in many instances. While considerable work has been done in some areas of the curriculum, there is need for an innovative surge that will unify the segmented and often unrelated parts into an integrated whole. The traditional subject-matter or "discipline" approach urgently needs to be supplemented or revised to include other approaches.

As state education agencies address themselves to the task of providing better learning opportunities by attempting to improve the curriculum, careful consideration of the following guidelines that have been suggested by Bebell[3] should prove useful:

- The curriculum should be based more upon process and less upon content;
- There should be a re-examination of the emphasis . . . of such content-heavy subjects such as English and history, and as a consequence, there may be a reduction in the relative amount of time given to them;
- Secondary school curriculums should be less oriented toward traditional academic fields and more oriented toward other areas;
- There should be greater independence on the part of each learner in building his own program; and
- There should be greater emphasis upon the . . . humanistic curriculum.

Utilizing guidelines similar to those suggested, state education agency personnel can provide the leadership and services that are required in the area of curriculum reform, and can help local schools and school systems to move noticeably closer to a zero-reject system[4] (devising a plan and program that will challenge and encourage "weak" students to continue their education, rather than to drop out of school) and thus enable all students to experience success in learning. If this is to be accomplished, the focus will have to be upon the learner.

But there are at least two cautions or pitfalls that should be considered:

1. *To try to balance, integrate and revamp the whole curriculum at once is too big a job.* The manpower, money and know how are not at once available. A more feasible alternative would be to divide the curriculum into two or three major streams of related studies such as science, mathematics or the humanities and begin a major overhaul of one or more of these areas of the curriculum.

2. *Curriculum development committees responsible for deciding on or recommending the kind of program needed should include a broad representation of parents and the public at large, and of students and professionals with a variety of backgrounds.* Too often curriculum committees are so narrowly represented that they lose the large perspective. A broadly representative committee, as suggested above, can help to move the emphasis in curriculum development back to where it belongs—to the purposes to be achieved—with subject matter playing its appropriate role as a vehicle for achieving the purposes.

There is nothing either new or novel about the concept of curricular change. "New" curriculums have been developed in the past, and new ones undoubtedly will continue to emerge. But many of those that have been developed have not considered, to any great degree, the needs of the learner. The result, in many instances, has been "the administering of aspirin when surgery is needed."

In attempting to effect the kinds of curricular changes that are necessary, it is essential that state education agency personnel recognize, understand, and be prepared to cope with the several powerful technological and other forces that affect or influence changes of this nature. They should also recognize—and help other educators to recognize—that certain of these forces may cause change to occur, while others may actually deter it. At least four such forces are identifiable:

- Groups and special interests that seek power over the curriculum;
- Those primarily concerned about costs;
- The rapid growth of knowledge; and
- The needs and concerns of people in schools and in the social milieu surrounding each school.

Both state and local education agencies are in a favorable position to recognize and attempt to deal with these and other forces to the advantage of learners. They must, however, do everything possible to prevent special interests that are contrary to accepted educational goals from prevailing.

Developing New Roles for Teachers

Learning opportunities are influenced by educational goals, and are related to *what* is taught and *what* is learned. But learning opportunities also are closely related to *how* subject-matter is taught, and *how* it is learned.

The concept of the classroom teacher as the "fountain of knowledge" may have sufficed in a day and age when the teacher was literally the major source for transmitting knowledge. But in an age characterized by almost instantaneous communication—and in which many learners enter the first grade with more "knowledge" than their parents possessed after several years in school—such a role will no longer suffice.

What is needed, both in the present and emerging educational environments, are teachers who perceive themselves to be *facilitators of learning,* rather than sources of knowledge. The traditional role of the teacher must change if the goals of education are to be met. As Rogers has observed:

> Teaching and the imparting of knowledge make sense in an unchanging environment. This is why it has been an unquestioned function for centuries. But if there is one truth about modern man, it is that he lives in an environment which is *continually changing.*
>
> We are . . . faced with an entirely new situation in education where the goal of education, if we are to survive, is the *facilitation of change and learning.* The only man who is educated is the man who has learned how to learn; the man who has learned how to adapt and change; the man who has realized that no knowledge is secure, that only the process of *seeking* knowledge gives a basis for security. . . .[5]

In an educational system in which *facilitation* of learning is the primary goal, the classroom teacher will necessarily have to devote major attention to the individual learner. All educational decisions, whether they relate to control, discipline, expectations, or to similar aspects, will have to be made with the learner foremost in mind.

State education agencies, in assuming their new and developing leadership responsibilities urgently need to attempt to find effective strategies that will assist classroom teachers to move from the more traditional role to the kind suggested above. To do so will require a high degree of expertise in working *with* people, and especially in helping local boards, administrators and teachers to understand the need for, and to effect this important change.

Improving Learning Procedures

Within the existing system of education virtually all responsibility for high quality and productive learning experiences is placed upon the individual classroom teacher. Typically, the teacher is in charge of—and almost totally responsible for—all of the essential factors and procedures that, hopefully, facilitate learning for the thirty or so students who are in the classroom.

Students, therefore, must rely upon the good fortune and/or good management of the school system if they are to have access to teachers who possess the attributes needed to diagnose learning difficulties and develop procedures designed to bring about optimum learning. Ideally every teacher should have: (1) a good understanding of the entire curriculum and of alternative teaching methods; (2) the ability to utilize and adapt a multiplicity of complex instructional media to provide variety and differentiation in order to meet the varying and different needs of students; (3) skill in diagnosing individual blocks and difficulties in learning and in adapting techniques to such needs; and (4) competency in teaching and tutoring small groups or individuals while, at the same time, using the time of all members of the unit as productively as possible.

Many educators doubt that any teacher can meet all of the above demands at a reasonable level of efficiency. Even providing for the efficient acquisition of knowledge of the subject matter on a level applicable to all learners in the unit is a formidable challenge. To provide additionally for the other desired outcomes of education is a near impossibility for any teacher.

Because of the understandable limitations that many teachers have in measuring up to these demands, the classroom unit system of teaching—the time-honored and traditional procedure for instruction—is giving way to other patterns of organizing schools and classrooms for instruction.

Commendable efforts have been made in several states and in many local school systems, and considerable improvements have been effected in procedures designed to facilitate learning. Differentiated staffing patterns, ranging from the kind of "team teaching" advocated by Trump and others, to the utilization of "teacher aides" or "paraprofessionals," have been developed and implemented in many local schools and school systems. Some states have made changes in their certification regulations that have facilitated and encouraged the use of such staffing patterns in local school systems. In every instance the goal has been—or should be—to meet, in more adequate fashion the needs of the individual learner, and to develop procedures that do this more adequately. In order to ensure effectiveness, any such procedures should include characteristics or provisions that place emphasis upon the student, including:

- The student is encouraged and helped to be in a position, and continuously in a frame of mind, to accept the responsibility for his own learning. Knowledge is something he himself must acquire, not that which is "shoved down his throat."
- Objectives of instruction (both for courses and topics) are defined in terms that are understood by the student and are made available to him. Students need to be helped to accept the objectives of instruction as their own goals.
- The student understands that performance measures are designed primarily to permit him to demonstrate his acquired competencies, and not merely to test his inadequacies.
- The measurement of performance is accomplished at frequent intervals for the specific purpose of permitting the teacher, student, and guidance counselor to determine what progress has been made, as well as what directions in future efforts should be planned by and for the individual student.
- Guidance will take on a new and added dimension within such a framework. It becomes a matter of helping each student to become informed about his progress and problems, the next steps to be undertaken, and the relationship of each curricular choice to his goals.
- The curriculum is sequential, and provides for continuous progress from one level of learning experience to another.
- Individual alternatives within courses of instruction are available to each student.

Curricular modifications based upon the preceding concepts are essential. However, the importance of decisions that are made regarding strategies for motivating students must not be overlooked. As Tumin has pointed out, motivation is something far more complex than "where there's a will there's a way." Rather, he implies that motivation is more appropriately described by "where there's a way there's a will."[6] It is important that strategies and procedures recognize that *learners are best motivated to pursue a goal when they perceive the goal as worth striving for, when they receive gratifica-*

tion in the process, when the achievement of the goal has an obvious payoff they can see and value, and when the attainment of the goal is feasible.

As educational leaders, parents and other concerned citizens attempt to examine and utilize the role of motivation as it applies to effective learning, serious consideration must be given to ways in which motivation can be achieved. Contingency management, negative contingency management, and contract learning are but three such approaches.

Contingency Management. In this approach to improving motivation, a deliberate use of consequences—probable or real—is made to increase the probability that the learner will choose one type of behavior in the place of some less appropriate kind of behavior in a given situation. The emphasis is upon overt visible responses such as a verbal act, a social act, or a manipulative act of some kind.

Contingency management has been present in some form in schools from the earliest days of education, and will undoubtedly be readily recognized as a variation on the "reward" theme. For example, "When you get all of your spelling words correct you can read in your favorite book," is one primitive kind of contingency contract. The consequence of an imposed contract for "getting all your spelling words correct" might consist of "being able to read your favorite book." This approach is being given more precise and appropriate form by advocates of motivation management.

Negative Contingency Management. This approach has perhaps been more widely used than any other relating to motivation. Essentially, it is a system of "motivation through threat of punishment." "In order to avoid punishment, you must perform such and such an act," or "Unless you finish that, you will have to stay after school."

To attempt to utilize this concept—to infer that those who don't achieve are lazy or lack desire and that punishing those who won't engage in a given learning task with enthusiasm or maximum effort—is to deny much of what is known about human behavior. Tumin has suggested that little will be accomplished in efforts to improve education, until teachers and others can demonstrate that school and education should and can be interesting and stimulating for every student.[7]

Contract Learning. The concept of "contracting to learn" is not new. It was embodied in the Dalton and Winnetka programs of an earlier era. A modern version of this concept has recently received a relatively high degree of acceptance. More and more teachers and educators are realizing that most students can accept a greater degree of responsibility for their own learning, as they must do when "contracting to learn."

As educators develop strategies relating to this approach to motivation, considerable care must be taken to avoid any tendency to arrange for "one-sided" contracts that are dictated by the teacher and accepted, often under duress, by the pupil. Contracts of this type, if they are to bring about the kind of learning that is desired, must be *mutually arranged* and *mutually accepted.*

Alternative Roles for State Education Agencies

There are a number of emerging strategies for influencing the quality of the learning opportunities and procedures provided by local schools and school systems, each of which has implications for roles of state education agencies. As has been suggested, perhaps the most important role is that of helping local school systems to become engaged in systematic problem solving and planning and, in the process, to help them to develop relevant goals and to examine all the options for achieving these goals. Toward this end, the state education agency must be willing to assume a positive leadership role, and be ready to provide, where needed, a wide variety of kinds of services as suggested in the following paragraphs.

Technical Assistance. Many local school systems do not have within their organizational structure or range of staff competencies the capability for assessing needs, analyzing problems, identifying resources, utilizing resources effectively (from within the district and elsewhere), and installing new programs. As a result, many local school systems do not utilize as extensively as they might such helps as: sources of outside funding, the products of regional educational laboratories, the new knowledge and its potential implications and applications being produced by the several research and development centers, and the miscellaneous innovative ideas being generated by projects, workshops, conferences and scholarly papers throughout the land.

State educational agencies should be in a favorable position to provide services that would help schools and school systems with their planning and with the more effective utilization of available knowledge in effecting educational improvement. Such technical services will require these agencies to develop a staff that is specially trained in helping and consulting, as opposed to developing and imposing state generated solutions or programs. Also, state education agencies will need to establish appropriate linkages with the sources of the products and information needed by the users (local school systems) and be able to respond effectively to user needs for information and requests for help in utilizing it.

Incentives. State educational agencies traditionally have attempted to regulate quality by specifying minimum program standards. While these agencies will probably need to continue to enforce minimum standards in the interest of safety and child health and welfare, incentives designed to encourage local school systems to move beyond minimum standards can be utilized to facilitate many needed improvements.

Accreditation. The accreditation of schools provides another important strategy for utilizing leadership to encourage changes in learning opportunities and procedures. Standard accreditation practices, in most states, provide for the state agency to perform two roles: (1) to serve as the coordinator for the activities of regular accrediting associations; and (2) to administer the school accreditation program for the state. Because of this dual role, the state education agency is in a good position to exert some positive influence upon the educational program.

Demonstration. Demonstration has proved to be one of the most effective means of publicizing new and promising educational developments that are based upon educational research. At demonstration centers, teachers and administrators can observe a new product or practice under actual operating conditions and can discuss with colleagues the problems and promises of the innovation.

State education agencies and local school systems can jointly sponsor and support demonstration centers or demonstration projects in various educational settings. Opportunities should be provided for teachers and administrators to observe new programs in action. The state agency should then encourage and assist local school systems in adapting worthwhile innovations to local school situations.

Defining the Role of the Teacher. Inasmuch as the role of the teacher is greatly affected by the specifications for the instructional system within which the teacher performs his role, state education agencies can help to clarify or establish teacher role definition when helping local school systems to set goals, examine options, and develop procedures that hold optimum promise for meeting the objectives. As services of these kinds are provided, attention should be focused upon the appropriate role of the teacher and the competencies needed to perform this role. As a result, in-service programs and activities designed to develop the needed competencies can be arranged.

In-Service Staff Development. There is an urgent need to prepare teachers for the new competencies that are essential in their changing roles. The approaches that may be necessary to meet this need may be as numerous and almost as varied as are the school systems themselves. A random multiplicity of approaches, however, may be wasteful and grossly inefficient. Why should every school system attempt to design its own in-service training program if there is agreement upon emerging teacher roles and needed competencies? Why should every system devote years of effort and talent in developing its own materials of instruction for its own in-service training program? State educational agencies can perform a valuable service by helping local school systems to develop and implement in-service programs that assist teachers to perform new roles and cope with the new technologies with competence and artistry.

As teacher roles change, new teacher competencies will be needed. Personnel of state education agencies should be prepared to coordinate and facilitate training that will produce the needed competencies in teachers. This can be done by working closely with and obtaining the cooperation of teacher training institutions, by contracting for resource persons outside of the agency who can respond appropriately to the varying in-service training needs of local schools and school systems, and by maintaining a high degree of awareness of the needs of local schools and school systems.

In Summary

In this chapter a number of options available to local education agencies as they seek to improve educational opportunities for all children and youth through improving the learning environments, curriculum and procedures have been discussed. At the same time, alternative strategies that state education agencies might employ as they provide encouragement and assistance to local school systems in solving critical educational problems have been suggested.

The ultimate objective of all efforts to improve education should be (1) to attempt to provide an environment that is conducive to learning; (2) to design and provide learner activities that enable the learner to cope effectively with his physical and social environment; and (3) to encourage teacher activities and procedures designed to ensure that successful learner activities will occur. The focus of learning activities, obviously, should be upon the student. Everyone concerned with education—parents, teachers, administrators, tax-payers and students—will need to direct their efforts accordingly. In many instances, however, the recognition and acceptance of the concept that "schools are for kids" will result in changes in the basic educational organization and philosophy at the local school level. The needed transition from *where education is to where it should be* will require systematic planning, many intermediate steps and probably some compromise arrangements. In order for these to be made, however, local schools and school systems will require much assistance.

State education agencies will need to help to identify and implement strategies that will make possible the kind of assistance that is needed. A partnership arrangement between the local school systems and the state education agency should be created—a partnership that should enable all concerned to achieve the only real purpose of education: effective learning on the part of each student.

FOOTNOTES

1. John S. Gibson, "On Quality in Education" (Unpublished paper prepared for the Committee on Public Education, Colorado General Assembly, April 1970), p. 1.

2. R. L. Johns, "The Economics and Financing of Education," in *Emerging Designs for Education*, Edgar L. Morphet and David L. Jesser, eds. (Denver, Colorado: Designing Education for the Future, 1968), p. 192. Republished by Citation Press, Scholastic Magazines, Inc., New York, N. Y.

3. Clifford F. S. Bebell, "The Educational Program," in *Emerging Designs for Education, op. cit.,* pp. 22ff.

4. The authors are indebted to Dr. Leon Lessinger, Calloway Professor of Education, Georgia State University, for important insights into the "zero-reject" concept.

5. Carl R. Rogers, in *Emerging Designs for Education, op. cit.,* p. xi.

6. Melvin M. Tumin, "Ability, Motivation and Evaluation: Urgent Dimensions in the Preparation of Educators," in *Preparing Educators to Meet Emerging Needs*, Edgar L. Morphet and David L. Jesser, eds. (Denver, Colorado: Designing Education for the Future, 1969), p. 10. Republished by Citation Press, Scholastic Magazines, Inc., New York, N. Y.

7. *Ibid.,* p. 11.

A HUMANISTIC PROGRAM FOR CHANGE
IN A LARGE CITY SCHOOL SYSTEM

Walter A. Dickenson
Car M. Foster
Newman M. Walker
J. Frank Yeager

This paper describes a series of new projects initated by the Louisville Public Schools and funded mainly by the U.S. Office of Education. These humanistically oriented projects were designed to reduce the bureaucratic rigidity of the traditional educational structure in a system which had the second highest dropout rate (43.6%) among large cities in the nation in 1963 (16).*

The school district reflects the national pattern of middle class white exodus to suburbia with all the attendant inner city problems. At present, of the 55,000 children in 68 schools, 25,000 (45%) are black and 73% of the teachers are teaching in inner-city schools. The poverty level based on annual incomes below $3,000 for the city is 39.7%, teacher turnover approximately 20% per year, and 71% of the pupil population is underachieving based on national averages.

It was recognition of the failure of the traditional educational approach to these problems that led the Louisville Board of Education, composed of three white and two black members, to hire a new superintendent on July 1, 1969. They had full knowledge of and were in full agreement with the changes he would institute despite expected opposition from some conservative quarters. These changes are embodied in the following programs:

---

*See References at end of article.—Ed.

From *Journal of Humanistic Psychology*, Vol. X, No. 2, Fall 1970, pp. 111-120. Reprinted by permission.

Project Focus. The organizational pattern of five elementary schools in the city's poverty area will be totally reorganized around groups of approximately 100 pupils assigned to 10 member teaching teams. These teams will consist of one experienced coordinating teacher, another experienced teacher, four Teacher Corps interns (110 college graduates without previous coursework in education will receive teacher training from the Universities of Louisville and Kentucky), two student teachers, and two para-professionals. The self-contained classroom of one teacher and thirty or more children will thus be abandoned for an open learning environment keyed to flexibility, individualized instruction, self-directed humanistic learning processes, and daily team critiquing and planning for the next day's activities. Insights into teacher training will be incorporated into university programs of teacher preparation.

Project Impact. One senior high, four junior highs, and two additional elementary schools will also be reorganized around eight to ten member differentiated teaching staffs responsible for "families" of approximately 125 students. The curriculum for all 12 schools will be radically reorganized around centers of interest that the students themselves will select such as important social issues, career opportunities, family life, skills related to group cooperation, and various problems actually present in the community. Reading, writing, and arithmetic subject matter will be woven into these centers of interest as they contribute to meaningful understanding and are relevant to *students'* needs and goals rather than teachers' needs alone.

Project Transition concentrates on the remaining 56 schools in the school system by initating a city-wide competition between all schools to plan and develop improved educational programs for their own school. A panel representing senior, junior, and elementary principals and teachers, the community, and the administration, will be chosen to judge prospectuses submitted according to Education Professions Development Act (EPDA) criteria. This panel will select two elementary, two junior, and one senior high school to receive up to $50,000 each of additional funds to implement their programs after an additional year of planning.

Approximately 500 principals, assistant principals, counselors, and top level administrators throughout the system have already been given an opportunity to participate voluntarily in a four-day basic laboratory experience designed to help them improve their skills in communication. This was deemed necessary to prevent principals and other middle management levels from subtly undermining grass-root involvement and creativity on the part of teachers. In many organiza-

tions middle management has been notoriously resistive to change
and can use specific training in the ways and means of facilitating
constructive change.

Career Opportunities Program. This cooperative effort of the
Louisville Public Schools and the University of Louisville institution-
alizes a career lattice on which non-certified employees and veterans
from low-income backgrounds can achieve horizontal (different
jobs), vertical (higher paying jobs), and diagonal (different jobs for
higher pay) mobility. High school graduates could thus become fully
qualified teachers with an A.B. degree in five years of work-study as
they support themselves while mastering established performance
criteria. The 100 para-professionals in this program will serve on the
differentiated staffs of both Focus and Impact schools.

Project IV. This project is based on Title IV of the Civil Rights Act
of 1964 and is designed to build more open and harmonious relationships between blacks and whites on the teaching staffs as additional
desegregation is carried out to achieve a greater degree of staff racial
balance. A closely related aim is to provide training in leadership and
process skills to promote black mobility within the administrative
hierarchy. Unless integrated black and white teaching staffs can set
before the students good human relations models, there can be little
hope that integrated student bodies can overcome racial prejudice
and bigotry.

Project VIII. A consortium of the Paducah and Louisville Public
School Systems, the University of Louisville and Murray State University was formed to salvage youngsters who have a high likelihood
of dropping out of school before graduation. Regular teachers have
been retrained to provide positive, accepting relationships with students built around flexible schedules and a broadened curriculum
geared to student needs and interests. Special emphasis has been
placed on procedures for rebuilding the self-concepts of alienated
youth and encouraging extensive involvement of parents in the
remediation process.

Change in Teachers' Role Definition

The basic goal of these projects plus others in the planning stage is
to gradually bring about a significant change in the self-perception
and role definition of all administrative and teaching personnel in the
system. The traditional role of the teacher as an authoritative manipulator of students' learning is to be replaced by a new role definition of the teacher as a *helping or facilitating person.* This definition
comes directly from Rogers' (13) premise that "significant learning

rests upon certain attitudinal qualities which exist in the personal relationship between the facilitator and the learner (p. 106)," but it also stems more broadly from the whole Third Force movement (9).

It is a change in this basic role definition that is believed to be crucial if this particular school system and perhaps American education in general are to ever develop a total learning climate in which pupils can increasingly become fully functioning, self-actualized persons.

Many educators today pay lip service to this goal while placing more relative emphasis on cognitive factors than on affective factors. It is granted that cognitive factors are easier to understand and deal with effectively, but children's cognitive development is often impaired by teachers who have an inadequate understanding of the affective domain and are therefore unable to motivate children.

Instead of helping children become increasingly self-directed, too many teachers are still striving valiantly to police the classroom and force children to study materials that have little relevance to their daily lives or interests. Conformity to rules and regulations is thus given higher priority than creativity in dealing with feelings, attitudes, convictions, beliefs, doubts, fears, loves, hates, and values in the classroom. This kind of traditional education is frustrating to most children, and especially so to inner city children. It is certainly not the freeing kind of experience that education is often intended to be.

Team Functioning

For these reasons the experimental projects to begin during the 1970-71 school year will emphasize process training[1] and function as near as possible to Bennis and Slater's (3) listing of five conditions necessary for any organization that seeks to function in accord with sound behavioral science practices. Thus to be a member of any team, a teacher will have to agree to: (1) full and free communication regardless of rank, (2) reliance on consensus rather than coercion to manage conflict, (3) decision making on the basis of technical competence rather than personal power or prerogatives, (4) an atmosphere conducive to emotional expression as well as task-oriented behavior, and (5) the realization that conflict is inevitable but can be mediated on rational grounds.

Rather than the traditional school principal, the teams in each school will be coordinated by a *Principal Learning Facilitator* who will be concerned exclusively with instruction and spend at least one-third of his time in direct contact with students. The administrative paperwork normally handled by the principal will be turned over to a *School Business Manager* who will order supplies, take care of the payroll, pupil attendance records, supervision of food, custodial services, etc. The school leader is therefore an instructional leader, sometimes called a master teacher, who is more skilled in group dynamics and curriculum than in administrative clerical work.

Laboratory training of the teams in each school will be designed to help them learn the group process skills necessary to function with openness and honesty. Individual anxieties, jealousies, misunderstandings, informational questions, and irritations are expected to be resolved as they arise. Time has been allotted for team critiquing daily. This continuous staff interaction should contribute to *healthy* friction between staff members, a reduction of negative feelings before they reach high levels, mutual evaluation of teaching efforts, innovative ideas, and a high degree of group cohesion, support, interpersonal responsibility, and productivity.

Research Base

This change in direction has a sound empirical base in recent, well-controlled behavioral science research. Truax and Carkhuff (19) cite some 118 separate research studies which support three facilitative conditions as antecedents to constructive personality and behavior change. These conditions are: (1) Accurate Empathy, (2) Nonpossessive Warmth, and (3) Genuineness. In the words of Truax and Carkhuff summarizing this voluminous research:

The finding that most human encounters can indeed be for better or worse suggests promising leads for research into the *prevention* rather than just the treatment of psychological disturbance and upset, of *under achievement, and the symptoms of psychological poverty.* The implications hold not only for the training and functioning of psychotherapists, but also *for the training of teachers and educators,* marriage partners, employers and supervisors, and parents. . . .

In essence, this is simply to say that the more we learn about how to *help* people, the more we also know about how *not to hurt* people. . . .

In part, one of the implications of the research just reviewed is *that the various related professions should take an active hand in weeding out or retraining therapists, educators, counselors, etc., who are unable to provide high levels of effective ingredients,* and who therefore are likely to provide human encounters that change people *for the worse.* (pp. 141-143 italics added.)

Thus, the delinquent, the underachiever, the mentally ill, the socially disadvantaged, the dropout, and even some of the mentally retarded can be seen as the end products of a sequence of interpersonal relationships that have failed to provide sufficiently high levels of these facilitative conditions. Low levels of these crucial conditions just will not produce the kind of individual who can succeed in the complex skills required in today's world.

Classroom investigations of these conditions have shown that third graders made significantly greater gains in achievement, as measured by the Stanford Reading Achievement Test, when their teachers provided high levels of these conditions (1). These effects were as great as the effect of high versus low intelligence quotients in normal classrooms. Truax and Tatum (20) used time sampling procedures with pre-schoolers and found that the degrees of empathy and warmth were significantly related to positive changes in children's pre-school performance and social adjustment.

Aspy and Hadlock (2) extended these findings to fourth and fifth graders. They found that students receiving high conditions made an average gain of 2.5 years in reading achievement in a five month interval whereas those receiving low conditions gained only .7 years in the same period. These attitudinal variables may well have accounted for Rosenthal's (15) widely quoted finding that the I.Q.'s of children expected to have high ability on the basis of a fake test actually did show significant increases.

Students' ratings of teacher competence also appear to be significantly related to the empathy variable (7). Christensen (5) found significant relationships between the teacher's warmth and the student's level of achievement in vocabulary and arithmetic. Students who had warmer teachers simply did better than those whose teachers were relatively cold.

Therefore, the evidence seems to strongly suggest that high levels of Accurate Empathy, Non-Possessive Warmth, and Genuineness have beneficial effects in a large variety of human encounters whereas the absence of these facilitative conditions has harmful effects.

Humanistic Personal Growth Model

One of the major goals of the extensive training programs funded in the projects has been conceptualized so far in terms of six areas of personal growth. These represent a tentative model of the kind of humanistically oriented teacher we are trying to develop.

Awareness

When a person is not growing, his self-structure operates like a filter to shut out painful perceptions that lower self-esteem and are inconsistent with the picture he has developed of "reality." For example, teachers often continue thinking they are "good teachers" even when they are unable to motivate their classes and actually wind up venting their frustration on the most troublesome children.

The person who is growing in awareness, on the other hand, is gaining increasing knowledge of the reality of himself and other people. Most of his energy goes into this search rather than into defensive distortion of reality to preserve his own ego and present picture of reality. Such individuals are open to their experiences and constantly modifying their perceptual world to fit the real world. This contributes to a natural spontaneity, freshness, and vitality in living rather than failure to react to aspects of life because they are never perceived.

Identity

Identity refers to that more specialized awareness or picture of one's own self and where that self fits into everything. A mature sense of identity stems ultimately from an accurate assessment of one's own strengths and weaknesses and a set of values that are in harmony with this identity.

Whereas the person who is not growing trys to support a more or less false identity, the growing person realizes all human beings are imperfect. He works at improving himself rather than hiding his problems. He therefore has the courage to be himself (18) and the satisfaction of knowing he is increasing his skills and competence.

Commitment

The growing person accepts responsibility for his own behavior and the person he ultimately creates of himself. He avoids being swept along by blind routine or trying to project blame onto others for his own shortcomings. Instead he experiences the exhilaration of pushing himself to achieve greater heights of excellence because he knows that real freedom can come from a "surrender" to life in all its reality, be it pleasureable or painful. He is therefore in the mainstream of life instead of on the periphery preferring to be mediocre rather than to take any risks. Thus he abandons his own egocentricity in his willingness to commit himself to living fully, honestly, and openly in the present without reservation.

Involvement

What is happening around the growing person affects him to the core of his being. He cannot remain detached and aloof; he must participate in the direction established by his sense of identity and his personal commitments. The children he teaches cannot remain separate, unrelated, and emotionally insignificant to him. Instead, he is likely to feel an increasing respect for their personhood, their feelings, and their individual uniqueness.

The uninvolved person responds mechanically and lifelessly and may not receive an influx of strength and self-confidence from successful execution of his responsibilities; his rigidity and defensiveness diminish the possibilities for enjoying life.

Meaning

The growing person gets satisfaction from developing the kind of value system that can stand the test of reality. And the test of any value system comes from living it, for unless it provides greater satisfaction in living, it is probably invalid. Man's search for meaning therefore may be conceived as a search for authentic being which could be defined as the degree to which he lives in accord with reality.

Lack of meaning strips life of richness and leaves a person emotionally constricted and impoverished. "Appearances and seeming" (8) increasingly become his bogus substitute for reality.

Becoming

The alive human being is constantly growing and changing; he is not a static, fixed structure that remains unaltered. Change is thus not as threatening to the person who knows he is not now and never may be a finished product.

Paradoxically, the non-defensive verbal expression of socially less desirable feelings (14) permits a person to move on beyond this point to a newer and higher realm of being. And teachers who are gaining increasing awareness of their own socially unacceptable impulses and desires can accept children who also display such emotions, thereby helping them to gain more control over such feelings before they erupt into destructive behavior. Teachers who have no real understanding of their own hostile and selfish impulses, because they are not personally engaged in a significant interpersonal experience of "becoming," can hardly be expected to do much more than barely tolerate such children. The rejection these children experience in school further intensifies their rage in vicious circles that eventuate in suspension, juvenile delinquency, and school dropout.

These six areas of personal growth are not mutually exclusive and are written in terms of ultimate expectations. Any movement in this direction will be acceptable. If Otto's (11) thesis that most normal, healthy people are using less than 10% of their potential is correct, then there would seem to be plenty of room for movement not only in the Louisville Public Schools but throughout our nation's antiquated educational establishment.

Decentralization of Authority

Although lay advisory councils are being established at every school in the system, the Focus and Impact Schools are being given virtual local autonomy. That is, control of each school is being turned over, in-so-far as this is possible within the limits set by state law, to an administrative council composed of the following three groups in approximately equal representation: (1) Parents and Community Representatives; (2) Teachers; and (3) Students. All representatives will be chosen by election and the Principal Learning Facilitator will be an ex-officio member of the council. Thus, schools could in time vary all the way from what is presently in existence to the pattern set by Fernwood (6), if local residents wanted to move in that direction.

Significantly, the idea for this council and its composition originated from a group of students who had been elected by their fellow students to represent them at the local Board of Education meetings. They were asked by the Board to present their own recommendations in regard to the experimental schools' operation next year. The Board subsequently decided to hire them during the summer months to help in the planning process. The distinguished psychologist, Carl Rogers, was present at that particular meeting and told the Board,

You are really making education history. To see a Board listening very intently to constructive ideas being thrown out by students is exceedingly rare in this country. I don't intend to be flattering, (but) you can't find this kind of thing in five systems in the country.[2]

FOOTNOTES

1. Along with basic encounter groups, or T-groups, training will include Human Potential Seminars (see manual developed at Kendall College, Evanston, Illinois under the leadership of Billy Sharp (17) and James McHolland), Self-Enhancing Education (Randolph and Howe, (12)), Experiential Encounter Tapes (developed by Joel Henning for the special needs of the Louisville Public Schools in a similar format as that of Berzon and Solomon, (4)), Interpersonal Communications and Higher Level Thinking Abilities (10) as well as time devoted to curriculum building. The intent is to help teachers acquire both conceptual understanding and experiences which will allow these understandings to be personally internalized and then applied from a background of skill training.

2. As quoted in the *Louisville Times*, April 21, 1970.

REFERENCES

1. Aspy, D. N. *A study of three facilitative conditions and their relationships to the achievement of third grade students.* Unpublished doctoral dissertation, University of Kentucky, 1965.
2. Aspy, D. N. & Hadlock, W. *The effect of empathy, warmth, and genuineness on elementary students' reading achievement.* Unpublished thesis, University of Florida, 1966.
3. Bennis, W. G. & Slater, P. E. *The temporary society.* New York: Harper & Row Publishers, 1968.
4. Berzon, B. & Solomon, L. N. The self-directed therapeutic group: three studies. *Journal of Counseling Psychology*, 1966, 13, 491-497.
5. Christensen, C. M. Relationships between pupil achievement, pupil affect-need, teacher warmth, and teacher permissiveness. *Journal of Educational Psychology*, 1960, 51, 169-174.
6. Drews, E. M. Fernwood: A free school. *Journal of Humanistic Psychology*, 1968, 8, 113-122.
7. Hawkes, C. R. & Egbert, R. L. Personal values and the empathic response: their interrelationships. *Journal of Educational Psychology*, 1954, 45, 469-476.
8. Jourard, S. M. *The transparent self.* Princeton, N. J.: Van Nostrand, 1964.
9. Maslow, A. H. *Toward a psychology of being.* Princeton, N. J.: Van Nostrand Company, Inc., 1962.
10. McCollum, J. A. & Davis, R. M. *Trainer's manual: Development of higher level thinking abilities* (Rev. Ed.) Portland: Northwest Regional Educational Laboratory, 1968.
11. Otto, H. A. *Explorations in human potentialities.* Springfield: Charles C. Thomas, 1966.
12. Randolph, N. & Howe, W. *Self enhancing education: A program to motivate learners,* Palo Alto: Stanford Press, 1966.
13. Rogers, C. R. *Freedom to learn.* Columbus: Charles E. Merrill. 1969.
14. Rogers, C. R. *On becoming a person.* Boston: Houghton Mifflin, 1961.
15. Rosenthal, R. & Jacobson, L. *Pygmalion in the classroom.* New York: Holt, Rinehart and Winston, Inc., 1966.
16. Schreiber, D. *Holding power/large city school systems, project school dropouts.* Washington, D.C.: National Education Association, 1964.
17. Sharp, B. B. *Choose success.* New York: Hawthorne Books, Inc., 1970.
18. Tillich, P. *The courage to be.* New Haven: Yale University Press, 1952.
19. Truax, C. B. & Carkhuff, R. R. *Toward effective counseling and psychotherapy.* Chicago: Aldine Publishing Company, 1967.
20. Truax, C. B. & Tatum, C. R. An extension from the effective psychotherapeutic model to constructive personality change in preschool children. *Childhood Education*, 1966, 42, 456-462.

PERCEIVED NEED DEFICIENCIES OF TEACHERS AND ADMINISTRATORS: A PROPOSAL FOR RESTRUCTURING TEACHER ROLES

Francis M. Trusty
Thomas J. Sergiovanni

Teachers and administrators have different needs which vary according to age, sex, and professional role. The almost universal failure of administrators, board members and citizens to recognize these different needs helps to explain educational rigidity, faculty dropout, and increased teacher militancy. In addition, federal involvement in traditionally local educational matters reflects a growing concern for solving problems created in part by this lack of discrimination.

One approach to individualizing the process by which a teacher's needs are satisfied is through the creation of a separate hierarchy for teachers. Restructuring teacher roles in relation to administrator and board-member roles to involve the teacher in allocating organizational resources is an important first step. Recognizing the educational primacy of the teacher-pupil relationship at each level of the teacher role hierarchy is a second important step. As teachers develop maturity and judgment in allocating resources and develop a wider variety of specialized role-competencies within a teaching hierarchy, administrators, board members, and citizens will better reward and recognize teacher contributions.

Design and Method

This study investigated need-fulfillment deficiencies for teachers and administrators in a school system. Maslow's theory of human

From the *Educational Administration Quarterly,* University Council for Educational Administration, Columbus, Ohio. Reprinted by permission.

motivation was selected as the conceptual framework.[1] Porter's[2] industrial management study provided the point of departure. In his study, Porter analyzed the role of five basic needs. From the lowest order (most prepotent) to highest order (least basic or prepotent) they were *security, social, esteem, autonomy,* and *self-actualization.* Questionnaire respondents included first- and second-level supervisors, department level managers, division and plant managers, vice-presidents, presidents, and board chairmen. The study focused on differences in perception between *actual* and *desired* need fulfillment for each level of management.[3] Porter assumed that the discrepancy between *actual* and *desired* need fulfillment was an index of job satisfaction. Our study assumed that the larger the deficiency in need fulfillment, the larger would be the dissatisfaction of respondents. This assumption is consistent with the speculations of Porter and of March and Simon.[4]

The general hypotheses of the investigation were: (1) there is no difference in the perceived needs of educators in one age group as compared with educators in other age groups; (2) there is no difference in the perceived needs of educators in one experience group as compared with educators in other experience groups; (3) there is no difference in the perceived needs of male educators as compared with female educators; and (4) there is no difference in the perceived needs of educators in one professional role as compared with educators in other professional roles.

Questionnaire

The questionnaire used in this study was an adaptation of the one developed and used by Porter. The instructions for completing the questionnaire were as follows:

> On the following page will be listed several characteristics or qualities connected with your school position. For each such characteristic, you will be asked to answer the following questions:
> a. How much of the characteristic is there now connected with your school position?
> b. How much of the characteristic do you think should be connected with your school position?
> For each of the 13 items, answer questions a and b above by writing a number from 1 to 7 in the corresponding space following each question. Low numbers represent low amounts or low importance, and high numbers represent high amounts or high importance.

The following items, listed by category, were included in the questionnaire:

Categories   *Items*

Security

  I–1 The feeling of security in my school position

Social

  II–1 The opportunity, in my school position, to give help to other people
  II–2 The opportunity to develop close friendships in my school position

Esteem

  III–1 The feeling of self-esteem a person gets from being in my school position
  III–2 The prestige of my school position inside the school (that is, the regard received from others in the school)
  III–3 The prestige of my school position outside of the school (that is, the regard from others not in the school)

Autonomy

  IV–1 The authority connected with my school position
  IV–2 The opportunity for independent thought and action in my school position
  IV–3 The opportunity, in my school position, for participation in the setting of goals
  IV–4 The opportunity, in my school position, for participation in the determination of methods and procedures

Self-Actualization

  V–1 The opportunity for personal growth and development in my school position
  V–2 The feeling of self-fulfillment a person gets from being in my school position (that is, the feeling of being able to use one's own unique capabilities, realizing one's potentialities)
  V–3 The feeling of worthwhile accomplishment in my school position

Procedures

All teachers and administrators in one school district, grades K-12 were asked to participate in the study. Of the 310 educators in the district, 223 completed and returned the questionnaire. Mean scores were computed for each question based on age, years of experience, sex, and professional role.

Need deficiencies for each category of respondents on each question were obtained by subtracting the mean response to Part A of an item ("How much is there now?") from the mean response to Part B of the same item ("How much should there be?").

Respondents included thirty-two administrators, seventy-three high school teachers, twenty-eight junior high school teachers and ninety elementary teachers. The sample included 119 male respondents and 104 female respondents. Fifty-six percent of the respondents were over age 34, and 58 percent of the respondents had less than 13 years of experience.

The data were treated by analysis of variance[5] to determine whether mean differences among educators within need categories were significant ($p = .05$). The F-ratio[6] was used to test each hypothesis related to age, years of experience, sex, and professional role. Hypotheses were confirmed where ($P < .05$) and rejected where ($P \geq .05$).

Findings

Treatment of the data related to the first three hypotheses revealed that Hypothesis 1 relating to age was rejected, Hypothesis 2 relating to years of experience was confirmed, and Hypothesis 3 relating to sex was rejected. The analysis revealed that respondents do have different needs and these are significantly associated with age and sex.

Educators differed significantly on the feeling of self-esteem they received from being in their school position and the authority connected with that position. The need deficiency of educators in different age groups also varied significantly. ($P = .001$) in relation to the prestige their school position had outside of school.

Experience was not significantly associated with need deficiencies. However, respondent need deficiencies were significantly different on specific items such as the opportunity respondents had in their school position to give help to other people and the authority connected with their school position. Educator need deficiencies also differed significantly ($P = .01$) on the opportunity for participating in setting goals and ($P = .001$) the prestige their school position had outside of school.

Sex of respondents was significantly associated with need deficiencies. The needs of men and women differed significantly on such items as the prestige of their school position outside of school, the opportunity for independent thought and action in their school position, and the feeling of worthwhile accomplishment they achieved. The largest difference ($P > .001$) was on the opportunity to develop close friendships in their school position. For each item, men expressed greater need deficiencies.

Figure 1, using mean scores, presents the need deficiencies for

Figure 1. Need Deficiencies of Educators Reported as Mean Scores*
by Need Category Items and Professional Role of Respondent

Need Category	Item	Professional Role				P
		Adminis-tration	High-School Teachers	Junior-High Teachers	Elementary Teachers	
Security	I-1	0.81	1.27	1.59	0.66	—
Social	II-1	0.72	0.92	1.48	0.81	—
	II-2	0.52	0.38	0.48	0.43	—
Esteem	III-1	0.69	2.25	1.81	1.41	.001
	III-2	0.63	1.53	1.59	0.83	.01
	III-3	0.84	1.97	2.93	1.10	.001
Autonomy	IV-1	0.84	1.26	2.37	0.87	.001
	IV-2	1.28	1.41	2.78	0.70	.001
	IV-3	0.72	2.03	1.85	1.22	.001
	IV-4	0.53	1.88	1.48	1.07	.01
Self-	V-1	1.09	1.58	1.70	0.87	.05
actuali-	V-2	1.19	1.90	1.74	1.10	.05
zation	V-3	1.79	1.79	1.67	1.06	—

*Low mean scores represent small need deficiencies. High mean scores represent larger need deficiencies.

For H_4 Λ = .593, F_{614}^{39} = 3.02, (P>.001): Hypothesis 4 (there is no difference in the perceived needs of respondents in one professional role as compared with respondents in other professional roles) is rejected in Figure 1. The difference is significant (P>.001 as computed by using an F-ratio where the degrees of freedom equal 39 and 614.

each item by professional role. An analysis of these data indicate that Hypothesis 4 is rejected. Professional role is significantly associated ($P > .001$) with need deficiencies.

The need deficiencies of administrators and of teachers at different levels vary significantly on the opportunity for personal growth and development in their school position (V-1) and the feeling of self-fulfillment they get from being in their school position (V-2). They also differ significantly ($P = .01$) on the prestige of their school position inside the school (III-2) and the opportunity to participate in determining methods and procedures (IV-4).

Finally they differ significantly ($P \geq .001$) on the feeling of self-esteem they get from being in their school position (III-1), the prestige of their position outside of school (III-3), the authority connected with their position (IV-I), the opportunity they had for independent thought and action (IV-2), and for participating in the setting of goals (IV-3).

Discussion

The need deficiencies of educators in this study varied according to age, sex, and professional role. Accordingly, educators value differently opportunities for achieving economic security, developing social relations, increasing one's self-esteem, having automony or becoming self-actualized.

Need Deficiencies by Age

The concern of young educators (age 20-24) with esteem contrasts with the concern older educators (age 45 and over) have for esteem, autonomy, and self-actualization. Specifically, older educators appear less concerned with the prestige of their position. Of all respondents, those between the ages of 25 and 34 report the largest need deficiencies for all items in the categories of esteem, autonomy, and self-actualization.

Although need deficiencies of educators in the 35-44 age group are only slightly less than in the 25-34 age group, the rank order of some items is considerably different. For example, while some educators want to achieve greater feelings of self-esteem from their school position, this is ranked tenth by 35-44-year-old respondents. The smallest deficiency on eight of the thirteen items is for educators in the 20-24 age group. In general, this group perceived more congruency between actual and desired need fulfillment for security, social, autonomy, and self-actualization items than did other age groups.

Significant differences among respondents in different age groups have to do with feelings of self-esteem, prestige of position outside of school, and the authority connected with one's school position.

Overall, need deficiencies tend to be smallest in the 20-24 age group, to be greatest in the 25-35 age group, to taper off in the 35-44 age group, and to be moderate in the 45-and-over age group. This observation is consistent with Herzberg's[7] extensive review of job satisfaction research. He concludes that workers between 20-30 years of age appear more dissatisfied with their jobs than younger or older workers. Morse[8] further confirms this phenomenon by concluding that job satisfaction for white-collar workers tends to be high early in service and late in service, with lowest satisfaction occurring at the intermediate point where level of aspiration is considerably higher than achievement.

Need Deficiencies by Experience

Although the hypothesis that years of experience would not make a difference was confirmed, some trends are evident. For example, educators with little experience tend to have greater esteem needs. Educators with five to twelve years of experience have greater need deficiencies in all categories than do other respondents, but their greatest need deficiencies are related to autonomy, self-esteem, and prestige. Respondents with more years of experience (13-24 years) tend either to achieve more or to expect less. With the exception of the opportunity to develop close friendships in their school position, and the opportunity for independent thought and action in their school position, the 25-and-over experience group shows lower need deficiencies than any age group. Finally, the expressed need for prestige appears to diminish with increasing years of experience.

Need Deficiencies by Sex

The hypothesis related to sex of respondents (H_3) was rejected. Only with regard to security do women have need deficiencies greater than men. Men's needs relate strongly to feelings of self-esteem, prestige of position, and worthwhile accomplishments. Women's needs relate strongly to feelings of self-esteem, participating in goal setting, and feelings of self-fulfillment.

Generally speaking, women appear more satisfied with their professional role than men. Further, they appear more satisfied with the opportunity their job provides for meeting social, esteem, autonomy, and self-actualization needs. Men appear more satisfied with the feeling of security their job provides. Possibly the difference between men and women in social, esteem, autonomy, and self-actualization need deficiencies is related to the greater concern men have with their status in society and success and how this is affected by their position.

Need Deficiencies by Professional Role

Professional role appears to be the variable most significantly associated with need deficiencies of educators. Assuming that need deficiencies are an index of dissatisfaction, it appears that the role of junior-senior-high-school teacher affords less opportunity for satisfaction than other professional roles. Elementary teachers by comparison have consistently smaller need deficiencies for all items but one.

Administrators in general report a high level of satisfaction with the exception of opportunity to develop close friendships in their school position. However, the areas in which administrators sense the most dissatisfaction are opportunity for independent thought and action, the feeling of self-fulfillment gained from their position, and feelings of worthwhile accomplishment.

On all esteem, automony, and two of the three self-actualization items, elementary junior-high senior-high teachers, and administrators differ significantly (P varies from .05 to .001) in need deficiencies. It appears that the job of administrator permits greater opportunities for incumbents to experience need fulfillment at all need levels. The job of teacher appears not to offer a similar consistent opportunity. However, it appears that the administrators and elementary-school teachers in this study are either more satisfied or less dissatisfied in their jobs than secondary and junior-high-school teachers.

This raises other important questions. How is need fulfillment related to expectations and opportunity? How do the needs of educators compare with the needs of persons in other professional roles or occupations? While satisfactory answers are not yet available, a review of Porter's[9] studies and of March and Simon's[10] theory of adaptive motivated behavior will serve to place the results of this study in perspective. Porter's research concentrated on the perceived deficiencies in need fulfillment as a function of job level. His research reports higher need-fulfillment deficiencies for higher-order needs (self-actualization, autonomy) than for lower-order needs (security, social). Further, his studies also suggest that the largest deficiencies at all job levels are in the highest order need areas, autonomy, and self-actualization. Teachers' need deficiencies differ from executives' need deficiencies in Porter's findings. Teachers, for example, have greater need deficiencies in the esteem area. School administrators, however, are similar to the executives in Porter's study. Porter's research tends to confirm Argyris'[11] theory of the dilemma between the needs individuals have for psychological success and self-esteem and the division of labor demands of formal organizations. Argyris hypothesizes that the probability of experiencing a sense of self-esteem, autonomy, and self-actualization will be greater for those at the top of the hierarchical structure and will be less for those lower in hierarchy.

One interpretation of the present study is that school administrators have greater opportunities for need fulfillment than do secondary and junior-high teachers. Elementary teachers, however, compare very favorably with administrators.

Conclusion

Largest need deficiencies for all educators, categorized by professional role, have to do with esteem, autonomy, and self-actualization. Administrators are less satisfied with their opportunities for self-actualization than are teachers. On the other hand, administrators report greater satisfaction in esteem category items than do teachers. The lack of self-esteem received from their school position represents the largest source of dissatisfaction for high school and elementary teachers.

Teaching as an occupation appears to have more potential for providing need fulfillment for women. A further interpretation strongly indicates that women teachers are more satisfied with their jobs. Lower need deficiencies are consistently reported by women for all need categories with the exception of security. This satisfaction tendency for women, in part, explains the congruence of actual and desired need fulfillment of elementary school teachers.

March and Simon's[12] model of adaptive motivated behavior may suggest a further explanation for this phenomenon. They hypothesize that satisfaction is a function of expected value of reward and level of aspiration. Essentially, the lower the satisfaction of a given individual, the more the search for alternative courses of action. This search leads to a higher expected value of reward. The incongruency between level of aspiration and the present state of affairs leads to increased job dissatisfaction.

It is possible that the level of job aspiration for men exceeds that of women. This may in part account for greater dissatisfaction among men teachers. Several alternatives appear available to men teachers with high need deficiencies. They may: (1) move from teaching into administration where opportunity for psychological success and personal aspiration fulfillment is greater, (2) leave teaching for the more diverse rewards of business or industry, (3) remain in the classroom, lower their aspirations, and accept what rewards are available, or (4) remain in the classroom and become militant in their efforts to gain control of the reward granting machinery.

In the opinion of the authors, teachers who lower their aspiration levels serve as major deterrents to the creativity and growth of students and to educational innovations. Further, teachers who militantly seek to change the environment do, in fact, aid administrators in their constant efforts to increase resources and find creative talent.

A Proposal for Restructuring Teacher Roles

Increased opportunities for professional advancement must be provided if teachers are to experience more need fulfillment at higher levels of the Maslow hierarchy. A reorganization of the internal role structure of teaching would provide needed opportunities for professional advancement. This would necessitate a re-examination of the role of the teacher and the role expectations held by administrators for teachers. The establishment of separate hierarchies for teachers and administrators would permit such reorganization. As administrators by comparison become less familiar with the task and content of teaching and subsequently become more involved in the administrative process, they are less a super teacher and more a professional administrator. It seems likely that under such a system, the professional teacher would tend to assume more responsibility for the content and methodology of his profession and for the behavior and evaluation of his peers.

Figure 2 represents a proposal for restructuring teacher roles. It should not be considered merely an overt attempt to relabel teachers. Rather, the purpose of the proposal is to redefine the working relationship within the ranks of teaching and to reallocate professional responsibilities among teachers. The proposal is based on the premise that as teachers increase in professional competence and maturity they should, and need to, be given more responsibility for their professional behavior and more opportunity for personal and professional growth.

A new teacher entering the profession, under the proposed plan, would function as an intern, being exposed to a variety of insight producing experiences while benefiting from cooperative working relationships with teachers at the fellow and associate level. The intern would be chosen on the basis of a strong formal preparation program and high promise for successful teaching.

Individual responsibility for instruction combined with continued opportunities for joint teaching would characterize the fellow level. Fellows would assume increasing responsibility for guiding the learning of students both in and out of the classroom, and cooperatively developing their own skills while working with teachers at other levels. Fellow teachers would constitute the nucleus of an emerging professional teaching core.

The associate level would represent, for many, fulfillment of professional aspirations. The associate would share with scholars and colleagues responsibility for the professional growth of interns and

Figure 2. A Proposal for Restructuring Teacher Roles by Redefining the Teacher's Working Relationships

Position	Salary Index	Professional Competence Required	Teaching Assignment	Other Responsibilities	Professional Relationship	Involvement in Allocation of Resources
Intern	1.00	Formal education Potential teacher	Joint teaching Small teaching load	Work with students and teachers in extra-curricular activities	Works with typical students in cooperative teaching relations	Consulted
Fellow	1.75	Knowledgeable Skilled teacher	Joint teaching Individual teaching Medium teaching load	Supervises student extra-curricular activities	Works with a variety of students in co-operative teaching relationships	Participates
Associate	2.75	Content specialist Competent teacher	Individual teaching Differentiated teaching Maximum teaching load	Cooperatively works with teachers and parents on educational problems	Has maximum exposure to students in individual and cooperative teaching relationships	Participates and advises
Scholar	4.00	Creative, productive Outstanding professional	Differentiated teaching Collaborative teaching Medium teaching load Curriculum research and development	Identifies and maintains contact with profession at large through research, writing, and developmental activities	Collaborates in a variety of teaching experiences; Serves as educational clinician; Develops experimental programs	Advises and allocates
OR						
Colleague	4.00	Collaborative, insightful Outstanding professional	Collaborative teaching Special teaching relationships Medium teaching load Human resource development	Cooperatively works with community, school administrators, and the board of education on broader educational issues	Functions as a coordinator of human resources, motivator, and assessment counselor	Allocates and helps secure

fellows. Movement from the fellow to associate level would be based on mature professional competence and demonstrated successful teaching. The associate would share fully in collaborative management efforts and would assume full responsibility for his professional behavior.

The associate could move to either of two levels: scholar or colleague. The positions would be considered equal in rank and pay but would provide a different emphasis in terms of professional responsibility.

The scholar would be characterized as one who identifies strongly with his professional specialty and with outside reference groups that exist to promote this specialty. At the same time, he would be a master teacher and student of his area of competence. His responsibilities would include joint teaching with fellows and interns, working with exceptional students, and research and development.

The colleague, on the other hand, would possess strength in organizational and human skills. He would serve as a consultant to other teachers and would be responsibly involved in selection, orientation, and assessment programs. He would have a strong voice in curriculum development, policy formation, and in allocating resources and would maintain close ties with the school administration, the school board, and the local community.

This proposal for increasing the hierarchical structure of teaching provides opportunities for movement within the ranks of teaching, while at the same time it increases the opportunity for growth at any given level. Associates, for example, assume responsibilities traditionally reserved for staff and administrative roles. Scholars are provided with the opportunity and autonomy to develop personal and professional competencies traditionally reserved for staff and administrative roles. Scholars are provided with the opportunity and autonomy to develop personal and professional competencies traditionally reserved for the collegiate community. Colleagues function as expert teachers and, at the same time, help other teachers administer their own professional behavior. This is a privilege long enjoyed by the established professions.

FOOTNOTES

1. A. H. Maslow, *Motivation and Personality* (New York: Harper & Brothers, 1954).

2. Lyman Porter, "Job Attitudes in Management: I. Perceived Deficiencies in Need Fulfillment as a Function of Job Level," *Journal of Applied Psychology*, XLVI (December, 1963), 375-384.

3. *Ibid.*

4. James G. March and Herbert A. Simon, *Organizations* (New York: John Wiley & Sons, Inc., 1958), pp. 83-111.

5. For reference to this technique see Allen L. Edwards, *Experimental Design in Psychological Research* (New York: Holt, Rinehart, & Winston, 1963), pp. 117-118.

6. For reference to this technique see E. F. Lindquist, *Design and Analysis of Experiments in Psychology and Education* (New York: Houghton Mifflin Co., 1953), pp. 39-40.

7. Frederick Herzberg *et. al.*, *Job Attitudes* (Pittsburgh: Psychological Services of Pittsburgh, 1957).

8. Nancy C. Morse, *Satisfactions in the White-Collar Job* (Ann Arbor: Survey Research Center, Institute for Social Research, University of Michigan, 1953).

9. Porter, *op. cit.* see also his "Job Attitudes in Management: II. Perceived Importance of Needs as a Function of Job Level," *Journal of Applied Psychology*, XLVII (April, 1963), pp. 141-148.

10. March and Simon, *op. cit.*

11. Chris Argyris, *Integrating the Individual and the Organization* (New York: John Wiley & Sons, Inc., 1964).

12. March and Simon, *op. cit.*